D1568827

Taking on
GOLIATH

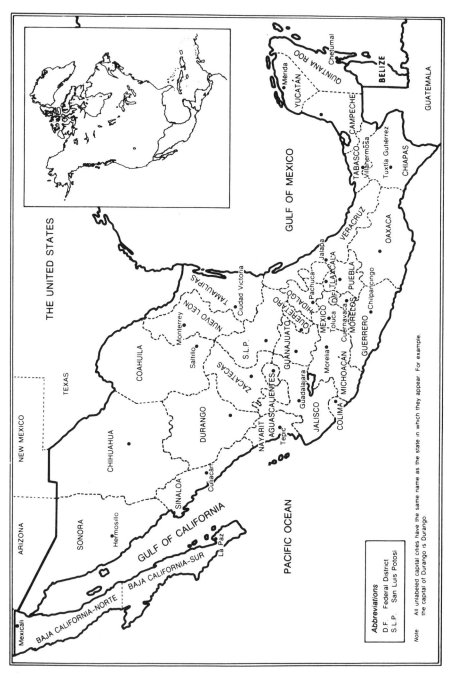

MEXICO

Abbreviations
D.F.   Federal District
S.L.P. San Luis Potosí

Note   All unlabeled capital cities have the same name as the state in which they appear. For example, the capital of Durango is Durango.

KATHLEEN BRUHN

Taking on
GOLIATH

THE EMERGENCE OF A
NEW LEFT PARTY AND THE
STRUGGLE FOR DEMOCRACY IN MEXICO

The Pennsylvania State University Press
University Park, Pennsylvania

Library of Congress Cataloging-in-Publication Data

Bruhn, Kathleen, 1963–
    Taking on Goliath : The emergence of a new left party and the struggle for
democracy in Mexico / Kathleen Bruhn.

        p.   cm.
    Includes bibliographical references and index.
    ISBN 0-271-01586-1 (cloth : alk. paper)
    ISBN 0-271-01587-X (pbk. : alk. paper)
    1. Political parties—Mexico.   2. Partido de la Revolución
Democrática (Mexico)   3. Partido Revolucionario Institucional.
    4. Mexico—Politics and government—1988–   5. Democracy—Mexico.
I. Title.
JL1298.A1B78   1997
324'.0972'09049—dc20   95-47061
                                                             CIP

It is the policy of The Pennsylvania State University Press to use acid-free paper
for the first printing of all clothbound books. Publications on uncoated stock
satisfy the minimum requirements of American National Standard for
Information Sciences—Permanence of Paper for Printed Library Materials,
ANSI Z39.48-1992.

FRONTISPIECE: Map of Mexico (reproduced from Daniel C. Levy and Gabriel
Székely, *Mexico: Paradoxes of Stability and Change,* second edition [Boulder:
Colo.: Westview Press, 1987], p. xxi).

*To William and Charlotte Bruhn,
my first, best teachers.*

Contents

List of Figures and Tables

Preface and Acknowledgments

In the course of writing this book I have been challenged, teased, and encouraged by many well-meaning individuals to hurry up and publish the story of the formation of the Partido de la Revolución Democrática, or PRD, before it fell apart without a trace and left me seeking employment in departments of history rather than political science. At the time of this writing the PRD faces another threat of a split that would reconfigure the Mexican left. In addition, some characteristic qualities of the Mexican political system that help explain outcomes in this book have undergone significant transformation. It is true that the PRD deserves a place in history if for no other reason than its dramatic impact on political change in Mexico. Nothing has been the same for the PRI since Cárdenas nearly beat the PRI's candidate in the 1988 presidential election and then organized his supporters into the most unified left party in contemporary Mexican history.

Yet the issues raised by the experience of the PRD remain among the most profound and significant problems for the future not only of Mexico but also of many other developing democracies: When will new parties form to represent marginalized sectors of the population? What are the obstacles to their effectiveness and endurance? How might party reform and party system change contribute to democratization, especially in cases of transformation from civilian authoritarian rule? And what is the future of the left in a post–Cold War, neoliberal world? Fundamentally, the story of the PRD raises questions about whether parties can represent popular interests effectively enough to prevent the polarization of deeply unequal but increasingly democratic Third World countries. This question should occupy the attention of many scholars for many years as new democracies face the challenges of economic reform, population growth, and burgeoning demands for political participation. Whether this participation takes institutional or noninstitutional forms may have a significant impact on the political stability and economic prospects of these countries. These are classic political science and comparative questions that continue to intrigue me as I develop further research.

This work required the support of many people. Above all, I owe a debt of gratitude to the men and women in the Partido de la Revolución Democrática who generously shared their time, their lives, and their stories with a young graduate student. I also appreciate the willingness of some members of the PRI and other political parties to talk to me candidly even though I was doing research on their political rival.

I have been fortunate to receive considerable institutional support as well. Most significantly, the Center for U.S.-Mexican Studies at UCSD graciously awarded me not only a Visiting Scholar Fellowship to support the initial writing of the dissertation but also a subsequent UC Fellowship for Mexican Studies to support its transformation into a book manuscript in 1994. The institutional resources of the center offered an ideal environment for writing; the human resources of the center made my experiences both pleasant and productive. I particularly want to thank Wayne Cornelius, Juan Molinar, Kevin Middlebrook, John Bailey, Van Whiting, Helena Varela, and John Lear, all of whom read portions of my thesis or helped shape the theoretical argument of the work in general. In Mexico my research was funded by the MacArthur Foundation, the Stanford Institute for International Studies, and the Stanford Center for Latin American Studies. I also am grateful for the institutional base offered at the Colegio de México by Soledad Loaeza and at the Universidad Nacional Autónoma de México by Matilde Luna.

In various stages of this project I have received critical advice and moral support from a number of scholars. I am most indebted to three individuals: Terry Karl, Richard Fagen, and Philippe Schmitter. All three read drafts of every chapter of the dissertation and offered thorough and constructive criticism. They have always supported me personally and encouraged me to grow as a scholar. In addition, I have benefited greatly from the advice and support of Larry Diamond, Rodolfo Stavenhagen, Gerry Hudson, Joe Foweraker, Keith Yanner, John Arquilla, Celia Toro, Ken Roberts, and Scott Sagan. None had a formal role in advising this research, but all have contributed to sharpen my critical thinking, and some have read portions of the book out of pure friendship. Keith Yanner in particular has read almost all of it and gave me very useful suggestions. I am also grateful to the reviewers from Penn State Press, whose careful and meticulous reading of the manuscript helped me considerably. Any errors which remain after their best efforts are solely my responsibility.

Last but never least, I want to thank my parents William and Charlotte Bruhn, for picking me up more times than I care to count, for always believing in me, for living as examples of courage and grace, and for teaching me their faith in God. They are a constant inspiration.

List of Abbreviations

ACNR	Asociación Cívica Nacional Revolucionaria
CCI	Central Campesina Independiente
CDP	Comité de Defensa Popular de Durango
CEE	Comité Ejecutivo Estatal
CEN	Comité Ejecutivo Nacional
CFE	Comisión Federal Electoral
CNAO	Comité Nacional para Auscultación y Organazación
CNC	Confederación Nacional Campesina
COCEI	Coalición de Obreros, Campesinos y Estudiantes del Istmo
COFIPE	Código Federal de Instituciones y Procesos Electoralés
COPLAMAR	Coordinación Federal del Plan Nacional de Zonas Deprimidas y Grupos Marginados
CTM	Confederación de Trabajadores Mexicanos
FDN	Frente Democrático Nacional
FEP	Frente Electoral del Pueblo
IFE	Instituto Federal Electoral
ISI	Import Substitution Industrialization
MAP	Movimiento de Acción Popular
MAUS	Movimiento de Acción y Unidad Socialista
MLN	Movimiento de Liberación Nacional
MRP	Movimiento Revolucionario del Pueblo
OIR-LM	Organización de la Izquierda Revolucionaria-Línea de Masas
PAN	Partido Acción Nacional
PARM	Partido Auténtico de la Revolución Mexicana
PCM	Partido Comunista Mexicano
PDM	Partido Demócrata Mexicano
PFCRN	Partido Frente Cardenista de Reconstrucción Nacional
PMS	Partido Mexicano Socialista
PMT	Partido Mexicano de los Trabajadores
PNR	Partido Nacional Revolucionario

PPM	Partido del Pueblo Mexicano
PPR	Partido Popular Revolucionario
PPS	Partido Popular Socialista
PRD	Partido de la Revolución Democrática
PRI	Partido Revolucionario Institucional
PRM	Partido Revolucionario Mexicano
PRONASOL	Programa Nacional de Solidaridad
PRT	Partido Revolucionario de los Trabajadores
PSOE	Partido Socialista Obrero Español
PSR	Partido Socialista Revolucionaria
PST	Partido Socialista de los Trabajadores
PSUM	Partido Socialista Unificado de México
RFE	Registro Federal Electoral
SPP	Secretaría de Programación y Presupuesto
UCD	Unión de Campesinos Democráticos
UCP	Unión de Colonias Populares
UNAM	Universidad Nacional Autónoma de México

1

Democratization and Party System Change

THE RISE (AND FALL?) OF THE CÁRDENAS LEFT

In the 1980s, as a wave of democratization swept much of the world, Mexico nearly experienced the end of one of the oldest and most stable authoritarian regimes anywhere—sixty years of virtually uncontested rule by the Partido Revolucionario Institucional (PRI). Backed by a new left coalition, independent candidate Cuauhtémoc Cárdenas came closer to ousting the PRI in the 1988 presidential election than any candidate since the founding of the governing party. Whether or not electoral fraud changed the outcome, as *cardenistas* contend, the real results of the vote were certainly much closer than official figures, which awarded Salinas a slim majority of 50.7 percent. Nevertheless, the PRI acknowledged more support for Cárdenas than any previous opposition presidential candidate: 31 percent.[1] Observers argued that "from the breakup . . . that the PRI is experiencing today, in less time than we imagine, a true system of parties will arise in Mexico. . . . the novelty that will permit this central change is the consolidation of a party [the *cardenista* party] with a social democratic orientation, but fed by profound national traditions."[2]

Barely three years later the Partido de la Revolución Democrática (PRD) formed by Cárdenas won only 8.3 percent of the vote in national congressional elections, 22.7 percent less than the left coalition in 1988, and just 3.3 percent more than the first left coalition to compete under the 1977 electoral reform (see Table 1.1). In 1988 Cárdenas won a majority in three states and carried two by plurality. In 1991 the PRD lost not only every state, but all three hundred electoral districts.[3] The PRI rebounded to 61.4 percent. Even the return of Cárdenas as a candidate in the 1994 presidential election could not lift the party to more than 17 percent of the vote, or recover second place in voter preferences. The most comprehensive left coalition assembled since the 1930s failed not only to hold onto its electoral gains but also to retain two of its most important achievements—its rare unity and its unprecedented alliance with popular movements that historically resisted electoral cooperation. The original coalition of parties and movements fell apart, while the remnant that formed the PRD suffered from internal divisions that damaged the party's image and effectiveness. The "viable alternative" offered by Cárdenas seemed to disintegrate as quickly as it had emerged.

The story of the PRD—its meteoric rise and subsequent agony—suggests answers to an intriguing theoretical dilemma: that explanations of party system stability often have trouble predicting party system change, especially through the creation of a successful new party, while explanations of new party formation and success frequently have trouble understanding their lack of persistence. The PRD is not the only new and apparently promising party that failed to hold on to initial gains. Why do such parties rise and fall?

In contrast to static explanations of party and party system fortunes based on institutions or social cleavages, I argue that the key to putting together the pieces of the puzzle lies in understanding the conflicting

1. Mexico, Instituto Federal Electoral (IFE), *Contienda electoral en las elecciones presidenciales*, ed. Jenny Saltiel Cohen (Mexico City: IFE, 1991), 7.

2. Hector Aguilar Camín, "The Mexican Transition," *Voices of Mexico* (June–November 1988): 9.

3. Mexico, Instituto Federal Electoral (IFE), *Relación de los 300 distritos federales electorales* (Mexico City: IFE, 1991).

Table 1.1. Patterns of electoral support, 1952–1994

	Independent Left (a)	PRI	PAN	Other (b)
1952	15.9 (c)	74.3%	8.7%	1.5%
1955	none registered	89.9	9.2	1.0
1958	none registered	88.2	10.2	1.5
1961	none registered	90.2	7.6	1.7
1964	none registered	86.2	11.5	2.1
1967	none registered	83.3	12.3	4.2
1970	none registered	83.2	14.2	2.4
1973	none registered	77.4	16.3	6.0
1976	none registered	84.8	9.0	5.8
1979	5.3 (d)	74.0	11.5	9.1
1982	5.9 (e)	69.3	17.5	7.3
1985	6.3 (f)	68.1	16.3	9.2
1988	29.6 (g)	51.1	18.0	1.3
1991	8.9 (h)	61.5	17.7	12.0
1994	16.7 (i)	50.3	25.8	7.2(j)

SOURCES: Mexico, Instituto Federal Electoral, *Contienda electoral en las elecciones de diputados federales*, ed. Jenny Saltiel Cohen (Mexico City: IFE, 1991); Silvia Gómez Tagle, *Las estadísticas electorales de la reforma política* (Mexico City: El Colegio de México, 1990); Mexico, Instituto Federal Electoral, *Relación de los 300 distritos federales electorales* (Mexico City: IFE, 1991); Mexico, Instituto Federal Electoral, *Elecciones federales 1994: Resultados definitivos según los cómputos distritales* (Mexico City: IFE, 1994). For comparability congressional vote is used for all years, including presidential election years. Presidential vote tends to correspond closely to congressional vote (though prior to 1988 most "other" parties co-nominated the PRI's candidate), except for 1976, when the PAN did not run a presidential candidate. Figures represent percentage of valid vote and may not sum to 100 percent due to rounding and omission of votes for nonregistered candidates from "other."
(a) The "independent left" changed organizational identities many times. I refer to those parties that defended leftist principles (from marxism-leninism to the social nationalism expressed especially in articles 3, 25–27, 123, and 130 of the 1917 Constitution) and that nominated independent candidates.
(b) This column primarily registers the vote of the "parastatal" parties, small, nominally independent parties that cooperated with the PRI to the point of co-nominating PRI presidential candidates.
(c) The congressional vote associated with General Henríquez Guzmán, an independent candidate from the left wing of the PRI linked to former president Lázaro Cárdenas.
(d) Left candidates in 1979 ran under the registry of the Mexican Communist Party.
(e) The vote of the Unified Mexican Socialist Party (PSUM, a fusion party formed mostly by the ex-PCM), plus the trotskyite Revolutionary Workers' Party (PRT—1.3%) and the Social Democratic Party (.2%).
(f) The vote of PSUM (3.4%), PRT (1.3%), and the Mexican Workers' Party (1.6%).
(g) The vote of the 1988 Cárdenas coalition: three parastatal parties (PPS, PARM, and PST/PFCRN) and the PMS (formerly PSUM). The PRT vote (.6%) has been added to the coalition vote for consistency.
(h) The vote of the PRD (8.2%) plus the PRT (.6%).
(i) The vote of the PRD. While leftist, the new Workers' Party (PT) has strong ties to the government and gets funding from unclear sources. Its independence is questionable.
(j) The vote of six parties; only one (the PT) won the 1.5% required to keep legal registry.

requirements of party formation versus party consolidation. The conditions that foster party emergence differ substantially from the conditions that foster their consolidation, organizationally as well as electorally. As a result, factors that encourage the creation of new parties and their early success do not necessarily support, and may even block, consolidation. Furthermore, party characteristics during formation leave traces that are hard to erase. Thus, though consolidation presents parties with common challenges, some adapt better than others. The very parties that have striking early success may be especially ill-designed for consolidation.

In addition, the case of the PRD suggests some hypotheses about the relationship between party formation and system change, the role of parties in the democratization of civilian authoritarian regimes, and the particular dilemmas faced by left parties in the post-Soviet world. The PRD has contributed significantly to the process of democratization in Mexico, though it has not benefited directly, in part as a result of its position on the left, in part as a result of its errors, and in part as a result of handicaps associated with newness. Indeed, while the left's initial success galvanized other parties to do a better job of seeking electoral support, its electoral decline probably made an equally important contribution to the likelihood of meaningful electoral reform by reducing the danger that reform would lead to an electoral victory by the ideological opponents of the ruling elite.

OPPOSITION PARTIES IN RESTRICTIVE REGIMES

Many authors have noted that institutions and laws, especially electoral laws, create incentives that favor some behavior and actors over others, and hence work as a source of party system durability.[4] Not only does party system type tend to persist but often the founding parties of an electoral regime persist as well, at least in part because they succeeded in setting up the rules to their advantage.[5]

---

4. The most well-known of these formulations is probably Duverger's hypothesis that proportional representation favors multiparty systems while the simple majority–single ballot rule favors a two-party system. See Maurice Duverger, *Political Parties: Their Organization and Activity in the Modern State*, trans. Barbara and Douglas North (New York: John Wiley, 1954).

5. According to Lipset and Rokkan, for example, party systems become decisively consolidated at a relatively early moment in the development of new nations. Lipset and

This is particularly true of hegemonic one-party systems like that which has characterized Mexico. In a hegemonic one-party system the same party always wins elections, not just because the majority happen to prefer it over time (as in predominant party systems), but because electoral rules and practices systematically favor it. Electoral opposition acquires a symbolic meaning at best, since the outcome is never really in doubt. According to Giovanni Sartori, these cases do not evolve into competitive party systems by their own inner logic or by gradual reform. The pragmatic-hegemonic party system "cannot escape the destiny of all monocentric systems, namely, that the party and the state *simul stant et simul cadent*, stand and fall together."[6] If the hegemonic party attempts to reform itself or electoral laws, it will do so in order to retain, not relinquish, its leading role. Those who have based their careers on the expectation that the hegemonic party will control state patronage will resist rules that might produce alternation in power. Thus, there is a fundamental barrier against a transition to multiparty democracy via any route but *ruptura*—a swift and successful challenge to the one-party system that results in a profound renegotiation of the rules of the game.

While most adapted to monocentric regimes, similar hypotheses could apply to party systems biased against minority parties. Two-party systems, for example, systematically overrepresent the two largest parties and make it difficult for new third parties to gain a foothold. The characteristic pattern of quick rise and equally quick decline shows up frequently in two-party systems. In the United States the dominance of the Republican and Democratic parties persists alongside the not uncommon appearance of independent candidates who do relatively well in a single election but fail to crystallize their political support into a consolidated, competitive party. In Great Britain the Social Democratic Party experienced a similar fate. Like the PRD, it originated in an elite

---

Rokkan identify this moment as the introduction of universal manhood suffrage. LaPalombara and Weiner identify the moment of party system consolidation as a more prolonged period during which political elites cope with three crises faced by nations on their way to modernity: legitimacy, integration, and participation. A crucial factor in this perspective is the persistence of party loyalties. Political socialization transmits and confirms party loyalties across generations. Party loyalties then normally keep voters from switching parties or supporting new ones. Thus, voters may remain identified with parties even if the content of party programs changes. See Seymour Martin Lipset and Stein Rokkan, eds., *Party Systems and Voter Alignments: Cross-National Perspectives* (New York: The Free Press, 1967); Joseph LaPalombara and Myron Weiner, *Political Parties and Political Development* (Princeton: Princeton University Press, 1966).

6. Giovanni Sartori, *Parties and Party Systems: A Framework for Analysis* (New York: Cambridge University Press, 1976), 281.

split within one of the dominant parties, attracted broad support for a very brief period of time, and disintegrated within a few years. One key barrier was the credibility problem, the party's inability to convince voters they would not waste a Social Democratic vote.[7]

Opposition parties have to take into account institutional obstacles and opportunities. Institutions and rules seem most helpful in explaining what happened to the PRD after 1989. They provided the ruling party with a set of tools that it used skillfully. However, institutions and rules explain only part of the problem. In the first place, there is considerable variation in the success of opposition parties in the same institutional setting. Within Mexico it is useful to compare the PRD with the more conservative, more consolidated, and more consistently successful PAN. Opposition party outcomes in other monocentric systems vary even more, depending on the extent of the limitations they face, but also depending on different social structures and opposition alliances.[8] Institutional approaches tend to underestimate the importance of strategy and leadership, and overlook opportunities offered by existing structures.

Thus, hypotheses based on the theory that institutions and electoral laws determine the potential for new parties did not predict the emergence of a new party, nor did institutions prevent Cárdenas from doing well in 1988. In fact, due largely to institutional restrictions "few observers expected the [cardenistas] to have much political impact once [the] PRI presidential candidate had been selected."[9] The 1986 electoral reform produced no major change favorable to opposition parties, nor did evidence surface that the PRI had renounced fraud; indeed, elections in 1985 and 1986 showed exactly the reverse. The PRI also continued to control labor and peasant organizations through corporatist institutions. According to conventional wisdom, corporatism as well as the PRI's origin in a popular revolution doomed the left to marginality.[10] Despite these odds, however, Cárdenas left the PRI in order to

7. The Social Democrats faced a plurality system with a support base distributed fairly evenly instead of concentrated in one region. Under proportional representation they might have survived.

8. A list of the hegemonic one-party regimes would include Taiwan after 1986, Turkey under the RPP, and South Korea under the Democratic Justice Party; a list of one-party predominant regimes would include the Swedish Social Democrats, Israel under the Labour Party, Italy before 1990, and Japan before 1993.

9. Kevin Middlebrook, "Dilemmas of Change in Mexican Politics," *World Politics* 41 (October 1988): 131.

10. For example, Needler explained lack of rebellion against the crisis by arguing that the PRI "[commands] the loyalty, through the unions affiliated with the party, of the organized groups most likely to be disadvantaged by the difficult economic period." See

challenge it electorally. His coalition included the weakest parties in Mexico, yet popular response to his campaign surpassed even his expectations. Mexico had virtually the same institutions and rules in 1987, when Cárdenas decided to leave the PRI and run for president, as it did in 1988, when he nearly beat the PRI, and in 1989, when his new party suffered its first serious problems.

LEFT PARTIES, NEOLIBERAL REGIMES, AND DEMOCRATIZATION

A second set of explanations, in hindsight of course, saw the left's rise as virtually inevitable but had a harder time predicting its swift collapse. For some, Cárdenas's strong performance suggested that Mexican politics had finally caught up to the dramatic demographic changes experienced since the foundation of the PRI. If parties reflect social cleavages, his ability to tap into bases "left out" by the PRI—including the urban poor and the progressive middle class—promised a bright future. Many interpreted Cárdenas's electoral alliance with urban popular movements as one of the most hopeful signs for the future of the new party, both because it was so unprecedented and because it improved the left's traditionally weak links to civil society; thus, "finally, the foundations were set for a party with strong ties to social movements and with the potential to articulate them politically."[11] Yet the party created by Cárdenas failed to keep either the electoral or the organizational support of most of these sectors.

Other explanations focused on the left's ability to fill a political vacuum opened up by the PRI's rightward shift, from promotion of import substitution and heavy state involvement in the economy toward promotion of a free market economy and open abandonment of revolutionary ideals. The only other major opposition party, the conservative National Action Party (PAN), supported the same basic neoliberal agenda of free trade, fiscal conservatism, and a more limited economic role for the state. Cárdenas seemed well-positioned to take advantage of

Martin C. Needler, "The Significance of Recent Events for the Mexican Political System," in *Mexican Politics in Transition*, ed. Judith Gentleman (Boulder, Colo.: Westview Press, 1987), 78.

11. Jaime Tamayo, "Neoliberalism Encounters *Neocardenismo*," in *Popular Movements and Political Change in Mexico*, ed. Joe Foweraker and Ann Craig (Boulder, Colo.: Lynne Rienner, 1990), 121.

opposition to neoliberal policies, a favorable factor for PRD consolidation. The PRD also benefited from support for democratization. The PRD resulted in large part from the struggle for democracy, made democracy a central demand, and convinced many that the PRI could actually be beaten electorally in their lifetime.

Yet the left's position with respect to neoliberalism and electoral democracy is far more complicated and less predictive than is often understood. On the one hand, the left may benefit from protest against the impact of neoliberal policies, particularly when they lift state protection of uncompetitive popular sectors in favor of market distribution of costs and benefits. Cárdenas benefited in 1988 from anger at what many saw as the state's *de facto* repudiation of its traditional alliance with workers, peasants, and popular classes. By implementing wage freezes, deep spending cuts, and trade restructuring, the De la Madrid government endorsed and enforced an unprecedented drop in living standards from 1982 to 1988, with no apparent end in sight. These factors triggered a specifically left electoral protest. One might expect, therefore, that the spread of the neoliberal approach could benefit left parties in a variety of settings.

On the other hand, ironically, the spread of neoliberalism coincided with and was fueled by the conspicuous collapse of socialist models of development, the left's traditional proposal. The failure of the left to offer a "discernible, coherent, and adequately financed alternative to the 'free-market' consensus" contributed to an ideological vacuum in which neoliberal policies were adopted almost by default, even by some who had campaigned on traditional left or populist platforms.[12] The goals of wealth redistribution and social justice seemed more urgent and vital than ever. Yet socialist prescriptions of a state-controlled economy and at least partial withdrawal from the world capitalist market appeared unable to provide economic growth and abundant consumer goods over the long term, despite advances in the distribution of income. Similarly, the debt crisis called into question the viability of the developmental state that had been a classic compromise for the left between socialism and free-market capitalism, as forced budget cuts eliminated or reduced state investment, subsidies, and services.

Thus, as neoliberalism spread, the left struggled to find an alternative to offer potential supporters that would "not [be] predicated on privatization, blind acceptance of export-led growth, and attacks on the living standards of working people" and that would guarantee political

---

12. Jorge Castañeda, "Latin America and the End of the Cold War: A Mixed Blessing for the Left," *World Policy Journal* 7 (Summer 1990): 481.

participation.[13] This new alternative is elusive; indeed, even within the left "the very idea of an overall alternative of any sort to the status quo has been severely questioned."[14] The often criticized failure of the PRD to produce a coherent, consistent alternative to neoliberalism, rather than indicating unusual laziness or incompetence on the part of PRD leaders in particular, fits within a much larger pattern of ideological confusion on the left.

The left's identity crisis also took place as many left parties and movements faced the additional dilemma of their role in democratic transitions. During a transition the left often plays an important part in mobilizing popular sentiment for democratization. If left parties participate in the negotiation of democratic rules and commit to be bound by them, they can reduce the danger of subversive or guerrilla threats, reassuring the military and removing a major threat to stable democracy. After transition the viability of the left may affect the persistence and scope of democracy. Left parties tend to specialize in demands like the redistribution of wealth, social services, and attention to basic needs for the marginalized and often unorganized poor. The systematic, effective articulation of such demands is vital to the quality of democracy, particularly in deeply unequal societies like Mexico. If the ideological spectrum narrows, democratic competition may cease to offer meaningful choices, in the long run alienating citizens and leaving social problems unchanneled and unaddressed until they reach crisis proportions and cause the regime to crack in unexpected ways. The guerrilla rebellion that broke out in the state of Chiapas in January 1994 illustrates this process at work.[15] If democracy becomes a mere matter of personnel—*who* exercises power, not *for what ends* power is exercised, the result may be a new kind of bureaucratic authoritarianism—in Malloy's terms, "hybrid regimes which . . . marry an outward electoral democracy with a technocratic and authoritarian policy process, especially in economic matters."[16]

13. Barry Carr, "The Left and Its Potential Role in Political Change," in *Mexico's Alternative Political Futures*, ed. Wayne Cornelius, Judith Gentleman, and Peter Smith. (La Jolla, Calif.: UCSD Center for U.S.-Mexican Studies, 1989), 384.

14. Castañeda, "Latin America and the End of the Cold War," 478.

15. The lack of a viable legal electoral opposition in the state of Chiapas, where the PRI won 90 percent of the vote as late as 1988, may have contributed to the rebels' perception that they could not get the government's attention in any way except armed rebellion. One major rebel complaint focused precisely on the way that PRI dominance of local government promoted complicity with local elites, deprived local indigenous and peasant groups of legal protection, and kept offenders from being held accountable.

16. James Malloy, quoted in Peter Smith, "Crisis and Democracy in Latin America," *World Politics* 43 (July 1991): 623.

Yet transitions also confront the left with its traditional ambivalence about representative, electoral democracy. On the one hand, democracy offers the left valuable opportunities to organize and conduct a Gramscian war of position for influence over the masses without suffering the repression targeted at left activists by authoritarian regimes. After the military regimes of the seventies, even bourgeois, capitalist democracy looked better than capitalist authoritarianism. Leftists who had defined socialism as "the historical fulfillment of the democratic ideal . . . that is no longer just formal but substantive as well"[17] seemed increasingly willing to value representative democracy as a worthwhile goal in itself, and as a more likely path to democratic socialism than revolution.[18]

On the other hand, much of the left had long seen representative democracy as a capitalist trap to trick people into giving up revolutionary forms of struggle in exchange for ultimately illusory promises of reform. Elections were not a reliable instrument for achieving socialism, as Allende tragically demonstrated in Chile. As practiced in many countries they did not even guarantee free and fair competition. Moreover, in order to secure a democratic system of questionable value the left often had to limit its substantive demands and its mobilizational power in order to convince conservative elites that democracy would not mean mob rule or attacks on property. Left parties sometimes formally negotiated such guarantees with elites in a political pact. While designed to win conservative support for a democratic transition, pacts tended to freeze in place concessions made by the left at a moment of vulnerability.[19] Moreover, if left parties commit themselves to representative democracy, they must often moderate their ideological program in order to get more votes (by appealing to the center) and convince elites they can safely allow leftists to take power. Thus, the left seemed to face "a situation which, in crude terms, offer[ed] two basic options:

17. Norberto Bobbio, *Which Socialism? Marxism, Socialism, and Democracy*, trans. Roger Griffin (Cambridge: Polity Press, 1987), 39.

18. "Democratic socialism" originally included not only substantive concerns but also a preference for direct democracy. Over time, it began to be acceptable in leftist circles to criticize existing socialist regimes for their failure to practice democracy. Some even argued that representative democracy was a more practical and thus preferable option given the difficulty (or impossibility) of direct democracy in modern mass society. See ibid., especially pp. 65–84. For a discussion of the relationship between the means of achieving socialism and the kind of socialism that results see especially pp. 31–46 and 103–20.

19. Terry Karl, "Petroleum and Political Pacts: The Transition to Democracy in Venezuela," *Latin American Research Review* 22, no. 1 (1987): 63–94; Guillermo O'Donnell and Philippe Schmitter, *Transitions from Authoritarian Rule: Tentative Conclusions About Uncertain Democracies* (Baltimore: The Johns Hopkins University Press, 1986), especially pp. 63, 69.

either capitalism with democracy or socialism without democracy."[20] Many leftists found it hard to choose.

Doubts about the left's willingness to abide by the democratic rules of the game hurt its chances of winning elections and taking office. The PRD position of criticizing electoral rules but asking for votes created confusion in potential supporters who were not sure why they were being asked to put a lot of effort into a process that the party argued was fundamentally flawed. Yet dissipating those doubts proved especially hard for the left. How can a party "prove" its commitment to democracy? For many left parties support for democracy at the regime level implied support for internal party democracy, but what kind of democracy, now that "democratic centralism" had gone out of style?[21] In addition to several models of representative democracy (majoritarian, proportional, and consociational), left parties more frequently confronted demands for direct democracy from popular organizations like religious base communities or urban popular movements, which had developed norms of participatory democracy. And if not all popular movements adopted these norms, and even fewer functioned as participatory democracies, nevertheless, the exposure of left parties to these norms challenged definitions of democracy as basically representative. What did a party need to do to be "democratic," or at least to convince popular movements that it was? And could this be reconciled with the party's status as an agent in the sphere of representative politics, participating in elections and assuming government responsibilities?

The difficulty of resolving these questions appears in the often troubled nature of left party relationships with popular organizations and their own elected officials. The heterogeneity of the modern left—which includes the remants of old left parties, unions, and "new left" organizations (from urban popular movements to movements based on "postmaterialist" claims like environmental protection)—tends to produce parties that struggle constantly with internal divisions and conflicting conceptions of democracy. Internal democracy in such parties may even aggravate these problems.

Thus, the dilemmas of dealing with neoliberalism and democracy

20. Bobbio, *Which Socialism?* 44.

21. A classic communist party formula, "democratic centralism" implied broad discussion and participation up until central authorities made the final decision, at which time absolute obedience to the decision became the rule. In practice, centralism succeeded and democracy failed due to the chilling effect party discipline had on discussion and the common lack of mechanisms to hold central authorities accountable. Most left parties found themselves in the awkward position of having to live down such practices in addition to their previous criticism of representative democracy.

confronted the PRD with a series of challenges common to many left parties. Yet common problems do not necessarily lead to common solutions. Depending on the characteristics of the party, especially its basic support, its foundation experience, its institutional context, and the party system in which it functions, left parties make different choices and accept different trade-offs. The PRD's answer is not the same as the answer of the Brazilian Workers' Party or the Italian Democratic Party of the Left. Lacking an identity rooted in either a coherent ideological alternative or organizational ties to unions, the more typical left party pattern, the PRD fell back on a loosely defined identity linked to diverse social movement struggles and early tactical choices. Defending this identity encouraged the PRD to make some unwise electoral decisions.

On the electoral level it is the pattern of rising support and then abandonment of the left that requires explanation. It is not immediately obvious—and the PRD still has trouble understanding—why voters that deserted one party in 1988 in order to protest neoliberal reforms and support a coalition that promised a return to Mexico's traditional economic model should almost at once, and without much perceptible change in party ideologies, return their support to parties promoting those same neoliberal reforms. While Cárdenas drew heavily on protest against economic crisis, protest had a distinctly leftist tinge. As Castañeda argued, "Cuauhtémoc Cárdenas touched a very basic fiber of the nation's soul in 1988. Under ideal conditions of sustained well-distributed and significant economic growth, it might be possible for a majority of the Mexican people to accept the abdication of a certain amount of sovereignty and autonomy in exchange for economic well-being. But in the absence of this best-case scenario, it is difficult to imagine how a people that probably elected a symbol of Mexican progressive, mestizo, egalitarian nationalism to the presidency in July 1988 would only a few years later approve of this kind of project."[22] Less than three years later they appeared to have done just that.

NEW PARTIES: EMERGENCE AND CONSOLIDATION

Ultimately, therefore, although the story of the PRD has implications for left parties and for opposition parties in restrictive regimes, it is

22. Jorge Castañeda, "Salinas's International Relations Gamble," *Journal of International Affairs* 43 (Winter 1990): 421.

fundamentally about what happens to a new party as it undergoes the traumatic shift from emergence to consolidation. Consolidation as I understand it is neither merely electoral nor merely a matter of internal organization, the focus of most studies of party institutionalization. A relatively small electoral party can have "blackmail potential," "governing potential," or "growth potential"—presenting a future threat to which other parties respond preemptively.[23] Electoral support does not imply corresponding institutionalization or influence. Consolidation of a party's organization affects its coherence, stability, discipline, and capacity to act as a unit, and hence its ability to influence politics above and beyond its level of electoral support. The *cardenista* coalition of 1988 had a lot of electoral support but could not translate this support into influence precisely because it lacked these qualities, while the PRD by 1992 could successfully confront the PRI under some circumstances despite a smaller electoral base. Finally, a narrow focus would miss important sources of party stability and influence. "Party consolidation," therefore, refers to the construction of stable norms and expectations for mutual cooperation, decision making, and conflict resolution in five key relationships: (1) among activists; (2) with voters; (3) with civil society organizations; (4) with other parties; and (5) with the state.

In this transition from emergence to consolidation, some common threads emerge. Whether the party under analysis is located on the right or left of the political spectrum, whether it was initially electorally successful or unsuccessful, and whether it emerged in the context of a one-party, two-party, or multiparty system, it must face the differences between detachment and reattachment, and between emergence and consolidation.

For a new party to permanently alter the structure of the party system two processes must take place: detachment of supporters from traditional parties and reattachment of supporters to the new option. Detachment and reattachment are not stages of a single evolutionary process but separate processes with their own causal dynamics.[24] In the first process, voters *lose* political identities; in the second, voters *develop*

23. Growth potential is my own term. The others come from Sartori's criteria for counting a party as "relevant." See Sartori, *Parties and Party Systems*.

24. These terms are analogous to dealignment and realignment but at the individual level of analysis. Detachment may result in observed system dealignment if detached voters do not vote at all or if they distribute their preferences in such a way that the distribution of votes in the party system is preserved. Reattachment results in realignment if voters acquire loyalties to different parties than the ones they supported before. However, hypothetically, parties may also win back lost loyalties, resulting in reattachment without realignment.

political identifications, in this case with a new party they at first know little about. Though the two processes are hard to separate empirically, their theoretical separation is a heuristically powerful way of understanding one of the major problems facing new parties, even those that have tremendous initial success: the consolidation of a stable electoral base and loyal activist cadres. New parties often depend especially heavily on detached voters (above all, the strategic protest vote) and detached elites (particularly "breakaway" leaders from an existing party). Thus, they should typically have trouble consolidating their political base.

Detachment

Without detachment, the formation of a successful new party is unlikely. If existing parties absorb political participation and loyalties, there is little space for new opposition and thus little incentive for leaders to undertake its organization. The causal factors that lead to detachment vary. Some causes build up gradually over time. Economic development, for instance, may result in the formation or growth of social actors unincorporated by the existing party system, or bring about the decline of sectors on which existing parties relied for support. Dissatisfaction with party performance can also accumulate slowly, especially in the case of a long-ruling single party. All policies anger some constituents, and hegemonic parties have sole responsibility for policy for extended periods of time. Their seemingly perpetual monopoly of access to power can by itself arouse resentment. Long-ruling parties also tend to become corrupt and overbureaucratized, which may alienate supporters, as in the cases of two other long-ruling parties: Japan's Liberal Democratic Party and Italy's Christian Democratic Party.

Other causes take the form of sudden conjunctural crises that accelerate detachment, especially if voters and potential new party leaders blame existing parties for the crisis and see them as incompetent to resolve it, or if they trigger the same groups drifting away from existing parties through more gradual social change. Thus, the same kind of stress that can lead to critical realignment in competitive party systems may also lead to the formation of new parties.[25] These parties become

25. Critical election theory, though often considered a narrow theory applicable mainly to two-party systems, offers an uncannily accurate picture of the Mexican electoral process in 1988, which, like U.S. critical elections, was "associated with short-lived but very intense disruptions of traditional patterns of voting behavior, . . . abnormally heavy voter participation, . . . abnormal stress in the socioeconomic system," and a "triggering

successful when for some reason existing parties cannot capture and express popular discontent. The question is therefore twofold. First, why would discontented elites choose to form a new party instead of exercising voice within existing parties, protesting outside parties, or withdrawing from politics? Second, why do existing parties fail to use the tools at their disposal to recapture drifting voters? Existing opposition parties seem naturally positioned to take advantage of protest against the governing party. Governing parties should rationally anticipate their loss of support and modify their positions.

Sometimes leaders of these parties miss the warning signs of defection for psychological reasons, like wishful thinking or cognitive routines that interpret present information in the light of past experience. The PRI clearly did not expect Cárdenas to do as well as he did in 1988, and this contributed to the willingness of some leaders to take a hard line that accepted and even encouraged his virtual expulsion from the party. Sometimes attempted ideological modifications are less than convincing. The PRI can trumpet its support for "democracy," but skeptics will never believe in their conversion. Sometimes the new is simply more appealing than the old that has already disappointed. And sometimes the crisis itself limits the alteration of party positions. As an opposition candidate Cárdenas had the latitude to promise what the government of a country could not publicly get away with promising, for example, promotion of a moratorium on debt payment. Thus, conjunctural crises may be particularly likely to lead to new party formation. They add to popular discontent, lock governing elites into "more rigid and dogmatic" positions that hurt them with the electorate, and alienate elites who could lead a new party. Thus they contribute, as in critical realignment, to the buildup of "the explosive 'bursting stress' of realignment."[26]

In the Mexican case gradual erosion of ruling party support contributed to the detachment of voters, which facilitated new party formation; but conjunctural factors dramatically accelerated this process and triggered the detachment of elites who organized the new left coalition. Until this occurred, the slow erosion of the PRI's electoral base, brought about by economic development and urbanization as well as increasingly public corruption, was not widely reflected in the party system. Despite limited opportunities to participate, a broad majority probably

---

event of scope and brutal force great enough to produce the mobilizations required from a normally passive-participant middle-class electorate." Walter Burnham, *Critical Elections and the Mainsprings of American Politics* (New York: Norton, 1976), 6, 8, 10, 170.

26. Ibid., 7.

supported the PRI until at least 1970, based on the country's excellent economic performance, legitimacy derived from the Revolution, and the PRI's commitment to share the gains from development with organized labor and peasants. These gains were virtually wiped out by the economic crisis. As the party in charge the PRI got blamed for everything: for incurring impossible debts, for corruption, for enforcing wage freezes, for incompetence in managing the crisis, and for implementing broad budget cuts just when people most needed social spending. Thus, by 1988 there was a large pool of potential protest voters detached from traditional loyalties to the PRI.

Second, and equally crucial, the economic crisis and the resulting transformation of economic policy produced a split within the ruling elite that eventually led to the defection of key figures from the left wing of the PRI, including Cuauhtémoc Cárdenas. Even after three years of crisis the 1985 elections produced no major reflection of discontent in the party system. Without the *cardenistas* there would have been no unified left alliance in 1988 and no PRD. Their political savvy and connections helped the *cardenistas* construct an opposition campaign fast enough to take advantage of a brief window of opportunity. Cárdenas attracted voters who had not confronted the PRI or participated in politics before. In addition, his candidacy further divided the PRI and prevented it from responding effectively. Most fundamentally, however, Cárdenas gave voters a way to move from passive detachment, or simple dislike of the system, to active detachment, or acting against it. While the opposition vote would probably have increased in 1988 no matter what, it would have been more fragmented and increased less overall without Cárdenas, a candidate whose ideological orientation, personal qualities, and symbolic identification with Mexico's most revolutionary president focused discontent around key issues. His roots in the system meant voters had a shorter trip to take away from previous loyalties to the PRI. Finally, to the extent that voters associated existing opposition with failure, preference for a new option increased.[27] In 1985 the PAN, the largest independent opposition in Mexico since the 1940s, increased its vote only 1.1 percent over 1982.[28]

27. Similarly, Dick Taverne explained his decision after breaking with Labour to support the formation of a new Social Democratic Party in Great Britain instead of joining the existing Liberal Party by saying, "I could never quite see the Liberals breaking through on their own. They had a smell of failure associated with them. They had been in opposition since 1920." Geoffrey Lee Williams and Alan Lee Williams, *Labour's Decline and the Social Democrats' Fall* (London: Macmillan, 1989), 112.

28. Mexico, Instituto Federal Electoral (IFE), *Contienda electoral en las elecciones de diputados federales*, ed. Jenny Saltiel Cohen (Mexico City: IFE, 1991), 10–11.

The detachment of elites with such long-standing loyalties to the system required drastic events, not just gradual demographic shifts or discontent with corruption. Eroding public support for the PRI—the result of both the crisis and these more long-term trends—did concern the *cardenistas*. Most were experienced politicians who had either held elective office or taken responsibility for electoral mobilization.[29] They saw a danger for the PRI in the social effects of the crisis and the government's unwillingness or inability to protect key voting blocs. Even more important, they found themselves increasingly marginalized within the system, leaving them helpless to prevent the implementation of neoliberal policies that conflicted at every point with their traditional ideological profile: where neoliberals promoted privatization and deregulation, *cardenistas* wanted a strong state role in the economy, including ownership of key sectors; where neoliberals supported wage freezes to hold down inflation, *cardenistas* wanted state support for labor demands such as wage raises to compensate for inflation; where neoliberals accepted fiscal austerity in order to pay the debt, *cardenistas* argued that Mexico should repudiate the debt if necessary in order to maintain state investment, jobs, and social services; and where neoliberals sought to lower trade barriers and court foreign investment, *cardenistas* defended traditional protection of national industry.

As the crisis deepened, the technocratic inner circle of De la Madrid increasingly refused to compromise policy in order to placate the *cardenistas*, fearing that dilution of austerity or restructuring would endanger Mexico's relationship with international creditors, business confidence, and ultimately any hope of recovery. To ensure policy coherence, De la Madrid excluded opponents from important positions. The PRI's hierarchical structure did not give dissidents an institutional niche to express their demands or encourage effective use of voice to bring about internal reform. Rather, De la Madrid's ability to control the PRI supported his attempts to marginalize the *cardenistas*.

These factors combined to produce an intolerable situation of increasing confrontation and polarization within the ruling party. The internalized beliefs of the De la Madrid cabinet, partly the result of education and training in the United States, coincided with IMF prescriptions in a policy package that alienated the *cardenistas*, driving them first to exercise voice in unprecedented public criticism and then to exit from the party.

29. Among others, this group included an ex-governor, ex-congressmen, and an ex-president of the PRI, who had also been a campaign coordinator for President José López Portillo in 1976.

Structural factors play a relatively minor role in this story of strategic interaction and conjunctural opportunity. The Mexican crisis affected too many sectors for the new option to have a well-defined structural basis. Thus, the effect of structural change was indirect, and worked primarily by swelling the pool of alienated voters to which a new party, if organized, could appeal. The availability of detached voters increases the likelihood that a new party will succeed in winning votes and therefore the likelihood that ambitious leaders will see the organization of a party as an attractive option.

Conjunctural crisis worked more directly and in multiple ways to increase the likelihood of new party formation. It alienated voters and potential leaders of an anti-incumbent coalition at the same time, though not necessarily for the same motives. The timing issue is not insignificant. The notion of triggers frequently shows up in studies of revolutions and social movements, both of which have to deal with the problem that while the social conditions that lead to revolt may be fairly common or of long standing, the experience of revolt is relatively rare. Theda Skocpol's argument that revolutions are more likely when international conditions lead to divisions within the state recognizes a specific manifestation of this general principle: people may have *reasons* to rebel most of the time, but *opportunities* occur more seldom.[30] Sometimes a trigger galvanizes public opinion into the recognition of social grievance. In party formation the trigger must affect potential organizers at the same time as potential supporters in order for the party to succeed. The very existence of such a pool of detached voters encourages potential leaders to see appeal to the electorate as a viable strategy for responding to the triggering events.

In the Mexican case detached voters entered actively into the process only after detached elites organized a coalition to support the alternative candidacy of Cárdenas. For the most alienated Cárdenas offered an electoral way to express their anger so that protest which had taken other forms could now show up in the party system. For others, voting for Cárdenas completed a detachment process that began with simple discontent with the existing system. Cárdenas thus benefited from and contributed to the detachment of voters from previous electoral identities.

Reattachment

However, the ability to take advantage of detachment does not imply the ability to reattach voters and activists permanently to a new politi-

---

30. Theda Skocpol, *States and Social Revolutions: A Comparative Analysis of France, Russia, and China* (New York: Cambridge University Press, 1979).

cal identity. This is not necessarily an intuitively obvious outcome. A new party, especially a successful one, fills some gap in the political system. Initial supporters find it meets their needs better than existing parties. There seems no obvious reason for them to suddenly cease to find it useful. Yet new parties often have trouble establishing a stable voting base (and older parties have trouble recapturing the loyalties of voters they have alienated) because reattachment confronts parties with a new set of constraints and opportunities, both different and more demanding than the task of attracting detached voters.

One can conceive of individual reattachment taking place through four main linkages. First, voters may identify with a party for ideological reasons because they share its worldview and political goals (ideological linkage). Second, they may support the party in order to preserve a valued social relationship with a friend, family member, social group, or organization that decides to commit to the party (social linkage). Third, they may support the party for reasons of self-interest, if the party proves itself able and willing to deliver payoffs to supporters (self-interest linkage). In order to attract an activist core, payoffs must include selective incentives as well as collective payoffs, though payoffs may take the form of either material resources or intangible rewards like prestige, participation, and power. Finally, supporters may identify with a party out of habit (psychological linkage): for short-term, strategic, or even idiosyncratic reasons constituents continue to vote for a party on a contingent basis until their pattern of voting convinces them they must really like that party. For a new party to win repeated strategic votes in the relative absence of other types of linkage (such as ideological sympathy), two conditions must generally persist: (1) continued protest against the incumbent party. (2) a relatively stark choice between the incumbent party and a single viable opposition. If a new party consistently chose the most popular candidate, it still might continue to appear the best option to defeat the incumbent party, but under multiparty competition the odds are against this. Psychological habit is therefore an unstable and unlikely path unless other linkages are called into play, as for example if the party wins an election and is able to use its victory to deliver some payoffs. Otherwise, each electoral failure diminishes the party's image as a viable alternative, which encourages volatile voting or the formation of additional new parties.

However, it is unusual for only one type of linkage to operate. First of all, the different factors are not independent of one another. Social groups contribute to the formation of ideological preferences, and similar preferences draw together social networks. Strategic choices are made in the expectation of future payoffs, and neglected payoffs may lead one to recalculate strategic choices. Interaction among these factors should therefore occur naturally. If a party's ideology appeals to peasants, it may recruit activists among peasants (activating a social linkage), seek to make payoffs to peasants, and thus win their loyalties.

Second, environmental and institutional factors can influence more than one linkage at a time. For example, socioeconomic characteristics may affect ideological preferences as well as the organizations of civil society, which can serve as mobilizational tools for a new party. Economic and social structures also shape the basic distribution of resources, which affects the payoffs a new party *can* deliver and the kind of payoffs supporters *expect* it to deliver. The supporters of a left party usually come from classes with many concrete demands but few economic resources to offer the party. The gap between needs and resources is likely to be huge. Finally, institutions—especially access to state resources—influence a new party's ability to deliver payoffs.

There are three key implications of this analysis. First, successful consolidation should be more likely when a party can call on multiple linkages. Second, if institutional and environmental characteristics shape the linkages available to a party to consolidate partisan loyalties, then manipulation of these characteristics can interfere with party consolidation. New identities take some time to form, and each path to reattachment relies to some extent on habituation. A one-time payoff may induce a one-time electoral reward, but reattachment requires trust in the party's ability and willingness to deliver future payoffs. In the meantime others will try to interfere with the transference of loyalties. Because new parties tend to get a greater percentage of their support from detached voters, existing parties have more latitude to interrupt consolidation. By shifting its ideological position, an incumbent party or parties can shrink the ideological space originally exploited by the new party. Incumbents can use their resources to break up incipient relationships with civil society and deliver payoffs to "buy" votes. Incumbents may also be able to interfere with a new party's ability to deliver payoffs. Last but not least, the use of fraud, intimidation, and manipulation of the media may make the new party appear less viable as a strategic vehicle for protest. In the Mexican case the PRI used all of these methods of interference with considerable success against the PRD.

Finally, this process clearly differs substantially from the process of detachment. The negative reasons an individual might have for renouncing previous loyalties and party identifications do not necessarily give him/her the positive reasons necessary to develop a new political identity or reassign loyalty. This difference between detachment and reattachment affects new parties most strongly because they have the smallest number of loyal voters/activists to fall back on, in contrast to older parties that may benefit from a short-term voting surge. And the more the new party depends on strategic voting for its initial support, the more precarious its path to consolidating a stable voting base.

Emergence vs. Consolidation

Several scholars have offered models of organizational evolution that stress the differences between new parties and mature, consolidated parties. Most connect these changes to bureaucratization and the professionalization of party leadership. For Robert Michels the end result is oligarchy—concentration of power in the hands of a few and the growing apathy of party rank and file.[31] Angelo Panebianco, drawing upon Allesandro Pizzorno's distinction between systems of solidarity and systems of interest, argues that "when a political party is founded, it is an 'association amongst equals' created to realize a common end" and therefore "cooperation in the realization of a common end prevails"; but "in time . . . the party tends to evolve from a system of solidarity into a system of interests. Through its bureaucratization and progressive involvement in daily routine, the organization diversifies from within" and as a result becomes a system in which "*competition* between diverging interests prevails."[32] Thus, "we see here the passage from a *social movement* type of participation . . . to a *professional* type of participation." Professionalization implies movement from "a phase in which collective incentives . . . prevail . . . to a phase in which selective incentives . . . prevail . . . from a phase in which organizational ideology is *manifest* (the objectives being explicit and coherent), to a phase in which organizational ideology is *latent* (the objectives being vague, implicit, and contradictory) . . . from a phase in which an aggressive strategy that tends to dominate/transform its environment prevails . . . to a phase in which a strategy of adaptation prevails."[33]

This transition takes place in large part because "parties, in the course of their organizational development, tend to go from an initial period in which certain needs prevail to a subsequent period in which

31. Robert Michels, *Political Parties: A Sociological Study of the Oligarchical Tendencies of Modern Democracy*, trans. Eden and Cedar Paul (New York: The Free Press, 1962).
32. A system of solidarity is "based on the concept of a community of equals in which the participants' ends coincide," and a system of interest is "a system of action based on the interests of the actor." See Angelo Panebianco, *Political Parties: Organization and Power*, trans. Marc Silver (New York: Cambridge University Press, 1988), 18.
33. Ibid., 19.

different needs prevail."[34] Panebianco does not elaborate on this difference but labels the transition "institutionalization" and presumes that parties naturally undergo the process. I argue that just as detachment differs from reattachment, emergence differs from consolidation—regardless of how much (if any) institutionalization occurs. The consolidation of a new party calls for different strengths and skills, imposes different tasks, and often takes place in different institutional/political arenas than its emergence.

Key differences in focus include:

	Emergence	Consolidation
Ideological Emphasis	personality of leaders global ideological vision promises of change	substantive issues specific policies payoffs
Tactical Attitude Toward Other Actors	challenge relationships mobilization/ confrontation	establish stable relationships steady activity/compromise
Arena of Action	public arena—plaza	institutional arena— government

The ideological emphasis of a new party is on criticism of the existing system. What catches voter attention is its global vision, in Sidney Tarrow's terms the "collective action frame" it employs to interpret the country's situation.[35] If its master frame is familiar to voters and it stresses key complaints, a new party may not need many concrete proposals. Yet in the long run no party can expect to consolidate voter loyalties solely on the basis of rejecting all that incumbent parties do. Repeated strategic voting is not as stable a basis for reattachment as propositive ideological development. New parties also highlight the personality of what at first will be relatively few, easily identifiable leaders. At the moment of emergence the very fact that they are challenging the "system" by forming a new party increases the likelihood that leaders will seem energetic, attractive, and fresh, while relative ignorance of their weaknesses exaggerates their personal strengths. Later scrutiny

34. Ibid., 18.

35. Sidney Tarrow, "Mentalities, Political Cultures, and Collective Action Frames: Constructing Meanings Through Action," in *Frontiers in Social Movement Theory,* ed. Aldon Morris and Carol McClurg Mueller. (New Haven, Conn.: Yale University Press, 1992), 177. See also David Snow and Robert Benford, "Master Frames and Cycles of Protest," in *Frontiers in Social Movement Theory,* ed. Morris and Mueller.

can tarnish the reputation of those whose weaknesses were less known at first.

In addition, the whole point of a new party is to challenge existing alliances and expectations. The more confrontational and dramatic this challenge, the more romantic, exciting, and appealing it may appear. Lacking other resources, organization, or established loyalties, new parties have to rely on public mobilization to connect to a mass base. Yet after a while the excitement wears off. Constant mobilization seems tedious and tiring. Permanent confrontation does not deliver payoffs without some willingness to negotiate and compromise. New parties may not be very good at negotiation until they develop the capacity to make collective decisions that are binding on their members.

Finally, the arena of action changes. The business of participating in government, of translating popular support into influence, payoffs, and policy results takes place in an institutional setting, not the public plaza. The plaza only gets the party as far as the offices where deals are actually made. Internal bureaucratization and institutionalization helps parties cope better with these demands. However, the change in tasks often produces changes in party behavior and success before any significant bureaucratization occurs.

Because of these differences between emergence and consolidation, the effect and importance of particular causal factors may change depending on the phase of party development. Features like institutions, social cleavages, or ideology may interact with the demands on parties to produce different results at different stages. Some factors that encourage the creation of new parties may do little for their consolidation, or actually inhibit it. Emergence itself may cause changes in the original factors that led to successful party formation. Thus, parties with unusual emergence strengths may be poorly designed for consolidation, and vice versa.[36]

The evidence suggests, for example, that institutions matter more to consolidation than emergence, and that it is critical to look at more than electoral law. The PRD suffered from intense discrimination, common to opposition in dominant party systems where institutions are designed to prevent party system change. Studying parties like the PRD presents a compelling picture of how such systems persist over long periods. In Mexico the normal advantages of incumbency accrue at all lev-

---

36. Margaret Keck makes the "vice versa" argument about the Brazilian PT, where she notes that "characteristics of the party that were thought to cause its 'failure' in the early stages of the [democratic] transition became key elements in its political survival and continued evolution." See Keck, *The Workers' Party and Democratization in Brazil* (New Haven: Yale University Press, 1992), 238.

els to a single party. Its position in the state gave the PRI a decisive advantage in resources. This stacked the deck against new parties in general, parties who attacked PRI policies even more, and left parties— whose supporters often cannot fund the party adequately—most of all. During emergence, alternative resources like charisma, mobilization, surprise, and denunciation of the government can compensate for structural and institutional disadvantages. Later on many of these resources vanish or prove ill-suited to consolidation tasks.

Likewise, new social cleavages may create opportunities for new parties, but the construction of solid ties to social sectors depends heavily on facilitating factors, like institutions, which may not be present. As a consequence, party performance may falter, and achievements possible during emergence—such as close electoral alliances with popular movements—become extremely difficult to sustain.

Similarly, the effect of ideology may vary. As a result of its ideological position the PRD shares many experiences with other left parties, suffers from common problems, and faces similar issues. However, ideological position may interact with institutions in different ways during party emergence and party consolidation. For party formation, the greater the difference between the position of the existing parties and the proposed new party, the more likely that potential benefits will outweigh potential costs for prospective party leaders and detached protest voters. There is simply more to gain from a risky switch to a new party with significant differences from incumbents than a new party that differs only slightly from incumbents. Yet in the long term, maximum difference with incumbents attracts proportionately more hostility and frightens voters in the center. In addition, the conditions under which voters tend to accept greater risks may not persist after emergence, increasing the negative effect of ideological distance. Voters are more likely to accept the risk of supporting considerable change when the cost of the status quo is especially high—that is, when fundamental interests are threatened. In such a situation cost/benefit analysis of the status quo may even turn negative (potentially greater continuity versus loss of key interests), enhancing the attractiveness of a vote for change. Again, if the threat to fundamental interests eases or reverses, the benefits of the status quo should rise, and the willingness of voters to accept significant risks diminishes.

These problems caused by the effects of newness should eventually be displaced by problems associated with characteristics of the party itself, such as its ideological position. The catch is that the circumstances of emergence shape party characteristics. If parties retain a genetic imprint, they may be unable to escape entirely the fate imposed upon them by the conditions and choices of their birth.[37] For example, the "social movement logic" that clearly characterized the PRD's formative period marked its organizational evolution and later strategic choices. If the PRD is any guide, many parties that do not act like unitary actors pursuing electoral victory may be responding not only to the pressures of well-positioned activists in the party bureaucracy but also to a social movement imperative to preserve salient features of movement identity, an imperative that may actually increase as prospects for success dim. In the case of the PRD identities forged in early experiences have a lot to do with some of its most apparently irrational electoral strategies, such as its prolonged refusal to negotiate with the government, its adoption of any and all social movements—including the Chiapas rebels—even when association with these movements scared off potential middle-class support, and the insistence of a number of top leaders on mobilizational campaigns rather than professionalized media campaigns.

Thus, this analysis highlights the long-term impact of choices made at a formative moment in a party's history. In essence, party emergence is a "critical juncture" for the new party and potentially for the party system. Styles, patterns of behavior, and decisions about party structure that emerge from the formative process have unintended and often unanticipated consequences for subsequent generations of party leaders. Parties may carry with them repertoires of strategies far longer than rational choice might suggest. And the difference between formation and consolidation suggests that the same set of characteristics may have different effects over time. "Newness" carries with it common challenges, but these initial characteristics influence patterns of success and failure.

STRUCTURE AND METHODOLOGY

The first three substantive chapters discuss detachment and the conditions that encouraged the emergence of a new party, combining statisti-

---

37. It is not clear exactly when Panebianco, to whom I owe the concept of a genetic imprint, would declare a party's genetic heritage complete. He seems to be speaking of emergence and early institutionalization when he argues that "organizational development is strictly conditioned by the relations that the party establishes in the genetic phases and after by its interactions." Later he suggests a longer period of genetic imprint, including "how the organization originated *and* how it consolidated" (emphasis added). I argue that one should limit the genetic imprint to an early phase, including conditions of

cal analysis of voting patterns with interviews of national elites. Chapter 2 focuses on the characteristics of the Mexican political regime and the stresses on the regime as it approached the crisis of the eighties, setting the stage for the emergence of new opposition in 1988. The third chapter analyzes what detached some elites from their traditional loyalty to the PRI as well as the role played in the emergence of a new opposition alliance by the accumulation of detached voters. Since party formation is a largely elite-driven process, I rely heavily on interviews with participants to trace the formation of the PRD, weighing the role of structural and institutional incentives that united opposition leaders to support the candidacy of Cuauhtémoc Cárdenas and later led to the creation of a new political party. Chapter 4 examines how the characteristics of the coalition contributed to its extraordinary electoral success and how they affected its performance in the critical moments when it first faced consolidation tasks. I supplement this with a statistical analysis of the socioeconomic basis of the *cardenista* vote, with particular attention to indications of reliance on strategic protest. Despite the shortcomings of questionable statistics, electoral results provide information that authors increasingly recognize as useful even in the study of semicompetitive systems like Mexico.

The second part of the book focuses on the problems of party consolidation and reattachment, and therefore requires the addition of local-level case studies. While strategic and institutional choices made at the national level affect local party organization, I look at the local level as well for two basic reasons. First, measurement of many dependent variables in consolidation requires looking at local or even individual results, including the spread of partisan loyalties, the ability of the party to penetrate society by building local organization, and the construction of working alliances with local popular movements. Performance of government responsibilities—a key part of a party's ability to deliver payoffs to supporters—took place almost exclusively on a local level, in municipal governments that the PRD controlled. Thus, an exclusively national focus risked accepting rhetorical accomplishments as real and missing much of what is interesting about the transition from emergence to consolidation. Second, local case studies expanded the number of cases, from one (the national party) to several. Though obviously these local cases are not independent, the considerable variation in success observed by region, state, and locality requires some explanation.

---

emergence and founding organizational decisions but before any substantial consolidation, in order to test whether a "genetic model" exists. See Panebianco, *Political Parties*, 20, 50.

The primary cases from Michoacán and the Estado de México fulfill two main requirements that make them interesting ways to look at the theoretical problems of emergence and consolidation. In the first place, these examples come from states where the *cardenistas* experienced their greatest success in 1988. Thus, these cases may suggest which variables are particularly important for success in emergence. Cases of successful emergence also maximize the contrast with consolidation. If success in emergence predicts success in consolidation, the party should have a better chance of consolidation in areas where it did especially well initially. If the characteristics of success lead at times to problems, it should be possible to trace this process in successful states. At the least, one cannot simply (and uninterestingly) attribute lack of consolidation to initial weakness. Support for Cárdenas was well above the national average in both Michoacán and the Estado de México. Michoacán is the home state of Cárdenas and the heart of his movement in many ways. In 1988 he received a higher percentage of the vote there (64.2 percent) than in any other state.[38] In the Estado de México, Cárdenas won more absolute votes, though a lower percentage of the vote, than in Michoacán; almost half the votes of the Frente Democrático Nacional (FDN) came from the Estado de México or adjacent Mexico City.[39]

Second, local cases were deliberately chosen from states with strikingly different structural conditions in order to assess how structural and socioeconomic variables affect support for new parties and prospects for consolidation. Modernization theory would hardly expect to find the vanguard of pressures for multiparty democracy in Michoacán—a largely agricultural state with deficient infrastructure, one of the highest illiteracy rates in Mexico and a weak, poorly articulated civil society. Its most striking structural characteristics are its high outmigration rate (mostly to the United States) and its relatively recent transition to agricultural production for the international market.[40] In contrast, the urban area of the Estado de México has high literacy rates, complex social and economic configurations, a more developed civil society, and relatively good communications and transportation infrastructure.[41] To the extent that the Estado de México resembles Michoacán

38. IFE, *Contienda electoral en las elecciones presidenciales*, 11.

39. Jaime González Graf, *Las elecciones de 1988 y la crisis del sistema político* (Mexico City: Editorial Diana, 1989), 339.

40. Jorge Zepeda Patterson, *Michoacán,* series "Biblioteca de las Entidades Federativas" (Mexico City: UNAM, 1988).

41. Edgar Morales Sales, *Estado de México: Sociedad, economía, política, y cultura,* series "Biblioteca de las Entidades Federativas" (Mexico City: UNAM, 1989).

not only in its initial success but in the problems local activists experience during consolidation, it suggests that common causal factors overwhelmed even these deep structural differences. To maximize the contrast, interviews and observations of municipal party organizations were conducted in rural communities around Morelia, Michoacán (mainly in the tenth electoral district), and in one case in urban Estado de México, adjacent to Mexico City.

Chapters 5–7 analyze how the differences between consolidation and emergence affected the new party's performance of specific consolidation tasks. The fifth chapter looks at party institutionalization, with special attention to how features of the coalition that made it successful during emergence affected the development of internal norms and discipline. It also examines the problem of internal democracy faced by the PRD as a left party, and its impact on the consolidation of party identity. Chapter 6 looks at PRD attempts to consolidate relationships with other parties and popular movements and to assume responsibility for local government. Many of these cases illustrate graphically the changing calculations that accompany consolidation. Finally, the seventh chapter focuses on electoral fortunes and strategies based on interviews, statistical examination of the relationship between PRD vote and socioeconomic structure, polling data, and regional patterns of PRD strength.

The PRD and Democratization

Chapter 8, the final chapter, reviews the theoretical implications of the case of the PRD for analysis of party system change and democratization. The broader implications of this argument about party emergence and consolidation for democratization depend to some extent on the role of party system change in the process of democratic transition. Party system change is associated with democratization almost by definition in the case of monocentric party systems, where the main limit to democratic competition is the existence of a monopolistic ruling party.[42] But what is the timing of change and the direction of causation? The *cardenista* gamble was (and to some extent still is) that only when popular

42. One point of view insists that democracy requires only internal democratization of the PRI—not an immediate transition to multiparty democracy. See Daniel Cosío Villegas, *El sistema político mexicano* (Mexico City: Editorial Joaquín Mortiz, 1973). However, this seems the least likely route to democracy. The PRI has failed to introduce any effective measures of internal democracy in the last sixty-five years.

mobilization forces the PRI to accept alternation in power—that is, only when the PRI loses the presidency—will a truly democratic regime change be possible. The PAN has relied upon a more dialectic approach, consolidating its position and pushing for small rule changes, hoping to wrest the levers of power away from the PRI one by one. Do significant changes in party strength and consolidation *precede* (and push for) or *follow* (and result from) significant changes in the rules of the game? And are parties the main actors or do other actors—like popular movements or guerrilla organizations—play a more important role in pressuring the ruling party to adopt reforms?

The answers to these questions may help determine the mode of transition. A scenario of strong, consolidated parties may be more conducive to an eventual political pact, with parties acting as the main agents of change. If parties cannot consolidate a stable presence and make compromises on behalf of broad constituencies, they may have less success in playing this role. The ability of left parties to participate in a pact may be especially crucial. No regime can be considered democratic, and no democracy can long endure, that refuses to tolerate left opposition or left electoral victories and permits electoral institutions to discriminate openly against left parties. Perhaps in part because of this Mexico's process of liberalization has more closely resembled the *abertura* of the Brazilian military dictatorship than either the pacted transition of Spain or the *ruptura* of Argentina: liberalization controlled from above.

In addition to the insights it contributes to analyses of party formation and party system change, therefore, studying the PRD may shed light on connections between party consolidation and the path of transition. This study also encourages a broader focus on institutional change as a source of democratization rather than just changes in electoral law. These institutions define the consolidation arena in which competition takes place. Finally, the argument presented here leads logically to the conclusion that if voters remain detached from partisan loyalties (as seems to be the case), considerable potential for volatility in the party system remains. The PRI has already seen evidence that the good performance of one president does not translate into permanent recovery of hegemony by the party. As some anticipated, the economic reforms introduced by Salinas created disruptions in the short term that hurt the PRI. Similarly, the PAN's ability to capitalize on Zedillo's economic problems does not guarantee its future success, especially in the context of a fickle electorate. New PAN governors could easily disappoint constituents, reducing the party's attractiveness. Economic recovery could improve the fortunes of the PRI. Most critically, PAN support for neoliberal policies that do not alleviate Mexico's profound inequalities could eventually backfire. In such a situation the problems of the left in consolidating an effective party structure might matter less than its ability to capitalize on popular discontent. Until then, suggests analyst Lorenzo Meyer, political democracy is still "only a horizon," "an imaginary line . . . that seems to separate earth and heaven but that recedes each time that we try to approach it."[43]

43. Lorenzo Meyer, "La democracia, sólo un horizonte," *Excélsior* (Mexico City), 14 August 1991, pp. 1, 3. Translations from Spanish sources by Bruhn unless otherwise noted.

2

Being *Priista* Is Like Being Catholic

The Institutional and Political Context

Unlike parties that emerge in the context of a democratic transition, where the very rules of the game are undefined, the *cardenista* coalition faced a well-established set of institutions and practices that shaped its destiny. During emergence this institutional context influenced the interests and strategies of key actors. It helps explain, first, why the ruling cohort followed policies that detached the *cardenistas* and why they thought they could get away with it; and, second, why the *cardenistas* reacted by challenging PRI candidate selection, why this proved ineffective, and why the next step was alliance with the independent left. The experience of the *cardenista* coalition mirrors that of previous movements; indeed, its roots in these movements contributed to its success.

Moreover, the consequences of earlier reactions to these movements contributed to the severity of the 1988 breakdown. As a result, in contrast to prior moments of left convergence, 1988 resulted in a permanent split within the PRI and the formation of an independent left opposition. Finally, in the consolidation phase, institutional arrangements gave the PRI tools to undermine the PRD. This chapter explores these contextual factors in three sections: (1) the key characteristics of the Mexican political regime; (2) the historical patterns of opposition; and (3) the sources of increasing stress leading up to 1988.

THE MEXICAN POLITICAL REGIME

Social scientists frequently marveled at the unique stability of the Mexican political system. While other Third World countries oscillated between repressive military governments and shaky semidemocracies, Mexico continued under the same basic political regime for more than sixty years. Yet prior to the 1920s Mexico's experience seemed similar to that of many less stable countries, with episodes of violent rebellion, military coups, and brief democratic experiments. If anything, violence in Mexico was more extreme and more frequently involved mass mobilization. Mexico's longest period of stability—the dictatorship of Porfirio Díaz (1876–1910)—ended in a civil war that mobilized peasants for revolutionary demands. Ironically, however, the experience of the Revolution gave elites powerful incentives for initiating a pact to control conflicts, what John Higley and Richard Gunther have called "elite settlements."[1] The Mexican Revolution did not result from the strategy of a revolutionary vanguard but rather the probably unintentional escalation of elite conflict between sectors of the new national bourgeoisie (led by wealthy northerner Francisco Madero) and the incumbent Porfirio Díaz, basically over access to political power. When Madero called on "the people" to defend his limited demand for political democracy, promising them resolution of land conflicts in return, he unleashed a series of popular uprisings that escaped elite control, resulting in civil war and ultimately in a much more radical constitution than Madero himself would have advocated. The Mexican Revolution demonstrated that elite conflicts, left unchecked, could lead to mass mobilization by

1. For example, see John Higley and Richard Gunther, eds., *Elites and Democratic Consolidation in Latin America and Southern Europe* (New York: Cambridge University Press, 1992).

competing elites, widespread violence, economic disruption, and loss of economic and political hegemony by the ruling classes.

In contrast, Mexican elites developed a stable political regime with three central features: presidentialism, hegemonic one-party rule, and state corporatism. All three features reflect a consistent principle, concentration of authority. Presidentialism concentrates authority in the federal executive. Hegemonic one-party rule concentrates authority in the hands of one political party. State corporatism concentrates authority in the hands of officially recognized interest associations. Together these features formed a state-party-society triangle that collected power and controlled its distribution to coalition members rather than allowing elite competition for power to destabilize the political system.

These features were also highly interdependent, and developed during the same process of national consolidation. Thus analyses that focus solely on the party and electoral system to the exclusion of the state and society cannot comprehend either the system's formation or its persistence. In contrast to the expectations of Lipset and Rokkan (1967), the initial extension of voting rights preceded the formation of the ruling party by more than ten years; later changes to the suffrage attempted to stabilize an existing system of parties and representation. In Mexico, on the other hand, consolidation of the party system reflected and resulted from consolidation of state authority and the establishment of a pact with interest associations. Here the approach of Joseph LaPalombara and Myron Weiner (1966) proves more useful for understanding the development of the Mexican political regime. In responding to crises of integration, participation, and legitimacy, the postrevolutionary leaders of Mexico developed the bases of a system that endured for more than sixty years.

After the turmoil of the Revolution, Mexico confronted severe and simultaneous crises of integration, participation, and legitimacy. The Revolution destroyed the national state and what centralization of power Porfirio Díaz had accomplished. Mexico disintegrated politically and militarily into regions dominated by local *caudillos* and menaced by local rebellions. As actual fighting subsided, aspirants to national leadership faced the challenge of overcoming centrifugal forces and rebuilding loyalties to a national government—a crisis of integration. They also faced a participation crisis. The masses mobilized in the Revolution demanded land and a share of power. Any national government had to satisfy some demands and provide some channels of participation, both to prevent regional *caudillos* from drawing on popular discontent to form armies to fight each other and to prevent a rebellion against the national state. Though national statebuilders may have wanted to demobilize the masses, they wanted even more desperately to make sure that if people *did* participate, they would support the national government and not a regional *caudillo*. The task of integration, therefore, led to the need to resolve the crisis of participation. Finally, a new national government had to build legitimacy so that rival regional elites and the general population would recognize its authority without the constant, debilitating need to use force.

Presidentialism provided a key integrating mechanism. As scholars have noted, the Mexican president represents the nation symbolically and controls it politically.[2] The president initiates virtually all laws, approved routinely by a weak and largely passive Congress. He can choose and remove ministers, prosecutors, and most government employees, including—*de facto*—even other elected officials, at least in his own party. He has tremendous influence over state and local governments through his control of the federal budget, on which they depend for most of their income. The main limitation to the president's power is temporal rather than political: he serves a six-year term and cannot be reelected. However, the outgoing president has had the informal right to name his successor since at least the 1950s. He may take into account the opinions of the political elite, but essentially he selects the candidate of the ruling party.

Many of these powers evolved over time, and do not appear formally in the Constitution.[3] In the early years after the Revolution, presidential power depended much more on statecraft than on constitutional privileges. Presidents could not take their authority for granted. They had not acquired an aura of invincibility, nor consolidated their control over the army, nor created the ruling party and its unions as instruments. In time, the concentration of national control over financial resources would allow the president to buy off or control regional *caudillos* through payoffs. President Alvaro Obregón (1920–24) made considerable strides toward controlling the military and improving the financial position of the federal government by cutting military budgets and getting foreign oil companies to agree to pay taxes to the national state. Still, in the beginning, presidents had to convince regional *cau-*

2. Víctor López Villafañe, *La formación del sistema político mexicano* (Mexico City: Siglo Veintiuno, 1986), 56; see also Daniel C. Levy and Gabriel Székely, *Mexico: Paradoxes of Stability and Change*, 2d ed. (Boulder, Colo.: Westview Press, 1987), 49–50.

3. These "metaconstitutional powers," as Garrido calls them, include control over the PRI, electoral institutions, the legislature, and presidential succession. See Luis Javier Garrido, "The Crisis of *Presidencialismo*," in *Mexico's Alternative Political Futures*, ed. Wayne Cornelius, Judith Gentleman, and Peter Smith (La Jolla, Calif.: UCSD Center for U.S.-Mexican Studies, 1989), 422–26.

dillos to accept national authority largely *without* using military force or money, since the national state had a monopoly over neither.

President Plutarco Elías Calles (1924–28) took a crucial step toward solving this problem of legitimacy and integration when he set up the National Revolutionary Party (PNR). In establishing the PNR Calles planned to win the consent of regional elites by creating a composite party that incorporated all their regional party organizations and that also controlled the national state. More immediately, he hoped to solve another succession crisis created by the murder of president-elect Alvaro Obregón in 1928. Though probably tempted, Calles declined to remain in office himself after this event. Several factors influenced his decision. To begin with, Obregón had been strongly criticized for violating the spirit of the 1917 Constitution's prohibition against reelection when he decided to run again in 1928, and Calles did not have Obregón's popularity to counterbalance this criticism. Even worse, some of Obregón's followers suspected Calles of complicity in the murder.[4] Although Calles wanted to choose his successor and perpetuate his influence, he also wanted Mexican elites to support the choice and believed Mexico could not afford continued violence over the succession.

Therefore Calles proposed the creation of a single national party (which he expected to control) as a means of reducing interelite violence, ensuring a peaceful succession, and bolstering the legitimacy of the national state. In his famous proposal to the Congress Calles attacked the principle of personalistic leadership, reminding elites that "our history shows us that [*caudillos*] only arise in periods of disturbance of the public peace, and that they produce, in the end, disorientation and anarchy." A country run by *caudillos* experienced divisive conflicts while they lived and chaos when they died. Calles suggested that since the death of Obregón left Mexico temporarily without an obvious *caudillo* in the wings, the country had a unique opportunity to "go from the category of a people and government of *caudillos* to the higher and more respected and more productive and more peaceful and more civilized condition of peoples of institutions and laws."[5] More to the point, a single party incorporating key political elites provided a way to avoid conflicts over succession by ensuring that all would support the same candidate.

The territorially based structure of the PNR reflected this goal of

4. There was ample precedent. At least two of the first three post-Revolution presidents were murdered by their successors: Madero (by Huerta) and Carranza (by Obregón).

5. Arturo Alvarado Mendoza, "La fundación del PNR," in *El partido en el poder: Seis ensayos* (Mexico City: Partido Revolucionario Institucional, IEPES, 1990), 31.

integrating regional elites. By including "all the parties, groups, and political organizations of the Republic, of revolutionary beliefs," as Calles's convocation indicated, it incorporated the political machines of particular local *caudillos* (since most parties at the time were not mass ideological parties) and dissolved them as independent entities.[6] The terms of the convocation allowed local elites to control the selection of delegates to the Founding Convention, subject in effect to a presidential veto. Each state was guaranteed one delegate for every 10,000 inhabitants, but delegates came only from existing parties and political groups. Delegate credentials had to be signed by the leaders of the participating organization, accredited by the municipal government, and validated by the national organizing committee, whose head was Calles. From the beginning, with certification by government officials "the border between State and Party was blurred."[7]

This time, in contrast to previous attempts to form a single "revolutionary" party, the lure of a national alliance worked. Perhaps as many as fourteen hundred associations participated in the foundation of the official party.[8] The number of registered parties dropped from fifty-one in 1929 to four in 1933.[9] The absence of a strong national *caudillo* like Obregón certainly encouraged an alliance in 1929. The fact that Obregón had no clear successor raised the specter of renewed elite conflict over the presidency and also presented an opportunity for influence over the succession. Calles won the voluntary participation of regional *caudillos* by offering them some autonomy in their own spheres and by promising them a share of the national power they thus accepted as legitimate. Hence, it was understood from the beginning—indeed, it was a condition for the pact—that this new national party would choose the president and control the national government. "Party" and "state" did not start out as separate entities but as Siamese twins.

President Lázaro Cárdenas (1934–40) contributed to the institutionalization of the state-party alliance and added the third pillar of the Mexican regime, state corporatism, by transforming the PNR "from a party of parties to a party of sectors."[10] The party-state alliance remained intact, but Cárdenas replaced the former regional structure with four functionally organized sectors that explicitly incorporated peasants, workers, "popular" classes, and the military into the party,

---

6. Ibid., 41.

7. Ibid., 46.

8. Ibid., 23.

9. Levy and Székely, *Mexico: Paradoxes of Stability and Change*, 37.

10. Samuel León, "Del partido de partidos al partido de sectores," in *El partido en el poder: Seis ensayos* (Mexico City: Partido Revolucionario Institucional, IEPES, 1990), 87.

now called the PRM (Mexican Revolutionary Party). The sectoral structure of the PRM helped Cárdenas address remaining problems of integration, participation, and legitimacy.

Most obviously, the PRM addressed problems of participation and popular legitimacy left unresolved by the foundation of the PNR. While the PNR had convinced powerful regional elites to accept the authority and legitimacy of the national government, *popular* unrest continued. In fact, "it was precisely at the moment of foundation of [the PNR] that the distance between the postrevolutionary state and the working class became total."[11] Obregón had come to power based in part on a close alliance with the CROM, one of the largest Mexican labor federations. However, this alliance had seriously deteriorated, in part due to Obregón's decision to seek reelection. CROM leader Morones, also accused of involvement in the assassination, was forced to resign his position in the government in 1928 and strongly opposed attempts to incorporate existing parties in the PNR, preferring to preserve the independence of the CROM's party arm, the Mexican Liberal Party. The CROM began to fall apart without state patronage, and a ferment of independent union organizing took place between 1929 and 1935.[12] Moreover, CROM had never managed to gain control of the nation's most important unions, in key areas like the railroad, electrical power, and petroleum industries.[13] Nor could the national state confidently claim support from the peasant majority. National leaders since the Revolution had largely neglected the peasants' single most important demand, major land reform, in order to avoid dangerous confrontations with powerful rural elites.

Lázaro Cárdenas believed that long-term stability and development depended on successfully confronting these entrenched elites and responding to popular demands. His strategy was to use popular organization allied to the national state as a counterweight to elite resistance. He called for the creation of a national peasant organization (the CNC, or National Peasant Confederation) and a new national labor federation (the CTM, or Confederation of Mexican Workers). Ultimately, such of-

11. Ibid., 100.
12. Rafael Loyola Díaz, "1938: El despliegue del corporativismo partidario," in *El partido en el poder: Seis ensayos* (Mexico City: Partido Revolucionario Institucional, IEPES, 1990), 143. For a history of labor in this period see also Barry Carr, *El movimiento obrero y la política en México, 1910–1929*, trans. Roberto Gómez Ciriza (Mexico City: Ediciones Era, 1981); Ruth Berins Collier and David Collier, *Shaping the Political Arena: Critical Junctures, the Labor Movement, and Regime Dynamics in Latin America* (Princeton: Princeton University Press, 1991); and Kevin Middlebrook, *The Paradox of Revolution: Labor, the State, and Authoritarianism in Mexico* (Baltimore: Johns Hopkins University Press, 1995).
13. Middlebrook, *The Paradox of Revolution*, 80.

ficially sanctioned unions incorporated peasants and workers into the ruling party. Cárdenas argued that only the combined power of the national state and national unions could overcome the opposition of economic elites and local *caudillos* to real change. He may well have been right.

However, these alliances also enhanced the power of the national state and Cárdenas personally, helping him counteract the influence of ex-president Calles in the PNR. Cárdenas deliberately divided the peasant and labor sectors, favored the CTM over independent unions that did not recognize his leadership, and maintained the leading role of the state in the alliance. In return for their loyalty Cárdenas distributed collective goods to peasant and labor unions, aggressively implemented agrarian reform, and promoted labor interests. He developed a reputation that lasts to this day as a reformer who supported the masses and respected popular organizations. However, he also used the power of the unions as his successors did, to support state initiatives, control popular participation, and enhance government legitimacy. Later presidents found they could use the unions more cheaply than Cárdenas by distributing a mix of payoffs that included more selective benefits to undemocratically elected union leaders and fewer collective benefits to large social groups. Thus, its recognition of popular sectors as part of the national social pact gave the ruling party a basis for laying claim to the legitimacy of the Revolution. But its incorporation of workers and peasants in official unions also gave the ruling party a way to be useful to the right (by regulating wages and strikes) and undermine challenges from the left. State corporatism blocked independent popular organizations and the left opposition from organizing among the classes that were their natural support base.

In addition to meeting demands for popular participation Cárdenas's sectoral innovation reflected ongoing attempts to strengthen presidential authority and national integration. The sectors replaced regional delegates as the basis for integration, undermining the independent power bases of regional elites. To appease them, Cárdenas specified that in addition to delegates named by the leaders of the unions, general "regional delegates"—over which local elites might have some influence—would represent labor and peasant sectors in the assembly of the PRM. The definition of "popular" sector left potential space for regional elites. Cárdenas defined it as "integrated by those members of the Party [i.e., the PNR] that did not belong to any of the other sectors; organizations of women, youth, professionals and small businessmen were also included."[14] These "members of the Party that did not belong to any of

14. Loyola Díaz, "1938: El despliegue del corporativismo partidario," 164.

the other sectors" could, of course, have belonged to regional organizations. In the long term, however, the sectoral structure of the party shifted the terms of conflict from a center-periphery contest to issues of class and function. The president used the authority and resources of the state to enhance his power by distributing favors and candidacies through the sectors rather than through regional parties. The frequent nomination of candidates with tenuous connections to the region where they ran for office also served to orient loyalties toward the national executive and to undermine attempts by local elites to develop regional power bases. Though the party would not change its name to the Institutional Revolutionary Party (PRI) until 1946, the basic building blocks of the Mexican political regime were in place.

The Role of Elections

Although the Revolution began in the name of effective suffrage, post-revolutionary institutions were designed primarily to help elites avoid the perils of elections. Competitive, pluralistic elections seemed to exacerbate elite conflicts rather than dampening them. Prior to 1929 elections often resulted in fraud, murder, and violence. National leaders created the party as a mechanism of control at the service of the state and modified electoral law to bolster its position. The PRI did not become antidemocratic by chance, but by choice and vocation. Elections never decided who would govern. PRI candidates customarily won such commanding victories that Mexican elections became a ritual untainted by the uncertainty of outcomes that accompanies democratic competition. In 1973 the PRI won more than 95 percent of the vote in almost a fifth of the country's electoral districts and more than 70 percent in 70 percent of all districts. Even after a 1977 reform that improved conditions for the opposition, the PRI won more than 70 percent in 57 percent of electoral districts.[15] As late as June 1985 the PRI controlled 96 percent of Mexican municipal governments, all thirty-one governorships plus Mexico City, 75 percent of the seats in Congress, and 100 percent of seats in the Senate.[16]

Since PRI candidates always won, the real selection of "elected" officials took place at the stage of candidate nomination—a notoriously un-

15. Leopoldo Gómez and John Bailey, "La transición política y los dilemas del PRI," *Foro Internacional* 31, no. 121 (July–September 1990): 69.

16. Wayne Cornelius, "Political Liberalization and the 1985 Elections in Mexico," in *Elections and Democratization in Latin America, 1980–1985*, ed. Paul Drake and Eduardo Silva (La Jolla, Calif.: UCSD Center for Iberian and Latin American Studies, 1986), 115.

democratic and secretive process controlled ultimately by the president. Personal connections to government officials distinguished the most successful aspirants. The president himself had considerable influence and almost certainly veto power over candidates for major offices. This was a key lever for presidential control of Congress as well as state and local governments. The future political careers of elected officials depended on satisfying their bosses, who controlled nominations, rather than their constituents. Governors and heads of PRI unions also had candidate selection prerogatives. Party conventions that formally nominated candidates essentially ratified choices made at other levels. Thus, at no stage did elections determine access to government positions.

Given that elections did not choose who would govern, it is at first difficult to understand why the PRI went to so much trouble and expense over such a long period of time, "electing" 15 presidents as well as "[500] senators, about 6,000 federal congressmen, some 500 governors, perhaps 6,000 local congressmen, and more than 50,000 municipal governments" between 1920 and 1988.[17] In contrast to other authoritarian regimes, from its foundation the Mexican ruling party held elections punctually with the participation of opposition candidates. In fact, Mexico's record of uninterrupted elections since 1920 surpasses the electoral continuity of many "developed democracies," including France, Italy, Germany, and Japan.

Elections *could* be held in Mexico because they were safe; they *were* held because elections contributed to the consolidation of one-party rule and to the stability of Mexico's political regime. By allowing opposition candidates to compete (and lose), the state reproduced revolutionary legitimacy. PRI electoral strategy stressed not just victories, but massive victories, of *"carro completo"* (every position available), by a huge margin, and with a large turnout. Whether fraudulently inflated or not, these margins of victory demonstrated the PRI's capacity for control, and—like good theater—identified the PRI with the whole nation, not just 50 percent plus one.

The goal of a big and impressive majority also gave party sectors an incentive to cultivate regional elites and popular allies through locally rooted patron-client networks, so that they could mobilize a good turnout. Presidential elections in particular encouraged a tradition of nationwide campaigning that forced PRI candidates to put in an appearance in places they might not otherwise have visited. These campaign visits gave local residents a sense of connection to the national

17. Juan Molinar Horcasitas, *El tiempo de la legitimidad* (Mexico City: Cal y Arena, 1991), 7.

regime, at least as personified in the president. In addition, the participation of opposition candidates bolstered the PRI's legitimacy, as the heir of a Revolution fought in part for democracy, and as the "safe center." For this reason the PRI tried to keep alive an opposition both to its right (the counterrevolution) and its left (the continuing revolution).

If the participation of opposition candidates contributed to popular legitimacy, the regularity and frequency of elections served the different function of guaranteeing rapid rotation in power, a key requirement for maintaining elite loyalty to the regime.[18] Elections stabilized authoritarianism by limiting the time in office of those individuals who controlled access to power. The regime could tolerate a high level of authoritarianism (including presidents, governors, and mayors who rewarded personal clients with positions and nominations) because it also had an electoral schedule for removing those people from office and because it adhered to that schedule with religious regularity. Elite consensus broke down under Porfirio Díaz not so much because he filled government positions by fiat as because he excluded sections of the Mexican elite over a long period of time. Studies of elite career patterns show a striking difference between the "extraordinarily static" prerevolutionary norm and the postrevolutionary norm of "relatively little repetition . . . [and] great flexibility."[19] Mexicans also used elections to distribute positions among different factions of the ruling coalition. High rates of elite circulation encouraged dissidents to remain in the system in the hope that their turn would come.

The hegemonic party system ensured that this regular leadership succession would take place in a controlled, gradual, and predictable manner. To make elections even safer, the ruling elite relied not only on the strong competitive position of the state-party alliance but on electoral laws unfavorable to opposition political parties. These laws made the PRI truly hegemonic. In 1946, even after the consolidation of the official sectoral party, eleven registered parties remained active. Following electoral reforms in 1946, the average number of candidates per district went from 5.3 in 1946 to 2.0 in 1949 and stayed roughly around 2.5 until 1961; at the same time the number of registered parties

18. This principle has been explored by writers like Gaetano Mosca, in *The Ruling Class* (New York: McGraw-Hill, 1939); and Vilfredo Pareto, in *The Rise and Fall of the Elites: An Application of Theoretical Sociology* (New York: Arno Press, 1979).

19. Peter Smith, *Labyrinths of Power: Political Recruitment in Twentieth-Century Mexico* (Princeton: Princeton University Press, 1979), 138, 148. Under Díaz 60–70 percent of the national elite had previous national experience; in contrast, in postrevolutionary Mexico "approximately two-thirds of the high national offices have been held by complete newcomers to the elite circles" (pp. 160–63).

went from eleven in 1946 to an average of four in the ensuing twenty years.[20] Among other things the "pivotal electoral law of 1946 . . . centralized the organization, monitoring, and certification of federal electoral procedures in the hands of the federal executive."[21] Government control over the electoral apparatus remained a consistent principle in all reforms because it gave the ruling party the ability to carry out fraud when necessary. More broadly, electoral regulations tended to make it relatively difficult to form new parties, bolstering the position of the PRI as the only effective national option.

If such restrictions seemed to endanger the continued participation of opposition parties—either by discouraging people from voting for the opposition a bit too effectively or by discouraging the opposition so much that it threatened to challenge the regime by nonelectoral means—the ruling party itself sponsored new reforms to revive opposition interest and strengthen its ability to compete in elections. These laws made it easier for opposition parties to get seats in Congress and to register new parties. However, the PRI did not relinquish control of the electoral process, revoke the state-party alliance, or show any willingness to endanger its electoral hegemony.

The process of ensuring loyalty within the ruling party followed a rather similar dynamic of incentives and punishments. The macrostability of elite loyalty to the ruling party did not reflect consensus around an enduring ideology but rather power sharing based on personal relationships to preserve the unity of an ideologically heterogeneous coalition. Analysts traditionally distinguished two major "wings" of the Institutional Revolutionary Party: (1) the *cardenistas*, who stressed equity and supported radical redistributive policies like agrarian reform and state intervention in the economy (including state ownership of companies) to promote the welfare of the working classes; and (2) the *alemanistas*, after President Miguel Alemán (1946–52), who stressed economic growth and followed a model of state capitalism more sympathetic to the needs of the private sector, intervening in the economy to protect national capital and promote capitalist development.

The power, resources, and positions of the state held these two wings of the party together. As long as those who held opposing ideologies agreed to share these resources, the party could keep the loyalty of those who had less influence in a particular administration, while regular elections offered hope that future administrations might be more favor-

20. Molinar Horcasitas, *El tiempo de la legitimidad*, 42.

21. Juan Molinar Horcasitas, "The Mexican Electoral System: Continuity by Change," in *Elections and Democratization in Latin America, 1980–1985*, ed. Paul Drake and Eduardo Silva (San Diego: UCSD, 1986), 108.

able. The "pendulum theory" argued that this did occur and that alternate control of the presidency by the two wings of the party produced a swing from more popularly oriented policies to more business-oriented policies and back again.[22] Whether a result of conscious candidate selection or not, successive presidents showed considerable ideological flexibility, accommodating significant changes in policy within the context of single-party rule. Thus, being *"priista"* primarily meant having access to power, access to the state. As one ex-*priista* put it, "Being *priista* is like being Catholic. You are, but you aren't."[23] Like another hegemonic institution in Mexico—the Catholic Church, to which more than 90 percent of the population formally belongs—the PRI created loyalty to the institution more than true believers in the faith. Just as many baptized "Catholics" in Mexico darken the door of a church only for baptisms, weddings, and funerals, to make the family happy, *priistas* could belong to the party nominally, flaunting or even acquiring party membership only at crucial moments, like elections. When the PRI had less to distribute or appeared less willing to share resources, loyalties faltered, and elite splits occurred.

Personal loyalties took the place of party loyalties in many ways, especially for the PRI elite. Personal advancement depended on a web of relationships known as *camarillas*, basically a patron-client network. Politically ambitious young men joined early, frequently through friendships with professors or classmates at the National University (UNAM). Getting ahead in government required good personal connections, loyalty and servility to superiors, and the flexibility to move from ministry to ministry, adapting to a variety of positions. Because of the personal basis of political advancement, candidates and officials were responsive not to their nominal constituents (voters or consumers of government services) but to their political patrons.

However, personal networks could also be turned against the state. Personal networks associated with the *cardenista* wing of the PRI played an important role in its 1987 split. Moreover, personalistic recruitment contributed to another division that would have an impact in 1987, between *"técnicos"* and *"políticos."* *Técnicos* specialized in disciplines like economics and engineering and followed administrative career paths, while *políticos* got more general training in disciplines like law and social science and followed careers that included experience in party and electoral politics. In the common perception, while *políticos*

22. See Dale Story, *The Mexican Ruling Party* (New York: Praeger, 1986), 30; Levy and Székely, *Mexico: Paradoxes of Stability and Change*, 117.

23. Personal conversation, Michoacán, May 1991.

stressed consensus building and compromise as elements of policy-making, *técnicos* tended to "underestimate the importance of human relations and politics," "stress the use of specialized knowledge for solving human and social problems," and "lack the political skills required for handling conflicts among large, autonomous groups, or between the state and one or more of those groups."[24] Technocratization occurs in part because of the greater need for specialists to advise state policy-makers as countries develop and as the state assumes a major role in the economy. However, as technocrats began to reach more responsible government positions, they nominated like-minded friends, "techno-cratizing" the upper echelons of Mexican government and increasingly excluding some parts of the Revolutionary Family.

The Central Characteristics of the Mexican Political System

The Mexican political regime was based on presidentialism, one-party rule, and state corporatism. Electoral laws safeguarded the control of the national executive over the conduct and outcome of elections. Personal loyalty drove candidate selection in the PRI and enhanced the authority of the president over Congress and local government. Unlike most cases of authoritarianism, the regime allowed opposition participation in elections (with the understanding that they would not win major offices) and incorporated popular classes. However, calling Mexico a democracy would confuse democracy with a plural ruling coalition. The principles of gaining access to state power followed more authoritarian than democratic lines, and the Mexican political regime remained fundamentally predicated on a state-party alliance in control of a strong presidency.

CONTESTED HEGEMONY: THE HISTORY OF ANTIREGIME OPPOSITION IN MEXICO

Up to this point I have emphasized the dominant characteristics of the Mexican political regime: its stability, its hegemony, its centralization,

24. Roderic Camp, "The Political Technocrat in Mexico and the Survival of the Political System," *Latin American Research Review* 20, no. 1 (1985): 111–12. A number of scholars question this dichotomy, arguing that technocrats do have political skills and politicians are not blind to the importance of rational, efficient policy. However, in terms of its effect on elite conflicts perception mattered more than reality, as Chapter 3 shows.

and its authoritarian nature. However, as the analysis has already suggested, stability does not mean the absence of change; authoritarianism does not mean the absence of checks to presidential power; and centralization does not mean the eradication of regional autonomies. Change could enhance regime stability. Establishing effective authority over critical areas of policy often required the president and the central state to leave local elites a free hand in other areas. From the beginning regime builders made mutually beneficial alliances with local elites, who became partner-clients to the national state. Above all, hegemony does not mean that no one protested. Often challenges contributed to stability. Protesters could highlight problem areas or issues, even as the fate of the protesters themselves (usually co-optation or repression) served as an object lesson for other potential protesters, maintaining hegemony. In looking at what happened to attempts to reform the regime, one sees most clearly its strengths and weaknesses, and its methods for adapting to challenges.

Protest came from many different groups and organizations. Peasant and indigenous communities, students, teachers, workers, and even business elites challenged state policies, presidential control, the PRI's monopoly, and state corporatism. The main independent party opposition developed to the right of the PRI, in the National Action Party (PAN). The PAN is a conservative, probusiness, Catholic party, formed in opposition to the "leftward drift" of the Revolution during the presidency of Lázaro Cárdenas.[25] The original Acción Nacional leadership came from the Mexican political and economic elite, but was less well placed in the Revolutionary Family, belonging mostly to old *maderista* families (followers of Francisco Madero, a northerner) and to Catholic organizations not integrated into the secular postrevolutionary regime.

Independent leftist opposition has come basically from three political currents: (1) the grass-roots popular movements; (2) the communist left; and (3) the *cardenista* left. The grass-roots movements generally sought specific benefits for particular groups and avoided alignment with political parties. The communist left splintered into many maoist, trotskyist, and marxist-leninist versions, but its strongest current origi-

25. The founders of the PAN objected to Cárdenas's insistence on secular public education and his enforcement of restrictions on the Church. Northerners objected to the dominance of the central state, more vehemently because, unlike Sonoran General Obregón, Cárdenas came from Michoacán in central Mexico. Businessmen objected to his radical programs, including agrarian reform, support of worker and peasant organization, and nationalization of oil. The PAN has relied mostly on middle- and upper-middle-class support, urban support, and regional bases in the developed north, but PAN support has grown steadily, reaching about 26 percent in the 1994 presidential election.

nated in the Mexican Communist Party, founded in 1919. For much of its history the communist left operated as a set of illegal, semiclandestine organizations, sharing an experience of government hostility and repression. Most of their longtime leaders spent time in prison; some were killed or disappeared. The last current existed within the PRI itself. As a more prosystem left, this current usually faced less government hostility. However, even the *cardenistas* could exhaust the tolerance of the regime with too fundamental or too public a challenge to its basic principles, incurring some of the same costs as the communist left unless they recanted and reached a new accommodation.

The periods of strongest left influence on politics coincided with moments when these strands converged in a cooperative project, like the Cárdenas candidacy in 1988. Analysis of two earlier moments of left convergence—*henriquismo* and the MLN—illuminates some of the personal and political connections that facilitated this coalition and some similarities in their formation and decline. The *cardenistas* tended to initiate contact with left opposition in order to exert public pressure for policy change when they felt marginalized within the PRI. Regardless of the issue that triggered convergence, the *cardenistas* usually ended up demanding democratization, which they invariably failed to get. Popular forces often played an important radicalizing role. The PRI responded to convergence with repression followed by liberalization. And these left coalitions fell apart in two to five years, its components returning to their previous independent existence.

Henriquismo

Some of these themes show up in the experience of *henriquismo*, which produced the most successful left opposition presidential candidate prior to 1988. General Miguel Henríquez Guzmán, a close ally of Lázaro Cárdenas, ran as an independent candidate for president in 1952 with some support from the illegal Communist Party.[26] Beginning with the presidential term of Cárdenas's successor Manuel Ávila Camacho in 1940, government policy began to drift to the right, excluding the *cardenistas*. Cárdenas chose Ávila Camacho because he felt stability required a moderate to soothe the nerves of business and conservative opponents, but Ávila Camacho moved farther to the right than expected,

26. Henríquez Guzmán played a key military role during the Cárdenas presidency. He fought the *cristeros* (religious zealots opposed to the secularism of Cárdenas), suppressed violent uprisings in Nayarit and Durango, and helped put down the rebellion of General Saturnino Cedillo in 1938–39.

then chose as his successor an even more conservative candidate, Miguel Alemán. Henríquez and the *cardenistas* protested this choice, and accepted it reluctantly. Toward the end of Alemán's term rumors began to fly that he planned to pick a relative, Fernando Casas Alemán, as his successor. At the prospect of yet another conservative president under the influence of Alemán, both Henríquez and Lázaro Cárdenas rebelled.

In principle, "what the *henriquistas* asked for was nothing less than that the party effectively participate in the designation of the presidential candidate, and that the opinion of its members be expressed freely and democratically."[27] When Alemán refused to open up the selection process or name a *cardenista*, Henríquez claimed that Cárdenas urged him to run an independent campaign. People close to Cárdenas, including his wife and seventeen-year-old son Cuauhtémoc, participated in the early stages of the campaign. However, when Alemán named Ruíz Cortines as the PRI candidate instead of his relative, probably to end the threat of a major elite split, Cárdenas publicly reallied himself with the PRI, declaring that "[Henríquez Guzmán] never received from me promises that I would participate in his campaign, nor did I encourage anyone to support his candidacy."[28] Without Cárdenas as a sponsor, harassment of Henríquez's party (the FPPM) increased. Henríquez lost the 1952 election. In January 1954 the government accused the FPPM of assaulting a military barracks in Chihuahua and dissolved the party as subversive and violent. Henríquez Guzmán and his aides accepted positions and rewards for their acquiescence.

The Henríquez episode illustrates the complex role played by the issue of democratization in convergence on the left. On the one hand, social reformers within the PRI often found that the road to influencing policy led through democratization. The hierarchical, centralized nature of the political system made it hard to get access to policy circles without the invitation of the president—a problem if the proposed policy differed significantly from the president's preference. Democratization offered a way for outsiders to force their way into power. This is why demands for democratization frequently began with demands for internal democratization of the PRI. The resistance of the PRI in turn encouraged reformers to seek outside alliances, to use public pressure and the threat of cooperation with the left opposition to leverage their way back into policy circles. The independent left sought such alliances

27. Olga Pellicer de Brody, "La oposición en México: El caso del henriquismo," *Foro Internacional* 17, no. 68 (April–June 1977): 480.
28. Carlos Martínez Assad, *El henriquismo: Una piedra en el camino* (Mexico City: Martín Casillas Editores, 1982), 25.

because they bought it political space, protection, and the hope of regime-level democratization to compete openly for power. Thus, these moments of convergence centered on common policy goals and a demand for democracy. However, the issue of democratization also divided the *cardenistas* from their left opposition allies. As long as they remained technically loyal to the PRI, focusing on internal democratization rather than electoral opposition, the *cardenistas* could accept policy concessions and reincorporation into power circles in lieu of democratization. When they did, the left opposition could not go with them, and cooperation collapsed.

The pattern persisted in part because of the depth of PRI resistance to internal democracy. As Luis Javier Garrido argued in "The PRI, or Impossible Democracy": "[The PRI] was from its foundation a state institution at the service of the official bureaucracy and as such the most important instrument of an authoritarian regime. The antidemocracy that has always characterized it is not an accident, but essential, and the failures of popular forces for over half a century to democratize it are the proof."[29] Even when party leaders sponsored internal democratization measures, they quickly repented. The classic case is that of Carlos Madrazo, named president of the PRI in 1965. As in other party-sponsored democratic reforms, leaders believed democratization would strengthen popular identification with the PRI after a challenge to its legitimacy—in the Madrazo case three years of criticism by the MLN (discussed below).[30] To "[stimulate] the democratization of the internal life of the party," Madrazo proposed replacing party leaders throughout Mexico, choosing candidates through primaries, and adopting individual affiliation instead of membership through the sectors.[31] Sectoral and

29. Luis Javier Garrido, "El PRI, o la democracia imposible," in *Democracia emergente y partidos políticos*, ed. Jorge Alonso and Sergio Sánchez Díaz (Mexico City: Centro de Investigaciones y Estudios Superiores en Antropología Social, 1990), 1: 68.

30. A second example is the democratizing movement sponsored by party leaders after the 1968 massacre of student activists who demanded democracy. In July 1972 the National Executive Committee declared that "the Revolutionary Party needs a change in its structure . . . and therefore in its methods of action"; in order to "extend more and more the possibilities of political participation of the population, . . . our party should have sufficient flexibility to interpret and understand this diversity of conditions and, in accordance with it, adopt the methods of selection of better candidates, according to specific regional or local conditions, with a view to achieving the best representativity for the candidates postulated by the PRI." This attempt did not make it past the proposal stage. See Ignacio Marván Laborde, "La dificultad del cambio (1968–1980)," in *El partido en el poder: Seis ensayos* (Mexico City: Partido Revolucionario Institucional, IEPES, 1990), 265–67.

31. "Panorama nacional," *Política* 5 (15 January 1965): 14.

local leaders objected to all of these measures. Individual affiliation undermined the sectors in particular, but both sectoral and local leaders feared losing their nomination powers, which they used to reward loyal *camarilla* members. Election of candidates would undermine their authority over subordinates, jeopardize their political advancement (since they had cultivated personal alliances with their superiors rather than popularity with the bases), and threaten the quota system that distributed congressional seats. With the consent of the president, Madrazo managed to carry out one internal election to choose the candidate for governor of Baja California. However, when he tried to use internal elections for mayoral candidacies in Sinaloa against the protests of the governor, his enemies united against him. The battle between the PRI and its president became a public scandal and threatened the party's image as a united monolith. President Díaz Ordaz forced Madrazo to resign after only ten months.[32] The president himself relied on nomination to control the party, the Congress, and hence the country. Thus, though presidents occasionally urged "democratic reform" of the PRI, these reforms always included a provision for selective application at the discretion of the president and national leaders, and never resulted in a lasting change in nomination procedures.

The MLN

The experience of the National Liberation Movement, or MLN, repeats some of the themes of *henriquismo*, but represents a more complete and sustained moment of cooperation among the various strands of the left. The MLN is the single most important organizational antecedent to the PRD. A list of its founders and sponsors reads like a "who's who" of the 1988 coalition. The members of the first National Committee of the MLN included twenty-seven-year-old Cuauhtémoc Cárdenas (representing his father), as well as leftist intellectuals and activists in the Mexican Communist Party and the Popular Socialist Party (PPS). Heberto Castillo—the 1988 candidate of the Mexican Socialist Party until

32. At that point Madrazo faced the same choice that Cárdenas faced twenty years later: submit gracefully or join the opposition. Madrazo considered forming a party. In late 1967 he called for a "national front" of "progressive men," and said conversations with the Mexican people convinced him that the PRI no longer had "the support of the immense majority." See "Panorama nacional," *Política* 8 (November 1967): 5. The question became moot when Madrazo died in a plane crash a few months later. Many felt his death was a little too convenient and suspected President Díaz Ordaz of having him murdered.

his resignation in favor of Cuauhtémoc Cárdenas—belonged to the MLN, as did—ironically—Eli de Gortari, a leftist university rector from Michoacán whose nephew Carlos Salinas became Cárdenas's PRI opponent.[33] MLN committees featured many young organizers who would participate in the Cárdenas coalition twenty years later, including Gilberto Rincón Gallardo, Arnoldo Martínez Verdugo, Rolando Cordera, and Ricardo Valero. Cárdenas relied on these personal and political connections in 1988.

The MLN started out as a nonelectoral pressure group to support the government of Fidel Castro in Cuba, under increasing attack by the United States, and to pressure the Mexican government to take a stronger pro-Cuba stance.[34] Like the Cárdenas campaign in 1988, the MLN began with an elite division in the PRI when Lázaro Cárdenas organized a "Latin American Conference for National Sovereignty, Economic Independence, and Peace" in March 1961. He invited nongovernmental organizations sympathetic to Cuba from all over Latin America, including the Mexican Committee to Promote the Struggle for Peace and International Cooperation, formed on July 24, 1959. The conference established a Provisional Committee for National Sovereignty and Economic Emancipation to organize a chapter in Mexico, and on August 5, 1961, this committee announced the foundation of the National Liberation Movement.

The MLN immediately developed a much broader and more domestic list of priorities, from regime change to the release of political prisoners. According to founder Lázaro Cárdenas, the MLN was to "contribute to the fulfillment of the principles of the Mexican Revolution." These principles included not only anti-imperialism and solidarity with Cuba but also support for municipal autonomy, proportional representation in Congress, decentralization, an active state role in economic development, agrarian reform, democratization and autonomy for unions and peasant organizations, and "absolute independence with respect to the International Monetary Fund."[35] These were combative demands. They would have increased the opposition presence in Congress, weakened presidentialism, and undermined corporatist control.

The MLN also began to engage in radical and confrontational action, especially as the time approached to select the PRI's candidate for the 1964 presidential election. In late 1962 rumors spread that the MLN

33. "Panorama político," *Política* 1 (1 March 1961): 7.
34. The first organized conference took place shortly after an unusually friendly meeting between President López Mateos and President Dwight Eisenhower in October 1960.
35. "Panorama nacional," *Política* 2 (15 August 1961): 5–7.

planned to organize a new peasant movement outside the PRI to push for government action on agrarian reform. The prospect of involvement in such a flagrantly aggressive enterprise caused the Popular Socialist Party to withdraw from the MLN in December 1962. In January 1963 Lázaro Cárdenas announced the formation of an independent peasant organization, the Central Campesina Independiente (CCI), to attack the PRI's "corruption and betrayal of peasant struggles." The PRI and PPS denounced his proposal, calling it "a new act of division, born of the old and sick sectarianism of the Communist Party and of the neotrotskyism that inspires the National Liberation Movement."[36] Nevertheless, some peasant leaders responded enthusiastically and began to organize a movement.

A few months later the Communist Party stepped up the pressure, criticizing "antidemocratic and antipopular" PRI candidate nomination practices and proposing that the MLN form a new political party to compete against the PRI in the 1964 presidential election.[37] Here Lázaro Cárdenas drew the line. Fearing the divisiveness of participation in elections, he had rejected electoral involvement by the MLN from the beginning, adding, prophetically, "the organization of new political parties belongs to the generations that follow us."[38] The National Committee of the MLN issued a statement that it would not become a party or officially sponsor any party.[39]

Nevertheless, the presidential election caused irreparable damage to the MLN. Conflict over how and whether to participate drove a wedge between the communist left and the *cardenistas*. Communist Party activists persisted in pursuing the formation of a party, hoping to take advantage of a 1963 electoral reform granting any party with 2.5 percent of the vote some seats in Congress. The Frente Electoral del Pueblo (FEP) presented its petition for registry in August 1963. It proved no more successful than the Communist Party at getting legal registry, and it increased government hostility toward the MLN. Several local organizers of the FEP were murdered; others, including its presidential candidate, were jailed. The FEP ran a largely symbolic campaign, nominating as candidates many political prisoners in jail since the failed 1958 railroad workers' strike.

36. "Panorama nacional," *Política* 3 (15 January 1963): 3–5; "Sección especial de documentos," *Política* 3 (15 January 1963): 2, 7.

37. "¡Forjar una alianza democrática y anti-imperialista para actuar en la lucha electoral!" *Política* 3 (15 April 1963): 23.

38. "Panorama político," *Política* 1 (1 March 1961): 15, 10.

39. Alonso Aguilar, "El MLN y la sucesión presidencial," *Política* 4 (15 August 1963): special documents section.

Meanwhile, Lázaro Cárdenas faced intense pressure to side with the PRI and its candidate Gustavo Díaz Ordaz. In the end Cárdenas could not bring himself to oppose the PRI in a presidential election. In June he endorsed Díaz Ordaz in a rally in the Las Balsas region of Michoacán. The endorsement infuriated MLN members, who complained that Cárdenas had no right to support the PRI candidate without "prior clear and public commitments" from the PRI, and accused him of contributing to the "disorientation of [the masses] . . . that believe in him and trust him as their guide and example."[40] The 1965 MLN board of directors included Cuauhtémoc Cárdenas, but his participation became sporadic, and in early 1967 he joined the PRI. Deprived of its powerful sponsor, the MLN found itself under increasing attack. Less than three months after the Las Balsas speech, the government went after the peasant organization created by Cárdenas. It supported and registered as the legal leadership a minority cohort friendly to the PRI. This leadership later affiliated the CCI with the PRI. The MLN finally disappeared after many top leaders were jailed for participating in the 1968 student movement.

The MLN demonstrates several common features of the formation of left opposition. First, it highlights the importance of elite division in creating space for strong left opposition. Lázaro Cárdenas initiated this division in 1952 (with Henríquez) and 1961 (with the MLN); his son Cuauhtémoc initiated it in 1986–88. Second, similar issues trigger convergence. The demands of the MLN sound uncannily like the demands that united the left in 1988. In 1988 as in 1961 a Cárdenas would call for independence from the IMF, state involvement in economic development, democratization of the PRI and its sectoral organizations, and political decentralization. Cuauhtémoc Cárdenas's 1988 statement that "the stimulation of our economy . . . [and] the improvement of living standards of the population . . . demand the support, the backing of popular forces, . . . and a broad democratic consensus"[41] echoes the 1961 MLN declaration that "only the action and the political organization of the great popular sectors . . . and the broadest possible unity of all the patriotic, progressive, and anti-imperialist sectors of our country will make feasible the solution of the great problems of the people."[42] Third, the *priista* element gets dragged toward real opposition as a result of exclusion from policy. The left coalition may start out with social justice

40. "Implicaciones del voto razonado de Lázaro Cárdenas en pro de Díaz Ordaz," *Política* 5 (15 June 1964): inside front and back cover.
41. Jorge Laso de la Vega, ed., *La Corriente Democrática: Hablan los protagonistas* (Mexico City: Editorial Posada, 1987), 42–43.
42. "Panorama nacional," *Política* 2 (15 September 1961): 9.

goals and anti-imperialist nationalism, but it soon raises demands for internal democratization of the PRI as well as broader political democracy. Finally, left coalitions suffer from internal contradictions and divisions that fragment it.

A Delicate Balance: Opposition, Regime Legitimacy, and System Reform

Although the MLN and FPPM ultimately disintegrated, these and other protests left their mark on the regime. The PRI made concessions in order to reduce protest, keep it occupied in legal channels (as opposed to violent or armed opposition), and reinforce overall PRI hegemony. For example, the PRI needed opposition party participation in elections. Opposition participation helped legitimize the regime by allowing the PRI to demonstrate its commanding majority and its hold on the safe center. However, the PRI also wanted to make sure the opposition could not threaten PRI control. The rewards for opposition parties were few, in terms of influence over policy or positions in government. Under these circumstances it was not always easy to get opposition parties to cooperate; they knew, as some members of the MLN board argued, that participating in elections does not achieve anything, "because all such elections are lost."[43] More than once opposition parties threatened to withdraw from elections or support violent antisystem behavior. The PRI responded with repression of the more serious threats but also with incentives to draw "safe" parties back into the legal electoral arena. Thus, "the great continuity of the Mexican elections must be understood not as stability without change but as continuity through change. It has not been the immobility of electoral processes that has kept them uninterrupted but, on the contrary, incessant and gradual change."[44]

Most incentives to participation combined crumbs to activist party elites with measures to forestall any real improvement in opposition competitiveness. In essence, the PRI gave with one hand and took away with the other. Toward the end of the 1950s, for example, opposition parties seemed barely able—and increasingly unwilling—to compete in elections. Between 1955 and 1961 a majority of electoral districts registered only one candidate.[45] The law also kept opposition parties from making significant gains in representation. As its percentage of the vote

43. Aguilar, "El MLN y la sucesión presidencial."
44. Molinar Horcasitas, *El tiempo de la legitimidad*, 29.
45. Ibid., 42.

increased steadily from 2.2 percent in 1946 to 10.2 percent in 1958, the PAN's percentage of seats in Congress held roughly constant.[46] With little to lose, PAN leaders took more aggressive action: initiating civil disobedience, withdrawing its representative from the Federal Electoral Commission, and—in 1958—ordering its victorious congressional candidates not to take office. In the nonelectoral arena the regime faced major strikes by independent organizers in the critical railroad and teachers' unions in 1958–59, which challenged its revolutionary, pro-union credentials. Peasant leaders like Rubén Jaramillo carried out land invasions. Cárdenas sponsored the CCI, perhaps "the most serious threat to the [main PRI peasant organization] CNC until recent times."[47] The regime response repressed the most dangerous groups (the railroad and teachers' unions) and introduced legal reforms that punished oppositions which remained outside the electoral system but rewarded those who participated on the PRI's terms. The 1963 electoral reform canceled the registry of parties whose candidates refused to take office but also offered minority parties more representation in Congress, through "party deputies." In the 1964–67 legislature twenty PAN congressmen won seats, only two fewer than the party's combined total from the previous four legislatures.[48]

Such reforms clearly did not give opposition parties real power. From the PRI's perspective that was the point: to ensure participation without giving up control. Despite the PRI's intentions, however, such reforms did slowly strengthen opposition parties. The 1963 reform encouraged opposition parties to run candidates even in districts they knew they would lose, since every vote counted toward the national total that qualified them for party seats. The percentage of districts in which only one candidate ran dropped from 33 percent in 1961 to zero in 1964. The number of congressional candidates presented by the PPS and the Partido Auténtico de la Revolución Mexicana (PARM) roughly doubled, and the number of PAN candidates grew 78 percent. Says Juan Molinar Horcasitas, "the importance of this increase in the level of participation of candidates in the federal elections could hardly be underestimated. The artificial stimulus to opposition electoral participation, even in unpromising districts, forced these parties to begin to recruit and form cadres in regions that otherwise would probably have been neglected. . . . The increase seemed to consolidate the party system."[49]

46. Mexico, Instituto Federal Electoral (IFE), *Contienda electoral en las elecciones de diputados federales*, ed. Jenny Saltiel Cohen (Mexico City: IFE, 1991), 2.

47. Molinar Horcasitas, *El tiempo de la legitimidad*, 55.

48. Ibid., 66.

49. Ibid., 71–73.

Contested Hegemony: Some Common Features

A summation of the most important of these generalizations produces six "rules of thumb" for understanding the role of opposition within the hegemonic, one-party system.

Rule 1: Strong political opposition usually originates in elite division.

Rule 2: Elite divisions in an election year tend to favor the electoral fortunes of the opposition. Elite divisions create political space (and weaken the regime's repressive capacity), which benefits opposition; and some conditions for an opposition-surge, especially popular discontent, may encourage elite divisions.

Rule 3: Antisystem electoral oppositions tend to arise during or shortly before a presidential election year. Prosystem electoral oppositions usually appear shortly *after* a presidential election.

Rule 4: Similar issues tend to trigger left convergence. The issue of democracy—how to build it and where to locate it—has played a key role in uniting and dividing opposition to the regime.

Rule 5: The regime typically responds to challenge with a mixture of repression and reforms designed to reinforce PRI hegemony and preempt future threats while offering the opposition incentives to enter or remain in the system.

Rule 6: Maintaining the relationship between hegemony and opposition required change to maintain continuity and therefore reflects a balancing act that is as much a characteristic of the Mexican political regime as its most enduring institutional pillars.

POLITICAL DECAY? INSTITUTIONAL, SOCIAL, AND ECONOMIC CHANGE, 1970–1985

By the early 1980s Mexico's balancing act had become increasingly difficult. Sociological change, accumulated institutional reforms, and the exhaustion of Mexico's historic economic development model made hegemony harder to maintain. Initial efforts to preserve the traditional model imposed financial burdens on the state that ironically made the ultimate crisis more severe. These changes shaped the opposition's incentives and opportunities in 1988.

Sociological Change and Alienation

Between 1940 and 1970 the Mexican economy grew at an average rate of more than 6 percent per year, a sustained growth rate matched by very few countries.[50] Along with this aggregate growth Mexico experienced significant socioeconomic development, transforming Mexico from a largely rural to a largely urban society. A mostly peasant population declined to about a third of the workforce.[51] A more complex social class structure developed, including a larger middle-class, service-sector, and industrial workforce. Mexicans increasingly lived in cities, especially Mexico City. By 1984 the population of Mexico City was estimated at close to 20 percent of the national population, compared to 6 percent in 1930.[52] People had more access to telephones, modern transportation, and communication. Levels of literacy and education improved.

These changes encouraged popular demands for participation and weakened PRI controls. Mexican society resembled less and less the society that the PRI had been set up to manage. PRI organizations incorporated the middle class incompletely, while much of the urban marginalized class in the informal sector remained outside the PRI umbrella. By the early 1980s only about 20 percent of the economically active population was unionized.[53] New social movements began to spread among this marginalized population in the late 1960s and early 1970s. These movements often deliberately stayed away from parties, especially the PRI, instead working as self-help groups to satisfy the material demands of the marginalized. Party sectoral organizations could not mobilize a population they did not penetrate. As one *priista*

50. Levy and Székely, *Mexico: Paradoxes of Stability and Change*, 132.

51. *Statistical Abstract of Latin America*, ed. James Wilkie (Los Angeles: UCLA, 1988), 26: 256.

52. Ibid., 95.

53. Pablo González Casanova, *El estado y los partidos políticos en México* (Mexico City: Ediciones Era, 1985), 48. See also Middlebrook, *The Paradox of Revolution*, 319–23, and corresponding footnotes. According to Middlebrook, reliable estimates by César Zazueta and Ricardo de la Peña put this figure at 16.3 percent in 1978. See Zazueta and de la Peña, *La estructura del Congreso del Trabajo: Estado, trabajo, y capital en México* (Mexico City: Fondo de Cultura Económica, 1984).

put it, 1988 made the PRI admit that "many more things [were] going on outside the party than inside it."[54]

Urbanization magnified the impact of new opposition. Opposition organizations tend to concentrate in Mexico's fast-growing urban areas, and opposition parties have always relied on Mexico City for significant support. However, it is one thing to have a strong urban opposition when the vast majority of the population lives in rural areas, and quite another when the majority of the population lives in those same cities. A single rally in the Zócalo of Mexico City can catch the attention of a national audience faster than a hundred rallies in the countryside. And as Mexico's population became more urban, the PRI's rural base became less able to compensate for the party's losses in the cities.

Finally, it became painfully obvious that despite some absolute improvements in living standards, neither the "economic miracle" nor the PRI's "revolutionary project" had lessened the gap between rich and poor. Between 1950 and 1969 the income share of the bottom 20 percent of the population declined from 4.7 percent to 4 percent, while the share of the richest 20 percent increased from 58.9 percent to 64 percent.[55] It is hard to sustain a claim to have promoted revolutionary justice when estimates suggest an increasing concentration of wealth: in 1958 the richest 5 percent made 22 times more than the poorest 10 percent; in 1970, 39 times more than the poorest 10 percent; and in 1977, *50* times more than the poorest 10 percent.[56]

Middle-class dissatisfaction with its share of the economic pie also began to manifest itself in protest against the regime, most notably in the 1968 student movement. Student complaints about the lack of postgraduation career opportunities added to an agenda that included demands for democratization, better living conditions for the urban poor, and an end to repression of independent movements. The spark was a rally held at the National Autonomous University on July 26, 1968, to celebrate the Cuban Revolution and call on the government to support Cuba against the United States. Police entered UNAM's campus to break up the demonstration, which faculty and students considered a violation of the university's legal autonomy from the state. They organized further protests. Frightened by cross-class support for the students and the probability that protests would embarrass the regime

54. Personal observation of PRI conference, April 29, 1991.

55. Levy and Székely, *Mexico: Paradoxes of Stability and Change*, 148. After 1969 (and the student movement), the middle class gained some ground, reducing the top 20 percent to 55.1 percent of income by 1977; the lowest 20 percent, however, declined still further, to 3.3 percent of income.

56. González Casanova, *El estado y los partidos políticos en México*, 88.

when world attention focused on Mexico as the host of the 1968 Olympic Games, only a few months away, the government ordered army snipers to fire on demonstrating students in the Plaza of Tlatelolco in Mexico City on October 2, 1968, killing hundreds. The massacre shocked the nation. Tlatelolco brought home the impact of authoritarianism to the families of the usually privileged and protected social classes and inspired the leaders of a generation of antisystem protest.

Political Liberalization and Institutional Change

Tlatelolco also contributed to the most significant of the institutional reforms that gradually improved the competitive opportunities for opposition: the 1977 electoral reform. After President Echeverría released imprisoned student leaders in 1971, several left political parties were formed, led by student movement veterans. The seed group for these parties was the National Committee for Consultation and Organization (CNAO), which splintered into several groups in 1972–73, including eventually the Movement for Socialist Action and Unity (MAUS), the Socialist Workers' Party (PST), and the Mexican Workers' Party (PMT) of Heberto Castillo. None of these parties could get legal registry under the restrictive laws of the time. They shared a deep antagonism toward the system and suspicion about the usefulness of electoral participation. Other student leaders spread out to organize popular movements.[57] The most alienated supported guerrilla struggles, to meet violence with violence. Guerrilla activity declined under military pressure, especially after the death in 1974 of one of the best-known guerrillas, Lucio Cabañas, but was not completely under control when Echeverría left office.

Existing parties failed to channel this discontent. The tiny "left" parties PARM and PPS had lost so much credibility because of their almost incestuous cooperation with the PRI that critics called them "parastatal" parties—virtual government companies bought and paid for by the state. On the right the PAN debated whether to legitimate PRI-style elections with their participation. Internal divisions over this and other questions kept the PAN from nominating a candidate for the 1976 presidential election. This was the last straw—leaving the PRI without any

57. See Vivienne Bennett, "The Evolution of Urban Popular Movements in Mexico Between 1968 and 1988," in *The Making of Social Movements in Latin America: Identity, Strategy, and Democracy,* ed. Arturo Escobar and Sonia Álvarez (Boulder, Colo.: Westview Press, 1992).

credible opponents on either the right or the left, except for the movements, parties, and guerrilla organizations that directly challenged the PRI's legitimacy outside the legal and electoral arena.

These threats led the government of President López Portillo to sponsor an electoral reform in 1977, in the hope of bringing protest into the system on the PRI's terms. The 1977 reform eased the requirements for new party registration, allowing the Mexican Communist Party and other independent left parties to compete legally in elections. Through a conditional registry procedure parties could prove they had sufficient support by actually competing in the election and winning 1.5 percent of the total vote, instead of having to hold assemblies and collect lists of notarized signatures before getting permission to compete. The conditional registry procedure also appealed to new parties because it did not require any particular geographic distribution of the vote.[58] In addition, the law increased the size of the House of Representatives to four hundred members and distributed the one hundred additional members according to proportional representation. A provision barring parties that won more than sixty single-member districts from getting proportional representation seats effectively reserved these seats for opposition parties. Finally, parties became eligible for financial support from the government for campaign expenses, and got limited free access to television and radio.

Like earlier electoral reforms, the 1977 law was designed to stabilize the system, not jeopardize it. Opposition parties could send their leaders to the House of Representatives—where their minority position (25 percent of seats) and the weakness of the Congress vis-à-vis the presidency would basically neutralize them. Nor did the reform compromise PRI control of the electoral process; it "barely modified the two fundamental principles that govern[ed] electoral participation and organization since 1946: the centralization of the process of organization and vigilance in a commission . . . presided over by the Secretary of the Interior, and the restriction of the right to nominate candidates outside national, registered political parties."[59] The fragmentation of the opposition produced by registering new parties even helped the PRI retain its commanding position.

58. Because definitive registry procedures required regional assemblies, almost all new parties after 1977 chose conditional registry, though a party needed more supporters to confirm conditional registry than definitive registry. Estimates based on an expected vote of 18,000,000, slightly more than the 1976 vote, suggest a contrast of nearly 270,000 for conditional and only 65,000 for definitive registry. See Silvia Gómez Tagle, *Las estadísticas electorales de la reforma política* (Mexico City: El Colegio de México, 1990), 26.

59. Molinar Horcasitas, *El tiempo de la legitimidad*, 98.

Nevertheless, the reform expanded the space for electoral opposition. Independent left parties could participate in elections, including the Mexican Communist Party (by 1979), the Mexican Workers' Party (by 1985), and the Socialist Workers' Party (by 1982). The first two parties later gave their registry to the PRD in the wake of the 1988 election; had they remained illegal, Cárdenas might not have been able to establish an independent party. The reform also encouraged the opposition to compete more effectively, even for municipal and state positions, by making available additional resources and rewarding efforts to campaign in all districts with an increased vote that qualified parties for more proportional representation in congressional seats. The percentage of municipalities in which only one party got votes dropped from 71.9 percent in 1975–77 to 41.4 percent in 1984–86, with at least ten states experiencing a more than 30 percent decrease in the number of one-party municipalities between the 1975–77 and 1978–80 periods alone.[60]

Moreover, the reform encouraged the ruling party to "[change] the rhetoric of self-legitimation. Instead of presenting themselves as . . . the heirs of the Revolution, they refer constantly to the sanction they have earned at the polls."[61] Electoral reform allowed the PRI to substitute a measure of electoral legitimacy for the revolutionary legitimacy that the system lost over time as the programs of successive presidents moved farther away from traditional revolutionary principles and as the generation of revolutionary leaders began to die. However, this eventually began to ensnare the PRI in a trap of its own making as the party tried to rely on an electoral legitimacy that it ultimately had not earned. Reference to electoral victories invited an ever closer scrutiny of electoral laws and procedures, raising the legitimacy costs incurred by electoral fraud and by maintaining institutional barriers to opposition parties.

The Roots of Economic Crisis

Finally, in the 1980s the PRI lost one of its remaining sources of legitimacy: its ability to deliver economic growth and prosperity. Mexico's "economic miracle" (1940–70) had been characterized not only by high average real GDP growth but also by a rise in minimum incomes unprecedented in Mexican history and by remarkably low inflation, under 5 percent. Mexicans refer to this period as the era of "*desarrollo estabilizador*," or stabilizing development. The economic boom bolstered the

---

60. Ibid., 116.
61. Molinar Horcasitas, "The Mexican Electoral System," 106.

loyalty of citizens to the PRI and made possible a system of broad class alliances. The system had the resources to offer some benefits to everyone. When the Mexican economy fell apart, these political alliances were put under enormous stress and created an opportunity for new left opposition. The responsibility for this economic crisis lay in part in tensions within the very model that produced these impressive results. However, some of the policies chosen to deal with growing protest and opposition also contributed substantially to the deterioration of the economy by saddling the state with a crippling debt and swollen bureaucracy. Differing evaluations of the weight of these factors fundamentally shaped the debate over economic policy in the 1980s between the *cardenistas* and their rivals in the PRI.

Like many similar programs for economic development adopted in Third World nations after World War II, *desarrollo estabilizador* assigned a key development role to the state and relied on partial protection of national industries from foreign competition as the main engine of growth and industrial development. The strategy of import substitution industrialization (ISI) promoted industrialization by encouraging domestic consumers to substitute goods produced nationally for goods previously imported from abroad. ISI required state investment and regulation but as a complement to rather than a replacement for private investment. The state built infrastructure and often owned key transportation and communication networks, including railroad, telegraph, and telephone systems. In Mexico more than 50 percent of public sector investment went to communications and transport during early ISI, declining gradually over time.[62] In addition, the ISI state invested directly in agriculture and industry, primarily in order to break strategic bottlenecks. Most Mexican agricultural investment went to develop the fertilizer industry and construct irrigation systems, especially from 1947 to 1952. The bulk of investment in industry went to secure sufficient oil, electric power, and steel for industrial growth.

Second, the ISI state used its regulatory power to encourage development in priority sectors. Laws protected national industries from foreign competition by imposing high tariffs, restricting foreign investment, and requiring import-licensing procedures that imposed costly burdens of paperwork and time for imports in nonemphasized sectors. The state could use taxation to encourage elites to reinvest capital and had the power to declare a given productive activity "saturated," thus preventing any new firm from entering that field and protecting profit margins. It controlled exports of raw materials to en-

---

62. Levy and Székely, *Mexico: Paradoxes of Stability and Change*, 135.

sure that the needs of domestic production would be met, and it regulated credit, influencing the distribution of private banking funds among sectors of the economy. While the state allowed considerable room for private enterprise, its intervention obviously made some activities more profitable than others. ISI policies were supported by a rhetoric of nationalism which argued that a strong national industrial sector was necessary to ensure sustained development. Finally, the ISI state frequently tried to control labor costs to employers through repression or control of labor (a goal made easier by state corporatist alliance with official PRI unions) and through subsidies of basic labor inputs like food and transportation.

This model contained a number of internal tensions that limited its capacity to produce sustained growth. The first problem was that most Third World domestic markets could not indefinitely absorb national production, especially in later stages of ISI, but often had difficulty expanding into foreign markets. The early stage of import substitution takes place in sectors that produce goods with low capital and technology inputs. It may then progress to sectors producing durable consumer goods like automobiles and appliances. These products cost more. Developing countries with high levels of inequality, like Mexico, have fewer domestic consumers able to buy them. However, these industries often have a hard time simply selling more abroad, in part because of some of the same measures that protect them from foreign competition, like overvaluation of the currency. If they produce for a domestic market too small to allow them to take advantage of economies of scale, their industry may remain inefficient and uncompetitive abroad. Second, continued protection becomes hard to sustain without increasing trade deficits and public debt. ISI industries usually import capital inputs from more developed countries, but protectionist measures limit exports and thus squeeze the supply of foreign currency with which to buy needed inputs. The state and private sector go into debt to make up the difference. Third, subsidy programs become hard to sustain without an effective method of internal tax collection (a common problem in Third World states) or a growing export base. In the Mexican case investment in agriculture also slowed, leaving the agricultural sector unprepared to keep up with population growth and the expansion of the urban, nonfood-producing workforce.[63] Mexico eventually had to import basic staples like corn. This increasingly affected government budgets, making food subsidies for the industrial workforce ever more costly.

63. Ibid. Agriculture's share of public investment dropped from 22 percent in 1947–52 to 11 percent in 1965–70.

All of these problems indicate some constraints on the ability of ISI to continue to deliver on its promise of economic growth. In some countries, like Taiwan, the state encouraged selective export promotion of labor-intensive goods, relieving some of the pressure on public finances and expanding employment. In contrast, Mexican leaders concerned about preserving the postrevolutionary class alliance and the hegemony of the PRI adopted populist policies that worsened many of the country's economic problems. The Mexican reaction was more the norm than the Taiwanese reaction. Many Latin American and African leaders who faced similar threats of political instability chose the same solution. The regime interpreted the 1968 student crisis as a warning that the young middle class was dissatisfied with opportunities for employment and consumption under ISI. To win their loyalty, President Luis Echeverría (1970–76) gave them jobs working for the state, in the bureaucracy or in public enterprises. In many cases the state simply adopted troubled and unprofitable companies in order to sustain employment. The number of enterprises with public participation increased from 84 in 1970 to 845 in 1976, while the number of state employees doubled to more than 1 million.[64] State expenditure in virtually all sectors increased. Since Echeverría also balked at tax reform to increase revenues, the chief results were spiraling public debt and unprecedented inflation, around 25 percent. External public debt ballooned from 4.2 billion dollars in 1970 to 19.6 billion dollars in 1976. One of every three export dollars went to debt service, a rate comparable to the worst years of the post-1981 debt crisis.[65]

Though they objected strenuously to any attempt to fix these problems by dismantling protectionism or taxing business, the regime's longtime business allies loudly complained about Echeverría's "leftist" populism. Thus, not only did the regime fail to stabilize the economic and political situation, but its (mostly rhetorical) attacks on the business community led to a serious breach between the state and business. Capital flight and capital strikes—the deliberate withholding of investment as leverage—made the economic situation worse. Echeverría finally found himself forced to devalue the Mexican peso in 1976 and sign a stabilization agreement with the IMF. The agreement included a ceiling on additional debt, which limited further expansion of the public sector.

After the discovery of massive new oil deposits in 1976–77, at the start of President López Portillo's term, these limitations became obso-

64. Ibid., 153.
65. Ibid., 153, 138.

lete. Oil let López Portillo satisfy all the elements of the political coalition behind the PRI and postpone the evil day of reckoning by borrowing and spending at an increasing rate. Euphoric government officials announced that Mexico had outgrown the problems of capital scarcity and entered into an era of "administer[ing] abundance."[66] Since it would take time for the oil industry to gear up for production at capacity, and since Mexican officials assumed (like almost everyone else) that oil prices would continue to rise, the government decided not to wait for abundance. On the strength of oil expectations it borrowed massive sums from international banks. Starting with an external debt of 19 billion dollars in 1976, Mexico quickly assumed responsibility for an additional 10 billion dollars by 1979, abandoning IMF borrowing limits with its tacit permission. Until Mexico could restructure its debt to a longer-term payment schedule with lower interest, this meant a staggering debt service-to-exports ratio of .62 in 1979: two out of every three export dollars went to service the debt. International bankers continued to lend money to Mexico, and Mexico blithely accepted what it then considered only an advance on its oil inheritance. López Portillo left a total foreign public debt of nearly 53 billion dollars when his term ended in 1982.[67]

Contrary to all expectations, the oil boom lasted only three years (1978–81), leaving behind a legacy of crushing debt and crushed expectations. When the bottom dropped out of the oil market in 1981, Mexico lost its principal source of dollars with which to make payments on the massive debt. It had to accept austerity programs that demolished the living standards of labor and the middle class, a failure exacerbated by the fact that these classes had hoped for so much during the López Portillo years. In addition, oil exacerbated Mexico's economic problems. Inflation resulting from the influx of oil money reached 20–100 percent in the latter part of the seventies, overvaluing the peso and hurting nonoil exports. Inflation also left the working classes in worse shape to face the onslaught of the debt crisis and austerity in the eighties.

A more subtle but critical transformation also took place during this period: the growing power of the banking sector within the Mexican government.[68] The influence of bankers grew naturally out of their in-

66. Carlos Monsivais, "Las repercusiones sociales y culturales del auge," in *El auge petrolero: De la euforia al desencanto*, ed. Rolando Cordera and Carlos Tello (Mexico City: UNAM, 1987), 35.

67. Levy and Székely, *Mexico: Paradoxes of Stability and Change*, 158.

68. For an excellent analysis of this institutional change, see Miguel Ángel Centeno, *Democracy Within Reason: Technocratic Revolution in Mexico* (University Park: The Pennsylvania State University Press, 1994).

creasing importance as mediators between Mexico and the international system—a position that became even more critical when oil prices fell and Mexico had to figure out what to do about a debt it could not pay. This shift brought to power men like Miguel De la Madrid, who blamed the crisis on protectionism, lack of budgetary discipline, and state interference in the economy. They decided to initiate a dramatic transformation of Mexico's economic model. The *cardenistas* strongly objected, stressing the historic achievements of ISI and state-led development and pointing out the dangers of opening up the economy, including loss of domestic industry, subordination to foreign capitalists, dependence on imported technology, and the social costs of poorly distributed growth. This debate defined the terms of the internal conflict in the PRI from 1986 to 1988 and mirrors debates in many former ISI countries, especially in Latin America, where the influence of populism was similarly strong.

CONCLUSIONS

In the political regime established between 1929 and 1940 presidentialism, one-party hegemony, and state corporatism functioned synergistically to complement and reinforce one another. In this political trinity elections played a role in legitimating the regime but mainly functioned as guarantees of elite rotation in power and as occasions to renew ties in the clientelistic network that bound the masses to the central government. However, the interdependence of presidentialism, one-party hegemony, and state corporatism also created vulnerabilities. For instance, the authority of the president over the party and official unions was based in part on his ability to distribute rewards, like candidacies, state resources, and government positions. Democracy in the PRI threatened the president's authority over the party and the Congress. A truly independent Congress could regularly block his initiatives, given the powers awarded to it by the Constitution. It is no accident that the regime paid so much attention over the years to assuring a commanding PRI majority in Congress, in part by nourishing a corporatist PRI-union alliance. Furthermore, if the PRI could not guarantee its control over the state and state resources, clientelistic networks could begin to starve and the party itself could disintegrate. Thus, the PRI could not easily accommodate demands for democracy, either internal or external.

Moreover, the Mexican political regime in the early 1980s faced dete-

riorating legitimacy and increasing challenges to its mechanisms of integration and participation. The political and economic reforms of the
late seventies offered opportunities for political opposition to take advantage of discontent with the system. The crisis exacerbated these
trends and brought about multiclass mobilization where the PRI-state
was most vulnerable and at the most vulnerable moment for the system:
the presidential succession. The transfer of power to a new president is
like a heart transplant for the system—its fundamental engine is replaced, presenting more opportunities for change than at any other
time, yet also the greatest danger of death in the transfer. The presidential election of 1988 would be, in truth, a "battle for the nation,"[69] a
struggle over Mexico's future economic model and political regime, between the neoliberals of Salinas and the social-nationalists of Cárdenas.

---

69. Rolando Cordera and Carlos Tello, *México: La disputa por la nación* (Mexico City:
Siglo Veintiuno, 1981).

3

The Birth of a New Political Option

ECONOMIC CRISIS, NEOLIBERAL POLICIES, AND DETACHMENT

Theoretical analyses of party formation highlight a number of important factors. Some approaches stress institutional incentives. New parties are considered much more likely, for example, in proportional representation systems.[1] Others expect institutional factors to have a "marginal bearing" on whether discontent will result in the formation of a party in particular cases, emphasizing instead a list of "political facilitators," including the behavior of existing parties, the strength of

---

1. A number of authors make this argument, most notably Maurice Duverger, in *Political Parties: Their Organization and Activity in the Modern State*, trans. Barbara North and Douglas North (New York: John Wiley, 1954).

mass commitments, and "what the elites, who could lead a new party, decide to do."[2] A third approach focuses on shifts in the electorate: on changes in the social cleavage structure (though "cleavages do not translate themselves into party oppositions as a matter of course"),[3] changes in the spatial structure of party ideologies, or changes in the size of the protest vote. Downsian modeling suggests that a lack of fit between party ideology and popular preferences might leave sectors of the electorate available for capture, though it is not clear from a strict Downsian point of view why lack of fit would become extreme and fixed enough to leave room for a new party, since parties are supposed to adjust to changes in the electorate. A contrasting argument claims that strategic protest voting governs the behavior of an ideologically unsophisticated electorate. The masses are "as likely to support a conservative movement as a progressive one, whichever is most available, when their conditions lead them to revolt." As there is nearly always someone willing to protest against an entrenched ruling party, "one-party dominance is conducive to the rise of third parties."[4] Each of these approaches points to an important influence on party formation. Somehow institutions matter, elite decisions (however arrived at) matter, and the availability of support matters.

The more interesting questions have to do with the relative importance of these factors and their impact on each other. While inherently less predictable than the general direction of the effect of institutions or angry voters, decisions by the prospective leaders of a new party seem especially crucial. Few parties are organized by individuals with no connections among political or economic elites. Even mass-based left parties benefit considerably from the resources, experience, and skills of members of more privileged classes. Institutions and the availability of popular support should be integrated into the explanation as factors conditioning elite choices and calculations. Clearly, party founders must consider what it costs to organize a new party in a specific institutional context. What are the requirements for party registration? How much support must the party have to qualify for matching campaign funds or to win representation in government? What will it cost in terms of time,

    2. Charles Hauss and David Rayside, "The Development of New Parties in Western Democracies Since 1945," in *Political Parties: Development and Decay*, ed. Louis Maisel and Joseph Cooper (Beverly Hills, Calif.: Sage Publications, 1978), 37–39, 46. For these authors elite choices remain largely within the black box of decision making.
    3. Seymour Martin Lipset and Stein Rokkan, eds., *Party Systems and Voter Alignments: Cross-National Perspectives* (New York: The Free Press, 1967), 26.
    4. Maurice Pinard, *The Rise of a Third Party: A Study in Crisis Politics* (Montreal: McGill-Queen's University Press, 1975), 95; 36.

money, expertise, and other resources to get that minimum level of support? Laws that make it harder to get party registration or win representation in government should discourage party formation. More generally, the institutional context offers dissident elites a set of non-electoral as well as electoral options for expressing discontent, some of which may cost less than forming a new party. Party founders must also anticipate popular receptiveness to a new party, especially if they plan to participate in elections. If voters seem loyal to existing parties, organizing a new party is less attractive. The more modest the electoral support needed to reach leaders' goals, the more easily this condition is met. It should not initially matter whether voters switch because of ideological affinity with the new party or simply to protest against existing parties, though this may matter considerably for consolidation.

Ultimately, however, even leaders with limited goals must feel that they cannot get what they want through existing parties and institutions. If likely to succeed, a strategy of pursuing goals through existing institutions usually requires less investment of energy than new party formation. Though reform of existing institutions seemed improbable in a hierarchical party designed to resist influence from below, the *cardenistas* tried virtually everything else before resigning themselves to the idea of an independent candidacy. Thus, the political marginalization of discontented elites often pushes them to form new organizations to achieve personal and/or policy goals. Sometimes the policy component appears almost vanishingly small, subordinated to the personal ambitions of leaders who feel unappreciated as individuals. Other examples, like the 1988 *cardenista* coalition, seem more affected by ideology. From a cost-benefit point of view the greater the costs of new party formation, the more likely it is that leaders must have broad goals, including significant policy as well as personal reasons. In either case, the marginalization of leaders with unmet goals tends to detach them from older political loyalties—close to a necessary condition for new party formation. While parties may be formed even in adverse conditions, by people with few resources and little immediate hope of success, parties are rarely formed by those who feel adequately represented by and in agreement with the policies of existing parties. As a result, factors that increase elite marginalization or ideological conflict should also find a place in the explanation of new party formation.

This chapter discusses why this occurred in Mexico and how it finally produced an independent *cardenista* candidacy in 1988. I argue that the formation of a new political option in Mexico resulted fundamentally from the detachment of key elites and voters from their traditional political loyalties. Both voter alienation from the PRI and the intraelite conflicts that culminated in a split began long before the economic crisis of the 1980s. However, the crisis and the government response to it dramatically accelerated popular rejection of the PRI and polarized elite conflicts. Increasing ideological polarization and political marginalization eventually led opponents of neoliberal policies to break with their PRI past and organize an electoral alternative, encouraged by the belief that they would find a receptive audience of detached voters ready to support their popular project.

During the 1980s President Miguel De la Madrid adopted policies in response to the crisis that contradicted fundamental principles of the traditional postrevolutionary compromise and excluded the *cardenista* wing of the party from policy influence and political power. Opponents accused him of abandoning the PRI's commitment to social welfare, endangering political stability, selling out the country to foreigners, and breaking the revolutionary pact that called for power sharing among party factions. They were particularly concerned about the prospect that their marginalization would continue past his term under the kind of candidate that De la Madrid would select if left to himself, and therefore concentrated initially on the issue of democratic selection of the PRI candidate. The result was the formation of a Democratic Current inside the ruling party. When De la Madrid's control of the state and party proved an insurmountable obstacle to internal reform, the founders of the Democratic Current carried their agenda outside the party, creating an alternative candidacy that criticized De la Madrid's policies. At the same time, the economic crisis presented the left with its best opportunity in years to challenge the PRI electorally. Dissatisfaction with PRI management had never been greater. In Cárdenas the left had a candidate able to capture that disaffection. The prospect of getting a piece of the action lured not only the independent left (the PMS) but also the normally PRI-aligned small parties and nonaligned popular movements. The National Democratic Front they formed with the dissident *priistas* was the first and most important step toward the formation of a new political party.

Structural and institutional features shaped this process. The crisis itself was not simply an unfortunate accident. The Mexican mix of distributive and business-oriented policies had long provided the political stability necessary for economic growth by satisfying some urgent social demands while respecting the interests of national capital. Nevertheless, as Chapter 2 suggested, these policies also contributed to the economic crisis that strained the old political coalition to the breaking point. Moreover, the *specific* outcome of the conflict between the *cardenistas* and the neoliberals—no internal reform and the creation of a new party—depended heavily on strategy and the institutional resources at the disposal of competing actors. In addition to domestic resources like its control of the presidency and the PRI, the neoliberal coalition had international backing and even pressure for its preferred policies. The *cardenistas*, in contrast, had little institutional leverage to force reform or reverse their marginalization from within. When their use of voice failed, they had few options left but acquiescence or exit.

PARTY REFORM RISES TO THE NATIONAL AGENDA: ECONOMIC CRISIS AND THE CORRIENTE DEMOCRÁTICA, 1985–1987[5]

The immediate catalyst for the economic crisis was a major decline in the world price of petroleum in 1981. Although intensive exploitation of oil had begun only a few years earlier, the Mexican state had already become dependent on oil revenue. In 1973 oil accounted for 1.7 percent of total exports and 13.7 percent of public sector income; by 1981, the oil sector contributed 75 percent of total exports and 30.5 percent of public sector income. Perhaps more important, oil provided 50 percent of total foreign currency income by 1981, making oil the single most important source of the dollars Mexico needed to make payments on its foreign debt.[6] As a result, when oil prices fell, the Mexican government suddenly faced a shortfall in anticipated oil income of 6 billion dollars—30 percent of expected oil revenues.[7] The disaster helped expand the public sector deficit to almost 15 percent of GDP in 1981.

At the same time, interest payments on the debt went up. About half this increase resulted from the initial strategy that the López Portillo government adopted to finance its budget shortfall: raising short-term borrowing rather than cutting expenditures. The government expected oil prices to recover soon, and sought not to disrupt the economy by suspending major development projects. While it seemed reasonable at

---

5. See Appendix B for a full chronology of these events through the foundation of the PRD.

6. Gabriel Székely, "La crisis de los precios del petróleo," in *México ante la crisis*, ed. Pablo González Casanova and Hector Aguilar Camín (Mexico City: Siglo Veintiuno, 1985), 1: 241.

7. Donald Wyman, "The Mexican Economy: Problems and Prospects," in *Mexico's Economic Crisis: Challenges and Opportunities*, ed. Donald Wyman, Monograph Series, no. 12 (La Jolla, Calif.: UCSD Center for U.S.-Mexican Studies, 1983), 5.

the time, the decision expanded short-term foreign debt from 1.5 billion dollars in 1980 to 11 billion dollars and over 50 percent of total public debt by the end of 1981.[8] The strategy committed the Mexican government to huge payments during fiscal 1982, due to the higher interest rates and immediate repayment obligations characteristic of short-term loans. Payments also increased because of rising international interest rates affecting Mexico's existing obligations to foreign banks. In 1982 interest payments alone equaled 37 percent of the value of Mexican exports of goods and services, compared to 30 percent in 1981 and 20 percent in 1977, before the oil madness.[9] To make matters worse, the availability of higher interest rates abroad and uncertainty about the stability of the Mexican economy encouraged capital flight and inflation. Thus, by 1982 "Mexico was in the midst of what one economist has called appropriately 'an old-fashioned financial panic.' "[10] As dollars left the country, the Mexican government began to exhaust its dollar reserves in debt service payments.

By August 17, 1982, the situation had become so critical that finance minister Jesús Silva Herzog went to Washington, D.C., to inform the U.S. government that Mexico had virtually run out of dollars and would soon be unable to make payments on the debt. A few days later, during his last "state of the union" address, López Portillo stunned his audience by announcing the nationalization of Mexican banks, a measure intended to give the state more control over currency and to stem capital flight. He appointed as its first director Carlos Tello—well known for leftist sympathies, dependency school economic analyses, and criticism of IMF stabilization plans. This only deepened the concern of international creditors. Mexico seemed to be heading toward a moratorium on payment of its debt, by then so large that default would affect the entire international banking system. United States banks and the IMF offered Mexico a bailout plan for immediate debt rescue, which Mexican officials signed in November 1982. Mexico would incorporate an IMF stabilization program into its own recovery plan, the Program for the Immediate Reorganization of the Economy (PIRE), which called for a drastic reduction in the public sector deficit, from 18 percent of GDP in 1982 to 3–4 percent of GDP by 1985.[11] In addition, in December 1982 López Portillo devalued the peso to recover export strength.

Nevertheless, President Miguel De la Madrid inherited a critical situ-

8. Ibid., 6–7.
9. Ibid.
10. Ibid., 9.
11. Judith Gentleman, "Mexico After the Oil Boom," in *Mexican Politics in Transition*, ed. Judith Gentleman (Boulder, Colo.: Westview Press, 1987), 43.

ation when he assumed office in 1982. He faced popular disappointment with the consequences of the PRI's economic management: increasing inflation and devaluation rather than growth. One early assessment argued that "if a social explosion is to be averted, Mexico must return to expansionary economic policies."[12] Yet the state's fiscal problems and the budget cuts they imposed not only ruled out Keynesian expansionary policies but aggravated the economic crisis by reducing domestic demand. Mexico's interest payments alone took up a good chunk of total revenue. No one rushed to lend Mexico more money. Even without pressure from the IMF, these problems would have resulted in cutbacks. New investment had to depend largely on the private sector, but thanks to the bank nationalization, state relations with business had rarely been worse. In short, De la Madrid found himself in an exceedingly unpleasant position.

To restore fiscal solvency as quickly as possible, the new government adopted an aggressive austerity program. Despite strict implementation, the plan fell short of its targets in the 1982–85 period. The external debt continued to grow. In part the plan may simply have set overly ambitious goals. However, additional cuts in oil prices made it even more difficult for Mexico to keep up with debt. Manufacturing exports began to collapse as well as a result of capital flight, an overvalued peso, and restrictions on imports (since manufacturing depended heavily on foreign inputs). Real GDP growth was negative in both 1982 and 1983, recovered slightly in 1984, but declined again in 1985.[13] In response to the worsening economic situation the government applied more of the same medicine, cutting or holding the line on expenditures. Targets included virtually every sector, from investment and social programs to state employment. The state's share of total investment fell by 40 percent.[14] Popular subsidies of basic goods like tortillas, fuel, and water were eliminated or reduced, undermining the living standards of the poor. To further cut expenses the government began to privatize state enterprises—not so much to make money from their sale as to avoid continued subsidies to unproductive companies.[15] Often the government simply closed down offenders, throwing many out of work. The state eliminated more than 20 percent of all positions by July 1985—

12. Wyman, "The Mexican Economy," 19.
13. Mexico, Secretaría de Hacienda y Crédito Público (SHCP), *El nuevo perfil de la economía mexicana* (Mexico City: SHCP, June 1991), 37.
14. Gentleman, "Mexico After the Oil Boom,"48.
15. Gentleman finds "no evidence . . . decision-makers believed that the measure would benefit the economy in any way other than simply reducing the public sector deficit" (ibid., 51).

representing 51,000 full-time jobs and more than 60,000 temporary jobs—and unemployment increased to 18.8 percent by the end of 1984, according to a study by the Economic Commission for Latin America.[16] In addition, the government made a sustained attempt to limit increases in wages. Lower wages were expected to contribute to a decline in domestic demand, resulting in lower inflation and a more stable investment environment. Later, as economic policy increasingly emphasized trade liberalization and attracting foreign investment, cheap labor would become part of the package offered to potential investors. In the short term, wage agreements negotiated with the official unions contributed to a dramatic decline in real minimum wages, perhaps as much as 30 percent between 1982 and 1985.[17] Competition for government favor among unions in the PRI helped keep unions motivated to accept even such enormous sacrifices in the hope of salvaging something.

By 1985 the failure of the economy to respond to these adjustment measures led the government to consider openly more fundamental reforms to the traditional model of Mexican development. Several events in late 1985 and early 1986 increased the sense of urgency of policymakers. The IMF suspended Mexico's drawing rights of $900 million in September 1985 because of poor progress in meeting budget and inflation targets. Part of this measure was immediately canceled when a major earthquake hit Mexico City on the day of the announcement. However, UN studies indicated that reconstruction costs could reach $4 billion, far more than the restored drawing rights. Then oil prices halved again in late 1985, with losses to the Mexican treasury of more than $2 billion.[18] The government had to throw out its 1986 budget and appeal to the United States for help. De la Madrid continued to stress Mexico's commitment to repaying the debt. There would be no moratorium. Instead, in late 1985 he announced that Mexico would seek entry into GATT, a decision that meant relaxing restrictions on direct foreign investment and dropping subsidies of some sectors of the economy—an attractive option anyway, from a budget-cutting point of view. GATT entry was a key step in the strategic shift from pure austerity to fiscal austerity plus trade liberalization, the basic neoliberal project. The decision to restructure the economy with or without a major restructuring of the debt was a significant departure from the policy followed from 1982 to 1985.

This decision was also the last straw for the left wing of the PRI. The

16. Ibid., 51, 55.
17. Ibid., 55.
18. Daniel C. Levy and Gabriel Székely, *Mexico: Paradoxes of Stability and Change*, 2d ed. (Boulder, Colo.: Westview Press, 1987), 164.

traditional progressive, social-nationalist faction inside the PRI strongly objected to all the main elements of the De la Madrid plan: wage restrictions, cuts in government investment and social spending, privatization, repaying the debt, trade liberalization, and deregulation of foreign investment. While social-nationalists argued that economic recovery required using state resources to expand domestic consumer demand, the De la Madrid government believed that economic recovery required contracting domestic demand (through state budget cuts and wage/price freezes) in order to hold down inflation, build business confidence, and create attractive conditions for private investment. International demand would replace domestic demand as the engine of growth. Conflict between these two projects certainly predated the crisis. However, the social-nationalist wing had succeeded in vetoing neoliberal policies in the past, such as the decision to enter GATT, which had come up before. As the economic crisis deepened, the De la Madrid government saw more fundamental reforms as the only alternative to short-term adjustments that had not worked. It became harder and harder to reconcile these reforms with the preferences of the left wing of the party, but the political risks seemed small compared to the risk of postponing or compromising economic reform. In September 1985 De la Madrid's annual "state of the union" address "drew upon elements of familiar political rhetoric, declaring that revolutionary nationalism continued to guide state policies. It was apparent, however, that the substance of the regime's political-economic agenda differed markedly from any revolutionary-nationalist program that could be envisioned."[19]

The Emergence of a Split in the PRI, 1985–1986: Ideological Polarization

As ideological conflict increased, politicians associated with the left wing of the PRI began to hold informal discussions questioning the political and class character of the De la Madrid administration. As these discussions achieved rudimentary consensus on the nature of the problem, a few politicians began to consider options and make connections. In 1985 three prominent *priistas* discovered a convergence between conclusions they had reached more or less independently. These politicians— Rodolfo González Guevara, Porfirio Muñoz Ledo, and Cuauhtémoc Cárdenas Solórzano—initiated formal conversations that resulted in the

19. Gentleman, "Mexico After the Oil Boom," 45.

creation of a Corriente Democrática (also referred to as the Democratic Current, or CD) in 1986. They did not intend to form a new party but planned to work through existing institutions, acting as a pressure group inside the PRI to influence policy and demand a more democratic selection of the next PRI presidential candidate. However, the independent candidacy of Cuauhtémoc Cárdenas and eventually a new party evolved from its activity. Its construction therefore merits close scrutiny in order to analyze what brought those who founded the Democratic Current into open rebellion against the PRI, and how their activity further marginalized and radicalized them.

Alone among the major organizers of the Democratic Current Cuauhtémoc Cárdenas had a substantial personal *camarilla*, developed largely during his tenure as PRI governor of Michoacán (1980–86). By 1985 Cárdenas had begun to turn this group into a political team for use after his term ended. He encouraged the formation of small discussion groups among trusted members of his government in 1984 and throughout 1985 to analyze the course of events in Mexico and the status of the Revolution. Composed mostly of *priistas*, these groups agreed by the fall of 1985 that the economic policies of the De la Madrid government and the worsening economic crisis posed a threat to the ideological goals of the Mexican Revolution. They discussed the problem of how to influence these policies but had not reached consensus on an appropriate solution.[20]

Cárdenas personally began to favor public pressure and criticism. On August 30, 1985, while still governor, he presented a paper at a conference on regional history in Jiquilpan, Michoacán, in which he synthesized the elements of the historical "revolutionary project" in order to "confront [these ideals] with the present situation of the country . . . to determine . . . what can or should be done so that the development of the country might *return to the paths* pointed out by the Revolution."[21] Innocuous as this might sound, especially buried in a flood of bland commentary on the Revolution, sitting governors in Mexico simply did not engage in such attacks on presidential policy. The national press interpreted the event as an accusation that De la Madrid had betrayed the

20. Interviews with local PRD activists and members of other (non-PRD) parties were assigned random coding by letters (A–Z, AA–AZ, BA–BZ, and so forth) in order to indicate which interviews led to which responses without compromising the privacy or security of sometimes vulnerable individuals. AB, June 1991; AG, July 1991; AC, June 1991; W, July 1991.

21. Cuauhtémoc Cárdenas Solórzano, *La revolución a futuro* (Jiquilpan, Michoacán: Centro de Estudios de la Revolución Mexicana "Lázaro Cárdenas," 1985), 11, emphasis added.

Revolution, quoting Cárdenas as saying that "contrary ideological currents" had gotten the Revolution off track.[22] His history of dissidence within the system and his status as the son of Mexico's most revolutionary president made Cárdenas an attractive ally for leftists in the PRI, but this speech also marked him as someone willing to confront the PRI publicly.

Meanwhile, the intellectual author of the Corriente Democrática was in Spain as Mexico's ambassador. However, like Cárdenas, Rodolfo González Guevara believed the PRI urgently needed reforms to keep popular support in an era of economic crisis—above all, internal democracy and endorsement of more socially protective economic policies. The problem was how to get the party to adopt these reforms. Inspired by firsthand observations of the Socialist Workers' Party (PSOE), which governed Spain at the time, González Guevara came up with the idea of forming a Corriente in the PRI. In particular, he was impressed by the organizational and political effectiveness of an internal current in the PSOE called the Corriente Crítica, which opposed Spanish entrance into NATO and the EEC. Based on his experience of forty years of activism in the PRI, González Guevara felt that a "Corriente Crítica" might correct the PRI's drift to the right and serve as a useful tool to push for more internal democratization.[23]

Yet the catalyst for the Corriente Democrática was the brilliant and volatile politician Porfirio Muñoz Ledo. If Cárdenas became the spiritual heart of the Corriente, and González Guevara its head, Porfirio Muñoz Ledo was its hands. González Guevara did not seek out allies in Mexico to put his idea into action. Rather, Porfirio Muñoz Ledo contacted him. In October 1985 Muñoz Ledo left his position as Mexico's ambassador to the United Nations and began a series of trips to Latin America and Europe to talk about the implications of the economic crisis and the need for internal democracy in the PRI. One of these journeys took him to Spain, where he met with González Guevara. Muñoz Ledo suggested the formation of a center for political studies in Mexico. González Guevara urged Muñoz Ledo to consider forming a "Critical Current" in the PRI. While the meeting did not result in an agreement, the two established a common interest in working together to promote democratization in the PRI. By the time Muñoz Ledo returned to Spain in early May 1986, González Guevara had also met with Cárdenas. He informed Muñoz Ledo that Cárdenas approved of the idea and thought

22. "La revolución mexicana, desviada desde 1941: Cuauhtémoc Cárdenas," *La Jornada* (Mexico City), 31 August 1985: 3.
23. Rodolfo González Guevara, interview by author, Mexico City, 22 September 1991.

it necessary to do something within the PRI. In this way Porfirio Muñoz Ledo, Rodolfo González Guevara, and Cuauhtémoc Cárdenas all began to think in terms of an internal current.

Shortly afterwards, Muñoz Ledo and Cárdenas met in Mexico City at the Consejo Nacional Extraordinario of the PRI, which convened on May 22–23 to discuss De la Madrid's proposal for responding to the debt problem. Their agreement on debt and other issues prompted them to decide to meet again to talk privately. Even before this meeting took place, both men, independently, gave further proof of their willingness to oppose the administration, foreshadowing the eventual course the Corriente would take in proposing internal democratization. Cárdenas made a statement to the press on May 28 calling for potential precandidates to announce their interest in running for president, implicitly ending the ability of the president to pick his successor in secret. At the same time a May 29 article in *La Jornada* reported that at an academic conference Muñoz Ledo had called for an open debate among potential PRI candidates. When the two met for dinner a few days later, they agreed to begin constructing an internal current. Muñoz Ledo asked Ifigenia Martínez, a mutual friend and a prominent leftist *priista* in her own right, to host a dinner for potentially interested allies. They set a date in June to coincide with the vacation visit to Mexico of Rodolfo González Guevara.

Thus, in the formal construction of the Corriente Democrática personal connections played a significant role. Some twenty guests attended the first dinner, with others joining later sessions. Figure 3.1 shows how key participants got involved through a web of personal connections; bold lines indicate a confirmed invitation, thin lines a probable one (confirmed by one side), and dotted lines a strong personal relation-

Fig. 3.1. Personal relationships among the founders of the Corriente Democrática

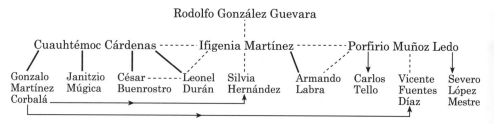

SOURCES: This diagram is based on interviews by the author, on biographies, and on Luis Javier Garrido, *La ruptura: La Corriente Democrática del PRI* (Mexico City: Editorial Grijalbo, 1993).

ship. Most originally became involved because of a connection to Cárdenas or Muñoz Ledo.

Not surprisingly, given the somewhat risky nature of the enterprise, only trusted friends were invited to join at first. Most of the relationships behind the diagram reach back many years. On the Cárdenas side they date to at least the sixties. Janitzio Múgica grew up with Cuauhtémoc Cárdenas.[24] Gonzalo Martínez Corbalá went to school with Cárdenas and participated in the MLN with him. Martínez Corbalá, César Buenrostro, and Leonel Durán worked with Cuauhtémoc Cárdenas in the ambitious development project overseen by Lázaro Cárdenas in the Las Balsas region of Michoacán in the sixties and early seventies. César Buenrostro studied with Cuauhtémoc Cárdenas in the engineering school at UNAM and worked in his state government. Leonel Durán met him in the mid-sixties when the two of them joined the PRI through the National Peasant Confederation and participated in its Consejo Técnico Consultivo (Technical Advisory Council) to promote agrarian reform.

The Consejo Técnico Consultivo also links Cárdenas to the middle figure in the diagram, Ifigenia Martínez. Martínez participated in the Technical Advisory Council as well as the MLN. She also served as alternate ambassador to Muñoz Ledo in the United Nations and worked closely with Muñoz Ledo and González Guevara during the congressional period of 1976–79: González Guevara was president of the Chamber of Deputies; Muñoz Ledo was president of the PRI; and Ifigenia Martínez headed a group of PRI representatives called the "*ifigenios*," who defended progressive, often dissident views in the Congress with the tolerance of the two other politicians. Silvia Hernández and Armando Labra were both *ifigenios*. Carlos Tello also served in the López Portillo government from 1976–77; however, like Vicente Fuentes Díaz and Severo López Mestre, his main connection is to Porfirio Muñoz Ledo. López Mestre worked for Muñoz Ledo when the latter was secretary of labor, and he served as secretary of finances for the presidential campaign team of López Portillo that Muñoz Ledo headed.

Yet despite the importance of personal connections in facilitating the organization of the Democratic Current, it would be a mistake to view the group as merely a random collection of political cronies. These new/old allies also shared an ideological discourse from the traditional left wing of the PRI as well as specific criticisms of economic and political

24. Their fathers (General Francisco J. Múgica and General Lázaro Cárdenas) were close friends and military allies. Cárdenas considered choosing Múgica as his successor, although powerful interests eventually forced the selection of a more moderate candidate.

trends under De la Madrid. Many of these "personal" relationships flourished because of their origins in a common ideological enterprise, as in the case of the *"ifigenios,"* for example. Thus, common diagnoses of events in Mexico as well as personal ties drew them together.

Working Document Number One, the first manifesto of the Corriente, provides an illuminating look at some of these diagnoses.[25] In it the CD defines itself as a "nationalist and democratic" group determined to contribute to the "progressive" transformation of the country through "resolute political action in favor of the historical constitutional project." It identifies several "grave threats" to national sovereignty: deterioration in the standard of living of the popular classes; increasing displacement of national productive capital by foreign capital; and indications of political alienation, such as high abstention and low credibility of election results. However, debt dominates this early diagnosis. Debt is blamed for social deterioration and policies that decapitalized the country and encouraged speculation, and democratic participation is promoted as the solution: "Only through the ever more intense participation of citizens in the adoption of fundamental decisions will it be possible to strengthen national independence, attend to the legitimate demands of all sectors, satisfy the aspirations of liberty and justice of Mexicans, and channel social inconformity within the institutional order." Specifically, the Corriente proposed to "invigorate [the party] through the most direct and permanent participation of the bases in the decisions that affect them, especially in the selection of candidates to posts of popular election at all levels." Thus, the Corriente's main economic proposal involved a moratorium on payment of the debt; its main political proposal pointed directly at democratic selection of the PRI's next candidate for president.

Former Corriente members consistently cite as reasons for the formation of the CD these common concerns about debt, the social effects of the crisis, and the lack of internal democracy in the party. Many members believed that Mexico *could* not pay its foreign debt; all of them seem to have believed that Mexico *should* not pay its debt at the same rate and at the same cost to the population, in part because much of the debt was "contracted in fact through corresponsibility of the lender and the creditor. Both parties were aware that commitments were exceeding the capacity to pay and still they continued."[26] Thus, debt reduction was

25. According to interviews, Porfirio Muñoz Ledo and Ifigenia Martínez wrote the Working Documents, with help and suggestions from other signatories. For the text of Working Document Number One see Jorge Laso de la Vega, ed., *La Corriente Democrática: Hablan los protagonistas* (Mexico City: Editorial Posada, 1987), 257–60.

26. Cuauhtémoc Cárdenas, in ibid., 44.

appropriate and possible with tough negotiation. With regard to "the [revolutionary] project of the nation," the Corriente observed "deviations in some matters—agrarian reform . . . ; abandonment of investments for all the projects and works dedicated to the . . . improvement of the living conditions of very large groups, concretely the indigenous groups, the campesinos, the workers . . . ; the lack of justice for the people of the countryside."[27] They described the De la Madrid approach as a decision "that it should be the market, production, the rules or the causes that determine the development of the economy, without the intervention of the state and without laws protecting the workers. In a word, without the social justice that the Constitution establishes."[28] And not only had the PRI drifted to the right but the conservative PAN had also increased its influence.

The Corriente's focus on internal democracy must be seen in the light of these social and economic goals. Corriente members saw internal democracy at least in part in instrumental terms, as a means for changing policy. As long as De la Madrid chose his own successor, it seemed doubtful that the next president would move in the direction desired by the CD. In the unlikely event that the Corriente achieved democratic selection of the presidential candidate, a more leftist candidate could win, given the unpopularity of the De la Madrid policies. Yet even if the PRI refused to choose its presidential candidate democratically, public demands for participation might force a national debate on these issues. It was in this context that the idea of proposing Cárdenas as a candidate for president first arose. According to interviews, González Guevara suggested from the start that Cárdenas run as a "precandidate of sacrifice."[29] In his view it was unlikely that Cárdenas would get nominated (hence the "sacrifice"), but his name would attract attention to the views of the Corriente.[30] A Cárdenas precandidacy was rejected at first because some felt it might provoke too strong a confrontation. However, the CD hoped that promotion of a public debate would reduce the president's freedom to pick a clone of himself by uniting a constituency for change. Says Cárdenas:

27. Confidential interview with CD founder, April 1991. Some interviews of people cited by name in other places will occasionally be cited as confidential interviews, either because the part of the interview cited need not be attributed to a specific source or because the respondent preferred to keep a particular answer confidential.

28. Confidential interview by author with CD founder, September 1991.

29. González Guevara, interview; Cuauhtémoc Cárdenas, interview by author, Morelos, May 1991); confidential interview with CD founder, April 1991.

30. González Guevara, interview.

In the Corriente Democrática we saw that it was not possible to draw a line between change in economic policies and political change. That is, the economic policy that had been imposed since '82 responded to the interests of those who make political decisions. So, for us it was clear that winning—winning political power or transforming, reorienting political decisions—was an indispensable condition for there to be a change in the orientation of economic policies. . . . we thought that only with a democratic change, that is, with an important popular backing, was it possible—I still think that only thus is it possible—to impose changes in the orientation of the economy.[31]

The economic crisis did not create these ideological conflicts. Just as many of those in the De la Madrid group had preferred a neoliberal approach since at least the seventies, many Corriente members advocated economic nationalism and party democracy throughout their careers. Cárdenas, for example, sought to democratize candidate selection in 1973 (after his father's death) by announcing his precandidacy for governor of Michoacán.[32] When PRI leaders named another candidate, he withdrew, accusing them of

interfer[ing] with popular action by invoking discipline, not the discipline of the principles and statutes of the party, but a discipline equivalent to putting the will and capacity of the members of the party unconditionally and unrestrictedly in the hands of the leaders. . . . for the party to truly fulfill its function of instrument of the people and promoter of the Revolution the demo-

31. Cárdenas, interview.
32. Other Corriente members had similar backgrounds. As a boy in the thirties, Rodolfo González Guevara belonged to the leftist Student Federation of the West. As president of the PRI in Mexico City in the fifties, he recognized defeats by the opposition. He once resigned a post as congressman to protest the imposition of a gubernatorial candidate, and he encouraged the *"ifigenios"* during his tenure as president of Congress. Ifigenia Martínez, one of Mexico's most prominent economists, consistently supported socially oriented economic theories of the dependency school. After receiving a master's degree in economics from Harvard in 1949, Martínez worked in ECLA under Raúl Prebisch, whose theories about Third World development were a precursor of dependency theory. Her publications called for a progressive state to promote development, defend national sovereignty, and ensure social justice. See, for instance, "La distribución del ingreso en México," in *El perfíl de Mexico en 1980.* (Mexico City: Siglo Veintiuno, 1972), vol. 1. Though the career of Porfirio Muñoz Ledo reveals a man of great pragmatism, his major government positions—as secretary-general of the Mexican Institute of Social Security (1966–70), secretary of labor under Echeverría (1972–75), and secretary of public education (1976–77)—give him credentials as a socially oriented politician.

cratic regeneration of its organizational structure and its mechanisms of decision is an indispensable condition.[33]

However, during the economic crisis the distance between leftist *pristas* and the national leadership increased. Particularly after the failure of early adjustment policies De la Madrid became convinced that only through a dramatic if risky departure from past approaches could Mexico recover economically. Mexico had to open up trade and investment, move toward privatization, and reduce state intervention in the economy. Corriente members argued that "shrinking the public sector as a solution to our financial woes amounts to cutting off the head of a man suffering from headache. Instead of recognizing the strategic usefulness of a strong public economy that can move with advantages in the market economy, . . . shrinkage is demanded, that enterprises be sold. . . . you can't have development with social justice like that."[34]

The Corriente and the De la Madrid government also reached different diagnoses on the role of debt in the origin of the economic crisis. The Corriente tended to believe that the economic crisis resulted from attempts to pay the debt, that "from the moment in which the priority, all the attention, all the economic efforts of the country are oriented to pay, prioritarily, the external debt, many sectors of the economy are neglected and we enter into an era of economic stagnation from which we still have not fully emerged."[35] Corriente leaders stressed that "changing priorities does not mean going to a moratorium or taking unilateral decisions about external debt but does mean covering the most urgent necessities of the country and then paying."[36] Meanwhile, De la Madrid insisted on keeping Mexico's commitments to international banks. His government argued that the economic crisis resulted from the *existence* of the debt, not attempts to pay it. In fact, they blamed Mexico's debt problem and economic crisis on the very policies that the Corriente advocated, including economic nationalism and state intervention, which they said promoted inefficiency and excessive spending.[37] To resume economic growth the government needed to re-

33. Miguel Ángel Granados Chapa, "Plaza pública," *La Jornada* (Mexico City), 9 July 1987: 1, 4.

34. Ifigenia Martínez, in Laso de la Vega, ed., *La Corriente Democrática*, 70.

35. Cuauhtémoc Cárdenas, in *20 años de búsqueda: Testimonios desde la izquierda*, ed. Eduardo Del Castillo (Mexico City: Ediciones de Cultura Popular, 1991), 40.

36. Cuauhtémoc Cárdenas, in Laso de la Vega, ed., *La Corriente Democrática*, 43.

37. See, for example, Pascual García Alba and Jaime Serra Puche, *Causas y efectos de la crisis económica en México* (Mexico City: El Colegio de México, 1984). Serra Puche's boss at the time was Carlos Salinas, De la Madrid's director of programming and budget.

duce the debt, attract foreign investment, restore business confidence, and control inflation. A moratorium would fatally undermine these goals by damaging Mexico's relationship with the business and investment communities. The government's analysis of the conditions for renewed growth led De la Madrid to accept enthusiastically the harsh austerity measures demanded by international banks.

The Emergence of a Split in the PRI, 1985–1986: Political Exclusion

In this context of increasing ideological conflict the *cardenistas* began to experience increased political marginalization. Technocratization had something to do with this. The division in the PRI in 1986–88 did not pit traditional conservative *alemanistas* against traditional progressive *cardenistas*. Some De la Madrid policies reversed elements of the traditional business-oriented model of state capitalist development, particularly the decisions to privatize and open up the economy. These changes took Mexico farther toward free-market capitalism than desired by many Mexican businessmen who relied on preferential treatment and protection from foreign competition. Moreover, the career patterns of the De la Madrid team differed nearly as much from those of previous business-oriented governments as from those of the Corriente. As Table 3.1 shows, De la Madrid accentuated the trend toward technocratization discussed in Chapter 2. In addition to their university education, fully two-thirds of the De la Madrid cabinet had some graduate training, often abroad.[38]

Table 3.1. Trends in university degrees held by cabinet members

	López Mateos Cabinet (1958–64)		De la Madrid Cabinet (1982–83)	
	Secretaries	Sub-secretaries	Secretaries	Sub-secretaries
Law/Medicine	55%	58%	30%	24%
Economics/Accounting	7	9	37	29
Architect/Engineering	15	20	13	21
Other	7	5	20	24
None	16	9	0	3

SOURCE: Roderic Camp, "The Political Technocrat in Mexico and the Survival of the Political System," *Latin American Research Review* 20, no. 1 (1985): 102.

38. Peter Smith, "Leadership and Change: Intellectuals and Technocrats in Mexico,"

Technocratization contributed to the split between neoliberals and *cardenistas* in two main ways. In the first place, the Corriente, with its *político* background, blamed the technocratic perspective for what they saw as reckless determination to implement a neoliberal program despite the damage it caused to popular support of the PRI. There were few if any leftist *técnicos*, and even fewer neoliberal *políticos* among those in power.[39] De la Madrid himself had never held any elective or party office, and only one member of his cabinet had such experience.[40] In contrast, most of the Corriente had experience in electoral and/or party politics. But the *técnico-político* division alone does not explain Corriente support. Relatively few *políticos* ended up in the Corriente, which was united more by ideological goals than by career experience or education. Traditional *políticos* in the PRI sectoral and local leadership—the "dinosaurs"—strongly rejected the Corriente's demand for internal democracy; other *políticos* supported the Corriente's demand for internal democratization but not its economic policy preferences. These groups tended to stay in the PRI. However, the Corriente's training clearly affected their perception of the potential costs of "technocratic" disregard for political realities.

In the second place, technocratization contributed to the Corriente's exclusion from policy-making by a government composed of an increasingly narrow policy perspective. CD founders like Ifigenia Martínez charged that "with the cabinet of Miguel De la Madrid a slow process of technocratization of the first circle of power has reached culmination, leaving the politicians completely outside. . . . there used to be a consensus that the president should be a *político*. But . . . the moment arrived in which the technocrats occupied all the posts of importance."[41] Their strong sense of exclusion, expressed in every interview of Corriente founders, led them to accept the risks of public confrontation in order to get some leverage against the president. The private pressure they attempted from 1982 to 1986 had the advantage of lower costs and little risk but the disadvantage that dissidents had to depend primarily on the unreliable power of persuasion. By 1986 it was clear that persuasion

---

in *Mexico's Political Stability: The Next Five Years*, ed. Roderic Camp (Boulder, Colo.: Westview Press, 1986), 109. For a nuanced analysis of changes in the political elite see also Miguel Ángel Centeno, *Democracy Within Reason: Technocratic Revolution in Mexico* (University Park, Pa.: Penn State Press, 1994).

39. Though some Corriente members had training in economics, like some technocrats, theirs usually dated to periods when economics as a discipline, particularly as taught in Latin America, favored economic nationalism and dependency theory.

40. Smith, "Leadership and Change," 109.

41. Ifigenia Martínez, in Laso de la Vega, ed., *La Corriente Democrática*, 59, 72.

had failed to prevent the government's policy direction from becoming more pronounced. The dissidents as individuals had no institutional position to give them leverage to demand compromise. De la Madrid packed the leadership of the PRI with his personal allies beginning in 1981.[42] More important, PRI progressives had virtually no access to the inner circle of policy-making: the presidential cabinet. Though every president tends to form a team dominated by allies, the Corriente felt De la Madrid had taken this to an extreme in a "silent coup d'état, by the financial group," referring to the high proportion of cabinet officials with backgrounds in finance or banking.[43] None of the Corriente founders held an influential policy-making post by the time of the CD's emergence.[44] As a result, the opportunity costs of participation in a publicly critical current were relatively low. They would not forfeit positions or viable channels for influencing policy. Finally, their willingness to break the code of silence and challenge the PRI was colored by their sense that De la Madrid had broken an informal rule of the game that required the government to share power, to "have in its composition people of different sectors of population, of different political currents, of different ages, of different parts of the country. [Before], it was a mosaic where somehow there was, inside . . . a capacity to influence the course of the country at a plural bargaining table."[45] In the Corriente's view the De la Madrid government deliberately ignored this tradition. The conflict between neoliberals and *cardenistas* became increasingly polarized.

The economic crisis encouraged political and ideological polarization (and therefore the ultimate breakdown of the PRI coalition) in three fundamental ways. First, it raised the saliency of concerns about social justice. The PRI had long ceased to make progress toward social justice, in the view of many CD founders, but the crisis seemed to move Mexico rapidly in the opposite direction. Second, by making a lot of people unhappy, the crisis encouraged the dissidents to "go public" and appeal to the masses for support. Some CD members explicitly say they thought of the economic crisis in strategic terms, as both a danger and an opportunity to use people's unhappiness as a source of leverage to "push a

42. In 1981 the president of the PRI even resigned his post, denouncing the "assault on the party by the bureaucratic team of one secretary of the state [De la Madrid—at the time secretary of programming and budget]." See María Xelhuantzi López, "La Corriente Democrática o la defensa de México," in *La Corriente Democrática: Hablan los protagonistas*, ed. Jorge Laso de la Vega (Mexico City: Editorial Posada, 1987), 204.

43. Porfirio Muñoz Ledo, *Compromisos* (Mexico City: Editorial Posada, 1988), 26.

44. Muñoz Ledo and Ifigenia Martínez returned from the UN in 1985. Cárdenas finished his term as governor of Michoacán in September 1986.

45. Confidential interview by author with CD founders, April 1991.

little harder" for reforms that they had long advocated.[46] Third, the urgency of the threat posed by the crisis encouraged a "radicalization" of the neoliberal-técnico and revolutionary-político positions. The crisis convinced the technocrats (or at least gave them an excuse to argue) that Mexico could no longer afford to compromise on neoliberal and fiscally conservative economic policies in order to hold the old semipopulist coalition together. They therefore decided not to appease opponents at the cost of policy, a decision bolstered by the demands of international banks and the IMF for strict austerity measures as a precondition for further loans. The revolutionary-políticos, meanwhile, saw the social and political situation that accompanied implementation of these policies as increasingly desperate. They did not think they could afford to wait six years for a more sympathetic president to come along.

The overlay of conflicting economic policy objectives made accommodation on the issue of democracy more difficult. Both the Corriente and the neoliberals needed to influence the selection of the presidential candidate to achieve their policy goals. As the faction that controlled the presidency, the neoliberals only had to defend the existing system of presidential designation to guarantee continuity in policy. The Corriente needed to change the system to influence the designation of the PRI candidate. Herein lay the seeds of the confrontation that would eventually result in the exit of the Corriente's most prominent leaders from the PRI. Thus, the drive for democracy both benefited from and was blocked by fundamental concerns about economic policy.

The Construction of the Corriente Democrática: August 1986–March 1987

From the beginning the Corriente's activity further marginalized its founders, increasing their exclusion and forcing them to choose between escalation and admission of defeat. As in a high stakes poker game, each defeat prompted Corriente members either to raise the stakes or fold their cards. Those who were willing to continue to escalate pressure gradually moved toward a position where continued membership in the PRI became untenable. Thus, PRI resistance to the Corriente's attempts to influence policy completed the detachment of those elites who created the PRD.

Characteristically, the public construction of the Corriente Democrática began with an unscheduled press leak. The original strategy, sug-

46. Confidential interviews by author with CD founders, April 1991, May 1991.

gested by Rodolfo González Guevara, had called for meetings to elaborate specific economic and political proposals before revealing the existence of a Corriente in the spring of 1987. However, during July the number of participants in Corriente meetings grew to between thirty and fifty. By mid-August rumors began to circulate. When Porfirio Muñoz Ledo returned from a trip abroad (to Spain, among other destinations), he decided unilaterally to clarify the legal and nonsubversive nature of the group by leaking a full account of their activities and purpose to a journalist at a national newspaper. On August 14, 1986, *Unomásuno* reported the existence of the group and described its goal as internal democratization of the party.

The premature emergence of the Corriente provoked the first set of defections among the original group of participants. In this and all subsequent splits, including the decision by some Corriente members to leave the PRI, variation in levels of tolerance for confrontation with the government divided members into escalaters and retreaters. The self-selection of those most comfortable with confrontation and bluff as the founders of the new party made it much more likely that the political coalition they formed would feel comfortable with confrontation. This is one of many paradoxes in the creation of new parties like the PRD: the very qualities that increased the likelihood that a new party would form made it harder for the new party to consolidate loyalties or achieve its political goals. Only leaders relatively comfortable with confrontation and risk would have broken away from the PRI to form an electoral opposition, but this leadership style also contributed significantly to the many seemingly unresolvable confrontations that divided the party internally and trapped the PRD in a confrontational strategy that increased state hostility and earned it a reputation as a troublemaker.

Several factors influence the tolerance for confrontation. First, personal ties to a government leader decrease tolerance; personal ties to a confronter increase tolerance. Second, broader goals increase tolerance of confrontation, since the potential payoffs increase. With limited goals the results of even successful confrontation may not seem worth the risk. In the CD's case confronters tended to have goals that went well beyond internal democratization. Third, strategic calculations of the effectiveness of additional confrontation affect acceptance of confrontation. Confrontation may provoke more concessions, but it may also incur a risk of repression and heavy political costs. Finally, individuals have different propensities to engage in confrontation, just as some people like to gamble more than others. Thus, those with more limited goals, close personal ties to system leaders, and a reluctance to believe that confrontation would promote those goals tended to drop out. Those with broad goals, close ties to other confronters, and a belief in the value of bluff and confrontation tended to agree to ratchet up the pressure.

Most defectors between August 14 and October 1, 1986, disagreed with the proposal that the group escalate to public criticism of the government by issuing a manifesto, Working Document Number One. PRI elites initially had responded cautiously to the "Corriente," some even expressing qualified approval. The head of the PRI in Mexico City called it "another of the contributions that we receive daily to enrich and perfect our processes."[47] A national leader of the main PRI peasant union (CNC) said the Corriente was consistent with the efforts of De la Madrid to improve the party and that it "should be welcomed."[48] Another top CNC official called the CD "a serious and valid effort to resolve the problems of democracy in the PRI."[49] Even the president of the PRI, Adolfo Lugo Verduzco, remarked that "the leadership of the PRI welcomes this initiative and the proof is that we already had the first meeting [with Muñoz Ledo]."[50]

However, meetings with leaders of the Corriente could not have reassured PRI leaders that the CD would fall into line. In an impromptu press conference after his August 22 meeting with Lugo Verduzco, Muñoz Ledo reaffirmed the right of *priistas* to form an opinion current in the party. Cárdenas got off to an even more aggressive start: speaking to students at the Polytechnical College in Michoacán on August 24, he criticized the use of oil revenues to pay Mexico's debt and called for discussions of party reform.

The PRI responded with increasing public hostility toward the Corriente even as Lugo Verduzco continued private meetings with Corriente leaders. On September 5 the PRI stripped Cárdenas ally Cristóbal Arias of his position as president of the Michoacán Executive Committee of the PRI. On September 10 the national press reported that in a letter published in the journal *La República* Lugo Verduzco

47. "Apoyo de diputados y un gobernador a la Corriente Democratizadora del PRI," *Unomásuno* (Mexico City), 16 August 1986: 1, 8.

48. "Es una gran corriente la que intenta democratizar al PRI: Muñoz Ledo," *Unomásuno* (Mexico City), 19 August 1986: 1, 8.

49. Roberto Santiago, Gonzalo Álvarez del Villar, and Raúl Correa, "Bremer: Toda sugerencia es útil al PRI," *Unomásuno* (Mexico City), 25 August 1986: 1, 7.

50. Miguel Ángel Rivera, "Se debe luchar por un PRI más plural y fuerte," *La Jornada* (Mexico City), 23 August 1986: 1, 6. At the time party leaders considered Muñoz Ledo the most dangerous, the leader of a group "seconded by Cuauhtémoc Cárdenas." Muñoz Ledo had held more important positions and had more national presence than Cárdenas, whose prior activities were mostly confined to Michoacán. See Bernardo González Solano and Alberto Carbot, "El PRI debe democratizarse para no quedar atrás," *Unomásuno* (Mexico City), 4 September 1986: 1, 5.

warned that "internal democratization must be forged on the basis of unbreakable unity. The unity of the revolutionary forces cannot be put at risk by the impatience of a few."[51] On September 15, as Cárdenas officially ended his term as governor, a book "evaluating" his governorship appeared in Morelia, Michoacán. The book—entitled *Cárdenas el pequeño* (Little Cárdenas)—depicted him as an "insignificant" man, "without talent," who suffered greatly from comparison to his father and who had brought about the "moral, social, political, and economic disaster of Michoacán."[52] The book also managed to single out the Corriente Democrática for special criticism, though it went to press only a couple of weeks after the August announcement of the Corriente's meetings.[53] On September 27 *Unomásuno* published a translation of an interview of President De la Madrid in *Le Monde*, in which he played down the importance of the Corriente, saying that it "calls itself new, . . . [but] is nothing new. . . . democratization is the banner of the whole party, not that of one group within the party."[54]

In the final days of September Lugo Verduzco held a group meeting with the majority of the Corriente. He urged them to be patient and asked them not to make public any demands until after the National Assembly of the PRI (scheduled for the spring of 1987), while continuing internal dialogue.[55] After Lugo left, the group remained to talk over their options. Some felt that the open criticism from PRI officials made it imperative to go public in order to clarify the goals and objectives of the Corriente. Others felt they had made a commitment in the course of the meeting to hold off on publishing a document critical of the PRI while they continued to talk to the PRI leadership. This faction argued that "putting out a document at that moment wasn't advisable, that it was going to lead to a confrontation with [Lugo Verduzco], with the whole government apparatus, which they did not believe suitable or useful, and at that point, they drew the line."[56] Only ten of the original participants signed Working Document Number One, which officially

51. Miguel Ángel Rivera, "Clase política," *La Jornada* (Mexico City), 10 September 1986: 2.

52. Romeo Ortega, *Cárdenas el pequeño* (Mexico City: n.p., 1986), 10, 22.

53. Ibid. It called the Corriente a tool to further the personal ambitions of Cárdenas. The book—printed by an undisclosed publisher, and written by an ally of new governor Martínez Villicaña—was obviously composed in a hurry. Nearly 40 percent of its pages are reprints of documents, letters, and texts of laws passed by the Cárdenas administration.

54. "La democratización del PRI, bandera del partido, no de un grupo: De la Madrid a Le Monde," *Unomásuno* (Mexico City), 27 September 1986: 17.

55. Confidential interviews by author with CD founders, April 1991, May 1991.

56. Confidential interview by author with CD founder, May 1991.

gave birth to the Corriente Democrática.[57] Nonsigners included Rodolfo González Guevara, Gonzalo Martínez Corbalá, and Silvia Hernández. All three opposed escalating confrontation with the government. Because of the premature unveiling of the CD, González Guevara had not yet resigned his post as ambassador and thus was limited in the support he could lend; he distanced himself as early as August 19. However, he also believed that internal reform would require the president's help and that publishing the document would guarantee a confrontation and doom the project. Martínez Corbalá had a connection in the De la Madrid administration that may have influenced his evaluation of the benefit of confrontation: young Carlos Salinas worked as his congressional aide in the 1960s. As the fortunes of Salinas improved, this connection tied Martínez Corbalá to the PRI.

After the publication of Working Document Number One on October 1, 1986, the PRI's response to the CD began to change. Within a week Adolfo Lugo Verduzco resigned as president of the PRI. His replacement, Jorge De la Vega Domínguez, had a reputation as a negotiator and conciliator. Many analysts outside the PRI viewed his nomination as a sign that Miguel De la Madrid wanted to accommodate the CD.[58] Corriente members themselves were pleased at the opportunity for negotiation they thought De la Vega represented.[59]

However, the De la Vega strategy between October 1986 and March 1987 combined private negotiations with escalation of public criticism and attempts to undermine CD support. On the one hand, De la Vega treated Corriente leaders with respect. He continued private talks, invited them to attend his taking the oath of office, even set up meetings with De la Madrid. He constantly told them the party wanted to see them continue to participate as *priistas*. According to interviews with both the CD and members of the 1987 National Executive Committee of the PRI, De la Vega does not seem to have offered top leaders a personal deal in return for cooperation, the classic co-optation scenario. He did offer them "spaces within the party": regular dialogue between individual leaders and the inner circle of power.[60]

57. The ten were César Buenrostro, Cuauhtémoc Cárdenas, Leonel Durán, Vicente Fuentes Díaz, Armando Labra, Severo López Mestre, Ifigenia Martínez, Janitzio Múgica, Porfirio Muñoz Ledo, and Carlos Tello.

58. See, for example, Roberto Santiago and Bernardo González, "De la Vega Domínguez, un político experimentado," *Unomásuno* (Mexico City), 8 October 1986: 7.

59. Confidential interviews by author with CD founders, April 1991.

60. Cárdenas, interview; Porfirio Muñoz Ledo, interview by author, Guanajuato, March 1991; Leonel Durán, interview by author, Mexico City, 19 April 1991; Ifigenia Martínez, interview by author, Mexico City, 19 April 1991; César Buenrostro, interview by author, Mexico City, 19 April 1991; Armando Labra, interview by author, Mexico City,

On the other hand, he refused to recognize the Corriente Democrática formally. Behind the PRI's refusal to recognize the CD lay its aver-
sion to giving institutional recognition to an independent pressure
group inside the party. Corriente members wanted recognition in order
"to create a platform of our own, a space of our own, in order not to
identify ourselves with those sectors of the party that were being criticized as antidemocratic."[61] However, a formal institutional position in
the party also "gave us, logically, the prospect of having a platform inside the party to participate with representatives in electoral processes."[62] The PRI distributed candidacies through recognized sectors.
An institutionally recognized CD could lay a claim on candidacies or use
its position as leverage to influence policy. The PRI leadership preferred
not to encourage the growth of a new institutional power base. As one
CD member recalls:

> The negotiation centered very importantly on the formal recog-
> nition of the Corriente *Democrática*. That was the dispute. . . .
> we naturally wanted life within the party, recognized existence
> in the party. And faced with this political pressure, they said,
> "Look—here are the statutes. And the specification of groups in
> our party is only within the Centrals [union organizations].
> There is no other type of affiliation. Join a Central, whatever
> one you want. The CTM, or the CNC, join." We said "No, we
> don't want that. We want our own space." They said no.[63]

Had they joined a Central, of course, the CD could have been absorbed
into the hierarchical structure of the unions—controlled, offered a few
token candidacies, but prevented from mobilizing around issues they
wished to address, like debt and candidate selection. Their concerns cut
across institutional channels for the expression of demands in the PRI.
And while PRI leaders told Corriente members their criticisms were
valid and emphasized their value as individuals, they refused to recognize them institutionally.

Similarly, as public criticism of the Corriente escalated, the PRI targeted the concept of a pressure group in the party rather than addressing its specific goals in a public debate. At least one original member,
Carlos Tello, withdrew from the Corriente during this period, appar-

---

26 April 1991; Janitzio Múgica, interview by author, Mexico City, 2 May 1991; and confidential interviews AW, August 1991, and BF, September 1991.

61. Confidential interview by author with CD founder, April 1991.
62. Ibid.
63. Ibid.

ently because he feared a "collision" and loss of employment in the state.[64] The PRI also put pressure on secondary CD leaders, particularly in Michoacán, where on October 9 a group of *priistas* published a Document of Support to the Corriente Democrática, signed by 1,290 PRI activists from all over the state.

The critical importance of Cárdenas begins to emerge at this point as the leader of a strong team of secondary cadres who could organize mobilizations like the petition on short notice.[65] No other Corriente leader managed a similar feat. It is no accident that the strongest criticism of the CD, the most intimidation of Corriente supporters, and the most reported attempts at co-optation are concentrated in Michoacán. A representative example is the scathing attack on the CD by the general secretary of the PRI (Irma Cué) and the state PRI president in Morelia, Michoacán, on November 4, 1986: "No group apart from the organizations and sectors of the party forms part of its militance. . . . Michoacanos condemn, here, the so-called "Corriente Democratizadora." . . . let them continue acting like what they are, a group of opposition . . . and let them do it from outside . . . [I]n the *priista* family, no spaces will be ceded, no cracks will open up, and we will not permit for any reason actions oriented toward disunity within the ranks of our party."[66]

A local columnist remarked, "Never before that we remember had such cutting remarks been made in a *priista* rally in the state. . . . Now there can remain not the slightest doubt of the forceful opposition of the national and state leadership of the party to these groups of opportunists."[67] Likewise, among local leaders interviewed in Michoacán and the Estado de Mexico, *michoacanos* most often reported personal threats and/or offers to get them to abandon the Corriente. Generally, the offer required leaving Michoacán for Oaxaca or some other suitably distant state. The Michoacán state government also decided to fire 30 percent of its employees for "budgetary reasons." Critics charged that many of those fired either signed the Document of Support or sympathized with the Cárdenas movement.[68]

---

64. Luis Javier Garrido, *La ruptura: La Corriente Democrática del PRI* (Mexico City: Editorial Grijalbo, 1993), 53.

65. It was also Cárdenas who secured the Corriente its first office, donated by Antonio Herrera, who had previously made the same office available during Cárdenas's campaign for governor of Michoacán (ibid., 124).

66. Jaime López Martínez, "Rotundo rechazo del PRI a la 'Corriente Democratizadora,' " *La Voz de Michoacán* (Morelia, Michoacán), 5 November 1986: 1, 2, 25, 30.

67. Alejandro Sandovál Álvarez, "Hechos y palabras," *La Voz de Michoacán* (Morelia, Michoacán), 5 November 1986: 1–2.

68. Teresa Gurza, "30% de los burócratas que laboran en Michoacán serán despedidos," *La Jornada* (Mexico City), 27 January 1987: 8.

If the PRI had succeeded in isolating the CD leaders from popular support, they might eventually have accepted the less desirable offer of regular contacts with the government. However, public attacks not only failed to destroy the Corriente's support, but, some argued, inadvertently publicized Corriente demands and "strengthened us, because they turned our movement into a great movement of opinion. *They* made us famous. . . . It was their first big mistake."[69] The strategy of isolation failed in good measure because of the economic crisis, which made popular support for the dissidents readily available. The Corriente as a group of nine men and one woman might have behaved quite differently from the Corriente as a group of opinion leaders able to command significant, if largely latent, popular support. The CD continued to attract sympathy and to speak out ever more explicitly about its goals for Mexico.

From Voice to Exit: The Corriente Democrática, March 1987–October 1987

The National Assembly of the PRI in March 1987 marked a major turning point in the Corriente's development, ending the period dominated by private negotiations. At the March assembly PRI leaders issued an ultimatum to the CD: shut up or get out. Between March and October 1987 some decided to shut up, but others got out, to support the candidacy of Cuauhtémoc Cárdenas. Analysis of the National Assembly thus provides critical clues about the dynamic that led some members of the Corriente from voice to exit. I argue that De la Madrid and the neoliberals preferred the risk of defections to the risk of opening up candidate selection and permitting members of the Corriente to compete. Ideological polarization continued to affect the calculation of relative costs and gains. Presidentialism also affected calculations and limited compromises, since only influence over selection of the presidential candidate would have an immediate, significant effect on policy. The president's alliance with PRI sectoral leaders on internal democracy gave him leverage to deny the CD control over policy and candidate selection. With no institutional niche the Corriente could only rely on popular support to force the president to listen. Thus, Corriente members who accepted

---

69. Confidential interview by author with CD founder, April 1991.

the risks of escalating confrontation eventually found themselves taking advantage of the only institutional opportunity available to translate popular support into influence—the general election.

The Thirteenth National Assembly of the PRI

Every three years a PRI National Assembly adjusts the party's program and statutes. Through these adjustments the party adapts to changes in national problems and in the policy preferences of the president. The National Assembly held the year before a presidential election gives the public an indication of which factions have the inside track in the selection of the next presidential candidate. Changes made in that year tend to set up the party to support the policy preferences of the true *tapado*— the hidden choice of the president. With the emergence of the Corriente it became evident that the National Assembly planned for March 1987 would decide important questions about the balance between the perspectives of the CD and President De la Madrid. The PRI leadership invited Corriente leaders to participate in the assembly as presenters in working groups on different areas of policy.

The presentations of the Corriente stressed all of the themes touched on earlier: debt repayment, pauperization of the working classes, denationalization, and—above all—internal democratization. In the key working group on political-electoral renovation Cárdenas warned that the PRI would lose ground to the opposition if it did not take the lead in democratization. He argued that "the democratic participation of militants in the selection of party candidates to elected office would favor the development of effective links between political leaders and the bases. . . . the security that democracy gives is today the only possible definition of national security."[70] He proposed that the assembly resolve to expedite the registry of aspirants to the PRI candidacy for president as soon as possible. After intense discussion the working group voted to reject the presentation. Corriente members in other working groups had similar though less confrontational experiences. In the end little of the CD's perspective was incorporated into the new program and statutes.

However, the climactic moment for the Corriente came during the closing ceremonies. The leadership prepared an unusual display of unity for the occasion. In addition to the sitting president, two former presi-

---

70. Cuauhtémoc Cárdenas Solórzano et al., *Corriente Democrática: Alternativa frente a la crisis* (Mexico City: Editores Costa-Amic, 1987), 104.

dents of Mexico (Echeverría and López Portillo) attended. Never before had an ex-president attended an assembly, since tradition calls for ex-presidents to stay out of politics in later administrations. The well-known antipathy between López Portillo and Echeverría made the image especially amazing. Then, in a closing speech that reporters called "unprecedented for the frankness of its language," the president of the PRI unleashed a scathing attack on the Corriente.[71] In response to the Corriente's criticisms of economic policy, De la Vega asserted that the PRI had "never abandoned the path of the Revolution, nor twisted it, nor deviated from it. If the life of the workers has deteriorated, that is something different. . . . [the crisis] is something the whole world suffers from and not the product of the economic policy of the government that the PRI supports."[72] He declared that the PRI was already "a party solidly united by our internal democracy" and that the participation of the CD in the assembly proved it.[73] Just as some CD members feared, their participation had legitimized a game with a predetermined outcome.[74] Then De la Vega brought the message home with a clear ultimatum:

> We exhort our comrades to assume their responsibility; in particular we invite all those who expressed ideas and assumed positions that the Assembly rejected. Let all *priistas* know that we will reinforce the sectoral structure of our party. That outside [the sectors] it does not have and will not have any other type of groups. . . . I convoke you, friends and comrades of our party, to close ranks with the national leadership. . . . We will not permit [anyone] to invoke the democracy that we practice in order to upset our party activity. From this great Assembly, we say to all those who from here on do not wish to respect the will of the immense majority of the *priistas*, that they resign from our party and seek affiliation in other political organizations. . . . In

71. Bernardo González Solano, "Sin procedimientos ocultos se designará candidato: De la Vega," *Unomásuno* (Mexico City), 5 March 1987: 1, 10–11.
72. Quoted in Samuel Maldonado, *Origenes del Partido de la Revolución Democrática* (Morelia, Michoacán: published by author, 1989), 30.
73. González Solano, "Sin procedimientos ocultos."
74. The decision about whether to accept the invitation provoked considerable discussion in the Corriente. According to one, "the more experienced said that we should not participate because it was going to cause a conflict, an aggression. The less experienced, like me, said that if our proposal was democracy and participation, independently of whether there were aggressions, we had to participate, because that was precisely what we were asking for. Participation. . . . That position won, and we participated." Confidential interview by author with CD founder, May 1991.

the PRI there is no room for fifth columns nor for Trojan horses. . . . In the exercise of our rich internal democracy we will not waste time fighting tiny minorities or persons that have other objectives, other purposes, and other banners. We will fight united against our adversaries outside; those inside, if they exist, have the doors open for them to act where it most suits their personal interests.[75]

Cárdenas took De la Vega's remarks as a direct challenge. A few days later he composed a letter to the National Executive Committee (CEN) of the PRI, stating:

The speech of . . . Lic. Jorge de la Vega, at the close of the Thirteenth General Assembly of the Party, announces for [the party] a period of antidemocratic authoritarianism [and] intolerance . . . contrary to the spirit, tradition, and conduct of men truly committed to the ideas and work of the Mexican Revolution. . . . These antidemocratic excesses and intransigence, norms of conduct in the highest party leadership, prevent any fitting and respectful collaboration with it.[76]

After showing the letter to some leaders of the Corriente, Cárdenas sent it under his own signature to the CEN—and the press. A similar letter by Porfirio Muñoz Ledo in support of Cárdenas's position appeared on March 12. The government's attempt to intimidate the Corriente into obedience had failed: the principal CD leaders refused to back down.

In talking with *priistas* about the logic of the decision to issue an ultimatum, its origin in the office of President De la Madrid becomes clear. Even among members of the National Executive Committee, no significant discussion took place prior to the ultimatum.[77] Close collaborators of Jorge De la Vega claimed that he had added some of the most damaging phrases—including the "fifth column" and "Trojan horse" references—since they listened to him practice his speech the previous afternoon.[78] *Priistas* outside the CEN sometimes claim they "have no idea" why De la Vega attacked the Corriente so furiously; or say De la Madrid made a mistake, that he ought to have known he would provoke a split.[79] One very high-level source suggested that in addition to the

75. González Solano, "Sin procedimientos ocultos."
76. Cárdenas et al., *Corriente Democrática: Alternativa frente a la crisis*, 131–32.
77. Confidential interviews by author, AW, August 1991; BF, September 1991.
78. Garrido, *La ruptura*, 76.
79. Confidential interviews by author, U, May 1991; V, May 1991; Z, May 1991.

political differences between the Corriente and the neoliberals, personal resentment played a role, particularly the long-standing rivalry between Porfirio Muñoz Ledo and Miguel De la Madrid, and the overreaction of a key presidential adviser (Emilio Gamboa) to the "betrayal" of his boss by Cárdenas and Muñoz Ledo.[80] Nevertheless, though the president and his advisers may have failed to anticipate the extent of the damage that Cárdenas could do outside the party, they did calculate that some of the Corriente might leave; De la Vega's own speech foresees this. Former CEN members state that the party line—"either they joined the team or they had nothing to do in the party"—was logical and consistent.[81] In fact, said one, "subsequent facts have demonstrated clearly that the then-president of the PRI was right [in calling them "Trojan horses"]. . . . [De la Vega] issued a call for internal discipline. . . . the call was not heeded."[82] According to another ex-CEN member, the party needed to arrive at the 1988 presidential election united, and "sometimes it is necessary to burst the pustule so that the fever can break."[83] Any damage the Corriente might do outside the party could not compare to the danger of letting it divide the PRI or influence the selection of the presidential candidate.

Once the challenge had been issued and thrown back, the eventual exit of at least some Corriente members became virtually certain. Party statutes gave De la Madrid effective control over the presidential nomination, in alliance with top party bureaucrats (mostly appointed by him), who controlled selection of convention delegates, and the sectors, which technically nominate the PRI presidential candidate. It may seem odd that labor, peasant, and popular organizations should support a president whose policies had brought hardship to their members. However, sectoral leaders had as strong an interest in denying the demand for internal democracy as De la Madrid. Not only did they keep their union positions thanks to undemocratic selection, but primaries to choose candidates would upset the traditional allocation of quotas of seats to sector and union leaders, which they used to build personal patron-client networks. Though union leaders might dislike the president's economic policies, they had much less interest in internal party democracy.

Therefore, the defiant response of Cárdenas and Muñoz Ledo implied a dramatic escalation in the level of confrontation. Only one day after

---

80. Confidential interview by author of highly placed *priista* insider, August 1995.
81. Confidential interview by author, AW, August 1991.
82. Confidential interview by author, CA, September 1991.
83. Confidential interview by author, BF, September 1991.

Cárdenas's letter appeared in the press the CEN "expelled" Cárdenas from the party.[84] Public attacks on the Corriente increased, and government employees were warned to stay away from CD events.[85] Meanwhile, Corriente leaders publicly acknowledged as their goal gaining decision-making positions in the government and nominating Cárdenas as a precandidate in the PRI.[86] Cárdenas stepped up tours of different parts of the country in an unofficial political campaign. His coy, on-again, off-again flirtation with a commitment to run as a candidate helped force the press to cover CD activities, keeping their issues on the national agenda, but also increased the level of tension and confrontation with the PRI leadership.[87] Harrassment of Corriente members increased. The secretary of Porfirio Muñoz Ledo was followed, detained, and interrogated; telephones were believed to be tapped; and notary publics appointed by Cárdenas while governor of Michoacán were suddenly stripped of their commissions.[88]

As government hostility grew, more CD members reached their level of tolerance for confrontation. Armando Labra did not publicly support the letter by Cárdenas condemning De la Vega's speech. Neither Armando Labra nor Vicente Fuentes Díaz signed a June 21 letter to De la Vega protesting the campaign of "satanization" unleashed by the PRI.[89] Janitzio Múgica began to distance himself shortly after a July 3 ceremony at which three thousand supporters formally asked Cárdenas to run, confirming his intention to seek precandidacy in the PRI.[90] This

84. The CEN had no real authority to do this. During the summer of 1987 the PRI put together a Commission on Honor and Justice in order to expel the Corriente, but when Cárdenas became a candidate for the PARM and joined that party, the PRI could expel CD members without recourse to a formal hearing.

85. On April 25, for example, Manuel Moreno Sánchez (a former PRI senator who left the PRI in 1980 to become the Social Democrat candidate for president) held a dinner in honor of Cárdenas at his house, "Los Barandales," in the Estado de México. Government officials considered sympathetic to the Corriente were explicitly told not to go.

86. These statements appeared in early June. See Garrido, *La ruptura*, 103.

87. According to reports from *La Jornada*, on March 18 Cárdenas said that the CD had no candidate, but "that doesn't exclude that we *might* have one." On April 25 he denied aspiring to any precandidacy. On May 14 he would not rule out the possibility of being a candidate of the left; and on May 20 he admitted in *Unomásuno* that he would like to be president. On May 28 Muñoz Ledo described Cárdenas as the Corriente precandidate, and on May 29 he again declined. See also Carlos Lugo Chávez, *Neocardenismo* (Mexico City: Instituto de Proposiciones Estratégicas, 1989).

88. Garrido, *La ruptura*, 126–27.

89. Laso de la Vega, ed., *La Corriente Democrática*, 315–20.

90. Múgica says he rebelled because Cárdenas did not consult the whole Corriente beforehand. Other sources said Cárdenas did talk with them before scheduling the July 3 event; possibly he did not talk with everyone, said one, but "why should he ask people he

probably contributed to the announcement of six "aspirants" to the candidacy by national PRI leadership on August 14; each would appear before the PRI to discuss his positions.[91] The list pointedly left out Cárdenas and did not officially convoke registration of precandidates, which would have given him an opportunity to apply. The list also served warning to the Corriente that its pressure had not affected policy: none of the candidates advocated Corriente positions, and according to CD leaders, none could have avoided a split.[92] The Corriente responded by issuing a "Democratic Proposal" on September 9 containing its central economic and political demands. During September more separations occurred, including a group of young CD sympathizers headed by Muñoz Ledo's former private secretary Alejandro Rojas. Only five of the ten signers of Working Document Number One supported the Corriente when Carlos Salinas became the PRI candidate on October 4, 1987.

By the nomination of Salinas it had become clear to Corriente members that voice had failed and only exit remained. With Salinas's formal nomination, the last hope died. The sudden announcement preempted Cárdenas's bid to register as a precandidate.[93] Furthermore, none of the six precandidates more strongly represented all that the Corriente rejected. As secretary of program and budget, Salinas had designed much of the De la Madrid economic plan. He was a classic technocrat, with training in public administration and political economy (including a graduate degree from Harvard), and an exclusively bureaucratic career as an economist and financial expert. If his goal had been to push remaining Corriente members out of the PRI, De la Madrid could not have chosen better.

Ex-Corriente sympathizers who remained in the PRI despite the unpromising nomination claim to have stayed out of conviction that the PRI could reform, that internal democratization was more effective than outside opposition to influence policy, and that waiting would not have permanent consequences for Mexico.[94] However, once they decided

---

knew would say no?" Múgica, interview; confidential interview by author with CD founder, May 1991.

91. The six were Miguel González Avelar, Manuel Bartlett Díaz, Ramón Aguirre Velázquez, Alfredo del Mazo, Sergio García Ramírez, and Carlos Salinas.

92. Only Sergio García Ramírez is mentioned (in one interview with CD founder, April 1991) as someone sectors of the Corriente might have had trouble opposing.

93. The PRI convoked registry of precandidates on October 3, and the sectors declared their support for Salinas on October 4. At this point Salinas was registered as a precandidate. PRI statutes required support from the sectors for registry, leaving Cárdenas out. As the only precandidate, Salinas automatically became the PRI nominee at the party convention in November, without even the formality of an actual vote.

94. For instance, young *priista* sympathizers of the Corriente (Alejandro Rojas, Ra-

to stay, many tried to salvage their positions by making overtures to Salinas.[95] Few of them later participated in the Corriente Crítica organized by Rodolfo González Guevara after the 1988 election to continue pressure for internal reform.[96] Others stayed in the PRI partly because of doubts about the *cardenistas'* economic nationalism and because of their "stubborn insistence on the discourse of the Mexican Revolution."[97] All who stayed in the PRI shared a strong reluctance to confront the government. External opposition was not their original project; it implied tremendous personal risks, and it seemed to have little hope of success, given the fate of past opposition candidates.

Nevertheless, Cárdenas quickly made plans to run an independent campaign; indeed, discreet conversations with potential party sponsors began in September, when everyone could see the writing on the wall. On October 12 the Partido Auténtico de la Revolución Mexicana announced that Cárdenas had accepted an offer to run as their presidential candidate. Those who left the PRI with Cárdenas would have preferred internal opposition, and many of them felt they would probably lose the election. But unlike those who stayed, they doubted the PRI's ability to democratize and believed that it was critical for Mexico to avoid another six years of austerity. They had no hope that Salinas would reverse the policies he had promoted in the first place and felt

---

miro de la Rosa, and their group) shared with the CD a concern about internal democratization; however, "in September *they* were beginning to talk about leaving the party. We were against it because we were not defeated, the struggle still had hope." Confidential interview V, May 1991.

95. Both Rodolfo González Guevara and Janitzio Múgica went to see Salinas shortly after his nomination "to offer support and solidarity," and cooperated in Salinas's presidential campaign. See Miguel Ángel Rivera, "González Guevara: Buenas condiciones en el PRI," *La Jornada* (Mexico City), 8 October 1987: 1, 6. González Guevara later organized a critical current to maintain pressure on the government.

96. The young *priistas* established a new internal current called Democracy 2000. Rodolfo González Guevara eventually changed his mind about the sincerity of Salinas and the PRI's ability to reform and joined the PRD. However, most simply continued their political career in some capacity under Salinas. Carlos Tello became Mexico's ambassador to Portugal, followed by the Soviet Union (in 1989); he also served as an adviser to the National Solidarity Program. Armando Labra took a job representing the government of Oaxaca in Mexico City. Silvia Hernández became head of the popular sector of the PRI and a senator in 1991. Severo López Mestre went to the Finance Secretariat of the PRI. Gonzalo Martínez Corbalá was elected to Congress for the PRI in 1988, became interim governor of San Luis Potosí (very briefly), and then was named director of the ISSTE. See Garrido, *La ruptura*, 196–97.

97. Confidential interview V with a member of the young *priista* group, May 1991. Said another young *priista*, "we do not believe in the mystification of the discourse of the Revolution" or in its relevance for Mexico's future, because "this generation was not formed in that concept of 'Revolutionary Mexico.' " Confidential interview T, May 1991.

they had no choice but exit if they wanted to continue to push for some of their original goals. The election offered an opportunity: if they won, they could bring about policy reform; if they lost, they would still have forced a national debate and built mass pressure for change.

Corriente members who left the PRI often argue that the conflict in social projects between the neoliberals and the revolutionaries determined the entire course of events. The resolve of the neoliberal group to remain in power and ensure the continuation of "correct" policies never wavered, in contrast to the self-doubt of many communist regimes in Eastern Europe. As one CD member put it, "the truth is that everything indicates, time has testified, that the commitment of the government is a permanent commitment independently of the person in power at the moment. . . . They had to maintain a political line, which has been followed."[98] They argue that the revolutionary wing of the party had no choice but to oppose this line. In the view of Cárdenas:

> Events simply precipitated having to make certain decisions. . . . these things are never determined in a voluntaristic manner. . . . Why is the Grito de Dolores [the Mexican call to the war of independence in 1810] given on September 16 at four in the morning and not one day before or one day later? For the same reason that the Corriente Democrática emerged like it did. . . . Political circumstances in the country coincided, the sensitizing of public opinion coincided with a group of activists who took the initiative and could respond in the way that we did to political events.[99]

Despite the opinions of participants, both Salinas's ability to incorporate more of a social perspective into his program after 1988 and the *cardenistas'* ability to accept NAFTA publicly suggest that a major split was not inevitable. The same concessions, made sooner, might have salvaged the alliance, although it is much less likely that they *would* have been made without the shock of the 1988 election and the threat of the PRD. Yet some rupture in the PRI, if not inevitable, was extremely likely. The severity of the economic crisis had polarized the party and made substantive compromise difficult.

However, unfortunately for predictability and theoretical neatness, the ultimate fate of the Corriente cannot be entirely separated from the decision of Cuauhtémoc Cárdenas not to bend to the "call to discipline"

98. Confidential interview by author with CD founder, April 1991.
99. Cárdenas, interview.

issued by Jorge De la Vega. Other *priistas* would probably have left the party if Cárdenas had remained, yet none of them could have aroused as much popular enthusiasm as Cárdenas, nor could anyone else have united all the center-left opposition parties. Moreover, it would have been much more difficult for someone like Porfirio Muñoz Ledo to reach the agreement with the Mexican Socialist Party (PMS) that gave the PRD institutional life. If it had depended on the uncertain trial of waiting for government approval, the opposition that emerged might never have gained legal registry. Thus, without Cárdenas the new party would have had somewhat different characteristics and quite a different impact.

THE COALITION AVAILABILITY OF CÁRDENAS ALLIES OUTSIDE THE PRI

Not until this point in the analysis do electoral laws become significant to explain the creation of a new party. Most obviously, if laws had not allowed opposition party competition, Cárdenas would have had to choose another way to oppose the PRI; either there would have been no new party, or it would have lasted a few months, like the FEP in the 1960s. Electoral law also shaped the form the coalition took. The law specified that several parties could nominate one candidate without losing their independent registry. This provided Cárdenas with the option he chose, a multiparty coalition. Ironically, the small collaborationist parties used the same law for many years to conominate PRI candidates for president before they used it to nominate Cárdenas in 1988—one example of how laws designed to ensure the hegemonic control of the ruling party had the unintended effect of presenting the opposition with an opportunity. Second, once he became a registered candidate, electoral laws gave Cárdenas additional resources, including government funds for his campaign, free air time on television, representation in electoral institutions (including polling stations), and the right to take office if he won the election.

Perhaps most important, electoral laws played a causal role in detaching the collaborationist parties from their traditional alliance to the PRI. The support of these "parastatals" gave Cárdenas his first electoral registry and early access to all of these benefits. An electoral reform passed in late 1986 (after the public emergence of the Corriente Democrática) further pushed him toward a parastatal candidacy by eliminating the provision for conditional registry that might have allowed Cárdenas to register a new party and run as the candidate of his own party. Cárdenas needed the support of at least one registered party. Registry intensified interest in the Cárdenas campaign, magnified its importance, and helped him attract maximum social mobilization. However, electoral laws and the desire for registry also stimulated the formation of an extremely heterogeneous coalition once the breach with the PRI became definitive. While the breadth of the coalition initially helped Cárdenas achieve electoral success, it later proved an obstacle to the rapid consolidation of a political party.

In addition to electoral laws, the economic crisis and policy conflicts contributed to the willingness of external party and nonparty actors to break with their traditional practices and support Cárdenas. By election day three major groups promoted his candidacy: the parastatals, the unified independent left (especially the Mexican Socialist Party), and most of organized civil society outside the PRI (specifically, independent unions and urban popular movements). While the parastatals had to renounce support for the PRI in order to support Cárdenas, the other two groups experienced the opposite problem: for them the major stumbling block was Cárdenas's history in the PRI and his ties to the official system, which they had refused to support. Their eagerness to become partners in the electoral campaign of 1987–88 reflected a series of changes in political coalitions.

The Independent Left

Of all of these groups, the independent left had perhaps the fewest changes to make to adopt Cárdenas as its candidate, but it was the last to do so. Two trends that developed over the course of many years prepared the left to participate in a broad center-left coalition. First, left parties increasingly moderated their ideological position, de-emphasizing "revolution" and "communism" as primary goals and stressing democracy instead. Second, the parties of the left began to converge in a process of unification. In 1981 these trends led to the voluntary dissolution of the Mexican Communist Party to form the Unified Mexican Socialist Party (PSUM) with other left groups. The Communist Party leadership, and above all its general secretary Arnoldo Martínez Verdugo, played a key role in this moderation/unification process.[100] After

100. For a more complete discussion of this process see Barry Carr, *Mexican Communism, 1968–1983: Eurocommunism in the Americas?* (La Jolla, Calif.: UCSD Center for U.S.-Mexican Studies, 1985).

the faction to which Martínez Verdugo belonged succeeded in over-throwing the leadership of Dionisio Encina (1940–60), the Mexican Communist Party moved away from strict adherence to the party line of the Soviet Union. Instead of forming a guerrilla front—the favored strategy in those days just after the Cuban Revolution—the Mexican Communist Party began to participate in 1961 in the MLN's broad front of progressive parties and intellectuals, arguing that the postrevolution-ary conditions of Mexico demanded a different strategy. It became the only communist party to condemn the Soviet invasion of Czechoslova-kia. Even when the Mexican government crushed the student move-ment in 1968, imprisoning many Communist Party activists, the main leadership refused to support guerrilla struggles in the early seventies. Rather, the party moved further toward unification by proposing the formation of a broad "coalition of all the antioligarchic forces" and by stressing the need for democratic rights in a transition toward social-ism, though they still rejected the "[solution] of forming a broad party in which would struggle progressive Catholics, democrats of different tendencies, and some groups hostile to the Party."[101]

The approval of the 1977 electoral reform gave trends toward unifi-cation and moderation a major push. Carr's study of the Mexican left suggests that electoral participation encouraged the Partido Comunista Mexicano (PCM) to cooperate with other left parties and that the PCM "carefully calculated and limited its program in order to win the sup-port of as broad a segment of the population as possible."[102] The PCM participated in the 1979 congressional elections in a left coalition with several nonregistered parties (notably the Movimiento de Acción y Uni-dad Socialista, the Partido Socialista Revolucionaria, and the Partido del Pueblo Mexicano, MAUS, PSR, and PPM, respectively). In 1981 the Partido Communista Mexicano formed the PSUM with these parties and the Movimiento de Acción Popular (MAP), which came out of demo-cratic union struggles. The new party abandoned the hammer and sickle emblem. (Appendix A discusses these different movements and shows how they fit into the PRD's genealogy.)

The evolution of the PSUM into the Mexican Socialist Party coin-cided with the period of conjunctural economic and political crisis that produced the Corriente Democrática. However, trends toward unifica-tion and moderation well preceded the crisis. The independent left re-sponded more to its sense of marginalization from the masses than to

101. Arnoldo Martínez Verdugo, *El Partido Comunista Mexicano: Trayectoria y pers-pectivas* (Mexico City: Fondo de Cultura Popular, 1971), 78; 11.

102. Carr, *Mexican Communism*, 22.

the crisis per se. After doing rather badly in the 1985 congressional elections, due in part to internal divisions, the PSUM renewed its attempts to bring the remaining left parties into a larger Mexican Socialist Party. Partial success crowned its efforts in 1987, when the legally registered PMT and several other nonregistered parties joined the PMS. Of the main left groups, only the trotskyist Partido Revolucionario de los Trabajadores (PRT) refused to participate.

Nevertheless, when the crisis pushed Corriente leaders to public criticism of government policies, the PMS leaders saw their own critique converging with critiques by the progressive wing of the PRI. As the conflict within the PRI deepened, the PMS publicly expressed approval of the CD's goals, particularly after the March 1987 National Assembly and the virtual expulsion of Cárdenas from the party. By April 26 various PMS leaders had begun to suggest supporting Cárdenas as their candidate for president if he left the PRI. Heberto Castillo, the eventual PMS candidate for president, offered several times to throw his support to Cárdenas if the latter participated in PMS primaries scheduled for September.[103] Primaries had become an important way for the left to distinguish itself from the PRI, win support from popular movements who demanded influence over party decisions about candidacies, and distance itself from the authoritarian practices of the old Communist Party. The PMS claimed the most democratic internal selection procedures of any party, with voting taking place throughout Mexico. However, Cárdenas delayed his departure from the PRI until the announcement of Salinas's candidacy, well after the PMS primary had selected Castillo. At that time it would have looked hypocritical for the PMS leadership to suddenly throw out the results of a democratic vote and adopt Cárdenas as the party candidate. Furthermore, when Cárdenas finally left the PRI, he immediately accepted the nomination of the parastatal PARM, for reasons discussed below. This made it even more difficult for the PMS to support him. As a result, the PMS did not name Cárdenas as its candidate until June 1988, barely a month before the election.

The Parastatals

In contrast to the lengthy twenty-year process of moderation on the left, the changes that prepared the parastatals to nominate an independent

103. See, for example, Alejandro Caballero and Rosa Rojas, "Heberto Castillo, por postular a Cárdenas si rompe con el PRI," *La Jornada* (Mexico City), 24 June 1987: 1,

candidate surfaced over a short period of time. Each party followed a slightly different path, but all shared four traits: (1) diagnosis that continued association with the PRI and its policies hurt their chances of winning enough votes (1.5 percent) to keep their registry; (2) fear that the hard-pressed PRI was no longer willing to save its smaller allies from this fate; (3) belief that the PRI had chosen the worst possible candidate in Carlos Salinas; and (4) belief that Cárdenas offered them a golden opportunity to boost their vote without going too far away from the "system."

The behavior of the parastatals (PARM, PPS, and Partido Socialista de los Trabajadores/Partido Frente Cardenista de Reconstrucción Nacional [PST/PFCRN]) started to change around 1983 after the disastrous electoral experience of the PARM in 1982 provided an impetus to reconsider alliance with the PRI. Since its foundation in 1952 the PARM had loyally supported the PRI—voting with it in Congress and electoral institutions, and even conominating PRI presidential candidates. The PARM had never nominated a presidential candidate of its own. Yet in 1982 the PRI allowed the PARM to lose its registry, not even bothering to use its control over elections to fraudulently boost the PARM vote over the minimum 1.5 percent that Mexican electoral law requires for legal registry. PARM leaders faced the unpleasant reality that their loyalty to the PRI did not win them popular support nor save them from the usual consequences of unpopularity. The 1982 election resulted in a leadership shakeup. The new president, Carlos Cantú Rosas, wanted to distance the party from the PRI. He announced a "new era" for the PARM and, after recovering registry in 1984, warned that the PARM would no longer support PRI presidential candidates. Meanwhile, other parastatals uneasily considered the implications: if the PRI would not go out of its way to save the PARM, arguably its most servile ally, they could hardly expect special treatment. Though popular support for the parastatals increased slightly in 1985, they remained at the edge of losing their registry (see Table 3.2).

The passage of the 1986 electoral reform shook the alliance even more. According to analysts, the 1986 reform "gave greater space to the stronger opposition parties, like the PAN or the PMS, [at the expense of] the small ones that will tend to disappear."[104] More important, the

---

5–7. As an engineering student, Cárdenas took classes from Heberto Castillo. They kept up a strong personal relationship, participating together in the MLN and at least one business venture. Castillo's ex-PMT faction supported the idea of inviting Cárdenas to become a PMS candidate more than some other factions of the PMS.

104. Jacqueline Avramow Gutiérrez, "Los partidos contendientes en 1988," in *Las elecciones de 1988 y la crisis del sistema político*, ed. Jaime González Graf (Mexico City: Editorial Diana, 1989), 30.

Table 3.2. Trends in parastatal support

	PARM	PPS	PST
1979	1.8%	2.6%	2.1%
1982	1.4	1.9	1.8
1985	1.7	2.0	2.5

law abolished conditional registry. The PARM had recovered its registry after 1982 through this procedure; abolition meant that parties would have a hard time regaining registry if they lost it in an election. Most important, the 1986 electoral law changed the composition of the Federal Electoral Commission and the electoral courts so that the PRI no longer needed the votes of parastatal representatives to have majority control of the commission. This provision removed the strongest incentive of the PRI to make sure the parastatals survived.

When the PRI cut them loose to sink or swim, the parastatals had to think of something else to save their seats. Never strong electorally, they could not count on a sufficient core of loyal supporters. Association with the unpopular economic policies of the De la Madrid government made no sense as a strategy to win additional support. Well before they could have known that Cárdenas would be available as an opposition candidate, they began to distance themselves from De la Madrid. The PPS took the most emphatic and ideologically defined steps. Documents from a biannual assembly held prior to the public emergence of the Corriente object to the "negative economic policy" of the De la Madrid administration—its sale of state-owned enterprises, its decision to court foreign investment, its dedication to paying the debt, its inability to control inflation, its willingness to enter GATT, and its lack of attention to social justice and basic needs. The PPS attributed the crisis to "the penetration . . . at the heart of the Mexican State, of elements without patriotic consciousness, technocrats of denationalizing mentality, of elements . . . [of a] counterrevolutionary current . . . [that] has been imposing, in important areas, decisions contrary to the national and popular interest."[105] Six months later, during its January 1987 assembly, the Central Committee declared that the PPS would not necessarily support a PRI candidate for president. Traditionally, the PPS justified support for PRI candidates as a common front strategy. In 1988 they repeated the call for a "common front of patriotic, democratic, progressive, and revolutionary Mexicans . . . [with] a common program and a common

105. Partido Popular Socialista (PPS), *Denunciar y derrotar la negativa política económica*, 82d Pleno del Comité Central (Mexico City: PPS, 1986), 18–22; 15–16.

candidate to the presidency," but they disqualified the most likely PRI candidates, singling out "Petriccioli, Alfredo del Mazo, and Salinas de Gortari" as part of the "reactionary, . . . conservative, . . . counterrevolutionary" group that served the "retrograde bourgeoisie."[106] By July 1987 PPS Assembly resolutions had become an explicit threat, showing special animosity toward Carlos Salinas as an official candidate:

> North American imperialism . . . is trying to influence by every means the correlation of forces so that the postulation [of a presidential candidate] that the government party makes will be in favor of an element that has established previous commitments in favor of imperialism, that guarantees docile conduct, [that is] ready to listen and obey the voice of the master in all matters of economic, social, and political life, as would be the case of . . . members of the economic cabinet, like Gustavo Petricioli, Alfredo del Mazo, Carlos Salinas de Gortari. . . . Overcoming the proimperialist and neocolonial thesis of the "slimming down" of the state, whose standard bearer is Salinas de Gortari, . . . is the key to overcoming the crisis."[107]

According to one interview, PPS leaders decided to support Cárdenas within twenty-four hours of the nomination of Salinas, although his acceptance of the PARM's offer made some rethink their initial enthusiasm, and it took until December to arrange an official nomination.[108]

The other parastatals moved more cautiously to distance themselves from the PRI, and did not burn their bridges until Cárdenas became clearly available. If they were to take the risk of abandoning their traditional PRI alliance and still keep their registry, it seemed best to go with a candidate who had more national presence and popularity than their own leaders. Cárdenas was perfect. Thus, the PARM declared in April 1987—after the PRI Assembly that attacked Cárdenas—that it would not support any PRI candidate for president. Yet unlike the PMS, the PARM waited to nominate a candidate of its own, leaving open the possibility of supporting the PRI or nominating Cárdenas. When the PRI's August 14 presentation of six officially blessed aspirants made clear to

106. Partido Popular Socialista (PPS), *Nos empeñamos en manejar con certeza la ciencia de la sociedad, el marxismo-leninismo*, 83d Pleno del Comité Central (Mexico City: PPS, 1987), 61–62; 12.

107. Partido Popular Socialista (PPS), *Es necesario y urgente poner otra vez en marcha a la revolución mexicana*, 84th Pleno del Comité Central (Mexico City: PPS, 1987), 15, 20.

108. Confidential interview AZ, August 1991. See also Garrido, *La ruptura*, 185.

the Corriente that opportunities for influence within the PRI were virtually nil, discreet talks began with PARM (and other parastatal) leaders, but no final agreement was reached until after the nomination of Salinas.[109] On October 12 the PARM leadership announced that Cárdenas would be their candidate, and on October 14, at its previously scheduled national convention, PARM became the first registered party to nominate him officially.

The second party to nominate Cárdenas, the PST/PFCRN, had also moved away from alliance with the PRI. In January 1987 the party began to discuss changing its name to the "Cardenista Party of the Mexican Workers," identifying with a quite different policy tradition than that represented by De la Madrid. The PST experienced greater internal conflict over the decision to challenge the PRI than the PARM or PPS, including a split in April 1987 between the faction of President Rafael Aguilar Talamantes and PST founder Graco Ramírez that culminated in the expulsion of the latter.[110] Ramírez, who had criticized the party's "servility" to the PRI, joined the PMS. The PST apparently planned to nominate Aguilar Talamantes as late as October, when the nomination of Salinas made Cárdenas a likely candidate. The PST formally nominated Cárdenas and changed its name to the PFCRN in late November, three days after De la Madrid devalued the peso by 33 percent.

Though the PARM nomination did not significantly discourage the parastatals from supporting Cárdenas, it had a disastrous effect on the relationship between Cárdenas and the independent left. PMS leaders wooed Cárdenas openly and persistently far earlier than any of the parastatals, trying to convince him to become their candidate. When Cárdenas accepted the offer of the PARM and actually joined the party, many PMS leaders viewed it as "not disappointment. It was a betrayal."[111] First, because of the PARM's "very disreputable" reputation as a "tool of the government,"[112] they feared that alliance with parties like the PARM would affect the substance and independence of the Cárdenas campaign and compromise the PMS. Thus, "there was mistrust, and I think justified. . . . never mistrust of Cárdenas, it wasn't that, but mis-

109. Some PARM leaders, including secretary-general Pedro González Azcuaga, thought a Cárdenas candidacy would be too big a risk for a weak party. When the PARM nominated Cárdenas anyway, González Azcuaga disputed the convention's legality and was expelled from the party.
110. Both factions claimed a majority to expel the other. The government sided with Aguilar Talamantes.
111. Confidential interview by author of former PMS member, August 1991.
112. Confidential interviews by author of former PMS members, February 1991, August 1991.

trust . . . toward the PARM and the FDN as such. . . . We thought that alliance would be a highly conjunctural one."[113] Second, according to the PMS, Cárdenas made the deal behind their back after rejecting a concrete PMS offer. The PMS saw this as a breach of faith; as one member put it, "the most elemental political courtesy [would require] saying that 'I am going to do this.' "[114]

Cárdenas apparently chose to go with the PARM almost entirely because of the factor of time, to get a quick start on the campaign. The PMS already had an official candidate: Heberto Castillo, selected in a national primary election. For the PMS to change its mind and nominate Cárdenas "wasn't easy. . . . the candidate we had chosen had been chosen by a very broad vote. . . . it wasn't a decision of the leaders, so we couldn't change it easily."[115] Even if Castillo resigned immediately, it would have taken time to organize a new convention and nominate a different candidate. Cárdenas would have had to wait to receive government funds and media coverage as the candidate of a party. In contrast, the PARM could easily nominate Cárdenas in a few days. In fact, the PARM had fortuitously scheduled its convention for October 14. This time consideration seems to have influenced Cárdenas's decision more than any other:

> It was not easy for any of the political parties to support my candidacy because that . . . meant a decision for independence . . . that put them in a totally different relationship to the government . . . of greater confrontation. So, we believed it was necessary to arrive at an agreement with the PARM as soon as possible. . . . We felt that it was necessary to hurry up the agreement and the sooner [an agreement] was consolidated, well, the sooner the candidacy would be consolidated as well.[116]

Some Corriente members argue in addition that a direct leap to the Socialist Party would have alienated potential support from moderate *priistas*, though it is not clear this calculation was made at the time. But implicitly, most participants assumed that the party vehicle and its associated program and organization mattered much less than the personality of Cárdenas. Thus, the prospect of a quick start to the campaign—wherever it came from—was a powerful lure. The offer of the PARM, "which had registry, therefore immediately gave [us] the capac-

113. Confidential interview by author of former PMS member, August 1991.
114. Ibid.
115. Confidential interview by author of former PMS member, April 1991.
116. Cárdenas, interview.

ity to have an electoral organization, representatives in the polling stations, representatives in the Federal Electoral Commission, and a whole series of operative things. . . . people asked, 'why the PARM?' [i.e., why such a disreputable party], . . . but the transcendent fact was that Cuauhtémoc Cárdenas, representative of our movement, now had a party to compete electorally."[117]

Once the other parastatals nominated Cárdenas, they formed a coordinating body called the Frente Democrático Nacional (National Democratic Front, or FDN). The FDN issued a common program and gave the groups supporting Cárdenas a forum to communicate with one another about campaign activities. The breach between Cárdenas and the PMS lasted until June 1988, when Heberto Castillo resigned his candidacy and the PMS Assembly voted to nominate Cárdenas. As Chapter 4 shows, the basic reason behind the PMS change of heart was growing concern that Cárdenas had captured the left's traditional support—constituencies like students and urban popular movements that the left had considered safe. However, the PMS refused to join the FDN officially. Rather, Castillo and the PMS leadership signed a separate pact with the Corriente Democrática and Cárdenas, specifying common program points and establishing a political commitment between the two forces. This political pact marks the real beginning of the alliance that would found the Party of the Democratic Revolution in 1989.

Civil Society

Organized civil society did not become heavily involved in the *neocardenista* movement until after the announcement of a Cárdenas candidacy. Like the left, independent popular movements and unions did not have to be detached from loyalties to the PRI, but they did have to be convinced to abandon traditional political practices—in this case, a general reluctance to ally themselves with any political party. Mindful of the fate of popular organizations incorporated by the PRI, most independent popular movements distrusted the motives of political parties and their ability to honestly promote popular interests. Nor did they believe that voting in elections, above all for the opposition, would advance the

117. Confidential interview by author of CD founder, April 1991. Another *cardenista* remarked, in similar terms, that "there wasn't time to form [a new party]. . . . Cuauhtémoc, [saw] that there was no other way and after all it wasn't so bad . . . it was a party. It had registry. They called him. They invited him. He accepts. And he is the candidate . . . and he can compete in the election. So it was very circumstantial but also very conditioned by the characteristics of the moment." Ibid., June 1991.

goals of their movements. Electoral alliance, in their view, could cause them to lose their autonomy in return for ephemeral and insubstantial gains.

However, in the mid-1980s many popular movements began to soften their traditional rejection of electoral cooperation with parties. One of the earliest and most successful electoral coalitions—an alliance between the Coalición de Obreros, Campesinos y Estudiantes del Istmo (COCEI) and the Partido Socialista Unificado de México—won the right to govern Juchitán, Oaxaca, in 1982. The COCEI experience encouraged other popular movements to consider temporary electoral alliances with parties. In February 1985 the National Revolutionary Coordinating Committee called for cooperation between movements and parties in local or regional coalitions, and several parties (PSUM, PMT, and PRT) accepted the idea. However, these steps did not result in widespread electoral alliances. Often, "not only did these [coalitions] experience electoral defeats that undermined the previously recognized mobilizational capabilities of the movement, but in some cases internal weakening, division, desertion, and demobilization clearly followed electoral participation."[118] Despite the increasing importance of electoral strategies, a doctrinal shift favoring electoral alliance with opposition parties did not take place.

During the Corriente phase of the formation of the new party these popular movements played no significant role. Key initiatives originated with the CD leadership, both to form the Corriente itself and to run an independent candidacy. Even the response of the public seemed lukewarm. As one Corriente leader remarked, "Cuauhtémoc had traveled around many places in the Republic. And he was received with sympathy by some, with enthusiasm by a few, with curiosity by others, . . . but one could not say that civil society in that moment had participation, no, it really didn't. . . . It was *ready* to participate, that is something else, that was the secret, . . . but that wasn't known for sure until later."[119] In Michoacán local CD committees were related to personal or political networks connected to the PRI, and for the most part they offered only vague support for whatever Cárdenas chose to do. Civil society organizations outside the PRI regarded the Corriente with cautious approval. While sympathetic to its goals, they remained understandably wary of committing themselves to a bunch of *priistas*.

118. Jaime Tamayo, "Neoliberalism Encounters *Neocardenismo,*" in *Popular Movements and Political Change in Mexico,* ed. Joe Foweraker and Ann Craig (Boulder, Colo.: Lynne Rienner, 1990), 127.
119. Confidential interview by author of CD founder, April 1991.

Nevertheless, changes in the behavior of this third group of Cárdenas allies had a definite impact on the course of the campaign once it became clear that Cárdenas would run. In many cases the participation of popular movements in the Cárdenas campaign resulted more from the initiative of their bases than from a deliberate decision on the part of their leaders to mobilize electorally. As Chapter 4's analysis of the FDN campaign shows, mass response to Cárdenas overwhelmed the organizational capacity of all of the parties and movements supporting him. People responded to his personal qualities, but, more important, they saw in his candidacy a chance to express their hostility toward the PRI and the effects of austerity. This hostility preceded the emergence of Cárdenas as an opposition candidate, as well as the emergence of the Corriente Democrática in the PRI. Thus while Cárdenas did not make Mexicans get angry at the PRI, his candidacy was vital in creating an opportunity for people to express their anger electorally.

In addition, popular discontent encouraged the creation of the Corriente and later the Cárdenas candidacy. Corriente leaders took action in part because they believed that popular discontent with the PRI had risen to dangerous levels that threatened future PRI dominance. They factored in latent political opinions not yet expressed through elections or through any organized movement. Indeed, perhaps the most important contribution of organized civil society was not its participation during the campaign but its contribution to creating this perception that PRI hegemony was in danger. The increasingly political and widespread organizational activity of civil society challenged the corporatist model of popular participation, especially after the 1985 earthquake, when slow government responses forced many Mexico City precincts to organize themselves to meet their own needs and rebuild their neighborhoods. Though civil society did not produce the split in a direct sense, this organized challenge as well as the patent discontent of ordinary citizens laid the groundwork for the progressive factions of the PRI to confront the De la Madrid government electorally.

4

A Trip to the Moon and Back Again

PARTY EMERGENCE AND CONSOLIDATION IN THE 1988
PRESIDENTIAL ELECTION

El cardenismo viene,
ya viene, ya viene,
y al pueblo le conviene.
El pueblo unido, jamás seŕa vencido
ya viene, ya viene,
Y nadie lo detiene.[1]

Cardenismo is coming
it's coming, coming now,
and it is what the people need.
The people united will never be defeated,
it's coming, coming now,
And nobody can stop it.

At the height of the euphoria aroused by Cárdenas's massive electoral mobilizations and near-victory, this campaign chant seemed prophetic. Yet something did stop the National Democratic Front. It failed to achieve its primary electoral goal and fell apart less than six months after the election, amid bitter accusations of betrayal. Of the four registered political parties in the FDN, only one—the Mexican Socialist Party—joined with Cárdenas in forming the Party of the Democratic Revolution.

---

1. Samuel Maldonado, *Origenes del Partido de la Revolución Democrática* (Morelia, Michoacán: published by author, 1989), 105.

The fundamental reasons behind the FDN's disintegration and the PRD's subsequent problems lie in the new conditions facing Cárdenas as he tried to consolidate his political force. Between October 1987, when Cárdenas launched his presidential campaign, and October 1988, when he called for the formation of a new party, his coalition made the transition from the emergence to the consolidation arena. During emergence, strategic, conjunctural, and structural advantages contributed to success on election day—July 6, 1988. But party consolidation imposes different tasks, which require different strengths and skills. New parties often perform these tasks poorly even when—perhaps *especially* when—they have had striking success in creating a new option with popular support. Moreover, the time frame changes, affecting the calculations of actors. What seems feasible and acceptable in the short term may seem neither feasible *nor* acceptable in the medium to long term. Problems within the *cardenista* coalition began to multiply as soon as the time frame and the nature of its tasks shifted.

Continuing from Chapter 3's analysis of the factors that encouraged emergence, this chapter analyzes the contextual factors and characteristics that contributed to the coalition's initial electoral success in 1988, and their effects on early postelectoral attempts to consolidate the "party of the sixth of July": to preserve the FDN, to defend the 1988 vote, and to use its popular clout to influence the regime. It thus begins to lay the foundation for two arguments more fully developed in the next three chapters: that the differences between emergence and consolidation and between detachment and reattachment help explain variation in performance and, ultimately, party system resilience; and that the characteristics and choices of a party in its early stages of formation have a lasting impact on the type of organization it becomes and on its success in consolidation.

In this analysis factors that encourage emergence and contribute to early electoral success do not necessarily promote and may even handicap consolidation. For example, the policy conflicts that motivated the formation of a new party and helped make it popular also made it a target of the ruling party. The PRI could not stop the new party from forming (and if anything its hostility raised the propensity of anti-PRI protesters to vote for the FDN). Yet while temporary advantages like surprise and charisma gave the new opposition resources to overcome the institutional advantages of the PRI at first, the structure of the institutional arena gave the ruling party the tools to hold on to power in 1988. Over time, the effectiveness of these tools increased, allowing the PRI to shape the conditions for new party consolidation and lay the foundations for its own at least temporary recovery. The coalition's ideological position on the left also complicated cooperation with the conservative opposition PAN, making unlikely a coalition of the opposition similar to the Campaign for the No in Chile, which effectively brought about a transition to democracy.

Neither the character of the FDN nor its reliance on mass mobilization and charismatic leadership proved as helpful for defending electoral support as for attracting it. Nor did the roots of emergence in socioeconomic structure guarantee consolidation; in fact, some of the groups most likely to voice protest by voting for the opposition, such as urban independent voters, may also be less inclined to develop new partisan loyalties. Finally, strategic calculations changed after the presidential election, driving apart the disparate group of allies. Thus, the coalition moved from a position of relative advantage during its successful electoral run to a position of relative disadvantage during its effort to consolidate electoral strength, stabilize relationships with party and nonparty allies, deliver on its promises, and institutionalize a party organization.

The FDN Presidential Campaign: Conditions Favoring Successful Emergence

Two sets of factors held the new coalition together and contributed to its success in 1988. The first set reflects the context of emergence, especially the political conditions for opposition (crisis and an available protest vote) and several "new party" advantages. The second set refers to the specific characteristics of the new coalition, including its foundation as a breakaway coalition of multiple organizations, its reliance on charisma, and its antineoliberal ideology. Some of these factors became liabilities for consolidation. Others compensated in part for the weaknesses of the FDN during the presidential campaign but later vanished or became less able to counteract the coalition's limitations.

Contextual Conditions Favoring Successful Emergence

The first significant contextual factor that contributed to the coalition's 1988 electoral success has already been introduced: the economic crisis and the neoliberal policies chosen to respond to it. The social consequences of the economic crisis, the PRI's handling of it, and the inability of most groups to influence policy essentially prepared voters to abandon traditional poses of either PRI loyalty or loyal apathy. When Cárdenas looked like the most likely candidate to punish the PRI, he won much of this available protest vote.

The crisis produced a sharp drop in living standards for Mexicans who could not protect their incomes by investing in dollars abroad. Inflation averaged 88.4 percent per year during the 1982–88 period, reaching a peak of 159.2 percent in 1987, the year the presidential campaign began.[2] Salaries did not keep up with inflation. Most estimates put the decline in the real minimum wage between 40 and 50 percent from 1983 to 1988.[3] By 1986 real minimum wages had fallen nearly to their 1938 level, wiping out the gains of almost fifty years.[4] Total wage income fell approximately 40 percent between 1983 and 1988.[5] Open unemployment rose, in part because of the elimination of state jobs.[6] The middle class, which depended more heavily on state employment and wage incomes, was hit especially hard. Agricultural incomes declined relatively less. Some urban workers were able to switch to informal sector or nonwage jobs to supplement their incomes. However, nonwage income declined by approximately 7 percent according to one estimate, and poverty increased.[7] Income per capita shrank in four of the six years before 1988, including the immediate precampaign years 1986 (− 5.9 percent) and 1987 (− .3 percent).[8]

2. Mexico, Secretaría de Hacienda y Crédito Público (SHCP), *El nuevo perfil de la economía mexicana* (Mexico City: SHCP, June 1991), 38.

3. For representative estimates see Nora Lustig, *Mexico: The Remaking of an Economy* (Washington, D.C.: The Brookings Institution, 1992), 68–69; Sidney Weintraub, *Transforming the Mexican Economy: The Salinas Sexenio* (Washington, D.C.: National Planning Association, 1993), 13; and Ruth Berins Collier, *The Contradictory Alliance: State-Labor Relations and Regime Change in Mexico* (Berkeley and Los Angeles: University of California Press, 1992), 128.

4. Esthela Gutiérrez Garza, "De la relación salarial monopolista a la flexibilidad del trabajo: México 1960–1986," in *Testimonios de la crisis: La crisis del estado del bienestar*, ed. Esthela Gutiérrez Garza (Mexico City: Siglo Veintiuno, 1988), 152–53.

5. Lustig, *Mexico: The Remaking of an Economy*, 68–69.

6. Gutiérrez Garza estimates this increase at 13.4 percent, from 6.3 percent in 1980 to 19.7 percent in 1986 ("De la relación salarial monopolista a la flexibilidad del trabajo," 161).

7. Lustig, *Mexico: The Remaking of an Economy*, 72. For analyses of some social effects of the crisis, including changes in diet and employment strategies, see Mercedes González de la Rocha and Agustín Escobar Latapí, eds., *Social Responses to Mexico's Economic Crisis of the 1980s* (La Jolla, Calif.: UCSD Center for U.S.-Mexican Studies, 1991).

8. SHCP, *El nuevo perfil de la economía mexicana*, 37.

This economic picture affected popular opinion. According to a 1988 survey, 89 percent of those polled rated the condition of the Mexican economy "bad" or "very bad," and 54 percent thought the country would "never" emerge from economic crisis.[9] Most people (53 percent) identified the top problem as inflation or low salaries. Many must have blamed the PRI: 18 percent thought the government almost never did the right thing, and 60 percent thought the government did the right thing only some of the time. Almost two-thirds said the political system should permit other parties to win elections more often. By 1987 government approval had fallen to less than 50 percent in every region and every class (see Table 4.1). Even more important, dissatisfaction undermined partisan loyalties. Between 1983 and 1987 the percentage of voting-age Mexicans who sympathized with the PRI dropped by an average of over 25 percent (see Table 4.2).[10]

As if the PRI did not have enough problems, economic expectations plunged again just as the presidential campaign got under way. Pushed by the October 1987 Wall Street stock market crash, President Miguel De la Madrid devalued the peso by 32.8 percent on November 19, 1987— only a month after unveiling Salinas as the PRI candidate. Thus, the election took place in the context of a population pessimistic about the future, dissatisfied with its government, and ready to look elsewhere.

Not all of this potential protest vote would necessarily have gone

Table 4.1. Government approval by region and class

Class		North	Center	South	Mean
			Region		
Upper	1987	46.7%	37.8%	45.0%	40.6%
	Change, 1983–87	+ 3.9	− 12.4	− 7.2	− 8.6
Middle	1987	30.5	29.1	31.8	29.6
	Change, 1983–87	− 6.8	− 17.0	− 10.3	− 14.3
Lower	1987	36.9	18.7	27.0	21.5
	Change, 1983–87	+ 2.1	− 18.2	− 9.9	− 15.1

SOURCE: Condensed and adapted from Miguel Basañez, *El pulso de los sexenios: 20 años de crisis en México* (Mexico City: Siglo Veintiuno, 1990), 249, 277.
NOTES: Regional figures report Basañez's calculations of average support within three "strata" classified on the basis of occupational data. "Upper class" includes "businessman" and "politician"; "middle class" includes "professional," "employee," and "bureaucrat"; and "lower class" includes "worker," "peasant," and "marginalized." "Mean" reports Basañez's calculation of average support within each strata nationwide.

9. William Stockton, "Mexican Pessimism is Found in Survey," *New York Times*, 16 November 1988: 16.

10. Miguel Basañez, *El pulso de los sexenios: 20 años de crisis en México* (Mexico City: Siglo Veintiuno, 1990), 249, 277.

Table 4.2. Percentage of voting-age Mexicans sympathizing with the PRI

Class		North	Center	South	Mean
			Region		
Upper	1987	49.5%	31.1%	41.0%	35.7%
	Change, 1983–87	−5.9	−33.0	−24.9	−27.2
Middle	1987	42.8	25.1	36.2	29.8
	Change, 1983–87	−8.8	−33.9	−18.0	−27.2
Lower	1987	22.8	22.8	36.5	25.0
	Change, 1983–87	−18.5	−33.2	−20.8	−29.0

SOURCE: Adapted from Basáñez, *El pulso de los sexenios,* 249, 277.
NOTE: Regional figures report Basáñez's calculations of average support within the same categories used in Table 4.1.

against the PRI in the absence of Cárdenas. Before 1988 popular discontent did not seriously affect election results or cause riots and disturbances; in fact, researchers found no evidence that the system was about to face a major legitimacy crisis.[11] The potential protest vote became an active protest vote in part because of the importance of presidential elections, in part because of the enthusiasm awakened by Cárdenas personally, and in part because of the fact that his coalition was competing in its first election as a new political force.

In the first place, newness itself can be an advantage. Unlike older parties, new parties have no record to defend, no broken promises to explain, no embarrassing mistakes to overlook. New parties may appeal especially to those who want change, a large group in 1988. However small a new party's chances of succeeding, other parties have demonstrably failed. Although the parties that supported Cárdenas were not new, their combination in a unified candidacy was not only new but unprecedented. What one party could not do alone, perhaps several could do together. Cárdenas himself had never led an opposition or lost an election. Moreover, what little voters knew of him tended to ease the fears and uncertainty that a complete unknown might have raised. His rhetoric and name linked him to a familiar past that most believed had been a better time. On this basis many voters trusted his promises to improve their economic position and perhaps even his capacity to beat the PRI. To put it another way, he was new, but not too new—enough of an outsider to credibly promise change, and enough a man of the

11. See for example Miguel Basáñez, "Elections and Political Culture in Mexico," and Martin C. Needler, "The Significance of Recent Events for the Mexican Political System," both in *Mexican Politics in Transition*, ed. Judith Gentleman (Boulder, Colo.: Westview Press, 1987).

system for change not to seem too scary. This favorable combination is particularly characteristic of many breakaway parties, which often enjoy early success.

Second, new parties frequently have the advantage of surprise. Since a new party has not yet competed in a major election, no one knows exactly where or to whom it will appeal most strongly. An incumbent party may be unable to tailor its campaign to address the concerns of the new party's potential supporters because it does not yet know who they will be. The PRI also lost several less savory tools for dealing with the opposition. One time-honored strategy involved eliminating opposition supporters from the voter registry—next to impossible without a fairly precise idea of who supports the opposition and where the registry needs "shaving," to use the Mexican term. Similarly, creative placement of polling stations in areas of PRI strength and away from areas of opposition strength requires detailed microlevel knowledge about which sections of communities support the opposition. This detailed knowledge was beyond the PRI in 1988 because the FDN represented a new political force. How much pull would Cárdenas have, with whom, and where? How much would component parties contribute? Would their support of Cárdenas undermine or reinforce their regional strength? Even Cárdenas would have been hard-pressed to give specific answers to these questions in 1988.

Third, the elite divisions that often accompany the creation of a new party complicate the mounting of a coherent response to the threat. As Chapter 3 showed, elite division was an integral part of the process, detaching some elites and freeing them to lead a new opposition. Though it relieved the pressure a bit, the departure of the dissident *priistas* did not do away with internal divisions. For one thing, new parties are risky ventures and some dissidents are bound to calculate that they are better off remaining in the system. In Mexico the long dominance of the PRI made a new party look especially risky. Therefore, many dissident elites played it safe by remaining in the PRI. Yet their decision did not imply tremendous enthusiasm for Salinas or a willingness to throw themselves wholeheartedly into a struggle against Cárdenas.

In addition, "elite divisions" can rarely be summed up by a single line of cleavage. The conflict between *cardenistas* and *salinistas* did not complete the list of conflicts in the PRI. Salinas also had trouble with other factions of the party, including the traditional union leaders. They too lacked enthusiasm for his campaign. Observers remarked on the strange "absence of the party sectors in their usual task of organizing big mobilizations in favor of their candidate."[12] Sectoral leaderships as important as Fidel Velázquez (lifetime president of the largest Mexican labor federation, the CTM) and Joaquín Hernández Galicia (longtime president of the powerful petroleum union) preferred other candidates. Hernández openly encouraged petroleum workers to vote for Cárdenas. González Graf explains the "poor effort of the sectors of the PRI," as a result of the "hatred of the political class toward the technocracy" and toward Salinas personally.[13] Austerity had further undermined the credibility and prestige of sectoral leaders with their members. Moreover, as secretary of programming and budget, Salinas had earned some enemies by his efforts to rationalize administration, eliminating sources of bureaucratic corruption like Hernández Galicia's control over oil subcontracts, which netted him personal profit and served as a slush fund for maintaining patron-client relationships. If they did not all oppose Salinas, such leaders did not go all out to drum up the vote.

In areas where many dissidents left the PRI the resulting disruptions in the party structure of dominance and control left serious holes. As a result, the PRI had trouble recovering in some of the very regions where party leaders could guess Cárdenas would get support, like Michoacán and Mexico City. Despite losing some of the benefit of surprise, the *cardenistas* did quite well in these areas. In Michoacán, where many PRI political elites had recently owed allegiance to Cárdenas and benefited from his political patronage, the PRI could not effectively mobilize in favor of Salinas nor mount a very successful fraud. The PRI made reorganization of the party structure in states that favored Cárdenas one of its first priorities after the 1988 election.

Advantages Based on FDN Characteristics

Its character as a breakaway coalition organized on the backs of existing parties helped the FDN get a quick start and gave it flexibility. For new movements under time pressure, amalgamating multiple organizations works as a shortcut to building a new party, although this strategy has some negative consequences for consolidation, as Chapter 5 shows. Founders of the Brazilian Partido dos Trabalhadores (PT) had to adopt a similar strategy in appealing to "leaders of already organized constitu-

12. Mónica Cándano Fierro, "Las campañas electorales," in *Las elecciones de 1988 y la crisis del sistema político*, ed. Jaime González Graf (Mexico City: Editorial Diana, 1989), 55.

13.. Jaime González Graf, "La crisis del sistema," in *Las elecciones de 1988 y la crisis del sistema político*, ed. Jaime González Graf (Mexico City: Editorial Diana, 1989), 145.

encies" in order "to meet the legal requirements in time to participate in the next election," and they too ended up with greater influence of old left party bureaucracies than might otherwise have been the case.[14] The *cardenistas* would have lost their best opportunity—the presidential election—if they had been forced to build a party from scratch instead of drawing on existing organizations with resources, infrastructure, and experienced cadres. The coalition parties came endowed with offices, telephone lines, bank accounts, political connections, and trained activists. Where Cárdenas could not count on opposition party organization, he could sometimes draw on ex-*priistas* with organizational expertise. In Michoacán, for instance, the FDN parties had virtually no presence or organization. Therefore, Corriente organizers, deputized to create a party structure in Michoacán, swarmed into the ranks of the PARM as soon as Cárdenas became the PARM candidate. They spread out to form local committees, participated as PARM candidates, nominated party poll watchers through the PARM, and joined the PARM's State Executive Committee.[15] In areas lacking a strong ex-PRI contingent and without an organizational presence of the FDN parties or a strong local popular movement, it was hard to put together an effective campaign in the short time available.

Moreover, the FDN's multiple organizations gave it flexibility. Local groups without much central control could tailor the campaign to local conditions and respond to changes relatively quickly. A flexible strategy is particularly necessary when local conditions differ dramatically. Mexico's social landscape offers a panorama of diverse social, economic, cultural, and political environments, with extremes of poor and rich, relatively isolated and highly interdependent, agricultural and industrialized, indigenous and European communities. In 1988 the FDN parties could appeal to local constituencies in their areas of relative regional strength: the PARM in Tamaulipas; the PPS in Oaxaca; the PSUM/PMS in Mexico City, the Estado de México, and Nayarit; and the PST/PFCRN in Veracruz and Hidalgo. Multiple organizations also helped the FDN monitor voting by providing backup systems to cover a larger percentage of the polls. Mexican law entitled each party to representatives in the polling stations; with four parties (after the PMS joined the campaign), someone was bound to send information to headquarters about election results from a majority of polling stations.

14. Margaret Keck, *The Workers' Party and Democratization in Brazil* (New Haven: Yale University Press, 1992), 94.

15. In 1991 the Michoacán PARM was still run by members who originally joined from the CD during this wave of organization, including state president Luis Coca Álvarez.

Nevertheless, the FDN as an organization could not take credit for Cárdenas's success. The FDN gave Cárdenas neither an efficient campaign machine nor a well-filled war chest in 1988. The three parastatal parties that nominated Cárdenas had virtually no national presence, a weakly consolidated base, and little organizational structure. They rarely won as much as 2.5 percent of the national vote, even when the PRI channeled them votes and money in exchange for their loyalty. Their 1988 vote bears only a superficial resemblance to historical patterns, as Figure 4.2 shows, jumping significantly before returning to near normal once they left the FDN. These parties did not have the activists, the support base, or the resources to mobilize the huge crowds that showed up at Cárdenas rallies. Nor did the nonregistered parties; some consisted of only a few dozen activists. Popular movements provided a larger activist base, but one unused to and sometimes even opposed to participating in elections.

Thus, a second major advantage of the coalition at this stage was its ability to call on the charisma of Cárdenas and, in general, on the appeal of a leftist ideology stressing equity and substantive social justice in a context of neoliberal transformation. The two features were not unconnected. The charisma of Cárdenas was partly personal, partly inherited from his identification with the social policies and personal qualities of his father, and partly situational, defined by Tucker as a type of charisma in which "a state of acute social *stress* . . . gets the people ready

Fig. 4.1. Parastatal vote for Congress, 1976–1991

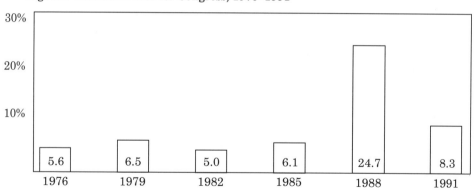

Sources: 1976–88 results from Mexico, Instituto Federal Electoral, *Contienda electoral en las elecciones de diputados federales,* ed. Jenny Saltiel Cohen (Mexico City: IFE, 1991), 3, 5; see also Silvia Gómez Tagle, *Las estadísticas electorales de la reforma política* (Mexico City: El Colegio de México, 1990), 22. 1991 results from Mexico, Instituto Federal Electoral, *Relación de los 300 distritos federales electorales* (Mexico City: IFE, 1991).

to perceive as extraordinarily qualified and to follow with enthusiastic loyalty a leadership offering salvation from distress."[16] Successful new parties almost always rely on a charismatic leader in the emergence stage. Indeed, they lack most other resources to legitimate their authority: with reference to Weber's classic (1964) identification of traditional, bureaucratic, and charismatic authority, new parties tend to have little traditional authority to rely on, and they have not yet developed an institutionalized bureaucracy whose procedures win it legitimacy. Only a highly ideological or issue-specific party may escape the characteristic reliance on charisma.

The early media image of Cárdenas did not emphasize this aspect of his leadership, portraying Cárdenas as a dour, humorless man, too poor a public speaker to appeal to the masses. Like many images, this one contains some truth. Cárdenas does not often smile in public, nor does he speak particularly well. However, people seem to listen to his quiet monotone more attentively than to more accomplished orators.[17] Other qualities also endear him to the public. Cárdenas has the capacity in a few moments to make people believe he is intently listening. His personal charisma lies more in this ability to listen than in his ability to speak. His Indian features gave him a visual connection to ordinary people not shared by the whiter Salinas; his name—Cuauhtémoc—honors the last Aztec emperor, who resisted the Spaniards and was tortured to death. He is believed to be scrupulously honest—rare for a Mexican politician. As a result, Cárdenas often inspires a fierce, protective loyalty, acknowledged even by those who feel he has let them down.

Perhaps more important, the Cárdenas name endowed the movement with some of the traditional authority of revolutionary symbols by identifying Cuauhtémoc with his father, one of the most beloved icons of the Mexican Revolution.[18] Though this is more specific to the Mexican case, a similar dynamic may operate for at least some new parties that appeal to traditional symbols. Letters written to Cuauhtémoc Cárdenas by ordinary citizens frequently mention Lázaro Cárdenas, his accomplishments for the people of Mexico, and what they personally owe to him—usually a bit of land, an education, a well. As the only son of such

16. Quoted in Angelo Panebianco, *Political Parties: Organization and Power*, trans. Marc Silver (New York: Cambridge University Press, 1988), 52; following Robert C. Tucker, "The Theory of Charismatic Leadership," in *Philosophers and Kings: Studies in Leadership*, ed. Dankwart Rustow (New York: George Braziller, 1970), 80–81.
17. Personal observations of Cárdenas in July 1989 and May 1991.
18. As recently as 1992, 29 percent of Mexicans polled—and only in urban areas— declared that Lázaro Cárdenas was the best president Mexico ever had. See "Instantaneas," *Este País*, no. 21 (December 1992): 38.

a father, Cuauhtémoc inherited this quasireligious devotion. Many of these letters are now collected in a volume edited by Adolfo Gilly. Analyzing their significance, Gilly writes: " 'They say that a son of the General is running. . . . we must support him,' said the peasants of Zacatecas. . . . In that sentence, I believe, is the key, . . . the myth of the son that returns to vindicate the betrayed father, the utopia of those who waited for the father who never returned and who now follow the son to avenge and erase the grievances received since then.'"[19] These remarkable letters, many infused with language more characteristic of texts referring to Christ than to a politician, reflect the transference of a powerful emotional loyalty from Lázaro to Cuauhtémoc Cárdenas:[20]

> Dear Cuauhtémoc Cárdenas Solorsano: your dad was our "tata" [a Spanish word meaning beloved uncle, close to "daddy"] and so we still feel, because he is not dead, he sends you to see how we his children are, so you can see if his commands are being fulfilled.

> We the peasants believe in you, because Tata Lázaro . . . came through for the good of all Mexicans.

> We have many people thanks to God and to your dear father General Lázaro Cárdenas who sowed the good seed to harvest the good crop.

> We want you to be like your dear father whom no one could defeat.

> All the peasants remember the name of General Lázaro Cárdenas because when he was president even the birds sang happily. As children we heard our parents say he should be president twenty more years. Because at that time, sir, it seemed that Jesus Christ walked on the earth.

> We are with Cuauhtémoc Cárdenas because we know that his ideals reflect his father.

19. Adolfo Gilly, ed., *Cartas a Cuauhtémoc Cárdenas* (Mexico City: Ediciones Era, 1989), 38.
20. Ibid., 47, 49–51.

May the spirit of your father be with you.

Or, playing on both Christian and pagan symbols (specifically the image of an eagle devouring a serpent, the mythical sign for the Aztecs to settle in the valley of Mexico):

> Our ancestors had courage like the eagle-man that [our national shield] symbolizes, not to mention the courage and power that my Lord Jesus Christ showed defeating and devouring the author of evil: the ancient serpent. May God be with you, Señor Ingeniero Cuauhtémoc Cárdenas.

In light of frequent criticism that the FDN had no political program it is important to stress that while the FDN may not have elaborated concrete alternative proposals, it had a basic ideological identity that drew on popular myths and symbols. Social movement theorists suggest that such symbolic identities motivate much social movement participation. "Collective action frames," for example, provide an "interpretive schemata that simplifies and condenses the 'world out there' "; they diagnose and prescribe remedies, and they "decode and 'package' in Gamson's terms . . . slices of observed and experienced reality."[21] A collective action frame "strikes a responsive chord in that it rings true with extant beliefs, myths, folktales, and the like. When that is the case, we suspect the frame is also considerably more potent."[22] Thus, movement organizers draw ideological symbols from underlying values, shape and apply them to interpret contemporary problems, and use them to mobilize support. In the *cardenista* case this identity involved reference to traditional symbols and discourses of the Mexican Revolution and the Aztec heritage, carried in large part by Cuauhtémoc Cárdenas. No other actual or potential opposition candidate could have drawn upon the legitimacy of these symbols in quite the same way. Cárdenas did well in areas where Lázaro Cárdenas had a strong historical influ-

21. David Snow and Robert Benford, "Master Frames and Cycles of Protest," in *Frontiers in Social Movement Theory*, ed. Aldon Morris and Carol McClurg Mueller (New Haven: Yale University Press, 1992), 137–38. There is a rich and varied literature on the construction of identity and its role in social movement formation, which cannot be adequately dealt with here. For representative analyses see *Frontiers in Social Movement Theory*, especially the chapters by Bert Klandermans, David Snow and Robert Benford, Debra Friedman and Doug McAdam, and Sidney Tarrow; also see Bert Klandermans, Hanspeter Kriesi, and Sidney Tarrow, *From Structure to Action: Comparing Movement Participation Across Cultures* (Greenwich, Conn.: JAI Press, 1988), vol. 1.
22. Snow and Benford, "Master Frames and Cycles of Protest," 141.

ence. In addition, the FDN consciously identified its political project
with the traditions of the Mexican Revolution, pointing out that:

> During the last five years the country has suffered the conse-
> quences of serious deviations from the revolutionary process re-
> sulting from the abandonment of the constitutional project by
> the governing class. . . . the parties and political, patriotic, and
> progressive organizations that sign the present document have
> decided to form a great National Democratic Front . . . to sup-
> port the candidacy of Cuauhtémoc Cárdenas, . . . a front that
> will become a bulwark against the advance of the reactionary
> sectors.[23]

The postelection struggle to form a new political party also identified it
clearly as "the party of democracy, of constitutionality, of the Mexican
Revolution."[24]

The very vagueness of the *cardenista* program beyond this basic identity probably helped Cárdenas attract a wide spectrum of protest voters.
All could agree that the PRI had led them into economic disaster, while
the alternate FDN program provided few solutions specific enough to
cause disagreement. What the FDN did was provide an interpretation
of the crisis based on the familiar discourse of traditional revolutionary
nationalism, focusing on goals and concerns (like social justice and democracy) that resonated with the goals and concerns of many protesters
in 1988. Thus, protest is not necessarily nonideological. In this sense
the Cárdenas vote was not a pure punishment vote but represented support for action on specific issues raised by the FDN, and salient to Mexican voters in 1988, including debt, decline in living standards, and the
corrupt authoritarianism of the PRI. At the same time, the *cardenista*
rhetoric and name evoked traditional commitment of the Mexican Revolution to social equity in a particularly timely way. Cárdenas was ideally
suited to capturing protest that focused precisely on the PRI's lack of
attention to popular needs.

Because of his ability to attract this ideological vote, strategic voters
who did not necessarily like Cárdenas or trust his movement came to
believe that he represented the strongest electoral threat to the PRI.
Not all Cárdenas voters expected or wanted Cárdenas to win, take office,
and implement his programs. Even if—perhaps especially if—a strategic

23. Partido Popular Socialista (PPS), *Plataforma común del Frente Democrático Nacional* (Mexico City: PPS, 1988), 5, 7.
24. Partido de la Revolución Democrática (PRD), *Documentos básicos: Anteproyectos*
(Mexico City: PRD, 1989), 3.

voter expected Salinas to win, he or she might try to limit Salinas's ability to implement undiluted austerity by threatening him with a strong vote for the candidate most opposed to austerity and presenting him with a Congress containing more antiausterity opposition congressmen. A pure strategic voter would take this principle to an extreme, voting for whichever non-PRI candidate seemed likely to get the most votes.

The ideological orientation of the FDN helped make Cárdenas the "most likely winner" for such strategic voters. In particular, his ability to mobilize crowds—attracted by Cárdenas and his ideological identification with popular struggles—helped the FDN overcome initial marginalization, convinced many that Cárdenas was likely to punish the PRI more severely than the alternative opposition candidates (Manuel Clouthier of the PAN, Rosario Ibarra of the PRT, Heberto Castillo of the PMS, and Gumersindo Maganda of the PDM [Partido Demócrata Mexicano]), and attract most of the available protest vote.

The Cárdenas campaign began slowly. Early trips to the north of Mexico attracted pitifully small crowds. The unallied left parties attacked the Cárdenas candidacy, calling it a government ploy "to undermine the more independent presidential candidates—in this case those of the PMS, the PRT, and the PAN."[25] PMS candidate Heberto Castillo challenged Cárdenas to explain his absence during critical moments for progressive causes in Mexico—the López Portillo decision to borrow heavily, the 1968 massacre of student protesters, and so forth.[26] According to a December 1987 poll, 29.6 percent of Mexicans supported Salinas, and only 5.6 percent supported Cárdenas.[27] However, 46.9 percent had no preferred candidate. The race was wide open, and the protest vote was up for grabs.

Over the next six months a series of important rallies held mainly in traditional *cardenista* strongholds mobilized unexpectedly large crowds, attracted media attention to his candidacy, and created an impression among uncommitted voters that Cárdenas was rising on a wave of popular support. The first such mobilization took place in the La Laguna region of central Mexico. During the presidency of Lázaro Cárdenas, peasants in this region organized against local landowners and were rewarded by special attention to La Laguna in the agrarian reform of

25. Azucena Valderrábano, "Heberto acusa a funcionarios de ayudar a Cárdenas," *La Jornada* (Mexico City), 27 January 1988: 32, 10.

26. Alejandro Caballero, "Arremete Heberto contra Cuauhtémoc, Porfirio, e Ifigenia," *La Jornada* (Mexico City), 7 January 1988: 32, 10.

27. René Delgado, "Simpatías y votación," *La Jornada: Perfíl* (Mexico City), 23 May 1988: 1.

Cárdenas, who expropriated many local haciendas and created *ejidos* (collectively owned farms) from hacienda lands. As a result, La Laguna has long been a *cardenista* bastion. Campaigning PRI candidate Carlos Salinas reached La Laguna on February 10, 1988. The Laguneros received Salinas with insults, stones, orange peels, and shouts of "Cárdenas! Cárdenas!" The next day, in a dramatic and politically effective contrast, the Laguneros greeted Cárdenas with a spontaneous outpouring of affection and a series of only partly planned rallies that attracted a total of perhaps one hundred thousand people. Neither radio nor television covered this event, but sympathetic journalists interpreted the reception as a reflection that "the General [Lázaro Cárdenas] came back no more, but now, in the most difficult moment of the crisis, his son has come."[28] Shortly afterward, a new poll reported that support for Cárdenas had jumped to 24 percent, second only to Salinas. If the votes of the PMS and PRT were added to the votes for Cárdenas, the article said, Cárdenas would win the presidential election.[29]

A second landmark mobilization occurred on March 18, 1988, the fiftieth anniversary of the oil expropriation by Lázaro Cárdenas. Refusing to attend the official celebration, Cuauhtémoc Cárdenas held one of his own, which reportedly drew some seventy thousand people to the Zócalo in Mexico City. The liveliness and spontaneity of the Cárdenas rally contrasted with the official rally, presided over by a tense President Miguel De la Madrid who seemed unwilling even to mention the name of the Expropriator. Again, Cárdenas invoked the *cardenista* heritage, and particularly its principle of Mexican ownership of vital national resources. He contrasted the still immensely popular expropriation with the "antipopular" policies of the PRI. Thus, where Lázaro Cárdenas

> confided in the support of the petroleum workers and technicians . . . in their capacity to keep the industry running . . . [and] always counted on the people, . . . the current government has been ceding the faculties of command to oligarchic forces and foreign powers. . . . the petroleum reserves have been used to guarantee an important part of the country's foreign debt, and the exportation of crude oil has become the main source of funds for the public sector, which uses them to cover commitments to

28. Hermenegildo Castro and Adolfo Gilly, "Los laguneros se volcaron para recibir a Cuauhtémoc Cárdenas," *La Jornada* (Mexico City), 12 February 1988: 40; 11.
29. "Juntos, FDN, PMS y PRT ganarían las elecciones," *La Jornada* (Mexico City), 15 February 1988: 40; 11, 12.

pay the debt. The people did not fight for expropriation to this end.[30]

A meeting in Apatzingán, Michoacán, on May 21 to celebrate the birthday of Lázaro Cárdenas began another series of important mobilizations in the home state of the Cárdenas family, rallies that drew the largest crowds yet.

Yet perhaps the most important rallies took place in Mexico City, where Cárdenas won more than a third of his total vote:[31] the first on the campus of the national university and the second in the Zócalo, the main plaza. The first rally clearly showed leaders of the Mexican Socialist Party, still reluctant to join the FDN, that the party had to throw its support behind Cárdenas or risk losing its constituency. On May 11, 1988, student groups issued a formal invitation to Cárdenas to speak on the campus.[32] On May 26 Cárdenas spoke at UNAM to a large and enthusiastic crowd. The response of the students strongly suggested they would vote for him in July; by a show of hands they "voted" in favor of a unified (Cárdenas) candidacy. Yet every left party from the Communist Party on had consistently won supporters and recruited much of its leadership from the national university. They depended heavily on this base, and usually considered the UNAM a safe constituency. When even the students seemed to desert PMS candidate Heberto Castillo, he decided to climb on the Cárdenas bandwagon. Two days after the UNAM rally Castillo told the press that he might withdraw his candidacy at the June Congress of the PMS. On June 3 Castillo offered to resign if Cárdenas would agree to a common program and some specific political commitments. Cárdenas accepted immediately, and the two leaders signed a pact four days later. PMS leaders say they continued supporting Castillo after the formation of the FDN, conscious that

30. Maldonado, *Origenes del Partido de la Revolución Democrática*, 141–43.

31. In the Federal District alone Cárdenas picked up 24 percent of his total vote, not counting the votes of residents of surrounding suburbs in the state of Mexico. Cárdenas got 44 percent of his votes from the state of Mexico and the Federal District. An estimate of over one-third of his vote from the populated area around Mexico City is more than reasonable. See González Graf, ed., *Las elecciones de 1988 y la crisis del sistema político*, 339.

32. These groups were the MAS (an excision from the PRT), the CEU (the student leadership of UNAM), and the STUNAM (the UNAM employee union). The invitation was preceded by considerable debate about giving candidates a forum in a university supposed to be above politics. Even the president of one of the parties backing Cárdenas (PFCRN) publicly asked him to decline, citing concern that the rally might provoke a confrontation. See Maldonado, *Origenes del Partido de la Revolución Democrática*, 155–56.

"the course of the campaign itself would tell us what to do."[33] Says Heberto Castillo:

> The tactic was simple. [Cárdenas] was gathering together one [group of] people, and my role was to unite all the people of the left. So, I will get them together and we will see how things go. . . . I saw the masses that we were mobilizing [and those he mobilized] and it was simple. The PPS, the PARM, and the Partido Frente Cardenista are never going to support me. Fine. And they *will* support Cuauhtémoc. The PMS supports me, and the PMS will also support Cuauhtémoc. So I just resigned, we joined forces, and achieved the [maximum] sum.[34]

Cynics might have found it even more simple: the PMS faced the desertion of its crucial, traditional base. They had to follow it.

Cárdenas's last important preelection mobilization took place a few days before the election, to close his campaign in Mexico City. No opposition candidate and few PRI candidates had filled the Zócalo before, but on June 25 Cárdenas did. Panoramic pictures of the Zócalo rally appeared the next day in national newspapers, giving the Cárdenas campaign an image of immense popularity right before election day, and perhaps influencing voters to believe in the chance of a Cárdenas victory.

Like popular mobilizations, electoral polls contributed to uncertainty and affected strategic voters. Newspapers published an unusually high number of electoral polls in 1988. Polls varied considerably, sometimes hinting that Cárdenas could win, sometimes that he would lose badly, but almost always putting him ahead of PAN candidate Manuel Clouthier, especially in key areas like Mexico City. Analysts usually dismiss the impact of polls as "almost nothing, because of the recent nature of the phenomenon . . . [F]ew people follow the results of these studies, and the people that do are the most politicized, whose decisions are more difficult to influence."[35] It seems logical that most people would ignore polls given the wide variation in results. Three national polls in June 1988 predicted that Salinas would get 43.6 percent, 61.4 percent, and 38 percent of the vote.[36]

33. Arnoldo Martínez Verdugo, interview by author, Mexico City, 23 April 1991.
34. Heberto Castillo, interview by author, Mexico City, 22 August 1991.
35. Irma Campuzano Montoya, "Una novedad: Las encuestas pre-electorales," in *Las elecciones de 1988 y la crisis del sistema político*, ed. Jaime González Graf (Mexico City: Editorial Diana, 1989), 102.
36. Ibid., 99.

However, this analysis misses a significant point: before 1988 Mexicans were not used to *any* uncertainty about election results. Precisely because of their fluctuations, polls created unprecedented uncertainty over the outcome of the presidential election. This prepared people to believe that a vote for Cárdenas might not be wasted. Furthermore, by revealing the novelty of a strong left candidate, polls directed attention toward Cárdenas and away from alternative opposition candidates, above all in the crucial Mexico City area. April polls in Mexico City showed Cárdenas with 26.3 percent of the vote, compared to 9.9 percent for PAN candidate Manuel Clouthier, but after the May 26 speech at UNAM support increased to 32–38 percent in favor of Cárdenas, compared to 12–23 percent for Clouthier.[37] Thus, the urban population most exposed to polls and considering how to use its protest vote might naturally have believed that Cárdenas had the best chance of defeating the PRI, or at least inflicting a severe blow.

The Voting Base of the FDN

Although "protest" responded to both the ideological and strategic appeal of the Cárdenas campaign, the FDN drew fundamentally on anti-PRI protest voters. Cárdenas votes clearly came at the expense of the PRI. At the state level of analysis the Cárdenas vote and the Salinas vote have a statistically significant (at .001) bivariate relationship ($r = -.78$). Where Cárdenas did well, the PRI did badly, and vice versa. Cárdenas did best in the center region where approval of the government and PRI loyalties dropped most (see Tables 4.1 and 4.2). Overall, he won about 21 percent more votes than the independent left and the parastatals averaged after the electoral reform of 1977, almost exactly the amount the PRI lost. Congressional vote behaved similarly. While the PRI congressional vote dropped by 16.4 percent, the congressional vote of the FDN parties increased by 19.7 percent.[38]

Statistical models of the FDN vote find less consistently significant relationships to socioeconomic structure than models of the PAN and PRI vote. The PRI vote comes disproportionately from marginalized, rural states with low levels of literacy. The PAN vote is a mirror image, associated with the most urban, industrialized areas. At the state level of aggregation, FDN vote bears no significant relationship to any of

37. Ibid., 100.
38. Instituto Federal Electoral (IFE), *Contienda electoral en las elecciones de diputados federales*. ed. Jenny Saltiel Cohen (Mexico City: IFE, 1991). PAN vote increased 1.1 percent over its 1982 presidential vote; congressional vote grew .5 percent.

these variables, whether the official vote or the unofficial FDN estimate of its vote is used.[39] At the level of the federal district Joseph Klesner (1995) finds significantly higher support for Cárdenas in less industrialized, less urbanized areas, with lower participation and higher literacy.[40] The signs of the association with industrialization and urbanization are the same as those in PRI models; the sign of literacy and participation is reversed. While difficult to interpret, this result could suggest that support for Cárdenas looked a lot like support for the PRI because it was taken from the PRI, but was higher in areas with relatively higher literacy once the effect of these factors was accounted for. Thus, the postelectoral diagnosis that "the terrible paradox of the current situation is that Carlos Salinas has the social base—rural and backward—of the project of Cuauhtémoc Cárdenas and Cárdenas has the social base—urban and modern—of the project of Salinas" gets it only half right.[41] The PRI vote is related to rural economy, a common phenomenon in the case of parties with a history of agrarian reform, but the Cárdenas vote was not strongly related to urbanization. Despite the appearance created by his strong showing in Mexico City, Cárdenas lost in other cities and won many votes in rural states like Michoacán and Morelos.[42]

However, by 1988 socioeconomic characteristics do not hold up well

39. See Appendix C.

40. In models based on congressional vote of the independent left parties Klesner finds few if any significant variables, perhaps because he seems to have counted only the PMS and PRT congressional vote. The PMS got fewer votes than any other FDN party; the PRT did not support Cárdenas. See Joseph Klesner, "Modernization, Economic Crisis, and Electoral Alignment in Mexico," *Mexican Studies* 9, no. 2 (Summer 1993), especially pp. 200, 203, 206; and Joseph Klesner, "Realignment or Dealignment? Consequences of Economic Crisis and Restructuring for the Mexican Party System," in *The Politics of Economic Restructuring*, ed. Maria Cook, Kevin Middlebrook, and Juan Molinar Horcasitas (La Jolla, Calif.: UCSD Center for U.S.-Mexican Studies, 1994. His 1995 analysis, in contrast, looks at the 1988 vote for Cárdenas in a model that also included four dummy variables for regional location. The larger number of observations (using three hundred electoral districts) may help explain the significance of variables. See Joseph Klesner, "The 1994 Mexican Elections: Manifestation of a Divided Society?" *Mexican Studies* 11, no. 1 (Winter 1995): 144.

41. Jorge Castañeda, "La manera como el PRI conservó el poder puede impedir que lo use como quisiera," *Proceso*, no. 617 (29 August 1988): 11.

42. Nor can one assume that "groups who opposed the economic reforms [by voting for Cárdenas] were often those who stand to benefit most from economic liberalization and vice versa." See Luis Rubio and Roberto Blum, "Recent Scholarship on the Mexican Political and Economic System," *Latin American Research Review* 25, no. 1 (1990): 190. The urban marginalized population that supported Cárdenas in order to protest insecurity, inflation, and deteriorating standards of living might experience relative deprivation under free trade if unqualified for industrial jobs, if growth failed to create sufficient new employment, or if cheap imported consumer goods drove out small business and artisanry.

at the individual level. In Jorge Domínguez and James McCann's sophisticated analysis, based on perhaps the best data sample available (two national polls taken in May 1988 and July 1991), only professional class and church attendance are identified as significant socioeconomic predictors (at .01) of the 1988 Cárdenas vote—both in a negative direction. Instead, Domínguez and McCann found that "the question of the ruling party's future was the central decision facing each voter. First and foremost the voter asked, 'Am I for or against the PRI and the president?' "[43] Thus, the 1988 Cárdenas voter was significantly more likely to perceive that the PRI was weakening, that the president had performed badly, and that the national economy would improve if another party won the election. These calculations even outweighed evaluations of the voter's personal financial situation, as well as specific issue preferences like the need to limit imports, pay foreign debts, control foreign investment, and so forth, though Domínguez and McCann do find a slight association between support for state-owned industries and support for Cárdenas in 1988. On this basis they propose a "two-step model" of Mexican voting, in which voters with "right-wing dispositions" chose the PAN once they decided that the PRI and the president were weakening, while voters with "left-wing dispositions" chose Cárdenas.[44]

Nevertheless, the strategic similarities between the PAN voter and the Cárdenas voter are striking. Voters for both parties were likely to perceive the PRI as weakening, to think the economy would benefit from another party in charge, and to disapprove of the president. This similarity probably made it easy for some voters to switch back and forth between opposition parties. It is telling that in 1988 a personal history of voting for the PAN was significantly and positively related not only to 1988 PAN support but also to support for Cárdenas.[45] The association had vanished by 1991. As Chapter 7 argues, the heavily strategic basis for the *cardenista* vote support made it much more difficult for the PRD to consolidate a loyal voter base.

The Weakness of the FDN

The presidential campaign of Cuauhtémoc Cárdenas succeeded beyond the wildest dreams of all but its most optimistic organizers, attracting

43. Jorge Domínguez and James McCann, "Shaping Mexico's Electoral Arena: The Construction of Partisan Cleavages in the 1988 and 1991 National Elections," *American Political Science Review* 89 (March 1995): 41.

44. Ibid., 44.

45. Ibid., 42.

massive popular support. However, its strength was deceptive. The political coalition that functioned well as a mobilizational tool contained fatal flaws that hindered its performance of consolidation tasks. To begin with, the FDN's organizational weakness and its character as a coalition of parties would come back to haunt it. Twelve separate organizations signed the *Common Platform of the National Democratic Front* on January 12, 1988: three political parties with legal registry, five parties without legal registry, and four popular/civic movements.[46] Even in 1988 organizational problems made the campaign difficult to manage. The multiplicity of organizations demanding to schedule events made Cárdenas and his team struggle to keep the campaign from flying in twelve different directions. No component of the FDN provided a strong enough organization to dominate the campaign.

In addition to the logistical difficulties of coordinating dozens of separate political groups, Cárdenas had to cope with the FDN's internal conflicts, which often obstructed the conduct of the campaign. The popular organizations had a long history of mistrusting political parties, particularly parties like those initially involved in the FDN, who had "sold out" to the PRI. The political parties did not get along either. In the FDN, old political enemies suddenly found themselves working on the same side. They resisted cooperation with people they did not trust. Enemies accused each other of infiltrating the FDN to work for the PRI, sabotaging FDN events, and passing information. Naturally, this did not improve communication.

Initially, however, the massive and largely spontaneous participation of millions of Mexicans made up to a great extent for the organizational failings of the FDN. Though the FDN was, as one of its leaders put it, "a semianarchic movement," it was a *large* semianarchic movement.[47] The mobilization of ordinary Mexicans surpassed and made irrelevant the weak organization of the FDN component parties, but such a level of mobilization is fundamentally limited to short periods of time. Therefore, it could not continue to compensate for weak organization in a *cardenista* party. Organization may not be strictly necessary for first-election success if mobilization conditions hold, but it becomes increasingly relevant to consolidation over time.

As a result, the organizational incoherence and internal contradictions of the FDN crippled it whenever the relevant time frame shifted from the short term to the long term and when goals shifted from the limited goal of supporting Cárdenas to the broader goal of consolidating

---

46. PPS, *Plataforma común del Frente Democrático Nacional*.
47. Confidential interview AZ, August 1991.

gains. For example, if the component organizations of the FDN had planned for the long term from the beginning, they might have made different choices about congressional candidacies that would have eased consolidation considerably and made it easier for the FDN to defend the 1988 vote. The FDN parties united only around the presidential contest—to elect Cárdenas, but more immediately to enhance their own vote by riding his coattails. Despite five months of negotiations over common candidates, the FDN only registered 70 common candidacies, for 300 plurality congressional seats, 200 proportional representation congressional seats, and 64 senatorial spots.[48] The obsession with enhancing party congressional vote reflects underlying conflicts of interest in the FDN as well as lack of commitment to and faith in the success of Cárdenas. If the FDN parties had believed Cárdenas would win a majority in many districts, they might have sought more common candidacies. Separate candidacies split the vote, even if Cárdenas won a majority in the district. Though fewer in number overall, their candidates under a unified candidacy plan would have had a better chance of winning. In fact, *cardenista* candidates won majority seats in only twenty districts in 1988, and fifteen of those were unified candidacies.[49] At the time critics protested that the inability to reach agreement on common candidates "testifies to the limitations of the Front. . . . [Primarily,] the National Democratic Front will serve to inject life into parties that only a few months ago . . . had few possibilities. . . . [There is no] clear course offering continuity after July 6."[50]

But injecting life into existing parties was precisely the point of supporting Cárdenas. Instead of adopting strategies that would commit them to share a common fate, the FDN parties tried to enhance their party vote in order to get a larger share of proportional representation (party list) seats in Congress. They named separate candidates in order to keep support for Cárdenas associated with their party's name.[51] This also affected the campaign. Individual parties worried about their share of the Cárdenas vote engaged in jealous rivalries over campaign schedul-

48. José Woldenberg, "FDN: Después de las elecciones, ¿qué?" *La Jornada* (Mexico City), 10 April 1988: 7.

49. Arturo Sánchez Gómez, "La contienda electoral," in *Las elecciones de 1988 y la crisis del sistema político*, ed. Jaime González Graf (Mexico City: Editorial Diana, 1989), 119.

50. Woldenberg, "FDN: Después de las elecciones, ¿qué?"

51. Congressional and presidential ballots came separately, and listed the FDN parties separately. On the presidential ballot a vote for any FDN party counted for Cárdenas, but parties believed voters were likely to vote for the same party on all ballots (which proved largely true), and therefore cared how voters expressed their preference.

ing. The presidential ballot—listing individual parties rather than an "FDN"—created some voter confusion over how to vote for Cárdenas. Individual parties could take advantage of this confusion to try to convince voters that support for Cárdenas implied support for a particular party. Events planned by only one party associated it with Cárdenas. Events planned jointly gave publicity to all of them. This incentive structure did not encourage cooperation.

From the point of view of consolidation the lack of unified candidacies hurt the FDN badly in 1988. Many majority seats went to the PRI in districts that Cárdenas won, simply because several candidates split the FDN vote. In part on the basis of these majority districts the PRI got a majority in the Electoral College to approve Salinas's election. The problem also reduced the influence of the *cardenistas* in Congress. The FDN's inability to reach agreement on common candidacies most adversely affected the Corriente Democrática, which could not get proportional representation seats without the cooperation of a party putting CD candidates on their party list. The resulting division of seats in the Congress gave the PRD a smaller contingent once the PARM, PPS, and PFCRN dropped out of the FDN and took their representatives with them.

In addition to organizational weakness and internal conflicts of interest, the FDN suffered from a major resource imbalance compared to its principal rivals, especially the PRI, although again the FDN's initial ability to rely on factors like surprise and mobilization compensated to some extent for this weakness. The FDN had serious financial problems. Though all the registered FDN parties got a government subsidy from which they contributed to the Cárdenas campaign, official subsidies reflect the percentage of the vote won by a party in previous elections. The FDN parties, as small parties, got small subsidies. One newspaper account claimed that in the last months of the campaign the three parties invested ten million pesos per month each in the campaign, a total of about $15,000 per month.[52] The FDN could not pay for much advertising. Free news coverage was in short supply. The government-controlled media relegated opposition parties to marginality, including the Cárdenas campaign. In the last trimester of 1987 the most-watched television news program (*24 Horas*) dedicated 113 minutes to the campaign of the PRI, 3 minutes to the PAN, and slightly less than 4 minutes to the FDN. The main news program of the other large television network

52. Alejandro Caballero, "10 millones de pesos mensuales aportó a su campaña cada partido del FDN," *La Jornada* (Mexico City), 2 July 1988: 11. The PMS was not counted, as it joined the campaign late.

Imevisión dedicated 258 minutes to the PRI between October and December 1987, 40 seconds to the PAN, and nothing to the FDN.[53] Printed media provided more balanced information. Table 4.3 shows the percentage of total coverage devoted to the different campaigns, based on a survey of three major national newspapers for the week of February 4–10, 1988. The PRT and PDM, marginal parties with less than 1.5 percent of the vote in most elections, are included to show how the press minimized the importance of major oppositions like the PAN and the FDN by equating them in terms of coverage with virtually irrelevant parties.

The FDN's third major flaw was its exposure to intense hostility from the PRI, related to its ideological position and its ability to threaten the PRI's voting base. Especially after 1988 the FDN was condemned by its own success. As his campaign attracted more public support and attention, intimidation and repression against the FDN mounted. Its offices were watched and its candidates followed. *Cardenistas* and FDN organizers began to receive death threats and face actual violence. The FDN reported that in mid-May one of its candidates had been kidnapped, questioned, and tortured, and that a violent encounter in Hidalgo between an FDN party and the PRI resulted in four dead and five wounded.[54] The most chilling event took place only four days before the July 6 election, when unknown assailants murdered Francisco Javier Ovando and Román Gil Heraldez, two top campaign organizers. Ovando was in charge of FDN arrangements to watch the polls and collect information about voting results on election night; Gil was his assistant. Their deaths were widely viewed as a warning to the FDN, particularly since the killers left the bodies where they would soon be found. As the FDN moved into the consolidation arena, where the PRI could more effectively structure opportunities for the opposition, PRI hostility toward the *cardenistas* would become increasingly important.

Table 4.3. Media coverage of presidential campaigns

	PRI	PAN	FDN	PRT	PDM
El Universal	46.4%	12.5%	11.4%	13.5%	7.3%
Excelsior	52.0	5.5	14.0	12.2	7.3
La Jornada	40.9	19.8	14.0	5.0	8.2

SOURCE: Raúl Trejo Delarbe, "Prensa y televisión en las campañas," *La Jornada* (Mexico City), 6 March 1988, sec. "semanal," pp. 14–15.

53. Raúl Trejo Delarbe, "Prensa y televisión en las campañas," *La Jornada* (Mexico City), 6 March 1988, sec. "semanal," 14–15.
54. Maldonado, *Origenes del Partido de la Revolución Democrática*, 158.

LOSING THE ADVANTAGES OF EMERGENCE: EARLY CONSOLIDATION TASKS

In order to consolidate its gains the *cardenista* coalition first had to try to hang onto its 1988 vote. The emergence strengths that compensated for the FDN's weaknesses and carried it through its first election did not equip it to perform this consolidation task. In trying to fight electoral fraud the FDN operated in an institutional arena dominated by the PRI rather than a plaza to which Cárdenas could attract voters. It had to cooperate like a political party with internal discipline instead of a loose, flexible campaign committee. The ideological position that helped it attract votes also hampered the construction of a common opposition strategy in alliance with the conservative PAN. Indeed, the *cardenistas*' antineoliberalism and their very success in mounting a threat only made the PRI more stubbornly determined not to make concessions to what it saw as a dangerous movement. Government hostility also made the Cárdenas alliance a less attractive proposition, and the nervous parastatals began to abandon Cárdenas as soon he could no longer help them get votes and seats. Surprise could not help the coalition in this situation, nor charisma. The *cardenistas* even forswore the potentially useful tool of popular mobilization. Though they could mobilize for the purpose of getting attention and publicity, leaders worried that they had no adequate institutional mechanisms of control to turn mobilization on only when needed to put pressure on the government and turn it off when negotiations were advancing. All of these changes contributed to their inability to defend their version of electoral results, and ultimately to the breakup of the FDN.

Nearly all observers agree that fraud marred the July 6 presidential election. Although it is impossible to prove that fraud changed the outcome, the evidence clearly shows that substantial electoral fraud benefited Salinas and that Cárdenas was the chief victim. To begin with, the electoral registry was inaccurate. A 1988 study by UNAM found that 23 percent of the voter registry in Mexico City listed wrong or outdated information.[55] A similar study by a northern newspaper found discrepancies in 36 percent and 49 percent of the voter registry in two Monterrey districts.[56] Altered voter registry lists could indicate a potential for

---

55. Andrew Reding, "Mexico at a Crossroads: The 1988 Election and Beyond," *World Policy Journal* 5 (Fall 1988): 622.
56. Ibid.

fraud, given that the PRI controlled the elaboration of the list and could eliminate opposition voters and/or add "phantom" voters to pad the PRI vote if needed.

Second, on election day opposition parties reported incidents of armed robbery of ballot boxes on their way to district counting centers. The ballot boxes would later arrive at the district with packets that did not match the original counts recorded by opposition representatives in the polling station. After the election thousands of partly burned ballots, many marked in favor of Cárdenas, appeared along rivers and in alleys.[57] PAN delegates at the final *Informe* of President Miguel De la Madrid in September 1988 would hold up some of these ballots in silent protest. The opposition also reported "flying voter brigades," which they accused of voting more than once. It seemed as though the PRI machine had met the expectations of CTM leader Fidel Velázquez, who announced less than a week before the election that 120 percent of his union members would vote for the PRI.[58]

A suspicious "computer crash" on July 6 heightened the fears raised by these observations. The government had installed a new computer system to tabulate the vote and speed up the national count enough to deliver preliminary results the same night. Yet on the evening of July 6 the government suddenly announced that it could not deliver results as promised because its brand-new system had "crashed." The opposition immediately accused the government of deliberately shutting down the computers after seeing the first polling results, which probably would have come from Mexico City, where Salinas took a severe beating—in order to give itself time to "fix" the results. At least two high-level PRI insiders admitted in interviews that the crash was deliberate.[59] Regardless of the reason, the "agonizing six-day delay in reporting even preliminary presidential election results for a majority of the country's polling places—which election officials blamed, at various times, on computer

57. For accounts see ibid., 622, 624; Miguel Ángel Rivera, "Silencio del PRI y gritos de la oposición ante la evidencia," *La Jornada* (Mexico City), 27 August 1988: 1, 15; Wayne Cornelius, Judith Gentleman, and Peter Smith, "Overview: The Dynamics of Political Change in Mexico," in *Mexico's Alternative Political Futures*, ed. Wayne Cornelius, Judith Gentleman, and Peter Smith (La Jolla, Calif.: UCSD Center for U.S.-Mexican Studies, 1989), 20.

58. Cristina Martin, "Clase política," *La Jornada* (Mexico City), 1 July 1988: 4.

59. One claimed that the decision resulted from concern that the PAN had illegally tapped into the government computer system (confidential interview H, May 1991). The other claimed that it was necessary for the government to hide the Mexico City results until other results came in, more slowly, from areas expected to be more favorable to the PRI (confidential interview, August 1995).

crashes, heavy voter turnout, and 'atmospheric conditions'—effectively destroyed the credibility" of the election result.[60]

Despite the lack of official election results from the Federal Electoral Commission, PRI president Jorge de la Vega immediately announced that Salinas had won a "decisive, legal, and incontestable" victory.[61] This further antagonized the opposition. As the PAN, FDN, and PRT opposition presidential candidates agreed in their *Call to Legality* on the evening of July 6, "the premature announcement of a supposed victory of the official party under these conditions, long before the process of counting and ratifying the vote results has been completed, reaffirms our suspicions that a fraud of gigantic proportions is taking shape which would distort the sense of the citizens' preference expressed in the polls."[62]

Official results did nothing to allay these suspicions. One problem was the curious behavior of those who did *not* vote. The overall abstention rate of about 50 percent—nearly double that of the presidential election of 1982[63]—seemed a "surprisingly low [turnout], given the intensely competitive contest in 1988, and despite a reported increase in the voter registration rate from 1982."[64] The pattern of variation in abstention compounded the problem. If higher voting costs and lower competition tend to result in less participation, one would expect lower abstention in developed urban areas and higher abstention in remote rural areas, where the difficulty of getting to the polls should have dramatically reduced participation. Mexican results revealed exactly the opposite, in a pattern of participation that favored the PRI: relatively high abstention in urban areas where the PRI did poorly, and extremely low abstention in some rural communities where the PRI got an unusually high percentage of the vote.[65] Some communities reported more

60. Cornelius, Gentleman, and Smith, "The Dynamics of Political Change in Mexico," 21.

61. González Graf, ed., *Las elecciones de 1988 y la crisis del sistema político*, 326.

62. Ibid., 324.

63. Silvia Gómez Tagle, *Las estadísticas electorales de la reforma política* (Mexico City: El Colegio de México, 1990), 19.

64. Cornelius, Gentleman, and Smith, "The Dynamics of Political Change in Mexico," 20. These authors argue that the apparent contradiction reflected fraud in previous elections to inflate rates of participation in order to increase PRI legitimacy, and that in fact the 1988 figure came closer to reality.

65. Participation varied more by community than by state. However, it is striking that overall participation rates in the heavily rural, extremely poor state of Chiapas nearly matched participation in Mexico City (55.4 percent to 57 percent). Gómez Tagle, *Las estadísticas electorales de la reforma política*, 228–29.

votes than the total number of registered voters.[66] In other heavily PRI *casillas* (polling stations), participation rates required heroic assumptions about the speed of voting. Observation of electoral procedures in 1991 (similar to 1988 but with one less ballot) suggests that a minimum of one minute and an average of a minute and a half was required to perform all the functions indicated by law—including checking the voter off the registry list, voting, and marking his finger with ink. According to official results, 432 *casillas* counted at least 1,200 votes each. Such *casillas* would have had to process a minimum of 100 voters per hour for twelve hours, or one voter every 36 seconds. One *casilla* in Pichucalco, Chiapas, even recorded a heroic 3,535 votes for the PRI, at a remarkable twelve seconds per voter.[67]

The refusal of the Mexican government to make public the vote count in 24,647 *casillas* (almost half of the total), as Mexican law required, also undermined the credibility of the elections.[68] In some districts in disputed areas like Michoacán as much as 98–99 percent of the *casilla* results remained hidden, with only global results reported. In 14 percent of the country's three hundred electoral districts the results of more than 70 percent of the *casillas* were never released.[69] In four districts (two in Puebla, one in Veracruz, one in Coahuila), PRD figures suggested that official votes for Cárdenas in released *casillas* came to more than his total official votes by 2,445 votes, 3,589 votes, 1,172 votes, and 7 votes respectively. In other cases the missing *casillas* behaved differently than released *casillas*. For instance, in Sinaloa district 3 Cárdenas got 3,051 total official votes, and 3,049 in the revealed *casillas*, leaving only 2 votes in the unrevealed 22 percent of *casillas*.[70] The government burned these hidden voting results several years after the election.

The *cardenistas* argued that the PRI inflated its vote in rural areas where the opposition could not place poll watchers in order to compensate for its decisive defeat in urban areas where opposition poll watchers prevented PRI fraud. Their analysis draws a distinction between one zone where the PRI got 96–100 percent of the vote and a second zone

66. For example see Juan Molinar Horcasitas, "Palabras pronunciadas por Juan Molinar Horcasitas," in *Las elecciones federales de 1988 en México*, ed. Juan Felipe Leal, Jacqueline Peschard, and Concepción Rivera (Mexico City: UNAM, 1988), 318–19.

67. José Barberán et al., *Radiografía del fraude: Analisis de los datos oficiales del 6 de julio* (Mexico City: Editorial Nuestro Tiempo, 1988), 80.

68. Cornelius, Gentleman, and Smith, "The Dynamics of Political Change in Mexico," 20.

69. Partido de la Revolución Democrática (PRD), *Elección presidencial* (Mexico City: PRD, 1989), mimeographed electoral results.

70. Ibid.

where the PRI lost. In 1,762 *casillas* the PRI got 100 percent of the vote, and in 5,968 *casillas*—one-fifth of the total polling places—the PRI got more than 85 percent. These *casillas* accounted for almost 40 percent of total PRI votes. There was also a strong correlation between 100 percent PRI *casillas* and those where the opposition had no poll watchers.[71] The division was not just a matter of a structural link to vote preference, with rural areas supporting the PRI and urban areas supporting the FDN and PAN. In the same city some *casillas* went 100 percent for the PRI, and in others the PRI got only 15 percent. To the *cardenistas* this proved Cárdenas won: "Mexico is not absurdly divided into neighboring but totally different communities; the only Mexico that really exists is that of the defeated PRI."[72]

Furthermore, in examining the voting results of the revealed *casillas* the *cardenistas* found an unusual pattern suggesting that the PRI inflated its vote by simply adding zeros on the end of vote counts. Assuming that the last digit of each *casilla* result should vary randomly, they expected a normal distribution of counts ending in each digit. They then examined 11,024 *casillas* in which the PRI got more than 60 percent of the vote and found that the PRI total ended in zero in 1,538, 438 more than predicted in a normal distribution. According to the *cardenistas*, the probability of this occurring naturally was "less than one in forty million trillion." In contrast, in *casillas* where the PRI got less than 60 percent, they found a statistically normal distribution of ending numbers. The *cardenistas* explain this pattern by saying that "in inventing a big number, in order to simulate the crushing victory of the PRI in a *casilla*, it more frequently occurred to them [to use] a number ending in zero than in any other digit. If the fraud had been more carefully planned, this would not have happened and the data would not betray this scar of the alteration."[73]

The Defense of the Vote: Strategies, Positions, and Alliances

At first, all the opposition parties stood together against the suspected fraud. The evening of July 6 the presidential candidates of the FDN,

71. Jorge Castañeda, "La manera como el PRI conservó el poder puede impedir que lo usc como quisiera," *Proceso*, no. 617 (29 August 1988). See also Adriana López Monjardín, "¿Derrota electoral del PRI o inconsistencia sistemática del electorado?" in *Las elecciones federales de 1988 en México*, ed. Juan Felipe Leal, Jacqueline Peschard, and Concepción Rivera (Mexico City: UNAM, 1988), 290.

72. Barberán et al., *Radiografía del fraude*, 49.

73. Ibid., 76; 71; 72–73.

PAN, and PRT went to Secretary of the Interior Manuel Bartlett (also head of the Federal Electoral Commission) with a joint petition, the *Call to Legality*, which denounced "numerous violations to constitutional legality" and the "determination of the governing group to consummate an imposition despite the popular will." The candidates emphasized that the gravity of these violations warranted annulling the election and warned that "we will not accept the results nor recognize the authorities that come out of fraud. . . . we urge the Government of the Republic to correct these deviations immediately and cause the popular will to be respected."[74]

Three days later Cárdenas raised the stakes, announcing that "the direct recovery of electoral figures [from FDN poll watchers] and, above all, information that deserves full credibility, coming from inside the government, permit us to affirm that we have won the presidential election. I give this information with a full sense of responsibility. I am conscious of its transcendence and its consequences." He also previewed tactics that would become commonplace in PRD electoral protests. First came a warning that "to persist in consummating the fraud" would make the country "ungovernable" because: "A president that takes power in such a way would lack legitimacy, moral authority before the people, and authority as well in the international arena. He would have neither credibility nor the confidence of the different economic and social sectors necessary to reorient national development."[75] Cárdenas exhorted De la Madrid and the Federal Electoral Commission to make known the true results of the election. If they did not, he would call on the FDN parties to contest the results in electoral institutions and then support peaceful mobilization. Since little could be expected from electoral courts, protest and mobilization would become more useful for making the prophecy of ungovernability come true. Perhaps most significant, he ended his statement by "confirming once more the commitment that I have made to the people, to those who gave me their vote and to the candidates of the [PAN and PRT]," that "I will not recognize authorities that might come out of electoral fraud" and that "there will be no transactions with the popular vote."[76] With this statement Cárdenas discarded as a matter of principle any negotiated settlement with the PRI that involved recognizing Salinas, and set the tone for future confrontations.

Despite his provocative claim of victory, the FDN parties stuck with

74. González Graf, ed., *Las elecciones de 1988 y la crisis del sistema político*, 323–24.
75. Maldonado, *Orígenes del Partido de la Revolución Democrática*, 201.
76. Ibid., 202.

Cárdenas, signing a Declaration for the Defense of Popular Sovereignty on July 12. The PAN, however, backed away. Joining in the FDN's denunciation of electoral fraud was one thing; confirming its electoral victory was something else again. It would mean, in the first place, an unprecedented and potentially violent conflict with the state. In the second place, if the PRI accepted defeat, the main beneficiary would be a leftist candidate whose program conflicted with much of what the PAN had defended since its foundation in opposition to the policies of the first President Cárdenas. Ideologically, most *panistas* preferred the neoliberalism of Salinas to the economic nationalism of Cárdenas. And third, successful transfer of power to a non-PRI candidate with the diverse party backing of Cárdenas promised political chaos, extreme uncertainty, capital flight, international hostility, and continued economic instability. Thus, the PAN stuck with the "Call to Legality" proposal of annulment, on the basis that fraud had so contaminated the process that no candidate had proof of victory. On July 11 Clouthier refused to confirm either claim of victory; on July 16 the PAN stayed away from the joint FDN-PRT rally that attracted more than 300,000 people to the Zócalo in Mexico City; and on July 19 Clouthier remarked in a press conference that "no one believes that [Cárdenas] won the election."[77]

The July 16 rally, one of the largest in the entire Cárdenas campaign, marked both the high point of postelection mobilization and—ironically—the beginning of the FDN's disintegration. After July 16, as election ratification got under way, Cárdenas began to lose momentum and have increasing trouble keeping his allies united behind one strategy. The FDN's internal contradictions, foreshadowed by the conflict over common candidacies, surfaced again in electoral institutions. Cárdenas brought the FDN allies together in emergence in part because he was not in a position to impose central control. This was not crucial during the campaign. Later, when the interests of the FDN allies began to diverge, the lack of a central decision-making authority left each free to go its own way. Cárdenas wanted the presidency, and he wanted to consolidate in one party the popular force that voted for him on July 6. The parastatal parties saw a Cárdenas presidency as an attractive but unlikely and not strictly necessary outcome. Of more immediate interest was the fact that the *cardenista* vote gave them more congressional seats than they could have dreamed of only a short time before. Ratification of the election would cement their claim to those seats as well as the higher state subsidies that went with a bigger share of the vote. It

77. *Las razones y las obras: Gobierno de Miguel De la Madrid* (Mexico City: Fondo de Cultura Económica, 1988), 681, 696, 699.

was clear that a serious attempt to force the PRI to accept defeat in the presidential election was risky and costly, while seeking only congressional seats promised a high probability of success, low risk, and significant profit. Thus, conflicts of interest between Cárdenas and those parties most benefited by the FDN vote intensified as the work of approving congressional majority district results began.

The price of congressional seats was implicit recognition of the electoral results. Once the FDN parties ratified the congressional election, they compromised their ability to claim that the PRI had not won the presidential election, both morally and practically. The FDN parties took what they could, but accepted that the PRI had won 52 percent of the congressional vote, giving the PRI majority control over the institution—the congress—with sole power to ratify the presidential election according to Mexican law. To some extent this outcome was implicit in the decision to participate in the legal process. Even the attempt to fight fraud through existing procedures put the FDN in an institutional environment that the PRI controlled: the Federal Electoral Commission (CFE) and the Court of Electoral Disputes.

The process of ratifying the election began with the Federal Electoral Commission, which issued *"constancias de mayoría,"* certificates confirming the election of individual congressmen in the 300 majority districts. All parties had representatives in the CFE, but the PRI controlled a majority of the commission.[78] In this stage opposition parties only got the CFE to hold back 13 *constancias de mayoría* claimed by the PRI—essentially postponing a decision on who would get the certificate. Some FDN representatives allegedly made deals to abstain on some cases, in exchange for getting other *constancias* for the opposition. However, the real fight came over proportional representation (PR) seats, awarded on the basis of the percentage of the congressional vote won by each party. Once the CFE approved the results in majority districts, this would seem easy, but the 13 held-back seats complicated matters considerably. Would the votes of those districts—officially favoring the PRI—be subtracted from the *total* vote on the basis of which the CFE assigned PR seats? If the CFE later decided to annul those districts, or award them to a different party, it should affect each party's percentage of the vote and change its share of proportional representation seats.

Furthermore, even if overall vote percentages did not change, the

78. If a party objected to the CFE's decision, it could take the case to the Court of Electoral Disputes. However, the Court of Electoral Disputes, also dominated by the PRI, dismissed 90 percent of the complaints it received in 1988. See ibid., 694-95 (the official government record of the De la Madrid administration); Cornelius, Gentleman, and Smith, "The Dynamics of Political Change in Mexico," 21.

missing 13 seats meant that the PRI and the opposition could not both sit all their representatives in the new Congress before *autocalificación* (self-qualification)—a procedure dating to Spanish colonial times by which newly elected congressmen vote to ratify their own election. With 52 percent of the official congressional vote, counting votes in the 13 missing majority districts, the PRI demanded 260 total congressmen. Since it had only 234 approved majority seats, the PRI asked for 26 PR seats—basically making up for the fact that it had lost (at least temporarily) those 13 seats. The opposition, meanwhile, had 53 approved majority seats. They wanted at least 187 PR seats to give them the 240 total congressmen to which 48 percent of the vote entitled them, and argued that they might deserve more if electoral courts later annulled PRI votes in the many disputed cases. Yet there are only 200 proportional seats, and $187 + 26 = 213$. If the PRI seated all its congressmen, they would have 260 votes against 227—a comfortable majority. If the opposition got all its representatives, the balance would be 247 (PRI) to 240. If only four *priistas* switched sides, Congress could annul the presidential election.

With control of the CFE, the PRI demanded and got all 26 representatives in a decree approved only by members of the PRI, the legislative commissioners, and the secretary of Gobernación. This required the CFE to count the votes of the missing 13 districts, and allowed the PRI to compensate for what they lost in those districts with proportional seats. Despite the still missing cases, the CFE declared its work complete on August 14, and on August 15 the Colegio Electoral met to ratify the congressional election. With a clear *priista* majority, it finally resolved the missing cases. Since the PRI insisted that its overall percentage of the vote (and hence its total share of 260 delegates) must remain unchanged, the Electoral College had to award some majority districts to the party that officially came in second.[79] The PMS and the *cardenista*

79. For example, the Colegio Electoral declared that "the results of the election are: PRI: . . . 24,000 votes; . . . PARM: . . . 9,000 votes; therefore, the election in the first district of Tamaulipas is valid and legitimate. . . . the candidates of the PARM are congressmen in this chamber." Aside from the oddity that two parties would get such round numbers of votes, this clearly violates the principle of majority election. Overall, the Colegio Electoral changed the total vote by only 4,900, despite a number of reversals of PRI claims to victory. See Molinar Horcasitas, "Palabras pronunciadas por Juan Molinar Horcasitas," 321. Overall, 5 majority seats were awarded to the second-place party; besides Tamaulipas I, the PARM got Guerrero 7, the PFCRN got Guerrero 2, the FDN (a coalition candidate) got Veracruz 22, and the PAN got Guanajuato 8. The PRI made up for these losses in proportional representation seats awarded on the basis of its allegedly majority vote in these districts. See Silvia Gómez Tagle, *De la alquimia al fraude en las elecciones mexicanas* (Mexico City: García y Valadés Editores, 1994), 137.

representatives walked out of the Electoral College on the final day of its labors rather than collaborate in the PRI's approval of delegates. The PFCRN (Partido Frente Cardenista de Reconstrucción Nacional), the PARM, and the PPS decided to stay, arguing that if they had left, the PRI would have done what it wanted anyway.[80] The FDN parties, especially the PFCRN, also made deals with the PRI to approve *constancias* in blocks of as many as 80 at a time, in order to speed up the procedure enough to get a new Congress by September 1, the date that the law fixed for the installation of the new Congress and the date of Miguel De la Madrid's final *Informe*.

On September 8, 1988, the new Congress became the presidential Electoral College, which certifies the presidential election. Once this was in session, the opposition reversed course and tried to keep Salinas from becoming president. The same elections they had just declared valid in their own case, they now declared invalid in the case of the president. But in ratifying the Congress, they had given the PRI majority control over the constitutional tool with which to ratify the presidential election. In the final vote the PAN delegation remained in the chamber and voted against the PRI; the FDN walked out. The declaration ratifying Carlos Salinas as president-elect passed by 263 votes to 83, and was signed only by the *priista* members of Congress.[81]

Between July 16 and September 10, when the Electoral College declared Salinas president-elect, the transition to multiparty democracy stalled, though the *cardenistas* did not realize it until later. Once Salinas had a constitutional edict from the Electoral College in hand, the opposition had far less leverage. At that point preventing his inauguration would have required some forceful action to compel him to resign—an extremely difficult task short of military intervention. Salinas's position was always stronger than it looked, due to the fact that his allies dominated the state, the military, and electoral institutions. Yet the improvement in his political position between July 7 and September 10 was much greater than the change between September 10 and the actual transfer of power on December 1.

The behavior of the *cardenistas* almost unconsciously reflects this strategic shift. The greatest popular mobilizations took place before the *autocalificación* of the Congress. Indeed, once the Congress as an Electoral College had approved its own election, Cárdenas explicitly re-

80. Miguel Ángel Rivera, "Clase política," *La Jornada* (Mexico City), 30 August 1988: 4.

81. Sánchez Gómez, "La contienda electoral," 133. The additional votes came from delegates elected by the FDN who decided to convert to the PRI after the election.

nounced further mobilization "until the presidential election is ratified."[82] The *cardenistas* apparently believed at first that lack of legitimacy would force Salinas to resign, as it had pushed other bureaucratic-authoritarian governments in Latin America to hand over power to elected civilians. They did not consider the significant difference that Salinas had already purged the regime of many soft-liners. His team was confident of its policy, its ability, and of the imperative need to keep Cárdenas from returning Mexico to economic nationalism. After the Colegio Electoral declared Salinas president-elect, the FDN parties began to pay less attention to preventing him from taking office and more attention to other urgent problems: upcoming municipal elections in Veracruz, a gubernatorial race in Tabasco, and, above all, the future of the FDN.

Given the importance of this moment for the future of democracy and the *cardenista* political force in particular, many critics analyzed it in detail and accused Cárdenas of a fatal lack of vision, offering alternative scenarios in which a different strategy could have led to a more optimal outcome for Cárdenas or for democracy. In the FDN some favored defense of Cárdenas's claim to the presidency; others favored annulment; and a third group favored negotiations, using the threat of annulment or mobilization to force the PRI to make concessions. Cárdenas himself supported all three positions at one point or another. Ultimately, the FDN could not unite around a single position. Even hindsight proves less than 20–20 when applied to the postelectoral juncture. There is little agreement on what alternative futures were possible, or how a specific alternative future might have been reached. Nevertheless, an analysis of this "turning point" suggests that one reason why these alternative futures failed to materialize is precisely the shift to the consolidation moment, for which the FDN coalition was much less suited.

Strategic Choices: The "Critical Turning Point" of July 6–September 10, 1988

The debate generally focuses on three decisions which some see as mistakes that "doomed" the transition and/or the *cardenistas*: the decision to play for the presidency and the resulting failure to ally with the PAN to annul the election; the decision to defend the vote in the Electoral College; and the decision not to negotiate a political pact as the price of

82. Hermenegildo Castro and Ricardo Alemán, "No se movilizará el FDN hasta que se califique la elección presidencial," *La Jornada* (Mexico City), 7 September 1988: 1.

legitimacy. Analysis of the first decision roughly posits as its alternative annulment with new elections. The second scenario suggests that a different strategy to defend the vote might have worked better. The third scenario states that negotiation could have given Cárdenas a pact with the PRI that dramatically improved conditions for opposition competition in exchange for acceptance of a Salinas presidency.

Each of these decisions also reflects a general dilemma for any political party trying to force a transition: the question of how much to cooperate with the regime and how much potential power to exercise. The decision to fight for the presidency is a maximalist option, requiring risky strategies of mobilization and the possibility of violence. For left parties this is a particularly sensitive issue given their historical debate over the use of violence to achieve socialist transitions. The decision to seek alliance with other opposition parties to defend the principle of clean elections and work for annulment required the sacrifice of the FDN's first choice (the presidency), but not necessarily cooperation with the regime. Whether this was possible depended heavily on levels of trust and conflicts of interest among opposition forces. The decision to negotiate a political pact with the regime implied significantly more negotiation with and concessions to the regime. A common path to transition, negotiation in the Mexican case nevertheless depended significantly on the characteristics of the regime and also the ability of opposition forces to maintain unity while bargaining for the best deal.

This simplification of the debate leaves one wondering how the Cárdenas left managed to decide on a strategy that underutilized its potential power to disrupt the system without getting at least a pact or a transition in exchange for its restraint. Fundamentally, the answer has less to do with unforced errors than with the weaknesses of the FDN and the often unnoticed strengths of Salinas's position. Even if Cárdenas had succeeded in taking office, the internal weakness of the FDN would have made it extremely difficult for him to govern well enough to consolidate his movement, quite apart from the likely problems with the United States and international banks. Nevertheless, the *cardenistas'* failure to take power at their peak in 1988 left them to face consolidation as an opposition party in a system set up to prevent just that. The inauguration of Cárdenas would at least have given them a common interest in holding together, as well as an opportunity to change the rules of the game enough to make a difference for democracy in Mexico.

Scenario 1: Opposition Alliance

The first scenario postulates a comprehensive opposition alliance in the Electoral College to annul the presidential election, forcing a constitutional interregnum followed by new elections. It makes three assumptions: (1) that the PAN would have carried through on its public support for annulment; (2) that Cárdenas could have held the FDN together for annulment; and (3) that at least eleven PRI congressmen would vote with the opposition. Agreement on annulment looked possible. Cárdenas did not reject annulment until August 9, though he never renounced his claim of victory.[83] The PAN, while not prepared to support a Cárdenas victory, repeatedly and publicly called for annulment. The Declaration for Democracy signed in early August by Cárdenas, the PAN, and the PRT rejected the entire 1988 electoral process. Nor was the PRI fully united behind Salinas.

Still, these remain relatively heroic assumptions. The key problem is the difference between support for annulment in theory and support for annulment in the Electoral College. In the case of the PAN, for instance, as long as the PRI could muster the votes to ratify Salinas, the PAN lost little by supporting annulment. On the contrary, the PAN reaped the reward of the righteous by upholding democratic principles. Yet how would the PAN have voted if it believed the result would actually be annulment? Although risk-taking PAN leaders preferred annulment, other risk-averse leaders would have opposed such a step, calling into question the PAN's ability to swing every vote in its delegation behind annulment. The PAN presidential candidate Manuel Clouthier, who called for annulment, was a risk-taker but a newcomer to the PAN; he had joined the party barely three years before. He faced opposition from influential old-guard *panistas* who preferred safer, more gradual strategies. Annulment would have meant a constitutional interregnum in which the PAN could have decisively influenced the selection (by the Congress) of a temporary president. However, the PAN would also have a lot of influence in a Salinas presidency, as the largest single party in Congress and as Salinas's natural ally on economic policy. Salinas would need opposition support to pass any constitutional reform since the PRI lacked the required two-thirds congressional majority. The PAN could exact a price for its cooperation. In addition, annulment meant a period of fourteen to eighteen months of uncertainty while a new election was organized, months in which capital flight would escalate, investment would virtually halt, and social divisions would increase. Manuel Camacho Solís, then Secretary of Ecology and Urban Development and Sali-

83. According to *Las razones y las obras*, 720, he "declared inappropriate" the PAN proposal to annul the elections, favoring an attempt to clean the process (by annulling fraudulent *casillas*) because annulment would create political problems. However, *Radiografía del fraude*, a book coauthored by Cárdenas and published in the fall of 1988, argued that "Salinas should resign in favor of a constitutional interregnum convoking new elections with broad guarantees of cleanness." See Barberán et al., *Radiografía del fraude*, 152.

nas's point of contact with the opposition, allegedly used this argument in private conversations with the PAN's presidential candidate and party president, winning their tacit agreement not to push the issue in exchange for a series of reforms to include economic and political compromises, changes in state relations with the Catholic Church, and educational reform.[84] Finally, what would happen after annulment in a new presidential election? Most at the time thought Cárdenas would win a clean election. And in terms of his economic policy preferences, Cárdenas was the worst scenario for the PAN. Thus, the PAN's ability to hold together a vote if they knew the consequences would be annulment is questionable.

What about the PRI? Could the opposition have gotten eleven votes? Certainly the Salinas team believed it possible. Indeed, this may be the most likely of the three assumptions. The doubts arise when one analyzes who in the PRI delegation might have voted for annulment, and under what conditions. Salinas's enemies might have voted for annulment. However, some of them (e.g., from the petroleum union) also had a lot to fear from democratization, since their own positions depended on nondemocratic elections in PRI unions. Still, assuming that eleven *priista* votes could be found, they would probably have depended on the ability of the opposition to convince them that it would hold together on annulment. Any *priista* who voted for annulment and got caught on the wrong side of the majority could expect retribution. Since the opposition could not prove its unity, the *priistas* held back on annulment.

Finally, the FDN had trouble holding together. The FDN had the most to gain if a new election was held and Cárdenas won. Yet this was contingent on the long term. In the short term the FDN parties had a strong incentive to approve the congressional election. This put an annulment vote in question and created suspicion that some parties had already made deals with the PRI. Salinas had on his side the long tradition of parastatal alliance with the PRI. Cárdenas could not have but wondered about his ability to hold the FDN together on annulment. In the end he did not put his delegates to the test but withdrew from the Electoral College in the moment of ratification.

Scenario 2: Maximizing FDN Goals

This scenario argues that the FDN made its critical mistake, not in its decision to fight for the presidency, but in its choice of strategy to

---

84. This conversation is reported in *Yo Manuel: Memorias ¿apócrifas? de un comisionado* (Mexico City: Rayuela Editores, 1995). The book allegedly is based on notes that were in fact stolen from the house of Camacho Solís. Many of the suggested reforms did take place, including a surprising warming of relations between the Mexican state and the Catholic Church.

reach that goal. Suggested alternatives vary: (1) do not participate in the Electoral College or ratify the congressional election; (2) fight one by one for congressional seats, taking the risk that this would provoke a constitutional crisis on September 1 if no full Congress existed; or (3) engage in confrontational mobilization that would use or risk provoking violence.

With respect to the first alternative, as one former FDN supporter argued, "it was very dangerous to ratify the Chamber of Deputies, because once it was ratified, and the PRI had a majority, it controlled the constitutional means to declare valid the election of Salinas. So we fell into a very difficult contradiction. . . . We did not recognize the election of Salinas, but we did recognize ours."[85] *Cardenistas* also argued that if the FDN decided to go to the Electoral College, it should fight tooth and nail for every case, even if this meant risking a constitutional crisis by delaying the ratification of the Congress past the deadline.[86] The PMS proposed "a rigorous examination of the documents, . . . throwing out those results that did not tally with the original count from each *casilla*, as well as the illegible documents, . . . [and] if the official party did not accept this procedure, the opposition response should be to try to get to the first of September without completely ratifying the Congress."[87] The problem was in the unwillingness of FDN parties themselves to take this risk; indeed, the PMS was the only holdout: "[T]he PRI signed a procedural pact with [the rest of the parliamentary groups of the opposition] to speed up the *autocalificación*. That was the first triumph of the official party in the Colegio."[88]

If legal means gave Cárdenas little leverage, what about mobilization and civil disobedience? Within the circle of Cárdenas advisers many voices urged more aggressive actions, like occupying the *Palacio Nacional*, the seat of Mexican government. Cárdenas could still draw huge crowds to the Zócalo. Had he called for such tactics, he would have found many volunteers. Many letters to Cárdenas even expressed a willingness to fight:[89]

85. Confidential interview by author of CD founder, April 1991.
86. The purpose of this, according to one former FDN supporter, had to do with negotiating leverage: "[S]ome of us believed that we had to mount a great parliamentary struggle, risking a failure to ratify a Chamber of Deputies, not accepting ratifications of packets of deputies [blocs accepted as a whole] . . . and that we had to arrive at the end of August with a very tense situation, with a risk of a constitutional crisis, in order to be in a position to negotiate effectively." Confidential interview BH, May 1991.
87. Pablo Gómez, *Mexico 1988: Disputa por la presidencia y lucha parlamentaria* (Mexico City: Ediciones de Cultura Popular, 1989), 21.
88. Ibid., 22.
89. Gilly, ed., *Cartas a Cuauhtémoc Cárdenas*, 34, 47, 49, 54, 55.

From Mexico City: "Don't be afraid. We know how to organize ourselves and help ourselves, we will not leave you alone . . . No surrender!"

From Michoacán: "All of us are ready to take up arms against the PRI. We are ready to fight for the liberty of the Mexican Republic."

From Durango: "Take the presidency any way you must. It does not matter to us to do as our ancestors and shed blood to win liberty."

From Veracruz: "We are with you in the defense of the vote and if it is necessary we are ready to take up arms. . . . you just get them for us from Fidel Castro or someone."

From Guerrero: "We will take you to the presidential seat with machine gun in hand if the PRI wants it that way."

From Puebla: "We are determined . . . if necessary to take up arms because . . . the population is prudent and not stupid like the *priista* rats believe."

How feasible was this strategy? Even had Cárdenas been willing to risk violence, he would have been taking an enormous chance, with the survival of the *cardenista* option at stake. Many who supported fighting in principle might have balked. Letters urging Cárdenas to fight often asked him to "send guns, because we don't have any."[90] Cárdenas made his own doubt quite clear in an interview shortly after the election:

> Let those who are determined not to use peaceful means demonstrate it by taking up arms. Personally, I would not recommend to them that they stand on a corner with a rifle to see who follows them. I think that . . . the very significant participation in elections . . . is an expressed political will, sometimes conscious and sometimes not so conscious, that change should and must come precisely through peaceful and electoral means. I found a generalized rejection of the use of violence for anything.[91]

90. Ibid., 54.
91. María Xelhuantzi López, "Una vida nutrida de México: Exclusiva con Cuauhtémoc Cárdenas," *Estudios Políticos* 7 (July–September 1988): 25.

In those days prior to the guerrilla rebellion in Chiapas few believed armed struggle would pay off. For Cárdenas in 1988 a call to arms would have been a shot in the dark, like Madero's call to arms in 1910. He had not prepared for such a struggle and did not have the organization to lead it. In addition, even though his restraint led many to doubt his leadership, Cárdenas personally opposed both violence and aggressive tactics like occupying public buildings because he did not want even partial responsibility for bloodshed by encouraging actions that had a high probability of ending in a massacre.[92]

Finally, the FDN could not use mobilization to extract concessions from the PRI without serious risk of escalation because it lacked the organization to direct mobilization, to communicate with the masses, and to keep track of local organizers. Arnoldo Martínez Verdugo expresses this conviction eloquently:

> In the last rallies that we held after the campaign, there began to be a cry, a slogan that the masses, the downtrodden [*la gente de abajo*] kept shouting that said, "if they impose the bald guy, there will be revolution" [referring to Salinas's baldness], and, well, it was understandable. But we as leaders could not allow this tendency to develop spontaneously because there was no organized base; it was very recent, it was still a very disorganized movement. It had no form of discipline, so that the leadership might make its position clear. So it could be the object of all kinds of provocation.[93]

Most important, the PRI controlled the state and would have the upper hand in an armed confrontation. Despite the sympathy of sectors of the army for the son of General Cárdenas, it is unlikely that the high command would have supported him against the state. The *cardenistas* would have paid a heavy price, and at the time they thought there were easier ways to get what they wanted. As Cárdenas argued in a speech on September 14: "[The PRI] would like us to call for a confrontation, to get them out of power by any means, in a disorganized and unprepared fashion, so they could respond with a bloodbath and a devastating wave of repression. They know that they are condemned historically either way, but they threaten us with an enormous cost in blood and suffer-

---

92. As one disillusioned *perredista* remarked, "Cárdenas just lacked the balls" to defend the vote in 1988. Confidential interview BI, July 1991.

93. Martínez Verdugo, interview.

ing."[94] Thus, given the organizational weakness of the FDN and the institutional position of the PRI, the scenario of Cárdenas taking power against PRI resistance is probably more an expression of frustrated hope than a missed opportunity.

Scenario 3: Negotiation with the Regime

This scenario, the most controversial as well as the most practical, suggests that Cárdenas should have realized the futility of trying to prevent the inauguration of Salinas and instead used his mobilizational power and/or his delegates in Congress as a threat to extract significant concessions from the PRI about future rules of the game. In this scenario both strategies for annulment and strategies to force the PRI to recognize a Cárdenas victory served the more immediate end of leverage for a negotiated pact that would lead to democratic transition. There was room for negotiation in 1988. The PRI genuinely feared it would fail to confirm Salinas. Differences of opinion exist about how far-reaching such a negotiation might have been and what the FDN would have had to pay to get a good pact. A cost-benefit analysis for the PRI and the FDN may clarify the dilemma. The PRI leaders wanted Salinas confirmed, preferably by a broad majority of all political parties, to enhance the legitimacy of a presidency already stained by controversy and protest. Yet would the PRI have made fundamental reforms to the system, reforms that would endanger its hegemony in the near future, in exchange for FDN acceptance of Salinas? As long as the PRI could get Salinas confirmed the party might prefer to endure the short-term stain of a fraudulent election and FDN condemnation rather than accept a deal certain to significantly increase electoral competition in the medium term.

Only if the PRI could find no other way of getting Salinas into office would it be necessary to give up a great deal, but here the internal weakness of the FDN came into play. Because the FDN was a new option, without a system of party authority and discipline, the PRI could try to buy the election more cheaply by making a deal with one of the former parastatals, instead of offering major reforms. After they finished ratifying the congressional election, PRI members controlled the levers to confirm Salinas with or without popular legitimacy. Cárdenas conceded unilaterally the only other thing the PRI might have wanted from the FDN: a promise to refrain from violence or behavior that might seri-

94. Cuauhtémoc Cárdenas Solórzano, *Nuestra lucha apenas comienza* (Mexico City: Editorial Nuestro Tiempo, 1988), 154.

ously upset public order. Therefore, the FDN would have had little to gain in a negotiation, since the PRI had no real incentive to make significant concessions *unless* (and this is an important exception) the FDN managed to annul the election with the help of the PAN. In such a situation the PRI would have had little choice but to accept negotiation on the rules of the game, possibly leading to a genuine transition.

Without the promise of significant gains and at least a moral victory over the PRI *cardenistas* believed the costs of a negotiation were high. They argued that people would desert Cárdenas if he endorsed Salinas after having claimed victory, and considered negotiating dangerous to his image. In their view even negotiations would give the impression that Cárdenas was prepared to sell his votes to the highest bidder. Higher gains might have tempted them more, but minor advances could hardly make up for the loss of such valuable political capital as popular trust in Cárdenas. In sum, negotiation, while possible, would probably not have had the immediate effect on democratization in Mexico that critics assume. Cárdenas gave up real opportunities to negotiate concessions, but a hypothetical deal might well have turned into a Pyrrhic victory.

Nevertheless, it is questionable whether rational calculation explains the entire outcome. On the one hand, many *priistas* felt Cárdenas had betrayed the party and endangered national stability. Credible sources in both the PRD and the PRI insist that so high was the sense of outrage that some figures close to Salinas proposed a hard-line solution to the *cardenista* problem, possibly involving an "accident" to remove Cárdenas as a threat.[95] On the other hand, *cardenistas* felt Salinas had betrayed and cheated them out of the presidency.[96] Years after the election some *perredistas* continued to refuse to call Carlos Salinas "president." One PRD mayor went to the extreme of addressing official correspondence to Mr. Salinas, Presidency of the Republic—acknowledging that

95. *Perredistas* say that warnings arrived from friends still in the PRI that such a plot might be under way. However, all sources confirm that powerful factions—including some influential military officers and the future Regent of Mexico City, Manuel Camacho Solís—opposed such a solution definitively. These rumors might seem completely ludicrous if not for the events of 1994, which implicated PRI officials in the assassinations of the PRI's first 1994 presidential candidate, Luis Donaldo Colosio, and the PRI secretary-general José Francisco Ruíz Massieu. In the latter case the president's brother, Raúl Salinas, was arrested and charged with masterminding the murder plot.

96. Estimates differed, with some saying Cárdenas won by 41 percent to 37 percent, with 22 percent for the PAN (see Barberán et al., *Radiografía del fraude* 139), and others arguing for a margin of 39 percent to 33 percent, with 25 percent for the PAN (see Maldonado, *Orígenes del Partido de la Revolución Democrática,* 198). In either case Cárdenas would hold office as president.

Salinas occupied the office of the president and could be found there, but not that he was president. Negotiation seemed to recognize Salinas's authority. The debate over whether and how much the PRD should negotiate with the government remained one of the dominant conflicts in the party through the 1994 presidential election.

The Breakup of the FDN and the Birth of the Party of the Democratic Revolution

The breakup of the FDN was implicit in its construction. The FDN parties sought a conjunctural electoral alliance "to form a great National Democratic Front, *with a view to the federal election of 1988, in order to support the candidacy of Cuauhtémoc Cárdenas to the Presidency.*"[97] Organizations in the FDN remained intact, their differences glossed over in the interest of promoting the presidential campaign. After the election ideological differences and conflicts of interest reemerged as tactical imperatives for union subsided. The behavior of many FDN members during ratification was an early symptom of this disintegration. Among popular movements who deserted, typical explanations sounded like that of one leader of the Movimiento de los 400 Pueblos, who announced that "the only thing left to [Cárdenas] is to negotiate with the government. My departure will not harm the Front, [but] the reasons that marginalize me and the Movement . . . are what will finish off the unity of the *cardenistas.* . . . the FDN has a lot to learn, it must resign itself to not getting the presidency."[98] Electoral alliance continued for a time, but once the presidential election had passed was more likely to intensify conflicts than to alleviate them. The FDN parties could not agree on common candidacies for Congress even in 1988, when electoral laws made it easier than it was by 1991.

In retrospect, the FDN's only real options were disintegration or merging into a single party. A loosely united front might cooperate in an electoral campaign, but one could hardly expect it to run a unified, effective parliamentary delegation. The tasks of a parliamentary bench require a delegation leader, a minimum of internal discipline, and some agreement on specific programs, policies, and tactics. The FDN lacked almost every requirement. Indeed, until some of the FDN parties resumed their alliance with the PRI, the new Congress "did not issue a

97. PPS, *Plataforma común del Frente Democrático Nacional*, 7; emphasis added.
98. Maldonado, *Origenes del Partido de la Revolución Democrática*, 227.

single law for three and a half months. The parliamentary debate was converted into an echo of the discussion over the elections."[99]

Thus, as the project for forming a new party progressed, tensions in the FDN mounted. The FDN parties had consented to a fling but were by no means ready for marriage. Cárdenas issued his marriage proposal on October 21, 1988, explicitly calling for the formation of the Party of the Democratic Revolution. His "Call to the Mexican People" responded directly to the limitations of the FDN. First, the existing FDN parties clearly did not organize a significant part of his support, which came from the "millions of unorganized Mexicans [and] the members of political and social groups that do not militate in a party."[100] These could seek shelter in a new party. In addition, the loose structure of the FDN presented serious deficiencies for pursuing its political project. Cárdenas argued that "for the tasks we have ahead of us," the most relevant reasons for the failure of the FDN to defend the vote in 1988 were first, "not having overcome the obstacles to presenting more common candidacies," and second, "the lack of organization. . . . voting is not turning out to be enough to achieve the necessary changes in the country, in the face of the strength of fraud and imposition. It is thus necessary to develop capacities."[101]

The "Call" did not require FDN parties to dissolve, and foresaw the possibility of continuing cooperation with those who did not join the new party. Nevertheless, the proposal to form a party accelerated the reemergence of ideological conflicts and the disintegration of the front. The PMS declared in favor of a party almost immediately, and offered its legal registry, but alliance with a socialist party made some FDN members uncomfortable. The PARM offered to admit the Corriente but rejected PMS participation on the grounds that "if a marxist party is to be formed, we would have nothing to do there."[102] The PPS, in contrast, ruled out participation because the new party would *not* be socialist. The PFCRN delayed only briefly in rejecting a new party; as its president put it, "those who urge the formation of a new party either don't have one or are unhappy with the one they've got."[103] Interviews with members of these parties three years later also reveal some squea-

99. Gómez, Mexico 1988: *Disputa por la presidencia y lucha parliamentaria*, 29.

100. Cuauhtémoc Cárdenas Solórzano, *Llamamiento al Pueblo de México* (Mexico City: PRD, 1988), 9.

101. Ibid., 5.

102. Hermenegildo Castro, "El PARM desaparecería al crearse el nuevo partido," *La Jornada* (Mexico City), 14 October 1988: 9.

103. Ricardo Alemán, "Sólo el PMS apoya crear el partido del FDN," *La Jornada* (Mexico City), 23 September 1988: 1, 8.

mishness about joining a party with the strident confrontational stance of the *cardenistas*.[104] The parastatals quickly came to terms with Salinas, supporting many of his neoliberal reforms. During early 1989, as the PMS and CD discussed a program and statutes for the new party, FDN cooperation deteriorated. The final breach followed a PPS and PFCRN decision to invite a *priista* speaker to a rally commemorating the March anniversary of oil expropriation.[105] According to the PRD, PFCRN president Aguilar Talamantes defended his decision in terms of "the interest of the PFCRN in establishing serious contacts with the PRI in order to formulate a programmatic platform on the basis of which we might establish political alliances."[106] Cárdenas reacted very negatively. For all practical purposes this marked the end of the FDN.

In light of the rapid disintegration of the FDN, the behavior of the PMS seems particularly curious. The PMS joined the Cárdenas campaign late and reluctantly. Yet only the PMS continued to support Cárdenas after the election, offering to change its structures, principles, and program in order to forge a new party in which the *cardenistas* would play dominant leadership roles. The June 1988 pact between Cárdenas and the PMS provides the basis for this postelectoral behavior. In contrast to the FDN pact, the PMS-CD pact centered on the principle of "a long-term political and programmatic alliance."[107] After listing twelve programmatic points to which both would commit themselves, the pact set down specific postelectoral commitments. If victorious, the parties agreed to collective designation of a Cárdenas cabinet; if defeated, they would "stay in the opposition . . . [and] dedicate all their efforts to strengthen the great alliance of democratic forces, to organize and promote the struggles of the people. Therefore, none of the leaders of the Mexican Socialist Party and of the Democratic Current will be able to accept a position of political responsibility in the government." In addi-

---

104. Said one PARM leader, "any Mexican knows that our political problems aren't so big that we should destabilize the whole country" (confidential interview K, April 1991). A PFCRN leader accused Cárdenas of saying "subliminally that it is necessary to resort to an armed revolution" (confidential interview BD, September 1991).

105. Cárdenas held a separate rally in Michoacán.

106. Maldonado, *Origenes del Partido de la Revolución Democrática*, 286.

107. According to Castillo's preamble to the June pact, "it is necessary to respond to [the popular demand for unity] with the unity of the democratic forces of Mexico . . . not with just any unity . . . [but] a long-term political and programmatic alliance to act together in today's electoral struggle and in the later struggles of the Mexican people to improve its conditions of life and win definitive liberty. . . . Let us build together a new national force and assume together the fundamental policy decisions that the moment demands." González Graf, ed., *Las elecciones de 1988 y la crisis del sistema político*, 269–70.

tion, both agreed to "maintain their alliance in all political and social spheres, and in all organs and institutions of popular representation in which they assemble. . . . Thus, the alliance that I now propose is the beginning of a commitment to pact in the local and federal elections of the coming years. The candidates in each election will be chosen according to procedures commonly agreed upon, which presupposes the possibility of primary elections."[108] This pact thus laid the foundation for the formation of a joint political party after the July 6 election. Heberto Castillo even suggested this publicly, though Cárdenas remained noncommittal before the election, saying only that if the FDN could not continue in unity, "then we'll see what kind of organization is most useful [conveniente] for us."[109]

The PMS sought such a commitment when other FDN parties avoided it in large part because it fit their trajectory. Unlike the parastatals, they had long rejected alliance with the PRI. Where the parastatals felt more secure returning to tried-and-true strategies of negotiation with the government, the PMS leadership had only to maintain their traditional stance. Their main concern was rather to make sure that Cárdenas remained independent and did not get into a party which would draw him back toward the PRI. Second, forging a new party with the ex-CD continued the drive toward unification on the left. The PMS had yet to celebrate its first birthday when it decided to offer its registry to the new party. As a new party itself, the PMS did not inspire dedicated loyalty or define the political identity of its members. More than one generation of politicians had grown up in the PPS and PARM, and the PFCRN dated to the early seventies. In contrast, all of the PMS leaders had relinquished at least one party in the course of the 1980s, with the formation of the PSUM in 1981 and the PMS in 1987. A merger thus seemed more natural and logical to the PMS than to leaders of the older parties.

Finally, the PMS suspected from the first that the FDN would not endure. They therefore made preparations to avoid another relapse from strong popular mobilization into business as usual. The PMS leaders did not trust the FDN parties. They also had learned from the experiences of previous "fronts" in Mexico and other parts of Latin America that such fronts either fell apart or were ineffective champions of democracy and progressive causes against the solid and well-financed op-

108. Ibid., 273–274.
109. Rubén Álvarez, "Anuncia Cárdenas campaña de difusión de la Corriente," *La Jornada* (Mexico City), 19 March 1987: 6.

position of the ruling classes. Using contrasting examples, one PMS leader explained the debate:

> [I]f Unidad Popular in Chile [under] Salvador Allende had been able to establish among them a party discipline, democratic, consensual, but party discipline, it would have been a different story, because in Unidad Popular everyone began to take different points of view and different positions. And that contributed to the defeat of Allende. On the other hand, in Nicaragua, the [successful] Frente Sandinista, which initially was a front where the individual organizations continued to exist, evolved toward a type of party. . . . So, we chose the form of a party.[110]

The PRD remained basically a breakaway party built on existing organizations. The PMS had not yet institutionalized an internal structure or a common identity to erase the loyalties of members of its component parties and, in fact, as Chapter 5 shows, in 1991 one could still find political currents traceable to parties that dissolved in the PSUM in 1981. Still, the mere legal fiction of being one party forced cooperation on key issues like candidate nominations. The PRD might "not [be] strictly a party structure in the old style [of Communist Party discipline]. But in any case it *is* a party. It has a single leadership, a hierarchization that culminates in its president, and its links are closer."[111] The *cardenistas* agreed, reflecting that the lack of common candidacies in 1988 revealed the "particular interests [of the FDN parties]. . . . by that time, three months into the campaign, the government must have begun to throw out little lures, offers, to discourage us or to reconstruct a certain . . . system of understandings that had existed before with these political parties. . . . all this made us understand the need for an organization to respond more to broader interests . . . the need to form a party."[112]

Conclusions

Thus, the FDN, though well suited to the task of creating a successful political option, did not adequately perform tasks necessary for Cárde-

---

110. Martínez Verdugo, interview.
111. Gilberto Rincón Gallardo, interview by author, Mexico City, 23 August 1991.
112. Cuauhtémoc Cárdenas, interview by author, Morelos, 3 May 1991.

nas's political force to consolidate its presence. In 1988 "the bases demanded [real unity], but we could not achieve it, and that was also another reason that carried us to the conviction of forming a new political party. A unified defense [of the vote] was not achieved in the Electoral College. . . . separate negotiations took place. Each party went its own way. And what might have been a successful defense if carried out together, a greater resistance, did not happen."[113] It did not happen because the logic of the consolidation arena had taken over.

The original broad coalition formed by Cárdenas succumbed to the forces that pushed it apart: pressure to act as one entity in order to perform consolidation tasks like defending the vote and running a parliamentary delegation, vulnerability to the manipulations of a PRI-government that controlled postelectoral rewards and structured the political options of the opposition, and internal ideological and political differences that surged to the forefront once the necessity for union around the single presidential candidate had passed. The coalition that joined in a new political party, the PRD, was thus reduced at the very first stage of consolidation. This political party would face its own troubles as the pressures of consolidation demanded more and more from it between 1989 and 1991. These troubles are the subject of analysis in Chapters 5, 6, and 7.

113. Ibid.

5

Problems of Party Building

DEMOCRACY, INSTITUTIONALIZATION, AND ACTIVIST
RETENTION

The breakup of the FDN and the transformation of the *cardenista*
movement into a legally registered party did not change the basic character of the movement or the fundamental consolidation problems it
faced. Though less heterogeneous than the FDN, the Party of the Democratic Revolution remained essentially a fusion party, merging preexisting political organizations and currents. The diversity of the groups and
organizations that supported Cárdenas (and the left in general) made
profound internal divisions very likely. The method chosen to register
the new party guaranteed it. After a rather half-hearted effort to organize the party via the definitive registry process of holding state assemblies, the ex-*priistas* accepted the offer of the PMS to transfer its party

registry to a new, jointly constructed party.[1] The *cardenistas* did not simply move into existing PMS structures. Even as organizers were setting up assemblies for definitive registry, negotiations proceeded with the PMS leaders to draw up new statutes and elect a new leadership. Since any party had the right to change its name and statutes, this process gave the PRD automatic legal registry—an attractive proposition to a group convinced that the PRI would never give a *cardenista* party registry.

However, the new party still faced all the challenges of any party making the transition from emergence to consolidation. After it became a legally registered party on May 14, 1989, the PRD had to construct an organization of activists, build relationships with civil society (especially the popular movements that supported Cárdenas in 1988), find a place in the party system, carry out government responsibilities as elected officials, and compete in elections. Its character as a fusion party on the left influenced how it approached these consolidation tasks. The PRD also had to cope with a particular type of regime—a one-party dominant system—that exaggerated the normal difficulty of many of the challenges it faced. Not only did the PRD have to learn new skills, it had to do so in an institutional environment controlled by its principal competitor.

Thus, party consolidation involved efforts to change the rules of a basically exclusionary Mexican political regime. I accept Schmitter's definition of a political regime as "the ensemble of patterns, explicit or not, that determines the forms and channels of access to principal governmental positions, the characteristics of the actors who are admitted or excluded from such access, . . . [and] rules determining how collective decisions are made."[2] However, different rules, norms, and expectations may apply within particular subsets of actors, each of

1. The PRI controlled two key levers: the body that voted to accept or reject proof that a new party held assemblies with the required number of attendees, and the government that issued (and could withdraw) permits to notary publics who must certify assembly records. These permits are very lucrative, highly coveted, and provide excellent incentives to cooperate with the government. One need only declare a few assemblies invalid to deny registry. At the time the Corriente could not seek conditional registry—proving one has supporters by getting 1.5 percent of the vote—because conditional registry was abolished in 1986 and not reinstituted until 1990. Anticipating rejection, the Corriente did not wait for the Federal Electoral Commission's final decision before accepting the PMS offer.

2. Philippe Schmitter, "The Consolidation of Political Democracy in Southern Europe," unpublished manuscript, 1988, p. 11. This mirrors the definition employed in international relations theory of "regimes" as "sets of implicit or explicit principles, norms, rules, and decision-making procedures around which actors' expectations converge in a given area." Robert Keohane, *After Hegemony: Cooperation and Discord in the World Political Economy* (Princeton, N.J.: Princeton University Press, 1984), 57.

which forms part of the whole pattern of access to decision making. One can think of these component patterns as subroutines within the larger political regime. Each subroutine consists of "rules of engagement" that characterize relationships among a specific set, or network, of actors. In the case of party consolidation it is the party's task to develop stable norms and procedures that will enable it to perform functions that require the cooperation of other actors in each network. Electoral performance alone cannot establish the party's place within these networks for several reasons. First, the sources of poor or good electoral performance cannot be reduced to electoral laws and campaigns. Performance of other tasks affects the ability to win votes. Second, the number and stability of votes do not necessarily reveal much about party influence or permanence. A party with 10 percent of the vote may be more consolidated than a party with 20 percent of the vote. Changing evaluations of the incumbent party may lead to vote volatility that obscures a consolidated opposition core. Finally, influence may depend less on size than on a party's ability to make binding decisions, forge lasting relationships with civil society, cooperate with other parties, and govern effectively.

Therefore, the next three chapters explore five subroutines, or tasks of party consolidation, through case studies of local party building in Michoacán and the Estado de México, based primarily on interviews with and observation of local activists.[3] Chapter 5 discusses the first of these subroutines, governing internal relations within the activist network. It examines the norms and procedures that determined access to party positions and the way in which the party made decisions. Chapter 6 discusses patterns of interaction with external actors. The interest subroutine deals with the interest group network, in the PRD's case primarily relationships with popular movements. The administrative subroutine looks at how the PRD exercised authority in elected positions. The partisan subroutine looks at interaction among parties. Finally, Chapter 7 examines electoral subroutines: those patterns of behavior and expectations that defined electoral strategies and efforts to consolidate voter loyalties.

THE ACTIVIST NETWORK

Subroutines developed within the activist network are key factors in party consolidation because activists carry out all other tasks of consoli-

3. Interviews with local PRD activists and members of other (non-PRD) parties were

dation. Therefore, it matters how a party selects leaders and candidates. It matters how members make collective decisions, and whether they see these decisions in particular and party rules in general as legitimate and enforceable. It matters whether decision making becomes institutionalized, defined as a function of increasing predictability (according to written or unwritten norms) and formality (channeled through formal institutions).[4] And it matters whether a party can attract and keep activists.

Equally important, the influence of party character is strongest in the activist network, the most autonomous partial regime. Only internally did *perredistas* have the freedom to determine rules according to their own goals and ideas about appropriate methods. In every other partial regime actors more or less hostile to PRD consolidation set many of the rules. External constraints and direct interference affected both rules and praxis even in the activist regime. Nor should one expect consensus about rules simply because activists have some interests in common. Nevertheless, the PRD enjoyed greater relative autonomy to realize a collective vision in the activist regime. As a result, some of the fundamental contradictions in the PRD project show up most clearly in this area.

Overall, the PRD made substantial progress in setting up collective decision-making structures. However, its consolidation of these structures left a lot to be desired. In its first six years the PRD did not become the united, democratic party intended by its founders, but was riven by divisions and rebellion against party decisions, tormented by persistent conflicts over rules, and plagued by resource problems that constrained its ability to institutionalize a permanent party structure able to penetrate the local level. Many of these problems were perfectly predictable and quite typical of new parties in general. Others particularly affect left parties (which at least in the 1990s seem compelled to deal with internal democracy in a context of considerable internal heterogeneity)

---

assigned random coding by letters (A–Z, AA–AZ, BA–BZ, and so forth) in order to indicate which interviews led to which responses without compromising the privacy or security of sometimes vulnerable individuals.

4. Huntington defined institutionalization as a process with four dimensions: adaptability, complexity, autonomy, and coherence. See Samuel Huntington, *Political Order in Changing Societies* (New Haven, Conn.: Yale University Press, 1968). This scheme is better designed to compare different organizations than to trace the progress of one organization over time, and is measured in large part by whether an organization has accomplished a specific task, like transition from founding leadership. I am interested in measuring institutionalization over a shorter period of time, for which a simple two-dimensional conceptualization seems more useful. This definition does not discount informal rules while still indicating the importance of formal institutionalization.

and parties formed by the fusion of preexisting currents. The PRD's situation as an opposition party under attack by ruling elites exacerbated these problems. Its image and performance suffered tremendously, limiting its prospects for consolidation.

THE PROBLEM OF DEMOCRACY: LEADERSHIP/CANDIDATE SELECTION AND PARTICIPATION

One of the most intractable problems in the construction of the PRD was the issue of internal democracy. The PRD inherited debates over internal democracy from both sides of its lineage: from an independent left that had long divided over the meaning and value of democracy, and from ex-*priistas* whose experiences in an undemocratic party led them to reject its undemocratic practices but left them with little training in democracy and often a sneaking admiration for PRI discipline. Popular movements also challenged the party to address democratic concerns in order to demonstrate its potential as a vehicle for political participation that would not try to manipulate and control them. The PRD's attempts to develop internal democracy, while they brought many benefits to the party, also lay at the heart of some of its most serious weaknesses, including its inability to cope with internal divisions and its difficulty in institutionalizing or legitimating party rules.

Debates about democracy raise complex and difficult questions for left parties. The initial decision to seek democracy at the regime level often involved painful trade-offs. On the one hand, historical experience encouraged skepticism about representative democracy as a way to achieve progress on the traditional left agenda—including social equity, development, self-determination, and reform of the relations of production. Compared to the electoral left in Europe, the Latin American left confronted societies with problems that seemed difficult to resolve through gradual nonthreatening change, including high inequality, underdevelopment, and poverty. In the rare cases where a radical left achieved power or influence through elections, right-wing opponents often refused to respect democratic rules and supported military dictatorship to curb the left. As Castañeda notes, "it did not make much of a difference if power was obtained through the ballot box or an insurrection . . . either way, there was the devil to pay. In fact, it seemed the only power worth winning was the one that sprang from the barrel of a gun: at least it lasted."[5] Critics charged that representative democracy tended to deradicalize and distract people from actions that might result in real change. Moreover, in many countries electoral rules did not create conditions for free and fair competition. As practiced in such countries, "democracy" did not allow left parties to win power, let alone carry out their program. Because of these problems the Mexican Communist Party's decision to seek registry and participate in the 1979 elections was "controversial. . . . important groups within the party remained (and still remain) unconvinced by the arguments of the party's leadership."[6] Within the PRD some activists questioned the value of electoral participation, especially when the PRI stole elections and the PRD's electoral presence was shrinking.

On the other hand, the experience of authoritarian regimes convinced many leftists that democracy mattered, despite its defects. For the left, emergence from the illegal, clandestine life of the 1970s meant relief from repression targeted at left activists and an opportunity to participate in political life openly, to organize and win influence over the masses. In addition, by the end of the 1980s revolutionary alternatives looked increasingly unviable and, in fact, later fell in Eastern Europe, the Soviet Union, and Nicaragua. Many leftists concluded that representative democracy offered the best hope for progressive popular causes, though they knew democracy did not come without strings. To take advantage of democracy, the left would have to accept limits on its behavior, implicitly or explicitly, and tolerate the knowledge that its electoral participation could help legitimate a government with which it might have serious policy conflicts.

The decision to fight for regime-level democracy and participate in elections also had implications for the internal structure of left parties. Internal democracy became a test of the left's democratic credentials, a demonstration that voters and elites could trust the left to abide by democratic rules and behave democratically if allowed to take power. To some extent the left invited this scrutiny by attempting to make democracy into a distinction between the left and the right-wing authoritarian regimes they fought. At the same time, opponents of left programs used lingering doubts about the left's commitment to democracy to justify resistance to its electoral victories and increased influence. They pointed to the undemocratic behavior of many left parties in

5. Jorge Castañeda, *Utopia Unarmed: The Latin American Left After the Cold War* (New York: Alfred A. Knopf, 1993), 335.

6. Barry Carr, *Mexican Communism, 1968–1983: Eurocommunism in the Americas?* (La Jolla, Calif.: UCSD Center for U.S.-Mexican Studies, 1985), 14.

power and to the telling silence of the "democratic" left in supporting these regimes without engaging in public criticism of their lack of democracy.[7] The left was also criticized for an "instrumentalist approach to democracy," which "neglected the intrinsic merits of democratic rule and tended to support democracy only when it supported them."[8] Both the Corriente Democrática and the Mexican Communist Party favored democracy in part for such instrumental reasons. The PCM came to appreciate electoral democracy earlier than many Latin American communist parties, perhaps due to its long experience of repression and illegality under a series of authoritarian governments or to the fact that it could not make much headway organizing workers unless unions became more democratic.[9] The ex-CD leaders were even more vulnerable to accusations that their commitment to democracy lacked conviction. Critics repeatedly questioned why—if they truly valued democracy—they had not done more to promote it while they had positions of power in the PRI.

Thus, the need to prove itself as a democratic subject involved the PRD, like many left parties, in debates about internal democracy. From the first the founders of the PRD defined "internal democracy in the Party [as] its fundamental political principle."[10] By making a commitment to internal democracy, they hoped to separate themselves from the PRI's history of authoritarian decision making and quotas of influence, prove internal democracy could work, and avoid the embarrassment of adopting nondemocratic procedures after criticizing the PRI for its lack of democracy. Equally important, PRD leaders found it hard to oppose internal democracy while calling for democracy in Mexico. Such exceptionalism seemed to justify the PRI position that Mexico was not

7. For example, Castañeda finds "unquestionable internal tension" in the statements of Latin American left leaders about Cuba, between a defense of Cuba's right to adopt whatever institutions it believes necessary while under siege by the United States (to "put self-determination first," as Cárdenas said) and admission that what they defended "was inherently and substantively different from what he [Cárdenas] was struggling for." See Castañeda, *Utopia Unarmed*, 341–42.

8. Ibid., 328.

9. The argument that the Mexican left's main goal should be "to secure the 'liberation' and democratization of the official labor movement" became a strong though minority position in the Communist Party in the late seventies. Carr adds that "the majority of the PCM leadership and active militants did not endorse the tone of this thesis nor share its explicit contempt for the struggles of groups outside the labor movement. However, its emphasis on the need to work within existing official trade unions struck a sympathetic chord." Carr, *Mexican Communism, 1968–1983*, 16.

10. Partido de la Revolución Democrática (PRD), *Documentos básicos* (Mexico City: PRD, 1990), 23.

ready for democracy. Finally, a display of internal democracy would distinguish the PRD as uniquely qualified to lead a democratic Mexico. Thus, its internal procedures became a litmus test of the PRD's commitment to democracy at the invitation of Cárdenas himself, who announced that the PRD should "show, in its democratic norms, in its internal life, . . . in [its] unity and respect for collective decisions, and above all in the personal conduct of each of its members, the tangible image of what it proposes for the country."[11]

Three critical problems complicated the implementation of this goal. First, not everyone in the PRD supported internal democracy, or even electoral participation. Some of the same activists who criticized the PRI for imposing candidates later suggested that PRD internal elections were "a trap we have laid for ourselves," which polarized the party.[12] This group grew after the first experiments with internal elections. Second, as a fusion of many different political currents, the PRD had well-defined and well-organized factions from the moment of its birth. Instead of constructing consensus, procedures intended to foster internal democracy pitted these groups against each other and exacerbated internal divisions, with devastating consequences for party image and effectiveness. The fact that most opposition candidates in Mexico reach the Congress through proportional representation lists instead of majority seats reinforced this tendency, by turning competition inward and rewarding better-organized factions that could negotiate as a group for good positions on the list. Third, party members continued to struggle over the definition of democracy, and specifically over two key questions: *What kind* of democracy and *who participates*? The first question deals with methods for translating popular input into outcomes. The second question deals with the identification of the *demos*, the subjects or citizens of democratic action. Because of these problems the PRD's attempt to prove itself democratic largely backfired.

In interviews lack of consensus about "democracy" as a goal and method became quite clear. Local-level activists defined democracy, variously, as:

—elections without fraud
—everybody participates; things are not done by "just a few"
—not having everything decided for you, outside your control.[13]

11. Cuauhtémoc Cárdenas Solórzano, *Llamamiento al pueblo de México* (Mexico City: PRD, 1988), 18.
12. Confidential interview I, April 1991.
13. Confidential interviews (respectively): ibid.; AO, June 1991; AX, July 1991.

This kind of response put democracy in political terms—but not necessarily *representative* political terms. The desire for "everybody" to participate tended to conflict with policies to hold elections and delegate responsibility to party leaders. Other definitions emphasized social goals:

—social and economic participation for everyone
—a system with "neither rich nor poor," where everyone is equal
—a government that doesn't rob people.[14]

Definitions of democracy also included rather contradictory traits:

—saying whatever you think in the party
—being able to question leaders
—[being able to] criticize the municipal government (PRD, in this community).[15]

But

—democracy "is not anarchy"
—put[ting] some of our people [of our *corriente*] in good positions
—*not* collective leadership. No one is responsible for anything, so there's no accountability.

Those who valued "say[ing] whatever we want" did not necessarily get along with those who rejected "anarchy," while those who supported letting everyone participate clashed with those who repudiated collective leadership or who valued democracy as a way of putting their people in power.

Despite this underlying confusion, the party's official statutes (1990) defined democracy in representative, majoritarian terms, and the *demos* in terms of individual citizens rather than according to social or organizational identity. The statutes explicitly rejected corporatist structures and defined membership as "strictly individual, free and voluntary."[16]

14. Confidential interviews I, April 1991 (first comment); AS, July 1991 (second two comments, from two individuals interviewed together in a single community).
15. First set, in order, I, April 1991; AS July 1991; AS July 1991 (this interview involved several participants in an indigenous community where people preferred not to be interviewed alone); second set, in order, AI, July 1991/AX, July 1991; campaign rally in Michoacán, June 1991/AF, July 1991; AH, July 1991; third set, in order, AD, July 1991; I, April 1991; observation of conversation, September 1991.
16. PRD, *Documentos básicos*, 26. These statutes were the first approved by a nationally elected congress. Earlier versions were approved by provisional organizing committees.

Individuals would join the PRD through direct application, not membership in another organization. Commitment to individual membership also resulted in the primacy of territorial representation over the representation of substantive interests.[17] Territorial criteria defined the jurisdiction of formal party institutions and the basis of access to power. PRD statutes established four levels of permanent party organization: (1) at the national level the Consejo Nacional (to meet at least once every six months) and the Comité Ejecutivo Nacional (the board of directors between meetings of the Consejo); (2) at the state level the Consejo Estatal and Comité Ejecutivo Estatal; (3) at the municipal level the Consejo Municipal and Comité Municipal; and (4) at the submunicipal level the *comités de base*, or base committees.[18] At all levels voting rights belonged to individuals, not interests, sectors, or organizations.

This structure meant that civil society organizations such as social movements, unions, and so forth did not have automatic access to candidacies or representation in leadership, though movement members could participate as individuals in the party. But PRD founders still wanted to encourage popular movement participation, especially in elections, not make it conditional on their leaders or members becoming formal members of the party. Therefore, party statutes included measures to give nonaffiliates access to party candidacies, and also left it up to the party convention that convoked internal elections whether only party members or the entire population of the relevant electoral district could vote in primary elections.[19] The flexibility built into the definition of the PRD voter extended in practice to the election of party leaders. Though the statutes said only affiliates could elect party leaders, the PRD simply had no way to distinguish between members and nonmembers. As a new party, it lacked a membership list; later, registration of members proceeded so slowly, in part due to resource constraints and fear of being identified as a PRD member, that the party still had no accurate registry years after its foundation. Characteristically, according to one Baja California PRD leader, a 1992 primary attracted about 5,000 supporters interested enough to cast votes, yet the party only had

17. Party statutes did give individuals the right to organize and register opinion currents, mainly to express differing ideological approaches rather than substantive class concerns (ibid., 28–29).

18. Ibid., 30. A congress was also supposed to meet at each level to elect the respective Consejo.

19. Specifically, the PRD could "nominate or support candidates that are not members of the party," if the appropriate party committee (municipal for a municipal election, etc.) decided to permit non-PRD aspirants to register as precandidates (ibid., 50).

about 700 affiliates on the books.[20] Thus, its statutes and practices encouraged a fairly ill-defined *demos*, which led to problems with the implementation of internal elections.

Party statutes also defined democracy in majoritarian terms. Though proportional representation is given as an option in some cases, the "free, equal, and majoritarian vote of the affiliates or of their elected delegates is required . . . to decide the policies of the Party, . . . the integration of its leadership, . . . [and] the nomination of its candidates."[21] Actual voting rules and procedures varied considerably and were frequently the subject of intense conflict at party congresses and conventions. For example, delegates to the PRD's first National Congress in November 1990 clashed over how to select members of the Consejo Nacional, or National Council—the broad, representative body with ultimate authority to make decisions between congresses held approximately every three years. Initially, the Committee on Candidates, a body appointed by the provisional National Committee, presented the Congress with a list of 96 people, which it asked the delegates to approve or reject. Delegates demanded and won the right to choose the members of the Consejo in a secret election from the full list of 340 self-declared candidates.[22] However, when the newly elected Consejo met in December 1990 to choose the members of the next CEN, they were again asked to vote for or against an official slate. This time a majority supported voting on the list, though a significant minority felt so strongly that when they lost the procedural question, they voted to reject the slate.[23]

In practice, most democratic selection was indirect, through delegates at conventions. PRD elections thus tended to resemble the older U.S. system of alliances, back-room negotiations, and bloc voting more closely than the modern primary. This reliance on conventions made internal democracy cheaper, compared to direct primaries, but also encouraged three trends inside the party. First, indirect election tended to dilute popular participation and give a small number of brokers extra influence, due to information constraints, participation costs, and voter apathy, especially about leadership selection. Elections to the smallest

20. Confidential interview, with local Baja California leader, July 1994.

21. PRD, *Documentos básicos*, 24.

22. The top 96 joined the Consejo Nacional. A number of those elected did not appear on the original list, and some had antagonistic relationships with Cárdenas or other top PRD leaders. Francisco Garfías, "No pudieron elegir los perredistas a su Consejo Nacional," *Excélsior* (Mexico City), 19 November 1990, sec. A, pp. 1, 28, 49.

23. The 23 dissenters included Heberto Castillo. See Alejandro Caballero, "Aprobó el Consejo Nacional el nuevo CEN perredista," *La Jornada* (Mexico City), 16 December 1990: 7.

elected party organizations, the municipal committees, had lower information costs in small communities where everybody knew the candidates, but in elections to state committees or large municipal committees participation was low and reliance on secondhand judgments by brokers increased.[24] Second, the convention system favored organized factions who managed to vote together and negotiate positions as a group. Those who could play the game advanced; those without an organized current tended to divide their votes and lose influence. This encouraged the solidification of factions in the party and factional dominance of party councils. Third, because the influence of a faction depended on how many delegates it controlled, leaders had a strong incentive to exaggerate the number of their supporters. Accusations of fraud tainted many internal elections, deepening divisions. These divisions, in turn, undermined cooperation and the legitimacy of decisions made by party committees. Consolidation thus seemed to pose disturbing trade-offs between internal democracy and party effectiveness.

Examples of leadership selection from Michoacán and the Estado de México illustrate some of these problems. When Michoacán held its first State Congress to elect a state leadership, local communities began by choosing delegates to the Congress. The number of delegates per community depended directly on the number of *"perredistas"* who showed up at an open, public election: a certain number of voters entitled the community to one delegate.[25] The PRD continued to use this apportionment rule for the practical reason that it did not have an accurate register of *perredistas*. The PRD would have excluded and alienated genuine PRD supporters by demanding proof of membership, and in fact I never witnessed a delegate election where certification was required. In the absence of universal party membership cards the PRD decided to rely on local activists to police themselves and recognize "fake" *perredistas*. This was far from a perfect solution. In the first place, divisions among local activists could embroil them in conflicts over the genuineness of the PRD militance of opponents and result in two separate sets of delegates sent to the congress or convention. In the second place, the apportionment rule itself gave less scrupulous faction leaders opportunities to cheat, to bring more delegates by lying about the number of voters attending the local convention. To control this the provisional State Ex-

24. In more positive terms one broker explained that his followers accepted his directions because they were not as familiar with the candidates and because they trusted his judgment; thus, he said, it is not always bad to "manage the people." Confidential interview AK, April 1991.

25. In 1991 participants gave different estimates, perhaps because the number varies according to the party convocation issued in each election.

ecutive Committee (CEE) tried to send a representative to each local election to see that the community had conducted its elections properly and deserved all its delegates. Given the number of communities in Michoacán that held elections this was not always feasible. Some small rural communities sent suspicious numbers of delegates to the State Congress, provoking charges of fraud. Unfortunately for the legitimacy of the leadership that this congress elected, the questioned delegates produced a majority for one of the two principal factions that dominated Michoacán. The minority faction had strong motives to discredit these elections. They could not prove their charges, and the national leadership did not intervene. However, the procedure lent itself to such charges, true or false. Local committees dominated by members of the losing faction often declined to cooperate with, obey, or even communicate with the state leadership.

The same procedure caused problems at the April 1991 State Congress in the Estado de México. One representative sent by the Provisional Executive Committee to certify the elections in a rural Valle de Bravo district was also a local *caudillo*/broker. According to opponents, he cheated, approving large numbers of delegates for small communities.[26] As in Michoacán, the questioned delegates could have determined the majority in the new Executive Committee, in part because they tended to vote as a bloc and in favor of one current in the state PRD. Conflict on the floor of the congress quickly escalated to disruptive shouting matches and even fistfights before opposing leaders arrived at a compromise through secret negotiations to accept some of the delegates.

Secret negotiations also ended up determining the composition of the state Executive Committee. The larger number of factions and their degree of organization encouraged such negotiation as a solution to conflicts in the Estado de México. In the PRD-Michoacán, in contrast, the fact that the party was composed almost entirely of ex-*priistas* who belonged to the Corriente meant that conflict quickly became polarized between followers of PRD Senator Cristóbal Arias and followers of PRD Senator Roberto Robles Gárnica. Yet in the Estado de México the presence of *various* left parties before 1988 translated into an equal or greater number of internal factions in the PRD, whose shifting alliances could allow the party to avoid polarization and reach compromise, at

26. These charges seemed well documented. His certificate for the disputed elections did not include lists of all those who attended, and in at least one case he presented a list of delegates to the organizers of the congress dated one day before the election in that community was held. See Gloria Pérez Mendoza, "Problemas de acreditación en el Congreso del PRD mexiquense," *La Jornada* (Mexico City), 14 April 1991: 6.

least in elections with a sufficient number of posts available for distribution among the factions. At the 1991 Congress, after two days of discussion, the three main candidates for the presidency of the party in the Estado de México agreed on a two-round voting rule, with the top two candidates in the first round going on to the determining round—a method nowhere specified in the statutes. The two-round election resulted in the selection of a compromise candidate as state president, after some clever maneuvering by his people.[27] Meanwhile, brokers worked out a *"planilla de unidad,"* or single slate, to fill the rest of the Executive Committee.[28] The slate gave representation to all major political currents present, including their brokers as well as the three contending candidates for the presidency. The Congress approved this slate virtually unanimously.

Nevertheless, these factional conflicts and charges of fraud deflected attention from the vital consolidation task of defining policy positions for the 1991 federal congressional election. Debates over accreditation of delegates took so much time that the Congress canceled a planned series of working groups to discuss the party's platform. Furthermore, the experience reinforced mistrust and divisions in the PRD. The carefully brokered Executive Committee fell into deadlock within a year. In April 1992 its minority president stepped down suddenly, citing his inability to overcome divisions in the party, and the Executive Committee chose a new president, this time from the majority faction, though not one of the contending candidates in 1991. Again, the incentives set up by internal democracy appeared to create problems for party effectiveness.

Local elections to municipal committees replicated this pattern. Often, purging of the opposition resulted in a more effective committee

27. Brokers for the third-place faction evidently told the ex-CD candidate that their delegates would vote for the ex-PCM candidate Alejandro Encinas in the second round, giving him the victory, unless the CD offered to swing some delegates toward candidate Jorge Gómez Villareal to eliminate the PCM candidate from competition in the first round. In the second round the PCM candidate's delegates voted for Jorge Gómez. Because the Encinas group and the CD group hated each other more than Jorge Gómez, the two-round rule resulted in his election.

28. In the initial procedure delegates nominated candidates from the floor. Candidates stood in front of the assembly, and as each stepped forward accredited delegates voted by holding up special "vote" cards. Problems arose because each delegate could vote more than once, up to the number of positions available. Not only did the disputed delegates vote as a bloc but they seemed to raise their hands more than the allowed number of times. As the real powers—the brokers—vanished again from the room, the "State Congress" degenerated into a sort of talent show, with delegates coming forward to sing folk songs or read poems. Personal observation, April 1991.

but at the expense of more public confrontations with purged factions. In the Estado de México the multipolar structure of divisions made possible the composition of brokered committees, but this just internalized divisions and often resulted in deadlocked committees unable to reach consensus on urgent decisions. In one case a conscious decision to include representatives of different currents led to the formation of a *comité municipal* in the Estado de México with personal and ideological conflicts that made debates rather heated. Because of the time it took to resolve these conflicts and the need to settle upon the decision that would arouse the least opposition, this committee frequently lost the initiative in conflicts with the municipal government or made decisions that allowed the government to preserve the status quo, instead of maximizing party gains. In at least one instance such conflicts nearly caused the committee to miss the deadline for legal registration of candidates for the 1991 congressional election.

These cases represent the upper end of the scale in terms of internal leadership elections. Most states did not manage to hold a congress in the first three years of the party's existence. Several states tried and failed. In both Baja California and Morelos—states Cárdenas carried in 1988—attempts to hold a congress failed more than once. The provisional Morelos leadership was primarily composed of non-*morelenses*, and according to a PRD account, "had to be installed in Mexico City because in the different installation attempts in Cuernavaca [Morelos], the conflicts unleashed over problems of representation did not permit such installation to be carried out."[29] Elected *comités municipales* seemed much more common than elected state leaderships, but there was considerable variation in the timing, representativeness, and quality of the elections for these committees.

Candidate selection initially offered more scope for direct primary elections. In states where the party had a strong presence, primaries predominated, particularly in the case of offices for majority election, though practice did not quite live up to theoretical commitment.[30] Technical and financial problems prevented the installation of more than a

29. Partido de la Revolución Democrática (PRD), *Informe sobre las elecciones en Morelos* (Mexico City: PRD, Comisión para la Defensa del Voto, 1991), 5.
30. The integration of proportional representation lists required a National Convention with delegates of three groups: delegates elected by the convention held to ratify or select the majority congressional candidate in each electoral district, majority candidates, and members of the Consejo Nacional. To encourage candidates to try for majority seats statutes specified that four of the first seven positions on the federal list (and six of the first ten candidates on the state list) should go to candidates already selected to run for a majority seat. See PRD, *Documentos básicos*, 51.

few polling stations. In its strongholds the PRD rarely managed to set up polling stations in areas outside the principal towns in a district. Though this disenfranchised much of the rural population, the PRD simply could not afford to duplicate the state's efforts in the general election. More commonly, the party did not hold primary elections due to lack of interest on the part of potential candidates. Party leaders sometimes had to exert themselves to dig up a suitable volunteer. Only where local PRD strength gave candidates a reasonable chance of success and provided a pool of candidates did the level of interest normally compel—and the activist infrastructure permit—primaries. Thus, the PRD's failure to hold primary elections in many states did not reflect lack of commitment to democracy but a more serious problem: lack of national presence. The PRD chose congressional candidates via primaries in fewer than half of all electoral districts in 1991.

Despite fundamental similarities between processes of leadership and candidate selection, some differences exist. On the positive side, the PRD held direct elections in many candidate selection cases. However, problems with internal elections manifested themselves more acutely in candidate selection, perhaps because the stakes were higher, potentially including government authority and a salary. While non-PRD activists had little reason to seek PRD leadership, they showed much more interest in public office. This caused serious problems in a number of cases where the party's candidate did not belong to the PRD. Primaries at times selected candidates that damaged the PRD's attempt to consolidate an electoral identity.

Second, representativeness may worsen, in spite of public pressure to present a slate that represents many potential constituencies. With respect to the representation of women nominated for office, for instance, the PRI, virtually without internal elections, came in ninth out of ten in 1991. The PRD, with perhaps the most democratic internal procedures of any party, came in dead last.[31] In 1994 the PRD abandoned primaries for congressional posts and significantly improved the representation of women to about one-fourth of all nominations.[32] Like-

31. María Luisa Cantú, "¿Qué tanto inciden las mujeres en los puestos políticos?" *La Jornada* (Mexico City), 8 August 1991, sec. Doble Jornada, p. 10.
32. Women represented only 12 percent of all PRD majority candidates, but in the more important proportional representation lists they accounted for 24 percent of the top twenty-five positions and 24 percent of the top fifty. This resulted from a negotiated agreement to select 30 percent women candidates. Candidate information from Mexico, Instituto Federal Electoral (IFE), "Reporte general de candidatos a diputados de representación proporcional por partido" (Mexico City: IFE, Dirección Ejecutiva de Prerrogativas y Partidos Políticos, 1994), computer printout.

wise, the 1991 convention to select candidates for the proportional representation (PR) list resulted in a skewed representation of political tendencies from the point of view of their probable popularity. The Mexican system awards PR seats to parties based on their vote in each of five *circunscripciones*, regions containing several states apiece. Parties present five lists, with the top five candidates in a region most likely to get elected. Candidates that belonged to independent left organizations before 1988 controlled 48 percent of these choice spots. Only four ex-CD members—16 percent of the total—won representation.[33] Candidate selection through negotiation did not result in a deliberately balanced representation of currents, but in aggressive attempts to grab as much as possible.

Third, resource exhaustion became a significant issue, particularly when candidates and the party had to spend money on a primary. Funds that could otherwise have been spent on the general election went into setting up polling stations, providing them with indelible ink to prevent repeat voting, printing ballots, and so forth. Many candidates conducted primary campaigns. While the winning candidate could consider his expenses an investment, at least partly recoverable in the general election, the defeated candidates lost resources that they might have put into the party pot or used in subsequent campaigns.

Sometimes losers simply took their resources—and supporters—out of the party altogether. Internal conflicts over the legitimacy of results seemed to cause definitive breaches with the party more frequently than in leadership selection. The difference between the kind of people who present themselves as candidates in the two types of elections may influence this pattern. Candidates with some loyalty to the party will exit less often when they lose elections than candidates whose only motive was to get the nomination or who never belonged to the party in the first place. However, even when contending candidates were unquestionably loyal to the party, internal campaigns could "exceed the limits of civility and cause wounds."[34] The 1991 battle for the senatorial candidacy in Mexico City provides a classic example. The three candidates were all top PRD leaders, but the contest quickly turned nasty.[35] Unlike leader-

33. Alejandro Caballero, "Ex-militantes de grupos de izquierda predominan en pluri-nominales del PRD," *La Jornada* (Mexico City), 27 May 1991: 3.

34. Confidential interview AB, June 1991.

35. The candidates were Rodolfo González Guevara, an original CD member who left the PRI just before announcing his precandidacy; Ignacio Castillo Mena, an ex-CD leader and member of the PRD National Executive Committee; and Heberto Castillo, also a member of the National Executive Committee and a longtime leader of the independent left. Castillo spent time in jail for his involvement in the 1968 student movement, supported the MLN, and founded the PMT, one of the parties that joined the PMS in 1987.

ship elections, the exigencies of campaigning for public support meant that it all took place in front of a large audience. Some of the more publishable comments accused fellow precandidates of everything from incompetence to nefarious dealings with the PRI. Public insults are even less easy to forgive and forget than insults in the privacy of a CEN meeting. In the aftermath, one losing candidate (Ignacio Castillo Mena) took Salinas's offer to become Mexico's ambassador to Ecuador and was expelled from the party, while the other (González Guevara) openly discussed his disillusionment with the PRD. The whole nasty spectacle contributed to the party's disappointing showing in Mexico City and tended to discourage PRI defectors like González Guevara, who joined the PRD shortly before announcing his senatorial aspirations, from seeking refuge in the PRD.[36]

Internal democracy per se did not cause these divisions. Thus, the accusations of fraud that so discredited the PRD, the fierce struggle for positions, and the unwillingness of losers to abide by the results does not prove that *perredistas* were exceptionally poor losers, exceptionally quarrelsome individuals, or exceptionally insincere democrats. There were two basic reasons for internal division. First, the PRD was a new party built by merging many existing organizations. The identities, feuds, and personal relationships created in these organizations continued to shape behavior in the PRD. Ideological and tactical differences connected to the party's character as a broad coalition with a vague umbrella ideology reemerged in the struggle for consolidation. Second, disputes over positions would have resulted in divisions regardless of the character of the party and regardless of the decision rule used to allocate candidacies or leadership posts. Conflict over positions and influence occurs in every political party. With different internal procedures the PRI and the PAN both have had trouble with divisions, including major splits, though in these cases one rarely hears the argument so often applied to the PRD, that its internal conflicts disqualify it from governing.[37]

36. One ex-president of the PRI (not Muñoz Ledo) commented afterward: "How lamentable. I received Don Rodolfo without problems; he had privileged treatment in the party. In the PRD, who would have guessed it, they treated him like garbage." See "De la supervivencia a la organización," *Este País*, no. 23 (February 1992): 13.

37. The PRI, of course, had Henriquez Guzmán, the MLN, the Madrazo movement, the Corriente Democrática, and many others. Virtually all opposition parties in Mexico between 1929 and 1994 originated in splits from the PRI. The PAN actually failed to nominate a presidential candidate in 1976 because of divisions, and has experienced many major public confrontations between party leaders and dissidents. In October 1992 similar divisions resulted in the departure of some of its most distinguished and longtime members, one of which actually became a PRD candidate for senator in 1994. For a discussion

Nevertheless, internal democracy had a number of negative consequences for the PRD. Like pressure applied to a flawed crystal, democracy deepened existing cracks and threatened to eventually shatter the party. The process of holding elections absorbed the party's energy and resources and encouraged party members to wash their dirty laundry in public, attacking one another as fiercely as the PRI could have wished. In the name of democracy and the right to be heard, party factions made conflicting policy statements, followed contradictory tactics, and generally made the party look indecisive, unpredictable, and unreliable. Overall, instead of proving its democratic convictions, the PRD proved that its democratic practices left a lot to be desired and contributed to its declining credibility as an alternative government. If the PRD could not hold fair, democratic, clean elections and abide by the results, how could the party promise democracy to Mexico? And if the PRD could not resolve conflicts among its own members, how could it govern the country?

In noting some of these dangers Jorge Castañeda argues that "distrust regarding the left's democratic convictions [is] so widespread and justified that there can be no excess in this direction for now. The inconveniences of too much democracy are preferable to the scourge of its absence or insufficiency. The left will have to make do . . . managing the perverse by-products as best it can."[38] In the case of the PRD the by-products of internal democracy amounted to more than an "inconvenience." It is possible, as Castañeda suggests, that time and experience and political learning will improve the left's practice of democracy and mitigate its negative effects, but this is not inevitable. Internal democracy does not necessarily provide a competitive advantage in general elections, especially since the diversity and complexity of its social base will probably continue to infect the left with divisions, making internal elections a risky strategy. This probably applies to most modern left parties as well as to the PRD. As a 1991 internal report (ironically, written by the PRD Committee for the Defense of the Vote) argued, the PRD's primary elections "are very far from succeeding in selecting good candidates, or even assuring consensus behind them in the popula-

---

of the early difficulties of the PAN, and the factors that "rent PAN with profound factionalism," see Donald Mabry, *Mexico's Acción Nacional: A Catholic Alternative to Revolution* (New York: Syracuse University Press, 1973), 50; for more recent decades see Soledad Loaeza, *Oposición y oportunidad: El Partido Acción Nacional en México* (Mexico City: Fondo de Cultural Económica, forthcoming), excerpted in Francisco Ortíz Pinchetti, "Acción Nacional no es un partido, sino una federación de organizaciones locales unidas por su anticentralismo: Soledad Loaeza," *Proceso*, no. 969 (29 May 1995): 22–26.

38. Castañeda, *Utopia Unarmed*, 361.

tion."[39] Party leaders might well decide to minimize the practice of internal elections for the sake of party competitiveness. One could imagine an alternative, semi-European model—a disciplined party with leadership control of nominations and perhaps the reservation of some seats for popular movements to fill autonomously. The PRD took a step in this direction in 1994 when it decided to use a national convention instead of primaries to nominate candidates for Congress, though the main reason for their choice had more to do with ensuring representation for candidates from "civil society," as the next chapter will discuss. And even so, some agreed with one participant that the convention was "excessively democratic" because it left the party at the mercy of pressure groups, to which "we should not be so subject."[40]

Yet the left cannot abandon all pretense to democracy. For the moment the left seems to have little choice but to accept the costs—in part to prove its commitment to democracy, but more directly because of pressure from key constituencies: the organized grass-roots and popular movements, which demand a higher standard of democratic behavior from their left allies than they expect from the right, and activists in left parties, who often get little from their activism except a sense of participation. Alternatives to democracy would not have resolved the sources of internal conflict or fights about candidacies and leadership posts. The PRI minimizes conflict over candidacies by employing its extensive resources, including government jobs, to compensate losers for accepting defeat gracefully. The PRD had nothing to use as compensation, making candidate nomination a very zero-sum game. Nondemocratic procedures to select candidates/leaders might well have increased the rate of attrition. Thus, as much as democracy cost the PRD, it would probably do worse without it.

PARTY INSTITUTIONALIZATION: PROBLEMS OF AUTHORITY AND ACCOUNTABILITY

Internal democracy should have made it easier for the party to solve a second problem: the development of legitimate institutions for making

39. PRD, *Informe sobre las elecciones en Morelos*, 1–2.
40. Confidential interview GC, September 1994. The pressure groups to which this participant referred were nonallied, "opportunistic" civil society organizations that he said threatened to denounce the PRD for antidemocracy if it did not award them candidacies. Ironically, he belonged to one of the most highly organized factions in the party—originally called the "Trisecta"—which was often criticized for its no-holds-barred approach to seizing candidacies.

collective decisions. This is key to the effective performance of a variety of consolidation tasks. The PRD needed to count on the cooperation of members to sustain coherent action as a legislative bench, as a party in local government, as a mediator for popular movements, and as an ally of other parties. These tasks require an ability to plan strategy, develop common long-term goals, and coordinate action. The FDN had no such institutions; its member parties had come separately to their common goal of supporting Cárdenas in 1988. But costs at that moment were not as high. Each group could plan its campaign activities more or less independently and accredit poll watchers under any one of several party registries. In 1991 the *perredistas* had to accomplish the same activities with only one registry and take on new tasks that the FDN did not have to perform, particularly once they assumed elected office. PRD statutes set up institutions to make collective decisions: the National Executive Committee, municipal committees, and so forth. The number of committees elected via more or less formal rules as well as the significant amount of party activity that ended up in formal institutions indicates improvement in institutionalization.

However, it is one thing to set up institutions for collective decision making and quite another for those institutions to make legitimate decisions through routinized procedures. Decision making did not become highly formalized or predictable, especially at lower levels. Many local committees had no clear boundaries. Members of the same committee often estimated committee size differently, or gave a range.[41] Participation in committee activity seemed quite flexible. Anyone could attend meetings and make comments, and in the Michoacán committees anyone could even vote, when votes were taken. Two individuals interviewed separately in one community identified each other as members of the committee—and denied belonging themselves, though they readily admitted PRD activism and involvement in many local party activities.[42] State and national committees had fairly clear rules of membership by 1991. Though the composition of committees changed frequently, informed people knew who was a member of the National Executive Committee and who was not. These institutions became important forums for discussing party strategy and policy but had trouble legitimizing their decisions among party members.[43] Instead, rebellion

41. This reticence may have come from a desire to protect committee members not present.

42. Confidential interviews AF, July 1991; DA, July 1991.

43. Debates in the Consejo Nacional proved instrumental in some policy shifts within the PRD, such as its ability to criticize its handling of the 1991 electoral campaign instead of relying entirely on denunciations of fraud, and its movement away from the line fol-

against party decisions hurt cooperation, resulted in vacillation and contradictory swings in policy, and generated an unattractive image of the PRD as an alternative government and alliance partner. When the party managed to reach internal consensus, its actions were effective, but it could not consistently act as a unit.

Three factors exaggerated the normal difficulty that new parties have in institutionalizing decision-making structures. First, conflict over the meaning and practice of democracy undermined its potential to legitimate decisions and institutions. Questions about the quality of internal elections led to questions about the right of the resulting committees to represent party members. Many did not see discredited committees as moral authorities whose opinions should carry even persuasive weight.

Beyond the problem of election quality, party statutes reveal an underlying ambivalence toward the idea of constructing party authority of any kind, associated in part with the problem of defining democracy and making room for the heterogenous groups in the PRD, but also with the "movement logic" that characterized spontaneous affiliations to the FDN. On the one hand, founders clearly saw a need for institutions with authority to make binding decisions in a timely way. Each party committee right down to the smallest, nonelected, and voluntary *comité de base* is charged to "carry out [or obey] and enforce [*cumplir y hacer cumplir*], within its sphere, the Declaration of Principles, the Program of Action and the Statutes of the Party, and the resolutions of the [respectively higher committees]"; each individual member has a duty to "respect and observe [*acatar*] the democratic elections . . . [to] bodies of representation, resolution, and direction of the party, as well as the agreements and resolutions taken by them according to these statutes."[44] On the other hand, party statutes protect individual and local autonomy in the name of democracy, defined implicitly as the right to decide one's own course of action. The member's right to "freely express his opinions inside and outside the party" supplements his right to "full liberty of action . . . inside and outside the organization," including support for internal currents to "use the resources and buildings of the party to organize themselves and make known their proposals," though they cannot claim to speak for the whole party.[45] The sanction of expulsion applies to five actions, only one of which refers to defying party decisions, and then only if it means "allying with any interest of the

lowed since 1988 that the Salinas government would fall from the weight of its own illegitimacy.

44. PRD, *Documentos básicos*, 47; 27.

45. Ibid., 26, 29.

government or other political party independently from the leadership of the party." Even decisions commonly thought of as normal party prerogatives, like party dues, were left to the individual member to "freely and voluntarily determine his contribution."[46]

This ambivalence toward authority and institutionalization as goals appears even more clearly in observation of party committees. One telling example arose during a 1992 meeting of the Consejo Estatal in the Estado de México. The state executive committee had raised several issues having to do with institutionalization and party authority: the need to make sure Consejo members actually appeared in the party's list of affiliates, the importance of regularizing the operation of municipal committees (including creating formal committees in the approximately one-third of the state's *municipios* without them), and the advisability of requiring new affiliates to pay a minimal fee to cover the cost of a party membership card. These measures—especially the last two—aroused substantial debate. Many delegates did not like the idea of enforcing universal compliance with rules or imposing obligations like an affiliation fee on members. One delegate protested the whole idea of formal committees. The term "institutional" made him think of the PRI, he said, and he didn't like it: the PRD should be a party of people, not institutions.[47]

Resistance to party authority had predictable effects on coordination. Local committees jealously guarded their autonomy and rejected "interference" by other levels of the party, undermining cooperation on such vital activities as poll watching.[48] Individuals often felt little obligation to obey decisions made by their own committees, even when they participated in them. The same activist might resist his committee's authority to compel him to attend meetings one day and the next day uphold the committee's authority to accept a deal he supported and force minority members who disagreed to comply with it.[49] Individuals who lost a vote might decide to do what they thought best anyway, even at the top levels of the party.[50] Such "double-dealing" could give the party a reputation

46. Ibid., 58; 27.

47. Personal observation, August 1992.

48. For example, the PRD commission to evaluate local Morelos elections reported "little coordination [of the CEN task force] with the Provisional State Committee, since they did not accept 'interference' from the National Executive Committee." PRD, *Informe sobre las elecciones en Morelos*, 29.

49. Personal observation, May 1991, in an Estado de México municipal committee meeting.

50. Cárdenas himself, for example, made speeches rejecting negotiations authorized by the party's CEN and carried out by the party's president.

as an unreliable partner for a pact. In its first six years the PRD failed to find a comfortable or even stable balance between freedom and discipline, between commitment to internal democracy and the party's need to make binding decisions on behalf of its members.

Second, resource constraints blocked the construction of strong communication networks and prevented the central party organization from using financial incentives to enforce general party discipline. Without communication no party can institutionalize a system to make authoritative collective decisions or coordinate actions. Popular input does not consistently reach decision-making committees, limiting the legitimacy of decisions. Members who intend to abide by the decisions of committees may fail to do so for lack of knowledge about what the committee decided. The PRD had trouble extending reliable communication down to the local level. It takes money to travel to party meetings, to make phone calls, or to post flyers with information. Many local activists have neither the money nor the time. As a result, they frequently reported feeling isolated and dissatisfied with communication in the party. In both Michoacán and Estado de México, coordination among municipal committees seemed limited. One attempt to create a network of municipal committee presidents in Michoacán experienced such a falloff in participation after a few meetings that no new meetings were scheduled. More effort was made to strengthen vertical links, with varying success. Michoacán's weak transportation and communication infrastructure exacerbated local committee isolation. One local committee member estimated that only 5 percent of his committee's communications involved the *comité estatal* and that the committee "never" communicated directly with national-level leaders, though they "listened to" the speeches of Cárdenas.[51] Most communications took place within the committee, or between the committee and actors in its local community. Urban areas close to Mexico City communicated more frequently with higher levels of the party, probably due to proximity and better infrastructure.

Differences in resources and infrastructure help explain differences in the operation of local committees. Urban committees tended to do more party work, scheduled meetings more regularly, and made some effort to restrict the vote to those who belonged to the committee. Higher institutionalization, particularly in the urban Estado de México, is also connected to activists' political training. Almost all municipal activists had previous party experience, usually in the bureaucratized old left parties. As one PRD leader put it, somewhat humorously:

51. Confidential interview AX, July 1991.

"Small groups that have party experience . . . take control of the directive organizations of the party because they have training for this. For example, the training to hold an eight-hour meeting. Other citizens after three hours want someone to call for the vote already, or say what to do, or what the conclusion is, period. *Now*, right? And so those without training leave, and those with training stay, and they end up in the party structures."[52] In the absence of "training," activists often ignored or bypassed formal structures, simply organizing for specific projects rather than at regular meetings. This did not necessarily make for a less effective committee, only a less institutionalized one.

Resource constraints also limited the leverage of party committees over lower-level committees or recalcitrant activists. Interviews at various levels in the party and in several different states confirm that the national party makes a quite limited contribution to state parties, and that state parties in turn hoard most resources to maintain a state-level infrastructure. Instead, state parties appear to depend heavily on the government subsidy allocated to them directly on the basis of their state-level strength. Indeed, the 1994 strategy of pouring virtually all the party's resources into the presidential campaign was intended to strengthen state party organizations by boosting the PRD vote and thereby entitling them to more support from the government. In part, the minimal financial ties between levels reflect the PRD's general impoverishment. In 1994—a presidential election year—the national party offices had only about fifty full-time employees on the payroll, plus thirty or so more flexible workers.[53] There is simply not much to go around. The desire to avoid internal conflict may also cause some reluctance to get into the business of dividing and distributing money. As one national leader argued, lack of money forces the party to choose among potential recipients, raising the danger of clientelism and factional competition.[54] The party sometimes allocates more money to states that are already strong, within striking distance of a victory, rather than to build up weak states, or—even less optimally—it gives money to state committees with stronger personal ties to national elites. However, the central party's limited financial role deprives it of a useful tool for exercising leverage. Divisions in the national leadership exacerbate the problem by making it hard for the party to use its slim resources strategically to overcome marginalization and lack of discipline at the subnational level.

52. Roberto Robles Gárnica, interview by author, Mexico City, 4 April 1991.
53. Confidential interview GA, September 1994.
54. Confidential interview GD, September 1994.

Third, two of the party's advantages during emergence—its reliance on charisma and its character as a fusion party—tended to create parallel channels of authority that overrode the legitimacy of party decisions, blocking institutionalization and acceptance of party authority. Cárdenas is the classic example. The PRD depended heavily on the charismatic authority of Cárdenas to draw together diverse political allies, recruit activists, and win support. Cárdenas could not transfer this authority to party institutions, in part because charisma remains stubbornly attached to individuals for some time and in part because—ironically—his charisma was not strong enough to dominate a party built by so many currents. Nevertheless, charismatic authority gave him unmatched influence over decisions, undermining development of the habit of deliberating decisions in party institutions and by majority rule.[55] Getting the party to adopt a policy depended less on debate or construction of a compromise than on convincing Cárdenas. Charismatic leadership also created a temptation for losers in party decisions to appeal to the higher authority of charisma by appealing to Cárdenas. The expectation of his intervention often led people to wait for him to define his position, and gave the impression that party decisions depended on what he thought.[56] When Cárdenas did intervene, he was accused of authoritarianism, sometimes justifiably, as when he threatened to resign if the party did not expel a local activist who accepted a position in the PRI-dominated government of Chiapas. When he did not intervene—and some evidence suggests that he initially tried to underutilize his authority—he was accused of letting the party drift or letting unscrupulous manipulators control it.[57] Therefore, critics like prominent activist Jorge Alcocer charged that "the truth is that the affairs of the party are not resolved in the formal institutions of the party but in private consultations [with Cárdenas]."[58]

55. Jorge Alcocer, "PRD: La hora del Congreso," *Nexos* 13, no. 155 (November 1990): 56.

56. As Heberto Castillo argued in a 1994 Consejo meeting, if there is *caudillismo* in the party, it is partly the fault of the *acaudillados*. Personal observation, September 1994.

57. For example, in 1991 he refused to present a list of candidates for proportional representation seats or to plead for the inclusion of particular candidates. Several *perredistas* who got left out complained that he had let tiny factions hijack the party.

58. Pascal Beltrán del Río, "El PRD se dividió en dos grupos y extravió el camino a la democracia: Jorge Alcocer," *Proceso*, no. 740 (7 January 1991): 8. Alcocer resigned from the PRD in December 1990, accusing Cárdenas of "putting all his authority on one side of the scale, . . . [though] he should be the neutral pointer registering the scale's balance." Even worse, according to Alcocer, Cárdenas put his weight on the wrong side, tilting the party toward a confrontational strategy that jeopardized the future of the PRD. Jorge Alcocer, interview by author, Mexico City, 19 February 1991.

Beyond the influence of Cárdenas, personal and political loyalties played an important role in defining divisions that led to rejection of collective decisions. In areas with a strong left presence before 1988, like the Estado de México, local factions tended to mirror political divisions among the old left parties and leaders, with the addition of the ex-*priistas*. Prevailing divisions reflected, remarkably, the original political experience of an individual—ex-communists versus ex-PMT members versus MASistas, and so forth (see Appendix A for a list of some of these factional forebears). Personal loyalties to individual leaders underlie these identities and help to explain why the original political experiences seem stronger than political identities forged in unification parties like the PSUM (1981–87) or PMS (1987–89).[59] At the national level, pre-1988 political loyalties gradually became less relevant, until by 1994 they no longer explained most key party divisions or predicted political positions. However, personal ties vertically connected national leaders to their previous political bases, preserving some remnants of older political structures.

In other Mexican states, with little pre-1988 left party presence, conflicts tended to follow personal lines rather than party origin. The principal division in Michoacán, for instance, reflected a rivalry between the two PRD senators elected in 1988 over control of the party and the PRD candidacy for governor of Michoacán. Some differences in perspective appear at the level of leadership, with allies of Cristóbal Arias slightly more "*político*" and allies of Roberto Robles Gárnica slightly more "*técnico*" in outlook. Arias had legal training and experience as a PRI party leader; his allies were generally younger people with local connections. Dr. Robles Gárnica belongs to the same generation as Cárdenas. Where Arias served as a congressman, Robles's most important elected office was a basically administrative position as mayor of Morelia. Robles's supporters included many former officials of the 1980–86 Cárdenas government,[60] who emphasized impartial, efficient administration to build

59. One of the best-organized of these factions (holding regular meetings and negotiating as a group) was the *Trisecta*, so named because it joined three currents dating to the 1970s or early 1980s: Partido Popular Revolucionario (PPR); Maoist Movimiento Revolucionario del Pueblo (MRP); and Asociación Cívica Nacional Revolucionaria (ACNR), which supported the guerrilla movement of the early 1970s. These organizations all participated in the PMS. For a while, in 1990, this group became the "six-pack" when it was joined by three others: the Partido de la Revolución Socialista, which split from the PST in 1975; part of the maoist coalition known as the Organización de la Izquierda Revolucionaria-Línea de Masas (OIR-LM), with roots in the 1960s; and participants from the leftist journal *Punto Crítico*, associated with former members of the 1968 student movement. See Appendix A for further information.

60. The battle between an Arias supporter and a Robles sympathizer for the PRD

party support, in contrast to Arias supporters, who emphasized old-fashioned political machine building.[61] Nevertheless, personal ambition and loyalties rather than party origin exacerbated this division. Indeed, at the local level supporters had trouble identifying ideological differences between the two. Initially a top-level split, it spread between 1989 and 1991, eventually becoming more intense at the local level than at the elite level as preexisting community conflicts became identified with divisions between *roblistas* and *cristobalistas*.

The split also revealed the incapacity of institutional rules to resolve such personal conflicts authoritatively. In 1991 Robles ceded the gubernatorial candidacy to Arias after internal negotiations in order to avoid a confrontation that would weaken the party. The intensity of the conflict subsided but resurfaced in even more virulent form in 1995 as the state faced a round of important local elections, including special elections to replace its interim governor.[62] A renewed battle for the gubernatorial nomination resulted in bitter public conflict, including claims of victory by both candidates in the primary, mutual charges of fraud and manipulation, and violent confrontation. When the state PRD decided to support Arias's claim, Robles Gárnica appealed on the grounds that the committee was fraudulently elected and biased toward Arias. The national Commission for Guarantees and Vigilance—statutorily responsible for resolving such problems—deadlocked on whether to uphold the state decision, largely on factional grounds. The National Executive Committee was forced to make the final decision, favoring Arias mostly on the pragmatic ground that while incidents of fraud had oc-

---

senatorial candidacy in 1991 illustrates these traits. Alfonso Solórzano Fraga, a young engineer and local congressman recruited initially into politics by Arias himself in 1988, represented the *cristobalista* current. He had some local political experience and a strong personal connection to Arias; he later married Arias's sister. His opponent Leonel Godoy sought allies among *roblistas* almost by default, since he did not owe his career or campaign to a connection with Robles. Godoy had little experience in local politics but an impressive resume as an administrator, serving in the office of the state prosecutor under Cárdenas, as head of the State Electoral Commission in 1986, and as FDN representative in the Federal Electoral Tribunal in 1988.

61. This assessment is based in part on self-evaluations of *roblistas* and *cristobalistas*. In municipal committees *cristobalistas* identified Arias as humble, more open to the natural leader, and representing the peasants, and Robles as representing the bureaucracy and ambition. *Roblistas* saw themselves as "well-prepared [educated]" and experienced administrators. They accused *cristobalistas* of authoritarian politics, "the same or worse than the PRI." Confidential interviews AI, July 1991; AE, June 1991.

62. Arias officially lost the 1992 governor's race, but he accused the PRI of stealing the election. PRD mobilization forced the naming of an interim governor. After considerable protest, the state scheduled special elections to select a new governor for November 1995.

curred, repeating the process would leave the PRD without a candidate until too late for an effective campaign. The conflict may well have cost the PRD the November election, which it lost by a narrow margin. It did cost the party the loyalty of Robles Gárnica, who resigned from the PRD in February 1996 to accept a position in the new PRI administration of Michoacán. Some of his personal supporters followed. Thus, personal loyalties defined divisions, blocked the institutionalization of decision making, and often led to public rebellion against party decisions.

Paradoxically, personalism could also improve communication and occasionally legitimated decisions. Significant intraparty communication went through personal connections. Committees without such a connection often had to rely on uncertain newspaper information. Some accepted party directives out of loyalty to a charismatic leader who favored them. Personal authority allowed the party to get away with not building institutional authority, but at least it kept the party on its feet. Getting rid of Cárdenas, for instance, would have left the party without its strongest unifying force. Even Alcocer—not his biggest fan— admitted that "without the presence of Cuauhtémoc Cárdenas, the PRD would have little future, at least for a few more years."[63] Despite his loss in the 1994 presidential election, Cárdenas remains an important reference point for many *perredistas*, giving him latitude to affect party policy against the preferences of the national leadership by making public policy statements, ingenuously identifying himself as just a PRD member with liberty to express his opinion, but fully aware of his impact.

Similarly, internal elections enhanced communication by bringing party members together and forcing them to talk to each other. The PRD did not rely entirely on personal, informal channels of communication and authority. Different levels of the party established organic links with each other through Consejos and internal elections. The Consejo Nacional was an important forum for comparing the experiences of PRD activists from all over the country. Members of the Consejo took information back to their state party organizations every six months at a minimum; in fact, the Consejo usually met more frequently, as often as every other month.[64] While Consejo members from more remote states could not afford to attend every meeting, most states tried to send at least one representative to key strategy meetings. Internal elections were also organized, carried out, and certified as a cooperative project between levels, providing opportunities for communication and the for-

63. Alcocer, "PRD: La hora del Congreso," 56.
64. PRD, *Documentos básicos*, 33.

mation of new personal connections. A Comité Estatal might send a representative to certify municipal committee elections and meet those elected. The election of candidates provided similar opportunities. For some communities internal elections were the most regular forms of contact with different levels of the party. Party institutions also tried to enforce binding decisions on members most frequently in the context of internal elections. And leaders tried to channel these decisions through party institutions, if possible, to validate them. Though the party did not always succeed in enforcing its decisions or convincing activists of their legitimacy, internal elections represented a significant attempt to make rules more predictable for activists, to channel them through party institutions, and thus to institutionalize an activist regime.

Nevertheless, as indicated in the PRD's own unsparing analysis, the predominant tendency remained

> acute institutional instability. At the margin of the variety and complexity of the causes, the effects of such a situation are obvious: relaxed discipline, political conduct divorced from the values of the party, arbitrary management of economic and material resources, insufficient information, improvisation or absence of work plans, deficient evaluation of activities, neglect of adopted procedures, a great many decisions that are never put into effect, et cetera. . . . a strongly institutionalized party has a well-developed national leadership, . . . operational homogeneity, among bodies at the same level, . . . diversity of sources of financing, . . . capacity of direction, not only in internal processes, but in what it does in the set of related social organizations, . . . [and] a high level of certainty about the rules of internal processes. . . . our party shows considerable lags [in each of these areas].[65]

ACTIVIST RECRUITMENT AND REATTACHMENT

As it attempted to consolidate subroutines governing activist interaction the PRD was also struggling with the task of simply keeping activ-

65. Partido de la Revolución Democrática (PRD), *Cuadernos del Tercer Congreso Nacional* (Mexico City: PRD, 1995), 28–29. This document was prepared as a basis for discussion of the party's organizational problems at the Third National Congress, held in Oaxtepec Mexico, in August 1995.

ists involved in the party. This is harder for new parties than it might seem because the demands made on permanent activists differ from the demands made on activists during new party formation in terms of time, level of commitment, and skills. It is one thing to mobilize activists to help in the exciting task of organizing a new party, and quite another to convince the same activists to contribute their time and resources on an ongoing basis. What I describe as permanent activism can take several forms. One can heuristically distinguish: (1) the paid party professional; (2) the regular (but unpaid) party worker, who contributes to routine party activity; (3) the reserve activist, who can be relied on to help out in moments of peak party activity, such as elections; and (4) the loyal participant, who turns out for rallies, marches, internal elections, and the like. Each group has a role in party consolidation. The bread and butter of a party, the first two groups make the biggest sacrifices and develop the most expertise. Fortunately, a party needs relatively few. The third group provides the party with a flexible, experienced, and trained workforce at key moments. And though loyal participants do not take on leadership roles, the fourth group's participation affects the influence of the party as well as the health of internal democracy.

In the PRD many activists who worked in the 1988 campaign did not continue as permanent activists. Neither party formation nor the 1988 campaign required more than a short-term, though intense, commitment. Regular activism, particularly in the first two categories, requires long-term, sustained effort and demands more surrender of freedom than coordinating schedules for a candidate or attending campaign rallies. Even reserve activists and loyal participants, though they mobilize only for short periods, make a greater commitment to the party than the original, unattached activist. Their willingness to pitch in repeatedly incurs costs and risks. Because permanent activists must make greater sacrifices of time, money, and autonomy, less dedicated or poorer activists mobilized during formation may become discouraged. Moreover, consolidation tasks often demand more skill, patience, and technical or legal training than organizing a rally, and certainly more skill than attending one. Those who make good campaign workers do not necessarily make—and will not necessarily become—good permanent activists.

These dynamics put the PRD in a different strategic position than the FDN. In rational action terms the costs of activism increased. Without a corresponding increase in the material rewards of activism, such as that provided by electoral or policy success, the rational choice should be a decline in activism. This is the first reason the PRD reattached fewer activists than the outpouring of support during the 1988 campaign might have led one to expect.

Nevertheless, the PRD kept many permanent activists. The use of alternative hypotheses reflected in the literature on social movements helps explain how the PRD managed to reattach activists despite many negative factors and what contributed to regional variation in rates of success. Overall, conditions that discouraged support for the PRD also discouraged activists, including government hostility, lack of resources, and internal divisions, which made activism unpleasant. However, interviews suggest that personal loyalties, antipriism, the potential for payoffs in areas with PRD support, and a shared social experience of sacrifice tended to reinforce PRD commitments.[66]

Ideological Linkage

One important hypothesis about how organizations attract and keep activists suggests that ideological program matters. People contribute to an organization because they share its goals, its principles, and its view of society. In the PRD promotion of leftist, nationalist principles characterized many of the people who continued to participate despite the party's recognized defects. Yet I would argue that ideological program did not become the primary source of activist loyalty, and largely failed to attract new activists. Because it was never altogether clear what the party as a whole stood for, individual activists tended to identify more strongly with subsets or factions within the party, and leave or enter with that faction. The PRD platform was not quite as vague as its opponents often contended, but it avoided defining a position on key issues, probably in large part to cover up substantial internal disagreement about specific policies. The PRD developed a worldview that included vague principles of support for national sovereignty, democracy, and popular classes, but not a plausible alternative with a consistent ideological justification.

Two brief examples indicate the nature of this problem. First, in the area of political reform, the 1991 electoral platform promised that the PRD would "promote a new electoral legislation to guarantee respect for the vote" by "preventing the government or any other political force

66. These interviews took place in 1991 and 1992 and cover local-level activists, primarily from municipal committees, but in no way should they be seen as equivalent to a survey of PRD activists. A survey would ideally interview *non*activists, *former* activists, and *current* activists in various types of party activity about the process of involvement. Unfortunately, I was unable to carry out such a survey.

from taking over the electoral institutions charged with the organization, holding, and monitoring of the elections" and by "the formation of a network of national observers."[67] The specific conditions that would constitute sufficient guarantees of free, fair elections do not appear—perhaps for a reason. In early 1994 PRD president Porfirio Muñoz Ledo participated in negotiating an electoral reform with the initial authority of the party and of Cárdenas. Among other provisions the final version of the reform offered all Mexican citizens formal accreditation to observe every aspect of the election, including vote counting, and changed the composition of the Federal Electoral Institute's governing board to reduce PRI control.[68] When Cárdenas reversed his position on the value of negotiating such a reform, the PRD congressional bench split, with nineteen voting in favor of the reform package and sixteen against. Then, at a very public rally to commemorate the oil expropriation, Cárdenas criticized Muñoz Ledo for supporting what he saw as insufficient reforms that might prejudice the party's ability to denounce fraud.[69] The party's equivocal stance on this issue reflected an underlying lack of ideological consensus on what it proposed in the way of electoral reform or on how to get to democracy, beyond common goals of fraud (how? a mystery) and "getting out the vote." Should the party shoot for gradual reform? A negotiated political pact? A *"ruptura"* with the system, carrying Cárdenas into power on the shoulders of the people? Differences persisted on these basic programmatic and strategic questions, leaving potential supporters unsure what the party would do next, or assuming the worst.

Second, and more critically, the party's leaders seemed curiously reluctant to attack the principles behind the main economic initiative of Salinas: the North American Free Trade Agreement. The 1991 PRD electoral platform does not openly reject free trade as a principle, but its version of free trade insists that "Mexico must preserve its power to vary the instruments of economic policy . . . [including tariffs, subsidies, exchange rates, and taxes]." Thus NAFTA should be "unmistakably rejected" because "it would commit Mexico not to use freely the opportu-

67. Partido de la Revolución Democrática (PRD), *Plataforma electoral para las elecciones federales de 1991* (Mexico City: PRD, 1991), 6–7.
68. The reform added six "citizen advisers," selected by a two-thirds majority of the Chamber of Deputies (a number the PRI cannot command under new limits), and reduced the influence of representatives of the national political parties to "voice but not vote." Mexico Secretaría de Gobernación, *Diario oficial* (Mexico City: Secretaría de Gobernación, 18 May 1994), 2–10.
69. Pascal Beltrán del Río, "Afloran las diferencias internas: Resbalón perredista en el día y el lugar de la apoteosis de Cárdenas en 1988," *Proceso*, no. 907 (21 March 1994): 8.

nities that the changing international market may present . . . [and] would accentuate and perpetuate the condition of dependence and asymmetry of Mexico compared to the U.S." Still, the party "recognizes that the processes of growing international economic interaction are not only inevitable but desirable in many ways."[70] Its programmatic alternatives are equally confusing. The 1991 electoral platform suggests as "alternatives" the renegotiation of parts of NAFTA (especially rules for foreign investment, environmental standards, and immigration) and a "Continental Development Agreement," which "by means of cooperation among all our countries would seek the improvement of the conditions of life of peoples, overcome backwardness and social marginalization, and achieve sustained economic growth."[71] This is the only statement in the 1991 platform that directly discusses the Continental Development Agreement. Interviews of local activists revealed suspicion of NAFTA, but also confusion about what it meant and what their own party stood for regarding it.

Given the fervor with which many *perredistas* describe their political activity and the sacrifices they make for it, the PRD's lack of ideological focus seems at first somewhat mystifying. Clearly, developments like the fall of communism pushed the left toward a vague umbrella ideology that accommodated all varieties of "leftism." Paradoxically, however, the PRD's ideological confusion is at least partly rooted in the factors that initially contributed to its success. During its early period the *cardenista* coalition drew strength from the vagueness of its ideological appeal, allowing it to reach out to a broad, multiclass group of activists. Its incorporation of so many diverse groups slowed the subsequent construction of an ideological identity. No single group dominated the PRD in its early years, unlike the Brazilian PT, to which the strength of the labor movement gave a certain identity. Many *perredistas* came into the movement with strong but different ideological goals. When the party had to come up with specific policies, as in the Congress, these differences made it hard for the party to take a united position. Yet attempts to mold these perspectives into something coherent drove away activists who found their goals less represented. To the degree that this internal diversity becomes typical of left parties in the post-Soviet era, left fragmentation will continue.

Yet the vague and even contradictory nature of PRD platforms could hardly be hidden—at least not with the PRI publicizing it. Thus, identification with PRD ideology did not significantly contribute to the re-

70. PRD, *Plataforma electoral para las elecciones federales de 1991*, 16–17.
71. Ibid., 17.

cruitment of new activists after 1988. Few people could join the PRD solely because of ideological affinity with the party's goals. In some ways PRD "ideology" resembled a Rorschach test, which every observer interpreted differently; it motivated activism in part by its openness, which made the party available as an instrument for a variety of political causes. The problem is that a "Rorschach party" may not be a very effective instrument. Attempts to use the party to pursue one set of goals were often blocked by party members going in other directions. Thus, activists with this ideological mix of motives could become frustrated and leave.

Self-Interest Linkage: Payoffs

A second potential answer to the problem of continued activism lies in the notion of selective payoffs. This is the answer preferred by Mancur Olson, for example. PRD activism did offer some payoffs, particularly to those who mastered the art of getting good positions on proportional representation lists or who got one of the few paid positions working for the party or its elected officials. Similarly, the lure of a candidacy motivated a lot of recruitment of disgruntled members of other parties or organizations, just as the denial of a candidacy motivated many defections. However, it is hard to explain the consolidation of a PRD activist core by reference to material payoffs. The PRD could not guarantee activists would get access to payoffs for several reasons: (1) it could not elect many people to office; (2) its internal selection procedures made renomination chancy; (3) Mexican law prohibits reelection to the same position in any case; and (4) some in the party thought it was important to make room for fresh blood rather than rotating among the same tired group. To make things worse, the party had little chance of enacting most of its preferred policies, as its electoral failures left it outnumbered in or absent from the major institutions of the national government. Thus, for most activists the rewards were less tangible: pride, influence, a sense of having contributed to a good cause, and, perhaps in some cases, pleasurable revenge.

But in return for these rewards activists paid nonnegligible costs. Few activists started off in 1988 with substantial resources to spend on political work. Especially at the local level, most activists in interview communities did not seem well-off. Such activists cannot subsidize a permanent organization. Moreover, activism tended to impoverish them further, making it more difficult for people to participate even as reserves in successive elections. Thus, far from relying on individual payoffs to recruit and retain activists, the PRD had to overcome the fact that many activists faced negative payoffs.

The progressive impoverishment of activists reflected the party's lack of resources. The typical activist was not paid. Second, he had to take time out of profitable work activities to dedicate to the party. This hit reserve workers as hard or harder than regular workers because of the huge demands on their time during important election seasons. Third, activists often paid operating expenses out of their own pockets. Virtually the entire budget of a *comité municipal*, both in Michoacán and the Estado de México, came directly from committee members. Efforts to supplement income by collecting dues or "taxing" the incomes of those who won elected office met with mixed success—from nearly complete failure at the local level to relatively strong cooperation at the national level. Thus, committee members paid rent on local party offices or met in homes, came up with cars and gas for trips to smaller communities in a *municipio*, and did all the publicity for party activities. Activism constituted a significant drain on time and resources.

Individuals can accept such costs during the short-term emergence period but cannot necessarily sustain them in the long run to fund consolidation. The PRD's position outside state power meant that resources were not as renewable; an aspiring professional politician could not simply move from elected positions to administrative ones as PRI politicians do. Some activists, especially at the state and national level, lost their jobs as a result of their party activity. Over time, frequent local elections and the daily expense of maintaining communication exhausted people's resources, forcing even committed activists to take time off to replenish their reserves and support their families. As one candidate for Congress in 1991 remarked: "[I]n '88 people were completely mobilized, and some spent all their savings, everything they had . . . to follow Cárdenas. . . . then in '89, in the July elections, they participated again in the same way. And in those [elections] of December of the same year. Well, then, no pocket can bear all that. . . . This campaign would have been easier for me if I hadn't spent so much in 1988 also. . . . People are spent economically, emotionally too."[72] Free-market capitalism does not guarantee even in theory a wide-enough distribution of resources to create countervailing centers of economic power, particularly among the marginalized Mexicans that the PRD aspires to represent. If the poor cannot work as activists because of resource requirements, the PRD may drift away from its intended constituency,

72. Confidential interview Y, July 1991.

leaving the poor to gravitate toward the PRI's offer of resources and limiting the PRD to a middle-class intellectual base.

The cost of activism seriously handicapped party consolidation and recruitment. One state activist in Michoacán blamed most organizational problems—including recruitment and retention of activists—on lack of resources:

> In the majority of our *municipios* there aren't any resources to establish an office where people can gather. All the people who form part of a municipal committee have to work to live. That keeps them from dedicating more time, full time, to the work of organization of the party, to travel to all the communities where *comités de base* were formed, . . . to inform and all the rest. . . . and this has permitted . . . a *decay* in party organization in many areas. It isn't that people have stopped participating in the PRD, but that we find them saying "hey, we just don't know anything, they haven't come to tell us," . . . and how do they go, if they find they haven't even got a car to travel around very extensive *municipios*?[73]

Though costs were higher in rural areas because of transportation, urban committees also had trouble meeting financial needs like paying rent on a local headquarters.[74]

In addition to these financial problems, the stress of PRD activism often discouraged activists. The hassles and irritations that resulted from internal party conflicts took a toll, particularly among those who had gotten involved in the first place in the spirit of unity that characterized the Cárdenas campaign. The party's defeats and the constant hostility it experienced also convinced some that their sacrifices would be wasted. Finally, intimidation and repression of party members forced people to consider the potential risks of PRD activism. Again, this was partly a consequence of the success of Cárdenas in 1988. The PRD represented a significant enough threat to the PRI and to Salinas's economic program that the party found itself pressured from all sides. The PRD Human Rights Commission lists 250 murdered activists and 9 dis-

73. Ibid.
74. For example, one municipal committee member in the Estado de México gave the party use of a room in her house for some time, going without the rental income she could have generated. When she finally asked the committee to help compensate her, three out of seven members present reported they were not regularly employed and could not contribute 30,000 pesos (about ten dollars) per month. Personal observation, May 1991.

appearances between July 1988 and May 1994.[75] The geographical distribution of deaths shows a pattern of greater violence in rural areas: Michoacán (27 percent) and Guerrero (22 percent) lead the list, with Oaxaca (16 percent) not far behind. Local activists know about PRD deaths, and some report personal threats. As a result, many try to keep a low profile—not the best method for winning converts.

Strategic Linkage

A third hypothesis suggests that strategic motives attract activists to the PRD as the party most likely to hurt the PRI. One might also see this as a "negative identity"; activists join the PRD in part because their identity is founded on rejection of the ruling party, as well as because of strategic calculations that the PRD has the best chance of helping them express that. Such motives seem to play a role in the spread of PRD activism. Conflict within the PRI over candidacies can be found at the heart of many such cases. In one rural community (Almoloya del Rio) in the Estado de México, for example, a faction of the local PRI defected to the PRD after losing a disputed PRI candidacy for the mayoral election. Prior to this election, the PRD had such a small presence in the *municipio* that it did not nominate a candidate. The PRI got into trouble all by itself, ironically, through a decision to hold a rare primary election. The disgruntled losing candidate, accusing his PRI opponent of fraud, decided to run as an independent. Though he won, the Electoral Commission refused to validate his victory because he had no legal party registry. *Only at this point* did the candidate join the PRD, to get legal registry for the special election proposed by the Electoral Commission. The strategic nature of his decision was painfully clear. The candidate himself told the media, "my group and I are still *priistas*. We only changed shirts, not ideologies." His attitude toward his new party was hardly flattering either. He spoke of the need to "erase from the imagination of the inhabitants of this community that the PRD is a 'shock' party. We will win again, and we will demonstrate to *perredismo* how constitutional elections are held correctly."[76]

75. Partido de la Revolución Democrática (PRD), *En defensa de los derechos humanos* (Mexico City: Secretaría de Derechos Humanos, Grupo Parliamentario del PRD, 1994), 319, 339–40.

76. Gabriel Ortega, "Mañana, comicios extraordinarios en Almoloya," *El Nacional* (Mexico City), 7 March 1991: 7. When he lost the special election, he kept this promise by refusing to engage in typical PRD protests, even though he lost by fewer than twenty votes.

However, such activism may not last. In general, strategic motives that played a role in the *emergence* of *cardenismo* appear less powerful in explaining the *consolidation* of activism. Theoretically, continued activism might result from strategic motives through one of two linkages: either anti-PRI sentiment combined with judgment of the PRD as the strongest competitor to the PRI in a particular region, or development of a new political identity (as a *"cardenista"*) after participating in the 1988 campaign. While anti-PRI sentiment remained one of the strongest beliefs uniting the PRD, the viability of the PRD came into question rather quickly in the year following the election, allowing little time for activists to acquire a "habit" before strategic motives weakened. Thus, theory would predict that only a small percentage of activists would acquire a durable identity in this way. Interviews of activists in 1991 do not contradict this interpretation.

Social Linkage

Finally, social movement literature has strongly stressed the role of pre-existing social networks in recruiting and maintaining a movement. The paired examples of Morelos and Michoacán support this interpretation and suggest that the production of identity as a PRD activist may depend significantly on social reinforcement. Although Morelos combined two factors favorable to strategic activism—anti-PRIism (Cárdenas won Morelos in 1988) and few alternatives for opposing the PRI—it retained fewer activists than similarly favorable areas, like Michoacán. In part, Morelos lacked the strong personal connection to Cárdenas unique to Michoacán. *Michoacanos* who support Cárdenas often refer to incidents during his term as governor—to his weekly open house, to his work building schools or wells, even to small loans some say they received from him during a personal crisis. Michoacán kept many activists on the strength of these experiences. Despite the messianic overtones of many discussions of Cárdenas, loyalty to him is in part a rational reaction to previous payoffs received from the PRD leader. More broadly, Morelos did not begin with the kind of wide network of intermediate activists that characterized Michoacán. In some ways activism tends to beget activism because strong personal and social linkages with other activists encourage continued commitment. Support for the PRD may become the mode and therefore an important identity in primary social groups. In Morelos nasty internal conflicts caused personal and social networks to break down. In Michoacán, personal loyalty to Cárdenas was reinforced by loyalties to intermediate leaders and networks of local-level activists. Similar breakdown in social networks caused by internal divisions could have the same effect in Michoacán.

It turned out to be difficult to create such social pressures artificially through devices like the promotion of base committees. The idea behind the *comité de base* was to provide party members with a small-group forum for discussion and participation. Many organizations that try to maintain active affiliation have found small groups helpful in forming committed communities, from ecclesiastical base communities to communist party cells. Party founders intended the *comité de base* to function in part as a membership recruitment and retention tool. PRD statutes gave the *comité de base* and not the *comité municipal* the explicit responsibility to "maintain a permanent affiliation campaign . . . [and] keep a current list of party members." Any eight *perredistas* could register a *comité de base*. Ideally, the PRD hoped for at least one *comité de base* in every electoral section (the area served by one polling station, at that time 750 voters). *Comités de base* could also cross electoral sections and form around an activity, either "the productive occupation . . . [or] the social dedication of the member . . . [such as] the promotion of human rights, of the environment, of culture, of sports, or any other."[77] In theory every party member would belong to a *comité de base*.

However, the *comité de base* never really caught on, whether because of its artificiality, because of apathy, or because of lack of promotion. In Michoacán quite a few *comités de base* existed. In 1991 Morelia alone had a directory of more than 90 base committees in its two electoral districts.[78] Yet many apparently existed mainly on paper or amounted to little more than an informal group of friends. Most other states did worse. The *comités de base* that did work often had an additional, nonpolitical function, like setting up a soccer league. These organizations may help retain activists, but in many cases it seemed that the *comité de base* resulted from the commitment of already dedicated activists, who formed a committee for themselves.

PARTY CONSOLIDATION AND SUBROUTINES IN THE ACTIVIST NETWORK

Party consolidation requires the consolidation of a permanent activist core (the basic labor force of the party) and the construction of institu-

77. PRD, *Documentos básicos*, 46–47.
78. Personal observation of party meeting, June 1991.

tions to coordinate them. The FDN worked well enough as a loosely articulated campaign committee only as long as its members could agree on a goal and delegate Cárdenas to resolve key coordination problems. It fell apart because it lacked a common set of rules for selecting leaders and making collective decisions about the broader range of goals and problems that a party faces in consolidation. The PRD developed this basic set of rules. It managed to select leaders, present candidates, and keep the loyalties of enough activists to survive its first six years. However, though the principle of internal democracy consistently prevailed as an expectation, the party did not achieve enviable levels of institutionalization. Conflict over the internal rules of the game continued throughout the period. This undermined cooperation, impaired party performance, and made overall consolidation more difficult.

The explanation of these patterns of incomplete consolidation differs materially from the explanation of party emergence. Both mass mobilization and economic crisis, which contributed to the recruitment of activists in 1988, become less relevant for explaining patterns of activism and almost completely irrelevant for explaining the basic principles—like democracy and individual membership—that shaped activist behavior. Economic conjuncture virtually disappears from the analysis. A worse economy would have depleted activist resources more quickly but would not have changed the basic direction of the trend. Though activist recruitment might have been easier under continued crisis, it would probably have focused on electoral mobilization (which can absorb more activists and promises quicker results than most consolidation tasks). In some ways, a continued influx of recruits might even have complicated the process of institutionalizing the party.

Other factors increase in explanatory importance—above all, the party's resource constraints, especially severe in its first two years. Factors like mobilization, which compensated initially for the relative poverty of the *cardenista* movement, began to decline due to progressive exhaustion. Socioeconomic structure begins to contribute as well. Though class does not "explain" who remained a PRD activist, differences in communication and transportation infrastructures affected the way in which elections and other kinds of intraparty communication occurred. The relatively modest position of many of its supporters also contributed to the party's resource constraints and its inability to use some strategies for reattaching activists, including payoffs in exchange for service.

A third set of factors switches from a generally positive effect during emergence to a generally negative effect during consolidation. The four important factors in this set are leftist positioning, vague ideology, internal heterogeneity, and charisma. While charisma united the *carde-*

nistas in 1988, it did not transfer well to party committees or local leadership, and in some ways slowed the institutionalization of party authority. The first three came as a package. Like many left parties today, the PRD combined leftist goals with a vague ideology and considerable internal heterogeneity, since it tried to include not only the old left parties and unions but also grass-roots popular movements with a wide variety of issue concerns. The internalization of heterogeneity guaranteed the perpetuation of internal conflicts and lack of consensus about tactics and ideology. The PRD's ideological imprecision initially helped bind a diverse movement around the specific short-term goal of electing Cárdenas in 1988; during consolidation it turned into a problem that permitted conflicts to become personal and sterile, blocked recruitment and reattachment of activists on ideological grounds, and kept everyone's eyes on a somewhat different prize. These internal conflicts became more acute as the stakes became more zero-sum under consolidation—positions in the party or candidacies rather than priority in campaign scheduling of Cárdenas, for example. Leftism and the history of the party's own founders also forced the PRD to deal with the issue of internal democracy in a way that few other parties in Mexico had to, at considerable cost to the party's image. Finally, leftism inspired special hostility from the state, including intimidation of potential activists and electoral pressure that exacerbated internal PRD conflicts by reducing the number of real positions for which factions competed.

The analysis highlights a number of paradoxes or trade-offs in the construction of an activist regime. Internal democracy as a means of leadership selection, for instance, relieved the burden on Cárdenas to choose leaders and thus helped preserve loyalties to him on the part of losers, provided opportunities for communication and building acceptance of party authority, and united the PRD around at least one ideological principle. Yet it also created incentives that increased division and confrontation in the party. Rather than encouraging activists to bring in new activists as allies in order to change the internal balance of power, the actual dynamic led to reinforcement of personal loyalties, with the balance of power shifting when existing leaders changed sides. The reasons may have to do with the reality that personal trust reduces the costs of collective action. Elites preferred to work with individuals who already controlled the loyalty of other activists, either because it is easier to trust and hold accountable a few allies than many newly recruited ones or because it is a convenient shortcut. Thus, personalism and charisma provided a focus for unity and legitimacy but also a focus for division.

Finally, the rules chosen to build an activist regime shaped the characteristics of the new party and therefore influenced party performance in other areas. Personalism and internal divisions affected most consolidation tasks, from elections and government to pact making and coordination. Most important, basic principles of democracy, individualism, and anticorporatism fundamentally affected how the PRD tried to establish relationships with civil society, how it tried to govern, and how it behaved electorally. These are the subjects of the next two chapters.

6

Cardenismo Under Siege

BUILDING RELATIONSHIPS WITH OTHER ACTORS

If consolidation of subroutines within the activist network is difficult, consolidation of stable networks between a new party and other actors is doubly difficult. In the first place, a party that fails to put its own house in order may not appeal to others as a reliable ally. In the second place, while new parties have considerable freedom to choose among alternative rules to structure activist relations, in other areas they must adjust to or try to alter established rules, institutions, and behavior, and contend with the resistance of other actors, some of which do not favor the party's consolidation. This dependence on the choices of actors hostile to the party marks a key difference between subroutines in the activist network and subroutines in the three networks discussed in this chapter.

In each area the switch from emergence to consolidation presented the party with new tasks. For example, in order to consolidate a stable alliance with the popular organizations that supported Cárdenas in 1988 the PRD had to learn to mediate for these organizations, deliver benefits, establish effective communication and accountability, and work out mutual obligations. In the administrative network the party's successful candidates had to assume responsibility for government, attempting to build supportive relationships with their constituents and with other levels of government. Finally, in the partisan network, the PRD sought party allies to consolidate its place in the party system. A party's ability to perform these essential functions affects its ability to consolidate stable relationships and, ultimately, to consolidate electoral support.

Though the assumption of these tasks does not doom new parties to failure, there is likely to be at least a period of adjustment when a new party will not perform them well, due to lack of experience and the fact that many questions about internal cooperation and party goals remain unsettled. Three further factors influence whether and how quickly party performance improves. First, the character of a party—a function of its ideological position, internal structure, and party origin—clearly affects its performance. Second, emergence changes the conditions for consolidation of relations between a party and external actors. For example, the emergence of the PRD gave popular movements better leverage in negotiations with the government over substantive demands, which in turn affected their need and willingness to remain allied to the PRD. Likewise, a new party may upset the party system, changing the spatial distribution of ideological positions or forcing reconsideration of past party alliances. But parties that see the new party's emergence as a threat will also try to plug the hole by adopting issues for which the new party found a constituency and/or by allying against it.

Finally, the effect of institutions on party fortunes changes during consolidation. The impact of institutions increases overall. Party performance depends more heavily on access to (or denial of access to) institutional resources than the decision to form a new party. Moreover, not all institutional influences that make party formation more likely will encourage consolidation. For example, presidentialism encouraged policy opponents to form a new party by limiting alternatives within the system for influencing policy against the will of the president. However, the concentration of authority in the executive also helped the president limit the consolidation of the PRD by controlling the flow of resources and shaping the party's ability to deliver on promises as a mediator for popular movements, as a local government, and so on. Especially after the reform of more restrictive electoral laws, institutions supported hegemonic one-party rule not so much by preventing new party formation as by undermining their consolidation.

THE INTEREST NETWORK

One of the biggest disappointments for the PRD was its failure to consolidate a permanent alliance with many of the popular movements that backed Cárdenas in 1988.[1]

Until 1988 most movements resisted party alliance and electoral participation, though the latter had become more frequent.[2] Their unprecedented and enthusiastic support for Cárdenas encouraged PRD founders to believe that "finally, the foundations were set for a party with strong ties to social movements and with the potential to articulate them politically."[3] At long last the *cardenista* project would succeed in overcoming the left's historic tendency toward "*partidos cupulares*" (elite-based parties) and build a mass base through alliance with the self-organized popular classes. The PRD made this not only a political priority but a central feature of its identity. Said Cárdenas, "We want to gather together and extend the great experience of self-organization. . . . We want our organization to be an instrument of society, and not

1. The definition of "popular movement" remains one of the thorny debates in this area. I follow Foweraker in understanding popular movements as the demand-making organizations of the popular classes (that is, excluding entrepreneurial organization). See Joe Foweraker, "Popular Movements and Political Change in Mexico," in *Popular Movements and Political Change in Mexico*, ed. Joe Foweraker and Ann Craig (Boulder, Colo.: Lynne Rienner, 1990), 4–7. In common usage authors often do not distinguish between popular movements as unions and as neighborhood associations. I do not assume that "popular movements" must be independent of parties. In my view, when, and under what circumstances popular movements ally themselves with parties is an empirical and theoretical issue. However, this discussion focuses almost exclusively on organizations not affiliated with the PRI, for the practical reason that the PRD made little progress within most PRI-affiliated unions. See Foweraker and Craig, eds., *Popular Movements and Political Change in Mexico*, especially chapters 6, 12, and 13.

2. For an analysis of the growing popularity of electoral strategies see Jaime Tamayo, "Neoliberalism Encounters *Neocardenismo*," in *Popular Movements and Political Change in Mexico*, ed. Foweraker and Craig, 126–28. However, "the electoral results . . . were not very significant."

3. Tamayo, "Neoliberalism Encounters *Neocardenismo*," 121.

just of its members or leaders."[4] Most *perredistas* remain convinced that
the future of their party lies ultimately in its ability to form a strong
working relationship with popular movements and—by extension—
their bases.[5] The decision of the PRD to reserve 50 percent of its 1994
congressional and senatorial candidacies for "external candidates" to
save room for the popular movements, and the meetings between Cárdenas and the Chiapas rebels in May 1994, both illustrate this aspira-
tion.

However, while many popular movements sympathized with PRD
goals, they found alliance less useful under consolidation conditions.
The PRD developed working relationships with some important popular
movements, like the Asamblea de Barrios and the Unión de Colonias
Populares (UCP) in Mexico City, though not without strain and conflict.
More often, popular movements distanced themselves from the PRD,
some within months of the 1988 election. The lack of a close relationship with popular movements deprived the party of electoral support, social reinforcement of PRD loyalties through organizations with
a strong group identity, experienced leadership, and channels of communication to civil society.

Given the political commitment of the *perredistas* and the apparent
enthusiasm of the movements for Cárdenas, why did this relationship
not last? And, where it continued, why did it not work better? I argue
that the relationship established during emergence differed considerably from the relationship required of a permanent ally, and therefore
the first did not imply the second. First, the shift from the electoral
moment to consolidation put the focus on issues, like the concrete resolution of demands, which the PRD was ill-equipped to handle successfully, particularly in the Mexican institutional environment. The PRD
could not offer selective benefits for alliance equivalent to what the government could offer for simply remaining neutral. The PRD was slow
to adjust to this situation. Its confrontational posture and its rejection
of negotiation with the Salinas government forced popular movements
to choose between achieving their demands and continuing to support
the PRD. In addition, parties and movements must overcome some competitive dynamics in their relationship, due to their common interest in

4. Cuauhtémoc Cárdenas Solórzano, *Llamamiento al pueblo de México* (Mexico City:
PRD, 1988), 16, 18.
5. For example, the PRD Third National Congress approved a resolution that "[t]he
PRD ought to aspire to be the natural political expression of the social movement[s]."
Partido de la Revolución Democrática (PRD), "Relatoría de la mesa de trabajo III: Situación de los movimientos sociales y las tareas del partido" (Mexico City: PRD, 1995), mimeographed copy.

commanding the support of essentially the same population. While mostly beneficial to popular movement autonomy, the continued organizational separation of movements and party tended to exacerbate tensions and mistrust, as did the roots of most PRD leaders in activism outside popular movements. Thus, alliances between movements and parties seem similar to alliances *among* social movement organizations: "more likely when [movements] appear to be close to the goal. . . . for then the costs of investing in the coalition seem small in comparison with the potential benefits, . . . [and] when there is one indivisible position or reward at stake, e.g., one governor or president can be elected."[6] Popular movements may accept short-term convergence during an election or during emergence, but for most movements, alliance remained a strategic, conjunctural option, not an attractive permanent goal.

Party-Movement Alliances: Conjuncture Versus Consolidation

Popular movement participation in the FDN implied a very different relationship to parties than the type of cooperation PRD leaders sought to institutionalize. As a new coalition, barely organized itself, the FDN lacked the capacity to demand anything from popular movements and, in fact, expected little—mainly endorsement of Cárdenas and voting support. Movements that participated did not have to accept anyone's authority, submit to deals made on their behalf, endorse all FDN candidates, or give up strategic flexibility. Cárdenas spoke for them only in the sense that his proposals coincided with their demands. In return, movements got an opportunity to shift protest against the PRI to the left (away from the PAN), to run candidates that could benefit from Cárdenas's coattails, and to use campaign events to mobilize people for their own purposes.

Many movement leaders *in 1988* stressed these strategic reasons— the same reasons that motivated other electoral alliances in the 1980s.[7]

6. Mayer Zald and Roberta Ash, "Social Movement Organizations: Growth, Decay, and Change," in *Protest, Reform, and Revolt: A Reader in Social Movements*, ed. Joseph R. Gusfield. (New York: Wiley, 1970), 529.

7. For example, the CDP of Durango participated in local elections in 1986 because, according to one leader, "the PAN began to capitalize on the popular discontent against the PRI. . . . To break the siege in which the state had put us, to win over or neutralize other sectors of the population, and to put a brake on the *panista* advance, we decided to participate." As a result "the electoral struggle gave us legitimacy and greater political weight. . . . the positions we won have allowed us to increase our capacity for administration [*gestión*]." See Luis Hernández, "Durango: De la lucha reinvindicativa a la democracia social," *Pueblo* 11, no. 125 (May 1988): 29.

For example, a leader of one urban organization (the Unión de Cuartos de Azotea e Inquilinos del DF) explained, "[We got involved] through a group of the Asamblea de Barrios, who see that tactically the personality of Cuauhtémoc Cárdenas is important for the movement. . . . it permitted us to think about winning in majority districts. Besides, the popular leaders of representative organizations could get a place in the Chamber of Deputies and push from there to resolve the demands of the population."[8] Similarly, a representative of the Unión de Vecinos de la Colonia Guerrero said, "the object was to use the electoral space to fix [our] influence, consolidate [our] work, and seek new spaces for organization and popular struggle."[9] Electoral participation benefited the Comité de Defensa Popular de Durango (CDP), in the view of one leader, because "in the heat of the campaign, we grew significantly. We could push the struggle against the contamination of our water at a higher level; we were linked closely with more than thirty peasant groups . . . establishing consolidated rural bases. . . . and if that weren't enough, we could equip ourselves with certain infrastructure for our permanent functions: . . . a small press, and a computer center."[10]

On the whole, the consolidation of a political party does not seem to have been a major priority for popular movements. It is questionable whether their participation in the FDN even contemplated the possibility of a permanent party alliance, especially since Cárdenas did not publicly propose the creation of a party until the campaign had almost ended. Rather, their goals probably remained, as in the past, the resolution of specific demands and "the construction of autonomous organizations of masses."[11] In the 1988 conjuncture, alliance with the FDN advanced these goals. Popular movements supported Cárdenas because their bases trusted him, because his popularity offered hope of getting their leaders into Congress, and because they did not have to give up much in exchange. When he could no longer deliver these benefits, and when the party began to demand more, many backed off. Alternative benefits that they might have expected from a permanent party ally— including an ability to mediate for the movement, place movement leaders in government, and deliver results on substantive demands—did not materialize, for reasons discussed more fully below. Thus, party found-

8. Armando Palomo, "Elecciones y movimiento urbano popular," *Pueblo* 11, no. 138 (August 1988): 9–10.

9. Ibid.

10. Luis Hernández, "CDP de Durango, la conquista del futuro," *Pueblo* 11, no. 138 (August 1988): 28.

11. This was the "strategic project" mentioned by Marcos Cruz, a CDP leader, in May 1988. See Hernández, "Durango: De la lucha reinvindicativa," 30.

ers should not have expected to resolve popular movement reservations by simply renouncing corporatism and committing themselves to "respect the independence and autonomy of social movements and organizations."[12] Whether or not it included formal integration in the party, permanent alliance entailed a different time frame, different expectations and obligations, and association with unpredictable party leaders whose actions no movement could ultimately control, even when they affected it.

Most PRD-movement relationships suffered from struggles over these issues, above all, movement obligations and party accountability. The easy interpretation of these conflicts—that movement leaders defended their autonomy against encroaching party leaders who wanted to use them as a source of support—is partly true and partly misleading. Certainly party (leader) goals often conflicted with movement (leader) goals, but movement goals also conflicted with each other. At the level of institutional design, for example, what method of linkage, what set of expectations and obligations could both guarantee maximum movement autonomy and strategic flexibility *and* ensure party accountability and responsiveness? By participating in PRD councils, movement leaders could promote communication and responsiveness, hold the party accountable, and guard against betrayal. Yet incorporation of movement leaders might give party activists a way to co-opt the movement, to use the movement's bases and mobilization capacity in support of party policy and electoral goals. Direct participation might also trap popular movements in party strategies—in the case of the PRD, intransigent opposition—and distract their leaders from action on member demands.

Initially, a strong party current argued in favor of a semicorporatist, dual-representation model. This idea prevailed in an early meeting of the Comité Nacional Promotor del PRD, when the working group on social movements concluded: ["It] is necessary to understand that the PRD has two legs of political action. These are, on the one hand, the territorial organization, and, on the other, the sectoral organization." Thus, a Peasant Council, Union Council, Student Council, etc., would "coordinate and direct activity . . . in each sector."[13] While organizations would not join the PRD, individuals would have representatives in the leadership according to their economic or social activity.

By rejecting this perspective, the PRD meant to guarantee the auton-

12. Partido de la Revolución Democrática (PRD), *Documentos básicos* (Mexico City: PRD, 1990), 48.

13. "Resoluciones de la mesa de movimientos sociales," *La Unidad* (Mexico City—PMS newspaper), 26 February 1989: 8. The first point was only one of two considered fundamental enough to put in bold print.

omy of popular organizations. The party's earliest statutes specify that
"linkage of [the party] with the movements and organizations occurs
through those militants of the party that at the same time participate
in the movements."[14] The resulting pattern of informal, overlapping
membership tended to favor institutional autonomy but failed to provide movements with a systematic way to keep the PRD accountable
and responsive, did not guarantee representation on candidate lists, and
discouraged coordinated decision making. One problem was that overlapping membership on a party committee and in a movement could be
quite haphazard. Some movements might have several representatives
and others none at all; rarely did the size of representation have much
to do with the size or importance of the movement. More often, dual
membership grew out of the political commitments of active individuals,
or the entrepreneurship of party activists who nominated movement
members in order to win support.

The PRD attempt to develop internal democracy often combined with
this method of linkage to deprive movement leaders of a sense of effective voice. The principle of one person, one vote gave them the same
formal influence as every other committee member. Regardless of the
size of their popular following, they could be overruled by a majority of
party activists. Committee members who took a less active interest in
party affairs—and this frequently included movement leaders—found
themselves less well positioned to defend their interests. They also felt
marginalized by candidate selection. When the party decided to hold
them, primaries offered movement members an opportunity to compete
equally with party activists for candidacies. More primary elections, especially for municipal elections, might have drawn more popular movement participation. However, it is not clear that primaries would
reverse movement marginalization. Small movements in particular
could easily get lost in an open primary. Primaries may pit a movement's leaders against party activists, other movements, and even rival
leaders within its ranks, with negative effects on the movement's prestige and unity. Moreover, even when a movement leader won a primary,
he still had to beat the PRI in order to get elected, since primaries were
used mainly to select candidates for plurality districts. The PRI lost only
ten plurality districts in the congressional elections of 1991—none of
them to the PRD.

14. Partido de la Revolución Democrática (PRD), *Documentos básicos: Proyectos* (Mexico City: PRD, 1989), 34. Later versions of the statutes dropped even this minimal provision. Except for a vague mention of "party affiliates and *comités de base* in the social
movements," the 1990 statutes do not establish a particular form of linkage. See PRD,
Documentos básicos.

The PRD could guarantee some seats through proportional representation. Yet proportional representation lists were negotiated by party conventions that tended to overrepresent party activists. Predictably, party activists fought for the plum spots with some success, and popular movements resented it. In the case of the CDP-Durango, for instance, conflicts over the PR list for local congressional elections in 1989 finally ended a crumbling relationship.[15] At the national level, identified leaders of popular movements got just four of the top twenty-five proportional representation positions in 1991, and two in 1994.[16] Movements did better on the top fifty slots in 1994 (eight candidates, most of which reached Congress), and much better in the list for the Federal District's Assembly of Representatives, almost entirely popular movement candidates. According to the PRD president in the Federal District, this reflected a deliberate decision to "compensate the organizations of the [urban popular movement], the majority of which had been left out of the nominations for congressmen."[17] Nevertheless, even in 1994 party activists and movements with strong connections to party currents generally managed to get the best positions. One of the identified "movement" leaders nominated in 1994 was also a past president of the Mexico City PRD and a member of the National Executive Committee. Said one observer, "the balance that had to be guaranteed internally eliminated the possibility of offering candidacies to more organizations of the alliance."[18] Such problems may help explain why more members of urban popular movements ran as candidates of the trotskyist PRT in Mexico City in 1991 than as candidates of the PRD, even though the PRT could offer candidates little hope of electoral success, and in fact seated no congressmen.[19] Unlike the PRD, the tiny PRT had to accept

15. Essentially, the CDP felt its local strength entitled it to more and better slots on the party list. At the PRD convention ex-PMS activists used party alliances to negotiate places. CDP outrage contributed to its break with the PRD and its decision to form a local party, which the PRI-state eagerly recognized after a quick reform of Durango electoral law. The CDP outpolled the PRD nearly two to one.

16. Alejandro Caballero, "Ex-militantes de izquierda predominan en plurinominales del PRD," *La Jornada* (Mexico City), 27 May 1991: 3; 1994 calculations by author, based on confidential interviews with scholars, one reporter, and PRD members. Nine of the top fifty candidates remained unidentified or unconfirmed.

17. Victor Ballinas and Alonso Urrutia, "La imagen de Cárdenas y las alianzas, cartas del PRD en el DF," *La Jornada* (Mexico City), 7 August 1994: 52.

18. Ibid.

19. Norberto Hernández Montiel, "El MUP: Del rechazo al sufragio a la lucha electoral," *La Jornada* (Mexico City) 14 August 1991: 39. Parties do not qualify for PR seats unless they get at least 1.5 percent of the vote, which the PRT failed to do in 1988 and 1991.

junior status in negotiations and simply hand over candidacies to the movements.

In addition, PRD statutes did not provide specific guidance about mutual expectations and obligations in party-movement alliances.[20] Disputes got worked out by negotiation at the local level, in concrete problems affecting organizations and local party committees. For instance, members of one committee in the Estado de México hotly debated the "obligation" of a PRD-allied union of street vendors to participate in the 1991 electoral campaign.[21] Several argued that the union as an organization had no obligation to participate. Another suggested that union members participate only as individuals in their district of residence. Others (most notably the union leader on the committee) accepted a duty to participate, but argued that union members should all participate in one district regardless of residence because a union member was the alternate [*suplente*] to the candidate for Congress in the district. This intriguing fusion of self-interest and duty discharged the organization's "obligation" to the party through support for a union candidate whose presence in government would give the movement a useful contact.

On another occasion debate focused on the obligations incurred by organizations that asked for PRD help in mediating demands.[22] Representatives of such organizations argued vehemently that neither PRD nor organization leaders could ask members to give up their own efforts—approved by the party or not—and wait for the PRD to fix it. Yet party activists felt equally strongly that once organizations submitted to PRD arbitration, they had a moral obligation not to accept a separate settlement, since it would damage party prestige and ability to handle the next arbitration. A consensus agreed that when several organiza-

---

20. Again, the trend was for the statutes to become more vague rather than less. In the 1989 version, which was vague enough, "members of movements and social organizations that militate in the party have a duty to promote its political line," but "the policy of the party in social organizations will be determined by its members in each one of them . . . The members of the party will respect the decisions that are democratically adopted in the social organizations of which they form part." *Documentos básicos: Proyectos*, 34. By 1990 the statutes even more obliquely remark that "the party will help resolve controversies . . . about the interpretation of the policy of the party with respect to the social movements and organizations. If differences persist, the organs of the party will respect equally the different positions framed in the [*Documentos básicos*]." If all else failed, "the party affiliates and the base committees in the social movements and organizations can petition the [party] . . . to convoke meetings, seminars, or general conferences . . . to illuminate and define the policy of the party." See PRD, *Documentos básicos*, 48.

21. Personal observation, May 1991.

22. Ibid., April 1991.

tions submitted a problem jointly, no one should make a separate deal. However, this compromise did not really address the party's position as mediator but rather reflected a desire for solidarity *among* popular organizations.

When the interests or strategy of the party conflicted with the preferences of a popular organization, the movement seemed to have the upper hand. Since the PRD could not offer immediate resolution of concrete demands, the PRD either ended up supporting the organization or the organization distanced itself from the PRD, which in the long run hurt the PRD more than the movement. In the view of some within the party, "the PRD has not developed its policy nor its structure in such a way that the undoubted prestige that it has in a large number of organizations is translated into real political influence. On the contrary, . . . it can be said that the social organizations influence the PRD more than the latter influences them."[23] Nevertheless, conflicts over party and movement responsibilities acted as an irritant, and occasionally as an excuse for ending a movement's alliance to the PRD.

Party-Movement Alliances: The Institutional Arena

A more important weakness lay in the PRD's inability to compete with the PRI as a mediator or service provider. The problem showed up in conflicts over negotiation with the government. Because the Mexican institutional context concentrates power and resources in the hands of a single party alliance, most popular movements end up bargaining with the PRI-state at some point, even if self-help and mobilization play a significant part in their strategy. Yet only days after the 1988 election, Cárdenas committed his supporters to a policy of intransigent confrontation with the "usurper."

This policy not only rejected a deal to accept the official results of the election, but extended in practice to any collaboration or compromise that might strengthen and legitimate the Salinas government. For the party, nonnegotiation provided a critical early basis for unity and a way to forestall co-optation of leaders, though not—as intended—a way to bring down Salinas by the weight of his own illegitimacy. Until Porfirio Muñoz Ledo broke the ban in February 1991, no top PRD leader pub-

---

23. Partido de la Revolución Democrática (PRD), *Cuadernos del Tercer Congreso Nacional* (Mexico City: PRD, 1995), 29. This document was prepared by the National Executive Committee as a basis for discussion at the Third National Congress of the PRD.

licly acknowledged meeting with Salinas. But nonnegotiation also cut off access to government funds and the means of achieving long-standing goals. As a result, the question of negotiations with the government probably provoked more divisions between the PRD and popular movements than any other single issue. Had PRD leaders chosen to look the other way instead of accusing popular movements of treason when they negotiated agreements with the state, the party might have salvaged at least limited cooperation with more movements. Instead, the PRD paid a terrible price for its stand against negotiation.

The damage was compounded, ironically, by the fact that the PRD's emergence increased popular movements' leverage against the state and gave them new opportunities to satisfy their substantive demands. In his first official act as president, Salinas announced the creation of a new social development fund called the National Solidarity Program (also known as PRONASOL or Solidarity), to win back popular support and divide the left.[24] Its funded projects included public works (especially extension of water and sewer lines, electrification, street paving, and road construction), scholarships and food baskets for poor children, school renovation and hospital construction, legalization of land titles, production credit to peasants, and a variety of other programs. Federal spending on Solidarity grew from just over one billion (new) pesos in 1989 to 6.8 billion in 1992.[25] Although a relatively small proportion of overall expenditure (less than 4 percent of programmable spending and 7.7 percent of total social spending), PRONASOL absorbed about 60 percent of all federal physical investment between January and June 1990, and by 1992 accounted for nearly half of all public investment in social development.[26] For many of the demands made by popular organizations, PRONASOL was the only game in town.

In addition, PRONASOL could offer popular movements the opportunity to co-administer projects. While the national PRONASOL board controlled the distribution of funding to different regions and states,

24. Apparently the IMF also required programs to offset social costs that accompany restructuring and to improve the political viability of economic reforms. See Peter Ward, "Social Welfare Policy and Political Opening in Mexico," *Journal of Latin American Studies,* no. 25 (October 1993): 628.

25. Oscar Contreras and Vivienne Bennett, "National Solidarity in the Northern Borderlands: Social Participation and Community Leadership," in *Transforming State-Society Relations in Mexico: The National Solidarity Strategy*, ed. Wayne Cornelius, Ann Craig, and Jonathan Fox (La Jolla, Calif.: UCSD Center for U.S.-Mexican Studies, 1994), 282.

26. Lourdes Cárdenas, "Las acciones de PRONASOL fueron políticamente favorables al PRI," *La Jornada* (Mexico City), 2 September 1991: 29; Contreras and Bennett, "National Solidarity in the Northern Borderlands," 282.

Solidarity attempted to avoid the overt paternalism of previous social development programs by requiring the formation of a local Solidarity Committee for any funded project. In theory the Solidarity Committee would propose projects, help administer the money, organize local contributions (if required), and act as watchdog.[27] The goal was to make communities coresponsible for development and to stretch a budget limited by fiscal austerity. While in most cases these committees were formed from scratch, independent popular movements could qualify as Solidarity committees, and Salinas encouraged them to apply. Through Solidarity, movement leaders could achieve community development goals, relieve government pressure on their organization, and develop connections in the administration. Larger movements could sometimes get access to PRONASOL production money to fund movement-run small businesses, an important potential source of funding.[28] These benefits convinced many popular movements to participate.

The desire to take advantage of Solidarity, not coincidentally, encouraged movements to keep their distance from the PRD. To begin with, the PRD's early insistence on nonnegotiation forced them to choose between achieving substantive goals and strengthening the party. Generally, they did not choose the party. In perhaps the most famous case, the influential Comité de Defensa Popular of Durango decided to sign a Solidarity agreement with Salinas in February 1989. The PRD accused the CDP of selling out to Salinas and of betraying the alliance by not including the PRD in discussions that led up to the deal.[29] Their mutual bitterness contributed to conflict over candidacies and eventually a split. Later the PRD became more tolerant. Many movements close to

27. In addition to contributions from state and municipal government budgets, PRONASOL projects often expected the local community to contribute some portion of the cost, either in cash, materials, or donated labor. Despite such mechanisms for participation, considerable evidence suggests that in many cases Solidarity committees did not represent genuine grass-roots participation, were connected to PRI activism, lasted only as long as the project, and had relatively little independent power in terms of oversight, administration, and project formulation. See Contreras and Bennett, "National Solidarity in the Northern Borderlands"; Jonathan Fox, "Targeting the Poorest: The Role of the National Indigenous Institute in Mexico's National Solidarity Program," in *Transforming State-Society Relations in Mexico: The National Solidarity Strategy*, ed. Wayne Cornelius, Ann Craig, and Jonathan Fox (La Jolla, Calif.: UCSD Center for U.S.-Mexican Studies, 1994).

28. For example, the CDP *Convenio* provided such funds.

29. For a discussion of the CDP-Durango and Solidarity's role in its breach with the PRD see Paul Haber, "Political Change in Durango: The Role of National Solidarity," in *Transforming State-Society Relations in Mexico: The National Solidarity Strategy*, ed. Wayne Cornelius, Ann Craig, and Jonathan Fox (La Jolla, Calif.: UCSD Center for U.S.-Mexican Studies, 1994).

the PRD received Solidarity money. However, even when the party began to encourage people to take advantage of Solidarity, it could not overcome its suspicion that Solidarity would co-opt popular movements and make them less reliable electoral allies. Nor could the PRD control perceptions that the PRI-state preferred to aid nonaligned organizations. While popular movements did not have to support or join the PRI to participate in Solidarity, most probably recognized that brazen support for the PRD did not improve the odds of a good deal. The PRI's conspicuously hostile relationship with the PRD gave movements an incentive to preserve their flexibility and avoid a close alliance.

In addition to Solidarity the PRD's limited mediation capacity undermined its relationship with popular movements. The party did go to bat for popular organizations even when this meant negotiation with the state. But the state institutions that heard many disputes resisted PRD efforts to help their allies, to the point that PRD congressmen sometimes worried they would "slow things up" by intervening.[30] In one case I witnessed in the Estado de México a PRD activist tried to mediate a dispute between the PRI municipal government and a community organization with two demands: repair of the old water supply system to provide more water, and revocation of water fees that the group argued had no legal basis. The PRD activist researched the issue, prepared a petition, and set up a meeting with the municipal government. He accompanied representatives of the organization to the meeting and presented their argument.[31] The *municipio* negotiator refused to budge. Finally, after nearly two hours he turned his back on the PRD mediator, walked to the other end of the table, and quietly offered to cancel fees on an individual basis for anyone who came to the municipal offices. The PRD mediator objected to this attempt to undermine the popular organization (and his place as negotiator). Yet his objections—and perhaps also his monopolization of the discussion—caused him trouble with the organization. Outside some members accused him of trying to tell them what to do, and told him he had no right to decide their tactics.

In another case even successful negotiation by the PRD left the popular movement without much confidence in its party ally. A popular movement in the Estado de México objected to the municipal government's removal of some movement-affiliated street vendors from prime selling posts and the use of police to break up their subsequent protest

30. Confidential interview DC, July 1989.

31. The process also revealed something about PRI culture. The meeting included a reception by the mayor, who received them graciously. He then claimed a prior commitment and turned them over to a subordinate who negotiated toughly. The mayor could later blame the subordinate for discontent.

march. The movement asked for help, and the state and national PRD
got involved, pressuring the governor to resolve the conflict. Negotiations eventually resulted in the government's dropping criminal charges
against the popular leaders, restoring the vendors to their positions,
and paying damages. Though the movement blamed its association with
the PRD for attracting government hostility in the first place, its leaders
felt satisfied with PRD negotiation. However, some PRD activists
threatened to demand the resignation of the chief of police as an electoral issue. This would have violated the government's main condition:
that the PRD not mobilize against the mayor or the chief of police. The
party managed to convince these activists that saving the alliance benefited them more than using the issue for electoral mobilization, aided
perhaps by the nomination shortly afterward of one of them to a high
spot on the party's proportional representation list for Congress. Nevertheless, the threat caused some tense moments for the popular leaders,
who faced criminal charges if the agreement fell apart. The crisis could
not have improved the popular movement's confidence in the PRD.

These divide-and-conquer tactics are hardly new, of course; indeed,
they are classic ways to channel opposition. Nevertheless, it is important to recognize how they inhibited attempts by the PRD to deliver
payoffs to individuals or organizations whose support it wanted. In the
consolidation arena the dominant party permeated institutions that the
PRD needed to deal with in order to deliver benefits. In the absence of
an electoral majority or significant legislative power, the methods available to an opposition party resemble those of a popular organization,
except that the latter may find it easier to get an agreement than parties
that directly challenge the PRI. The PRD's confrontational stance made
alliance particularly costly for popular organizations. As a result, many
preferred to remain uncommitted, cementing an alliance with neither
the opposition nor the government in order to maximize their bargaining leverage and independence.

Despite these incentives, not all popular movements abandoned the
PRD. While these hypotheses remain tentative, successful PRD alliance
with movements like those in the Asamblea de Barrios and the Unión
de Colonias Populares may reflect three basic factors: (1) greater ideological and tactical affinity with the PRD, and particularly similar elements in their movement/party identity; (2) strategic location; and (3)
selective incentives. Popular movements that remained close to the
PRD seemed to value confrontation and electoral participation more
than negotiators that distanced themselves. These tactical similarities
are hard to pin down because all movements experience divisions over
tactics, and most accept government aid. Negotiation and confrontation

may be part of the same process of extracting resources. Still, the PRD-allied Asamblea de Barrios tended to share with the PRD a belief in electoral participation and suspicion that negotiating agreements with the state would demobilize, divide, and disarticulate the opposition. Solidarity may have tempted the Asamblea less because its demands as a mostly renter organization make it ineligible for key programs, but this cannot explain the support of the PRD-allied UCP, which shared many demands with movements that chose to negotiate for Solidarity money. Like the Asamblea, the UCP agreed with many PRD tactics, particularly electoral participation, even before the emergence of the PRD and despite harsh criticism from the dominant leadership of the CON-AMUP, to which it then belonged. The question of tactical coincidence deserves further investigation.

Second, many of the PRD's strongest allies were concentrated in Mexico City where the PRD had a strong constituency. Popular movements are more likely to commit themselves to the PRD where the party is stronger and hence more valuable as an ally. Further, outside Mexico City the federal government can balance the power of local oligarchies, which may lead popular movements to favor ties with the national state, which is controlled by the PRI. Where the federal government *is* the entrenched local oligarchy, as in the Federal District, this may favor seeking non-PRI allies. Finally, movements may stay closer to the PRD when they have connections in the PRD leadership. This may reinforce regional location, as the proximity of Mexico City movement leaders to national PRD activists enhances their access and importance to party leaders.

Thus, the general institutional environment inhibited the consolidation of close alliances between popular movements and party. PRD attitudes exaggerated but did not determine the direction of this trend. Prospective alliances eventually ran up against the reality that opposition parties did not have the resources to bid effectively against the PRI. Paradoxically, though the emergence of a strong left party benefited movements by improving their bargaining leverage with the state, they had to abandon the party to take maximum advantage of the opportunity. Popular organizations may ally with an opposition party during a brief period, like emergence, but close alliances should constitute an exception to the rule.

Parties and Movements: Allies or Competitors?

Ultimately, however, the relationship between parties and movements may stumble over an even more fundamental obstacle: the intrinsically competitive element in relationships between organizations that attempt to draw upon the same resources for different purposes. Parties do not always rise at the expense of movements or vice versa, but neither do they always rise and fall together. This problem complicates alliances between parties and movements in many different settings. First of all, competition reflects the bureaucratic imperatives of organizations with separate internal rules of advancement, separate budgets, and separate programs. Organizations try to enhance their own power and control over their environment. The relative size of national parties versus local popular movements makes it hard for the latter to control their environment if they become deeply involved with a larger organization whose decisions they—as smaller movements—cannot control. More personal motives also affect dual members. If advancement in one organization does not lead automatically to advancement in the other, activists will pursue their ambitions according to different rules, creating divided loyalties and disputed turf. Questions of personal power or promotion easily turn into questions about the authority of each organization. For instance, popular movement leaders had to accept majority rule in party committees, an irritation when they brought more support to the party than others. The ambiguous status of the leader would then turn into a conflict between organizations over who had authority to make binding decisions. As movement leaders competed for party connections to enhance their prestige or candidacies and thus increase their value in the movement, party leaders tried to enlist movement support in internal party battles, spreading factions from one organization to another.

Second, parties and movements do not pursue identical goals or, more accurately, they do not always have the same priorities. All may agree on the value of satisfying popular demands, winning elections, and encouraging democracy, but while parties tend to prioritize electoral success and national regime change, most popular movements put substantive goals and local struggles first. As a result, the tactics a party adopts to achieve its goals may undermine a popular movement's attempt to achieve its goals. The problem of intransigence versus negotiation is one example of this dilemma. More commonly, conflict between goals manifests itself in choices about the allocation of scarce or shared resources, such as the limited attention and energy of common constituents. For dual leaders the scarce resources over which party and movement compete clearly include their own energy and time. For those who make a serious commitment to both movement and party, this is a major conflict. They often have to withdraw from intensive movement activism to attain influential positions in the party or complain about exhausting schedules. Popular movements fear with reason that elections will distract their leaders from the movement's original goals. And supporters worn out by mobilization for elections may have less ability to mobilize again for other purposes.

At one extreme, subordination to party priorities nearly destroyed the fledgling Unión de Campesinos Democráticos (UCD). The UCD was created by the PRD out of frustration with the party's lack of progress inside PRI unions and because of the scarcity of independent civil society allies in regions like Michoacán. In 1989 Cárdenas called for the formation of a new independent peasant union as a shortcut. The UCD's first national convention in April 1990 elected as its national leader a PRD senator, Cristóbal Arias, with extensive party connections but little experience in peasant organization. Despite some links to independent peasant organizers, the UCD relied on PRD activists for its early members and leaders, and became strongest in areas where the PRD had a political presence. Membership of local PRD/UCD committees in Michoacán often overlapped nearly 100 percent. Local PRD committee members called the UCD "a branch [*dependencia*] of the party," or "a branch [*ramo*] of the party itself, . . . an official organization within our party."[32] This close relationship caused serious problems for the UCD, threatening its effectiveness and its future. Though alliance to the PRD exposed the UCD to PRI-state hostility, the organization never seriously considered alternatives. Worse yet, its closeness infected the UCD with PRD divisions. By 1992 the UCD had at least three rival national leaderships: one sprung from prior peasant groups, one associated with Senator Arias, and one allied with Senator Robles Gárnica. Each set of leaders claimed legitimate authority.

Similar though less severe problems occurred in organizations closely tied to the PRD. Activists in the Asamblea de Barrios reported constant government harassment and attempts to ban it from extending its presence into the Estado de Mexico.[33] Party divisions also contributed to a 1993 split in the Asamblea that resulted in two rival leaderships that closely parallel two internal PRD currents. While government harassment and divisions might well have occurred in the absence of the PRD

32. Confidential interviews AR, July 1991; AI, July 1991, from different communities. In two of seven Michoacán interview communities, the UCD and PRD shared an office. PRD candidate entourages also traveled in trucks with UCD logos. Personal observation, June–July 1991.

33. Confidential interviews with three leaders of the Asamblea de Barrios, August–September 1994.

alliance, party problems clearly contributed to strains on the Asamblea.[34]

At the other extreme, parties that continually subordinate their needs to popular movements may fail to consolidate an effective electoral presence. Unless a party can survive electorally, it cannot be very useful to popular movements. The initial problems of Mexico's Partido del Trabajo reflected in part its greater dependence on movements. Created in 1991 by several regional popular movements, the Partido del Trabajo is highly decentralized, a "federation of various parties and organizations" that is "far from being a national party."[35] It lacks a presence in many areas, as well as a program, a party structure, and an intellectual base. It failed to win 1.5 percent of the vote to keep its legal registry in 1991. Only when it acquired a unifying national candidate and an alliance with the PRI did its fortunes improve enough to win it registry in 1994.[36]

From the point of view of the PRD attempts to include popular movement leaders sometimes led to problems with party unity and consolidation, recognized even by some movement leaders. One top leader of the Asamblea de Barrios and former president of the Mexico City PRD suggested that the tendency for PRD organization to coalesce around preexisting pockets of movement organization had inhibited the consolidation of party structure.[37] Similarly, the policy of encouraging "openness to civil society" sometimes led to the nomination of candidates without party loyalties, or actually hostile to the PRD. In one Estado de Mexico primary, for instance, the winning candidate had previously supported abstention. He refused to sign a statement supporting the PRD platform. According to his campaign managers, he would "coordinate" with the PRD if he won but would not "take orders" from the party.[38] Far from requesting PRD help in organizing his campaign, the candidate often failed to inform the local PRD committee of upcoming events. Instead of working with him to win the election, party activists worked to prevent the disaster of a public defection. Only

34. For a history of the Asamblea de Barrios see Angélica Cuéllar Vázquez, *La noche es de ustedes, el amanecer es nuestro* (Mexico City: UNAM, 1993).

35. Luis Hernández, "El Partido del Trabajo: Realidades y perspectivas," *El Cotidiano*, no. 40 (March–April 1991): 22, 26.

36. Close ties to the PRI and Salinas helped the PT, financing a lavish electoral campaign that no new party should have been able to afford with its own resources, much less a party based on popular movements. Rumor had it that the PT even owed Salinas its charismatic presidential candidate, Cecilia Soto—a PARM congresswoman until her PT nomination, and not a popular movement leader.

37. Marco Rascón, interview by author, Mexico City, September 1994.

38. Confidential interview P, May 1991.

days before the deadline to register candidates, his alternate [*suplente*] resigned, citing concern about the candidate's lack of identity with the PRD. When the PRD municipal committee scheduled an emergency meeting to name a substitute, the candidate did not show up, and the committee eventually had to accept his non-PRD nominee in order to register a candidate. The PRD lost that election.

However, a bench full of such congressmen could be even worse, preventing the PRD from coordinating action, providing effective leadership, building a common program, and posing a credible alternative. Indeed, the PRD's 1994 attempt to assign 50 percent of its candidacies to non-PRD members raised serious questions about how its bench would cooperate in the 1994–97 congressional term, given the diverse ideological origins of winning candidates, including *panistas*. Party activists worried about this even as they lamented failing to achieve more alliances with unaffiliated civil society groups. Relaying the demands of popular movements does not give a party a consistent ideological perspective to offer the electorate, especially since popular movements represent a small percentage of the total voting population. Popular movements need parties that defend their interests in institutional arenas to which they have no other direct access but that can also survive electorally. This is not easy to achieve.

THE ADMINISTRATIVE NETWORK

The institutional environment also affected PRD performance of another crucial consolidation task: governing. Demonstrating an ability to govern effectively can help a party consolidate support, change policy, and prove its viability and value as an alternative administrative body. Yet to govern effectively a party must successfully extract resources and cooperation from other state institutions and actors. In Mexico resources are highly centralized, at the federal level and in the presidency. In 1984 the Mexican national government controlled 84 percent of public revenue and 89 percent of public spending, compared to 51 percent of revenue and 56 percent of spending in the United States.[39] The con-

---

39. John Bailey, "Centralism and Political Change in Mexico," in *Transforming State-Society Relations in Mexico: The National Solidarity Strategy*, ed. Wayne Cornelius, Ann Craig, and Jonathan Fox (La Jolla, Calif.: UCSD Center for U.S.-Mexican Studies, 1994), 105. Of seven countries Bailey analyzed (Australia, Brazil, Canada, Chile, Mexico, the United States, and Argentina), the only one with a higher fiscal concentration was Chile, which does not have a formal federal system like Mexico.

centration of resources in PRI-dominated institutions gave the ruling party the power to interfere with opposition performance, severing the connection between electoral victory and consolidation through strong performance in government.

Mexican opposition parties tend to win positions that emasculate them: in municipal governments and legislatures, where success depends particularly heavily on cooperation from the ruling party. The opposition might improve its strategic situation by winning governorships, as the experience of the PAN may demonstrate, but even a governor needs help from the national executive. Opposition congressmen constitute the largest category of elected opposition representatives. However, until the PAN won in Chihuahua in 1992, no Mexican opposition party had ever controlled a legislative majority at the state or national level. Absent a majority, the weakness of Mexican legislatures and the individual position of opposition congressmen gave them little authority to resolve concrete problems. Where PRI candidates could promise to exploit connections with the federal executive, PRD candidates could expect less cooperation; indeed, in 1991 they often tried to lower expectations by pointing out that congressmen could *not* deliver funds to their districts. This was not a particularly effective campaign tactic. In addition, PRD legislators presented relatively few initiatives (about 10 percent of the total presented in the 1988–91 term), due in part to insufficient legislative staff and resources.[40] In the 1991–94 Congress the PRD had a more substantial independent presence. Nevertheless, from December 1991 to July 1993, PRD deputies proposed only 16 initiatives or constitutional amendments out of a total of 178.[41] Three came to a vote: one was rejected; the other two (on religion and education) were approved together with those of other parties. This is not an impressive performance. While the PRD made public statements about issues to come before Congress, these statements often came from noncongressmen and were limited to condemnation of proposed changes without suggesting an alternative.

PRD candidates did win majority control over municipal govern-

40. Based on a survey of all issues of the congressional *Diario de los debates* for the period in question. More than half these initiatives were constitutional reforms, many very basic or obviously unacceptable to the PRI. In comparison, the PAN presented 33 percent; the executive branch, 15 percent (this category accounted for virtually all bills passed)' and PRI legislators (the majority party!), 6 percent of all initiatives.

41. Leonardo Valdés, "Partido de la Revolución Democrática: The Third Option in Mexico," in *Party Politics in 'An Uncommon Democracy': Political Parties and Elections in Mexico*, ed. Neil Harvey and Mónica Serrano (London: Institute of Latin American Studies, 1994), 73.

ments—more, in fact, than any other opposition party in the 1988–91 period. Between December 1988 and April 1991 the PRI won 1,568 municipal elections; the PAN, 31; and the PRD, 89, nearly 60 percent of them in Michoacán.[42] Municipal governments have little independence. Their weakness together with geographical concentration has led some to underestimate the significance of these victories. Nevertheless, until the 1981 victory of COCEI in Juchitán, Oaxaca, left oppositions did not control *any* municipal governments. PRD control of 89 *municipios* thus represented an important advance for the left.

In carrying out their responsibilities, PRD municipal officials had to balance relationships with actors at other levels of the Mexican state, the population they governed, and the PRD party structure. However, their experiences suggest some limits to municipal government as a path to party consolidation in a centralized political system. Winning a municipal election gives an opposition party credentials as a credible threat to the PRI. As a "most-likely-winner" it may benefit from anti-PRI protest votes. But winning also exposes the party to determined efforts on the part of the PRI to "recover" the *municipio*, especially in larger cities. Municipal governments depend heavily on PRI-dominated levels of government for approval of many local regulations and for supplementing their tiny budgets.[43] This makes it difficult for an opposition municipal government to improve performance dramatically or to effect significant change. Decentralization would raise the significance of this testing ground for opposition parties. The breakdown of state corporatism could also help. (The PRI used its control of local unions of state employees against the PRD.) Similarly, the PRI-state's ability to manipulate the media shaped perceptions of the PRD's performance. In addition, the mobilization necessary to win in the first place may raise expectations and encourage people to make demands that an opposition government is even less equipped to meet than a PRI government. As one PRD municipal official put it, "it is extremely difficult to be an opposition government . . . [because] we are faced with a more active, more participatory society, but we must do it with fewer resources."[44] Due in large part to these factors, PRD governments failed to convince most voters of the party's superiority or to convert its initial victories into

42. José Ureña, "Clase política," *La Jornada* (Mexico City), 18 August 1991: 6.
43. Municipal officials in PAN-governed states also depended on higher levels of government, but the PRD feels pressure to behave more cautiously in such situations. As one PRD municipal council member in Tiajuana suggested, the fact that many former Cárdenas supporters voted for the PAN governor in 1989 meant they could not attack him aggressively for fear of alienating their own base.
44. Confidential interview EC, July 1992.

stable majorities. In the 1991 federal congressional elections the PRD beat the PRI in only twenty-seven of the fifty-two Michoacán *municipios* it governed, and widened its margin of victory in just two.[45]

Limits on Municipal Government

The centralization of resources in the federal government imposes basic constraints on municipal governments of every party, but presents particular problems to opposition mayors that cannot count on extra federal help. Municipal governments usually raise less than half their income. For the rest they depend on contributions from the federal government, distributed according to federal law as a small percentage of federal taxes collected in the *municipio*, adjusted by population. Although PRD officials question the honesty of PRI officials responsible for determining apportionments, municipal budgets collected in Michoacán do not confirm systematic prejudice against PRD governments. In order to test for partisan bias while holding constant other reasons for differences in municipal income (like population and economic structure), PRD *municipios* were matched to PRI *municipios* in four size categories.[46] Though too small for statistical significance, the comparison suggests that the size and weight of contributions varied more with the size of the *municipio* than with the party affiliation of its mayor (see Table 6.1). Small *municipios* got relatively larger contributions and depended more on federal income, probably because of the weakness of their own tax base and administrative infrastructure. For instance, they tended to get less from *predial* taxes imposed on real estate. In small rural *municipios* this mostly meant land. But *ejidal* land escaped transfer taxes because it could not be sold, and other land often failed to yield much income because of inaccurate and outdated land censuses.[47] Small municipal governments lack the capacity to bring a census up to date, especially in the face of resistance by local landlords. In many cases they did not collect "municipal" taxes themselves; rather, the state government collected the tax, kept an often large portion to cover administrative costs, and returned the rest to the *municipio*.

Federal and constitutional law restricts the tax powers of local government, making it difficult for independent municipal governments to

45. Partido de la Revolución Democrática (PRD), *Tablas comparativas de los resultados electorales* (Mexico City: PRD, Secretaría de Defensa del Voto, 1992).

46. A complete set of budgets for PRI and PRD governments was not available.

47. The 1992 agrarian reform law reversed this clause, permitting *ejidos* to sell off land.

Table 6.1. Municipal income, 1991

	Small *Municipios* (population 1–15,000)		Medium *Municipios* (population 15,001–30,000)	
	PRI	PRD	PRI	PRD
Federal funds budget share	77%	81%	61%	76%
Federal funds/capita	68,416	115,140	37,255	31,766
Predial tax budget share	3%	2%	3%	5%

	Large *Municipios* (population 30,001–100,000)		Super-Large *Municipios* (population over 100,000)	
	PRI	PRD	PRI	PRD
Federal funds budget share	64%	61%	42%	41%
Federal funds/capita	29,326*	31,317	28,026	26,947
Predial tax budget share	8%	8%	5%	40%

Sources: Condensed from Kathleen Bruhn and Keith Yanner, "Governing Under the Enemy: The PRO in Michoacán," in *Opposition Government in Mexico,* ed. Victoria Rodríguez and Peter Ward (Albuquerque: University of New Mexico Press, 1995), 121. Budget data from Annual Reports (Informes de Gobierno) or from municipal treasury books. Municipal size information from INEGI, 1990 Census.
*In this budget the month of November did not appear to be included. Hence, absolute per capita figures are low. Percentage figures may or may not be affected.

supplement their federal income. At the first Michoacán encounter of PRD mayors only two *municipios* (Morelia and Jiquilpan) reported increasing income enough to base most of their budget on their own resources.[48] Sometimes escaping financial dependence on the state meant adopting unpopular measures. One local government improved the accuracy of the catastral census and the efficiency of tax collection, substantially increasing *predial* income. However, few enjoy being taxed more efficiently. Similarly, the PRD government of Morelia responded to the heavy inherited debt of its water district by raising fees 100–300 percent, eliminating what amounted to a subsidy of the service.[49] Naturally, people resented the fee increase, since the quality of service remained about the same. The PRI exploited this dissatisfaction by

48. Partido de la Revolución Democrática (PRD), "Conclusiones de la primera reunión estatal" (Morelia, Michoacán: PRD, 1991), mimeographed minutes.
49. Patricia Ávila García, "Estudio preliminar sobre el deterioro socioambiental en la ciudad de Morelia: El caso del água," in *Urbanización y desarrollo en Michoacán,* ed. Gustavo López Castro (Zamora, Michoacán: El Colegio de Michoacán, 1991), 253.

organizing popular protests against the PRD's "antipopular" behavior. Another strategy to raise municipal funds involved restructuring investments toward higher-risk accounts that yielded higher interest income. Yet such a strategy not only risked the reputation of the municipal government (as the scandal created by the failure of one Morelia investment proved), but was only available to large *municipios* that had income invested.[50]

Thus, the real significance of dependence on federal money is the cap it places on total municipal budgets—not the partisan withdrawal of this money to threaten opposition governments. Locked into an inadequate budget, "the *ayuntamiento* receives the pressure of social demand. . . . But the mayor doesn't have the wherewithal . . . so he can only do 1 percent of what they are demanding, and that only with help . . . [with] the support of higher levels of government."[51] If a municipal government wants to carry out a development project in the community, it must seek additional funds from the state. Unlike budget contributions, this money is discretionary and therefore subject to partisan favoritism. It is difficult enough for a PRI municipal government to get help; imagine then the difficulties faced by an opposition municipal government. The PRI has little reason to help the PRD perform well by turning over scarce resources to a PRD government.

PRONASOL—one of the most important programs providing additional federal funding—reached opposition *municipios*, but not necessarily in a way that fostered municipal participation and influence.[52] Therefore, simply saying that Solidarity money reached a *municipio* did not say much about the level of participation or discretion of the municipal government. Indeed, both PRD and PRI municipal officials in Michoacán claimed they did not know how much total Solidarity money reached their communities. In interviews they listed three main pro-

50. Other risky strategies allegedly included an attempt by one PRD government to extract a "fee" from a beer company in exchange for a prohibition against selling other brands in the *municipio*. The money involved, according to one source, amounted to more than the total federal contribution. While technically legal (and apparently not invented by the PRD), the policy did not survive public disclosure.

51. Confidential interview with former *priista* mayor (now in the PRD), April 1991.

52. The federal budget divided Solidarity into three broad rubrics—Solidarity for Production, Solidarity for Social Welfare, and Solidarity for Infrastructure Support—and subdivided into programs administered by different agencies and directed at different beneficiaries. Not all operated through the municipal government. See John Bailey and Jennifer Boone, "National Solidarity: A Summary of Program Elements," in *Transforming State-Society Relations in Mexico: The National Solidarity Strategy*, ed. Wayne Cornelius, Ann Craig, and Jonathan Fox (La Jolla, Calif.: UCSD Center for U.S.-Mexican Studies, 1994).

grams as channels for Solidarity money: *Escuela Digna* (repair and maintenance of schools), *Niños de Solidaridad* (scholarships and food baskets for needy children), and *Apoyo a la Producción* (production credits to farmers with marginal land). These programs did not offer much scope for a municipal government to reshape priorities. PRD officials in large PRD *municipios* complained they simply received lists of names, perhaps indicating relatively more marginalization.

Nevertheless, in both PRD and PRI *municipios* the federal government retained ultimate control over the distribution of PRONASOL money. In the case of the special aid to municipalities called *"Fondos Municipales,"* for instance, John Bailey's 1994 analysis finds several points at which the central government directed how a municipal government could spend its money. Central government employees in negotiation with governors determined the overall budget and identified *municipios* to get money. Municipal officials participated in a Municipal Solidarity Council (with state representatives) that could solicit proposals and pick projects to forward to federal officials, but only according to specific criteria; for instance, the committee had to spend most of its money outside the municipal seat, avoid "agrarian problems," and select only new projects that could be completed within a fiscal year.[53] Solidarity field officers had final approval of proposals. Municipal officials paid contractors or neighborhood committees from a checking account separate from general municipal funds and prepared reports monthly (quarterly after 1993) for the Solidarity field office. The state field office of the Federal Comptroller then did a final audit. Bailey concluded that *"Fondos Municipales,* like all PRONASOL programs, comes in a grant-in-aid package, densely wrapped in red tape and thoroughly tied up in procedural strings that ultimately reach Mexico City."[54] Solidarity decision making bypassed the state legislature, reduced municipal government officials "to the status of equal partner with popularly elected representatives from the neighborhoods," forced state governments to devote the little left over after essential spending to qualifying for PRONASOL matching funds, and basically "magnifie[d] central control, exercised ultimately by the president."[55] While local officials might have some input on projects selected, Solidarity did not give them discretionary money to alter federal priorities.

Moreover, in some ways the relative input of PRD versus PRI munici-

53. The municipal seat could spend relatively more money if at least two-thirds of its population lived there, although it was still limited to less than 50 percent of the total.
54. Bailey, "Centralism and Political Change in Mexico," 116; 113–16.
55. Ibid., 111, 117.

pal governments did not matter. Whether or not they helped choose beneficiaries and projects, PRI municipal governments automatically shared in the credit. Solidarity programs came painted with Solidarity colors—the same as those of the PRI and the Mexican flag. This is possibly the biggest difference between PRD and PRI municipal governments. PRD governments found, as one municipal official complained, that Solidarity programs "stick us with the cost of distribution, but we don't get the credit."[56] Federal construction projects are explicitly identified with Solidarity—even "tripartite" works, to which the municipal government must contribute a share of its own resources. Interestingly, PRD protests did not focus so much on marginalization (three of the four PRD governments in the sample felt they had some influence over project selection) as on popular perceptions of their contribution, arguing that the government robbed them of credit for PRD ideas by "baptizing" everything Solidarity.[57]

In addition to income restrictions PRD governments complained of attempts to manipulate expenditures, but available evidence could not confirm two common charges: that the Federal Electricity Commission charged PRD governments more, and that the state held them responsible for inherited debts allegedly scheduled to be written off until the PRD won. Though expenditures are harder to compare because *municipios* did not use standardized categories, sample data (see Table 6.2) do not suggest extraordinary differences. Indeed, the similarity between PRD and PRI budgets is quite striking. Daily administration of essential services ate up most of the budget. Personnel (mostly salaries and benefits) took about a third. Expenditure on basic municipal services (not shown) took another 15–25 percent. This left little room for municipal governments to create budgets that reflected different priorities or made dramatic improvements in the *municipio*.

Federal influence over the performance of local governments did not necessarily end with municipal finance. Some methods of influence were virtually invisible, such as slow harassment and foot-dragging. The PRI-state might deliver required federal contributions but delay delivery through "bureaucratic foul-ups," paralyzing a municipal government. More obvious methods included manipulation of PRI-controlled unions to discredit the opposition government by interfering with its ability to deliver services. While PRI governments reported few conflicts with popular organizations, PRD governments in cities over medium size re-

Table 6.2. Municipal expenditure, 1991

Budget share of:	Small *Municipios* (population 1–15,000)		Medium *Municipios* (population 15,001–30,000)	
	PRI	PRD	PRI	PRD
Personnel	NA	32%	26%	NA*
Public works	20	10	25	NA*
Light/electricity	10	11	8	15
Public debt	none	none	7%	NA*

Budget share of:	Large *Municipios* (population 30,001–100,000)		Super-Large *Municipios* (population over 100,000)	
	PRI **	PRD	PRI	PRD
Personnel	30%	39%	50%	30%
Public works	19	9	11	17
Light/electricity	NA	NA	14***	14***
Public debt	3%	15%	6%	10%

SOURCES: All data noted in Table 6.1.
*This budget was too disaggregated to place accurately in comparable categories.
**This budget was missing figures for November. It is impossible to say whether this would have affected percentage figures calculated on the basis of the available months.
***This figure for both cities represents general services—light plus garbage service, etc.

ported frequent public clashes with unions. Strikes by garbage workers (which, as unions of state employees, officially belonged to the PRI) seemed a favorite tactic, perhaps because uncollected garbage quickly becomes a visible public nuisance. In Morelia the PRI-affiliated garbage workers went on strike shortly after the PRD took over. As garbage piled up, local and national newspapers proclaimed Morelia a dirty city and called the PRD incompetent. Interviewed two years later, PRD municipal officials insisted that their solution of the garbage problem attracted national interest, even from PRI governments in other states.[58] However, the public image of unresolved conflict remained, sending a clear message—even to some PRD sympathizers—that costs would follow an opposition victory. Use of public police forces, particularly police controlled by the state or federal government, as in capital cities, may also present a problem for opposition *municipios*. Again, Morelia stands out. As a state capital Morelia depended heavily on the state police. According to the PRD, the state police permitted actions against the public interest to make the PRD look bad. For example, PRD officials claim

58. Confidential interview W, June 1991; EA, July 1992.

they informed police about a tip that vandals associated with the PRI planned to dump garbage in the downtown area, but the police did nothing. More than a ton of garbage ended up in the public square.

These tactics worked best in combination with a media campaign to publicize PRD mistakes. The PRI-state used its control of media to shape the PRD's image, identifying the party with conflict and violence. While national media have more independence, many local newspapers openly side with the PRI. For instance, in the 1992 campaign for governor in Michoacán the PRI candidate portrayed the PRD as a band of uncivilized, vicious malcontents. Using "Peace and Progress" as his slogan, he urged *michoacanos* to vote against violence by voting against the PRD. Local newspapers dutifully predicted electoral violence and riots. The governor called in the army to protect public order from expected PRD provocations. In part due to fear, abstention rose.

In the same election a survey of local newspapers during the three months before election day found a striking disparity in the coverage of PRI and PRD campaigns. The PRI candidate appeared on the front page 180 times to 37 times for the PRD candidate; as a party the PRI made 419 front-page appearances to 150 for the PRD.[59] Even worse, many PRD "appearances" amounted to front-page condemnations of a PRD action or predictions of PRD violence. In some ways the PRD might well have been grateful it did not appear more frequently. PRD governments come in for more than their share of this kind of attention. Articles reminded readers of the failures of PRD governments, especially those of large *municipios* that the PRI was anxious to recover. Even if voters appreciated PRD performance, understood its difficulty, and did not hold it responsible for failure, the media reminded them that a PRI government could establish a cooperative relationship with state and federal authorities. Shortly before the election in Michoacán a PRI-affiliated union of street vendors occupied Morelia's city hall, forcing the PRD mayor to set up his office under a tent in the street. After two weeks of fruitless negotiation by the local government, the PRI governor got the union to leave voluntarily, one day before the election. The subliminal message, published on election day in a local paper, was that only a PRI government could manage social conflict.[60]

Despite these external pressures, PRD municipal governments must bear some responsibility for performance failures. While it is difficult to

59. Ricardo Alemán Alemán and Mireya Cuéllar, "El caso de Michoacán hace indispensable una profunda reformal electoral en el país," *La Jornada* (Mexico City), 31 July 1992: 1, 14.
60. The PRD mayor later claimed responsibility for solving the problem, but by then the election was over.

disentangle the relative contribution of the PRD to poor performance, given the pervasive effect of PRI hostility, it is possible to pinpoint five problems. First, budget comparisons reveal the tantalizing possibility that PRD governments actually spent less on public works than their PRI counterparts. In fact, the PRI outspent the "popularly oriented" PRD by two to one in two of the three pairs available. This may indirectly indicate greater Solidarity expenditure in PRI *municipios*, since many Solidarity projects required municipal contributions. Whatever the reason, in at least this small sample, PRD governments did not devote as much to the highly visible category of public works. Second, in some cases, especially in very small *municipios*, PRD officials did not have the skills to do a good job. This problem seems less important when one considers the large number of underskilled PRI mayors in such communities. Nor can lack of skill explain the problems of big PRD governments like Morelia, where many administrators had served as top-level state officials under Cárdenas.

Three other related problems were more serious: internal divisions, charges of authoritarianism, and employment practices in PRD municipal governments. The problem of division has already been discussed. Divisions occurred within municipal governments, and between municipal governments and party committees. The divisions that affected the party also affected municipal governments. Where the elected mayor belonged to a different faction than the dominant group in the *comité municipal*, friction between the PRD-government and PRD-as-party became severe. The special situation of a PRD official added new wrinkles to the problem of institutionalizing party authority. Municipal officials occupy an awkward position with respect to the party. Their legal position gives them resources and authority independent of the party leadership. Government officials may see themselves more as public servants than as party servants.[61] They may attribute their election to their own popularity among a broader constituency, and interpret their responsibility to the party (at best) as an efficient, honest performance that brings it credit, rather than obedience to party committees. Thus, of all party members, PRD officials are among the least likely to accept party discipline. Yet their performance in office reflects most on the party. Hence, the party has a direct interest in monitoring and influencing these members. Party activists often attribute electoral victory to the party's hard work and expect to be consulted regularly; if they are not, they feel insulted and betrayed. The fact that PRD officials had to enter into dialogue with the PRI-state often exacerbated party suspi-

61. For example, interviews EA, W, EC, July 1992, June 1991.

cions. While rejecting negotiation between Salinas and national leaders, PRD policy stressed the "legitimate right" of a PRD mayor to negotiate with the PRI-state as a "necessity," and even "a natural part of his duty."[62] In practice, however, local activists wondered about PRD mayors who got along "too well" with the PRI.[63] This resulted, ironically, in suspicion of the very mayors who had the most success in getting Solidarity money. Party statutes maximized this separation by prohibiting mayors from belonging to municipal committees.[64]

Many of these problems, while not unique to the PRD, are common to new left parties, especially in centralized political systems. The Brazilian PT had very similar experiences in several of its first local governments, including Diadema, Saõ Paolo, and Fortaleza. Brazil's public finances are highly centralized, leaving municipal governments with limited resources. Like the PRD, the PT "did not enjoy a sympathetic national press; there was extensive reporting of intraparty conflict and of the PT's mistakes in Diadema, and very little coverage of successful efforts." Further, "internal factors" kept the party from using municipal victory to "showcase" its capability, including "lack of prior programmatic consensus within the local party on priorities for municipal policy," factional intraparty struggles, and conflicts between party and administration.[65] The local administration's denial of party authority over appointments to posts in the government and its refusal to submit administrative decisions to the PT delegation for prior approval also sparked bitter conflicts.[66] Such conflicts between elected officials and party leaders mark the history of all parties. As in the case of the PRD, the PT's problems seemed particularly severe in large cities, which face more diverse *cabildos* and often greater elite resistance, and in early governments, before the party accumulated experience and developed an official policy of pragmatism. Less successful PT governments shared with the PRD problems with intransigent factions reluctant to compromise.

62. Roberto Robles Gárnica, interview by author, 4 April 1991.

63. For instance, in one personal conversation an activist told me she would never trust a certain mayor because he had dinner with Salinas and called him "Mr. President" publicly. She felt that this implied recognition of Salinas as the legitimate president of Mexico and therefore betrayed Cárdenas.

64. PRD, *Documentos básicos*, 55. One PRD government asked all PRD members not to participate in the *comité municipal* in order to concentrate on performing their jobs well. This widened the separation between government and party, fostered misunderstandings, and created resentment among party leaders.

65. Margaret Keck, *The Workers' Party and Democratization in Brazil* (New Haven: Yale University Press, 1992), 199–201.

66. Ibid., 204–5, 211–12.

One potential difference with the PT, less easy to explain, is the PRD's relative neglect of measures to encourage popular participation and access to local government. Complaints about the authoritarian attitudes of PRD mayors (and, to be fair, many PT mayors as well) usually sprang from perceptions that a particular mayor did not consult "the people"—especially *party* people—before making policy. Yet some PT governments made efforts to set up popular councils, usually to promote coparticipation in public works, similar to Solidarity committees. In contrast, the PRD invented few institutions to increase participation. Possibly Solidarity committees in Mexico preempted opportunities for the kind of organization attempted in Brazil by the PT, but many PRD administrations did not even try, or tried only half-heartedly, to improve popular access.

However, complaints about a mayor's openness to democracy seemed less related to community participation than to his willingness to take party considerations into account and to allow easy personal access. Ironically, two of the Michoacán mayors most often accused of authoritarianism had set up nonpartisan "urban councils" through which citizens could propose solutions to urban problems, though these councils were not very effective and were shut down.[67] Rather, a major source of complaints about authoritarianism may be nonpartisan employment policies. Only one of the four PRD governments in the budget sample reported replacing *priista* employees with PRD activists. This *municipio* also had good party-administration relations, and was the only one of the four that the PRD won in 1991. Officials in other PRD governments volunteered—sometimes without a direct question—that they constantly had problems with PRD people who wanted them to fire *priistas* and hire *perredistas*, or who expected special treatment, like preference in contracts, because of their party affiliation.[68] They had trouble honoring such requests. Some cited nonpartisan administration as a moral response to decades of PRI corruption and favoritism. More practically, most municipal employees in large *municipios* belong to PRI unions and are hard to fire. Further, PRD governments face constant state scrutiny. Some have been audited more than once. Special treatment for *perredistas* would certainly be used to discredit the party.

Nevertheless, greater access to the mayor might resolve some concerns about participation. In addition, the more successful PRD govern-

---

67. In one case popular apathy made the council ineffective; in the other the municipal government dissolved the council because it claimed "*priistas*" on the council tried to "usurp government functions." Confidential interviews EA, EC, July 1992.
68. Confidential interviews EA, EB, EC, EF, July 1992.

ment published detailed accounts of municipal finance and kept open channels to party and citizens. This might be a cheap way to improve evaluations of opposition government.[69] The result of later elections in PRD towns suggests that good performance in technical terms does not alone consolidate party loyalty. In Morelia, by many standards, the local government significantly improved efficiency and services, yet reports on the night of the 1991 congressional election indicated that the PRD had failed to win a single polling station in the city. The key to converting government into electoral success may go through stronger party-government links, not performance per se.

PRD Governments and Electoral Change

Statistical analysis suggests that other factors—including PRI effort—might play an important role in electoral success as well. Multivariate regression analysis of municipal-level voting data from Michoacán shows no negative relationship between experience of PRD government and either PRD vote or PRD losses. Instead, PRD vote is significantly and positively related to previous PRD government as well as to levels of illiteracy, and negatively related to *municipio* size (see Appendix C for sources and tables). The PRD did not lose more votes in towns that it had governed than in towns that it had not. However, the PRI improved its performance significantly more in PRD-governed towns, as well as in towns with larger populations and lower illiteracy. This result tends to confirm the notion that the PRI exerted its maximum effort in larger cities and that the experience of PRD government mobilized formerly apathetic or abstentionist voters to vote against the PRD. However, the net effect would be more lost elections even when the PRD did not lose more votes.[70]

THE PARTISAN REGIME

Although much of what has been said about PRD municipal governments could apply to any opposition party, the PRD did differ from

69. A similar style of openness by the PAN administration of Mérida, Yucatán, including public postings of monthly municipal expenditures, may well have contributed to the consolidation of PAN support there.

70. These results should be viewed with some caution: due to lack of municipal-level data on some variables (especially income per capita and Solidarity expenditures), the models may be misspecified and the significance of individual variables could change. Still, they pose tantalizing questions about how PRD governmental performance might affect party consolidation as well as electoral success, and are included in that spirit.

other opposition parties in one important respect: the special PRI hostility it attracted as a left party that criticized the Salinas project and competed with the PRI for a similar constituency. In contrast, the PAN had a different voting base, supported Salinas's economic program, and by the early 1990s faced much less PRI hostility than it had in the past, even winning PRI acceptance of three PAN governorships. Greater PAN-PRI cooperation undoubtedly had a lot to do with the fact that changes within the PRI brought the regime into greater ideological congruence with the conservative PAN than ever before.

Yet the PAN's changing relationship with the PRI was also directly connected to the PRD's emergence. Any successful new party upsets the balance of power and presents an opportunity for different alliances. In the first place, the new party may attempt to build alliances with other parties to pursue common goals and buy tolerance. This may include cooperation with other parties to reshape norms and expectations about party behavior in the legislature, the electoral arena, and so forth. Its success depends largely on two factors: (1) whether it poses a threat to the goals and interests of potential allies; and (2) whether the new party is perceived as a reliable partner. The PRD largely failed to construct stable alliances or alter norms of behavior in its favor. In the second place, the emergence of a new party may affect alliances and expectations among other parties not shared by the new party itself. In this second sense the PRD "succeeded." Its emergence created an environment in which cooperation between the PAN and PRI became significantly more likely. However, this warming relationship undermined the PRD's chances of electoral consolidation, as it was intended to do.

The PRD's failure to reshape the partisan network as it wished had a good deal to do with the difference between emergence and consolidation. Its success trapped it, especially as the time frame switched to the long term. The PRD claimed a place in the party system that directly attacked the long-term interests of the two largest parties. Based on 1988 the PRD defined its profile in the party system as the party of the majority, the party that would slay the PRI dragon. This obviously threatened the PRI. So did the fact that Cárdenas went after the PRI's traditional base and appealed to traditional symbols. The PRD won support in the countryside, among peasants, as well as in highly developed regions. It arrogantly declared itself the inheritor of revolutionary principles, a historic right of the PRI. And it came close enough to winning at a national level that some in the PRI felt it could endanger stability. At an internal PRI conference on "Democracy and Modernization" one speaker characterized the PAN as a "loyal opposition" that "will legitimize [our] institutions," while the PRD was as an "antisystem" party that could prove "very destabilizing."[71] Another protested that the PRD wanted to "occupy the place of another party . . . to abandon the Noah's Ark . . . constructed to survive the flood of 1910."[72] While most *priistas* said the PRD was not dangerous (as one put it, "no party that partici-pates in elections can be destabilizing"), many thought the PRD suf-fered from delusions of grandeur. For them, the PRD's true "place" corresponded roughly to that of the old left parties, marginal to power but an escape valve for a certain highly ideological constituency.[73] Yet even the PAN, though willing to accept considerable support for Cárde-nas in 1988, had no intention of allowing the PRD to keep either the protest vote or second place in the party system. While the FDN did not attract most of the PAN's historic class base, it did steal protest votes from which the PAN had benefited, leaving the PAN behind the left even in traditional PAN strongholds like Baja California, which Cárde-nas carried in 1988.

For both the PAN and the PRI natural resistance to electoral dis-placement was compounded by rejection of the PRD's ideological prefer-ences. As this book has argued, such conflicts lay behind the split in the PRI that created the PRD in the first place. On the right the PAN's reluctance to put political democracy ahead of its economic program made cooperation with the PRD difficult. In contrast, a powerful faction in the PRD, including its secretary of interparty relations, Graco Ramí-rez, initially favored a broad electoral alliance of all opposition parties to beat the PRI. This group argued that ideological differences mattered little compared to getting democracy: ["To]morrow we can discuss eco-nomic and political proposals, and there differentiate ourselves [from parties with other ideologies]. . . . [Today] the only program that the party needs is . . . to get the PRI out of the *Palacio Nacional*."[74]

Neither the PAN nor key groups in the PRD bought this reasoning, especially when it came to constructing a common candidacy in 1994. PAN president Luis H. Álvarez argued that common candidates would confuse the electorate and dilute the ideological content of electoral choice.[75] More pragmatically, only a common presidential candidate could effectively bring about a national transition. This idea never had a chance. After nearly winning in 1988, Cárdenas, the PRD majority, and even the PRD faction most receptive to the idea of an electoral alli-

---

71. Personal observation, April 1991.
72. Ibid.
73. Confidential interview Z4, May 1991; also H6, T6, and U5, May 1991.
74. Graco Ramírez, interview by author, Mexico City, 6 March 1991.
75. Statement in UNAM Seminar, "The Effect of the 1990 Electoral Reform," 13 February 1991.

ance had no inclination whatsoever to support anyone but Cárdenas in 1994; yet the PAN had absolutely no inclination to support Cárdenas—of all people, the son of the man whose policies had inspired its creation.

In addition, the PRD's internal problems made it a less attractive ally. To an established party like the PAN, the chaotic internal politics of the PRD seemed bewildering and unpredictable. Though the PAN has never lacked internal conflicts, fifty years of experience may give parties a more secure identity. Furthermore, the same suspicions that poisoned PRD activist relations must have affected the PAN. After all, the PAN spent many years fighting the manipulations of the very party in which some of the PRD's most prominent leaders once participated. Porfirio Muñoz Ledo had served in the detested government of Echeverría in the 1970s, as the campaign director of López Portillo, and as president of the PRI. Cárdenas had signed into law a state electoral reform as governor of Michoacan that made competing difficult for opposition parties. The joke that the PRD knew how to defend the vote against PRI tricks because some of its activists had spent years organizing electoral fraud hit uncomfortably close to home.

Finally, the implacable hostility that developed between the PRI and PRD even before the 1988 election made cooperation with the PRD risky. It was obvious that the PRI was determined to marginalize the PRD, while the PRD was determined to taunt and defy the state. In this context alliance with the PRD meant endless confrontation with the state. While the PAN pioneered the tactics of civil disobedience to protest electoral fraud, and knew the costs of this strategy, applying it in all situations as a "matter of principle" did not appeal to pragmatic PAN leaders.[76] Experiences with common candidacies tended to bolster these concerns. In 1992, for instance, the PAN ran two strong candidates for governor, one in Durango and one in Chihuahua. Both had local support and were former mayors of the largest city in their respective states. The Chihuahua candidate sought and won an understanding with Salinas that the PRI would commit itself to a clean campaign, restrain campaign expenditures, and respect the results. He won the election by a narrow margin and the PRI conceded immediately. The Durango candidate sought an alliance with the PRD, against the advice of the national leadership. He lost the election, engaged unsuccessfully

76. The PAN leadership argued that protest of fraud without proof is counterproductive. In addition to complaints about "cybernetic fraud"—fraud by computer program—the PRD viewed fraud more broadly as unequal conditions for competition, not just falsifying votes. In many cases this appeared to amount to generic denunciation of all elections won by the PRI—the very impression the PAN wanted to avoid.

in mobilization against "fraud," and in the end was deserted by some of his PRD allies. The PAN-PRD alliance behind Dr. Salvador Nava for governor of San Luis Potosí in 1991 experienced a similar fate, except that it was the PAN that backed away.[77]

Even more ideologically sympathetic parties participated in fewer electoral alliances with the PRD after 1988. Often the PRD itself resisted alliance, either because no other parties were available in a community (except the PRI), or because the disintegration of the FDN left PRD activists with little confidence in the reliability of electoral alliance. Electoral reforms also made alliances much more difficult. The most successful 1991 alliance matched the PRD and the PPS, the only registered party that still defined itself as marxist/leninist, in support of common senatorial and gubernatorial candidates in Guanajuato, Mexico City, and several other states.

Yet PAN cooperation with the PRI cannot be explained solely by referring to the weakness of the PRD. The PAN had gotten along for years without an alliance with either the left *or* the PRI. The PAN had come through the previous six years of increasingly conservative economic policies without the significant warming trend on both sides that developed almost immediately after 1988. The emergence of the PRD made this development much more likely by providing the PAN and PRI with a common enemy. To the extent that PAN electoral advances, including control of state and local governments, contributes to democratization in Mexico, the PRD ironically made democratization possible by promoting its chief opposition rival.

It is typical that one of the key examples of PAN-PRI convergence was also a PRD failure to convince opposition parties to join a coalition for electoral reform. Between 1988 and 1991, for the first time, the PRI lacked the two-thirds congressional majority required to amend the constitution. Nevertheless, the PRI passed a 1990 electoral reform, the Federal Code of Electoral Institutions and Processes (COFIPE), with the help of all opposition parties except the PRD. This reform made coalitions behind a single candidate more difficult and the majority of the PRI more secure.[78] As the largest opposition party in Congress, the PAN

---

77. Dr. Salvador Nava ran as the PRD-PAN-PDM candidate for governor in San Luis Potosí in 1991. Dr. Nava demanded a full opposition coalition as a condition for running, and his local popularity gave him the leverage to force a common candidacy. When he accused the PRI of electoral fraud, the PRD supported his claim and the PAN held back. PAN reluctance particularly annoyed the PRD because it had immediately supported a PAN candidate's claim of fraud in the Guanajuato governor's race held the same day.

78. The law made coalitions come up with common nominees for a significant percentage of positions. No longer could four parties agree only on a single (presidential) candi-

provided critical support for this package. What could have persuaded a party known for its long and courageous struggle for democracy to pass up an opportunity to blackmail the PRI into an electoral reform law that met more of its demands? Why did the PAN approve a law that hurt its own prospects in such obvious ways that some PAN congressmen refused to obey party commands to vote for it? Although the PAN congressional vote fell less than 1 percent between 1988 and 1991, it qualified for 12 percent fewer congressional seats (from 101 to 89 deputies) under the new electoral law it was instrumental in approving.[79]

Paradoxically, the emergence of the PRD both created the opportunity for meaningful opposition cooperation by limiting the PRI's control of Congress and also encouraged the PAN to cooperate with the PRI. In order to deflect the danger of a left advance that might derail the economic program or result in instability, PAN leaders apparently made a conscious decision to settle for a reform that at least hurt the left worse, by making FDN-type coalitions more difficult, for example. After the 1991 congressional election PAN leaders admitted publicly that in signing the COFIPE they chose to prioritize economic reforms, because "the country needs and needed then to create the conditions for an economic recovery [in order] for a democratic transition and to resolve the social problem. We said this is the first step, creating the conditions, as a necessary base to take the second step"; they also argued that "there is an incorrect analysis when it is believed that something more could have been gotten out of the system. If we had radicalized our position . . . the only thing we would have generated was a climate of uncertainty and instability."[80] While the PAN leadership criticized the PRD for refusing to see compromise and the COFIPE as a desirable step forward, most *perredistas* and some *panistas* thought the PAN gave up too much.[81]

---

date. It also guaranteed a congressional majority to the party that got 35 percent of the popular vote.

79. "La crisis de ser gobierno y ser oposición," *Este País*, no. 23 (February 1993): 9.

80. Ricardo Alemán Alemán, "No fue ingenuidad del PAN la negociación del Cofipe," *La Jornada* (Mexico City), 26 August 1991: 14.

81. Some *panistas* argued that "it was not naive to sign the . . . COFIPE with the PRI, and much less is the result of the elections [of August 1991] the coresponsibility of the PAN. . . . we wanted . . . to create the conditions for a peaceful democratic transition, but [the PRI] did not take advantage of that magnificent opportunity." This group claimed that PRI "dinosaurs" perverted the intentions of a fundamentally sound law. See ibid. Another group of *panistas* argued that the COFIPE "propitiated the attack" on democratic legality and that the PRI designed the COFIPE to stay in power. See Evangelina Hernández, "El Cofipe propició el fraude: Altamirano Dimas," *La Jornada* (Mexico City), 29 August 1991: 8. The public declaration of PAN priorities for economic over political reform clouded the party's image and produced such internal dissension that the PAN National Council two weeks later "reaffirmed" its rejection of "the government thesis of

Without the emergence of a strong left threat, it is hard to imagine this kind of cooperation on the part of the PAN. Indeed, the PAN's "collaborationist" strategy provoked a major internal split, with some of the party's most prestigious national leaders—including two ex-presidents of the party—resigning in 1992 over what they saw as a sellout of the party's principles.[82]

It is also hard to explain the PRI-state's sudden willingness to accept PAN electoral victories without reference to the emergence of the PRD. Cooperation paid off handsomely for the PAN. For the first time the PRI accepted defeat in an election for governor, allowing PAN candidates to take power in the border states of Baja California and Chihuahua—the very same states where only a few years before, in 1985 and 1986, disputed and dirty elections shut out the PAN from the governorship and key municipal governments. As Chapter 7 discusses more fully, these PAN victories fulfilled three key functions for the regime. First, they established the basis for PAN cooperation on electoral reform: some political liberalization, at least toward PAN candidates. Second, they gave the PRI credentials to claim that Mexico was a democracy and hence deserved international support. The highly visible concessions to the PAN looked very democratic, even though they essentially resulted from discretionary, top-down decisions rather than permanent changes in institutions. Publicity over PAN victories drew attention away from the fact that the regime simultaneously used fraud to deny PRD victories in other local elections. Thus, PAN victories helped the PRI channel protest away from the left by attracting strategic protest votes out to defeat the PRI. If the PAN could win, went the lesson, then some flaw in the PRD must account for its losses.

Legislative alliance also failed to materialize among parties ideologically closer to the PRD. Differences in attitudes toward cooperation with the PRI were major reasons. PRD intransigence frequently isolated it as the only party opposing a particular reform. Its sometimes disruptive, confrontational behavior in Congress broke the traditional

---

postponing the political reform until the economic reform has been completed; we maintain that there will only be genuine economic reform if at the same time there is genuine political reform." See Ricardo Alemán Alemán and Juan Manuel Venegas, "PAN: Incumplió Salinas la promesa de ampliar la democracia en México," *La Jornada* (Mexico City), 9 September 1991: 3.

82. These leaders—José González Torres, Pablo Emilio Madero, Bernardo Bátiz, Jesús González Schmall, and Jorge Eugenio Ortíz Gallegos, among others—organized what they called the "Foro Doctrinario y Democrático" (Forum for Doctrine and Democracy) in 1989 to protest cooperation with the PRI as well as exclusion from power in the PAN.

rule that congressmen should be seen and not heard. Lack of predictability created additional problems for the PRD, which had trouble producing a unified vote among its own members in the legislature; this reduced its reliability as an ally to other parties.

Limited, short-term cooperation occurred mostly for "defense of the vote" in specific elections. In several cases this went well beyond rhetoric. The PRD supported candidates of other parties who claimed fraud deprived them of victory, like 1991 gubernatorial candidate Vicente Fox (a *panista*) in Guanajuato. PRD activists mobilized, wrote legal briefs, and provided information to non-PRD candidates. Nevertheless, its support was not reciprocated when the PRD accused the PRI of fraud.

Opposition parties also missed opportunities to improve the cleanness of elections. For example, opposition parties never recruit enough poll watchers to cover every polling place, and usually have trouble covering more than half. Absent coordination, one polling station might have representatives from several parties, while others remained unwatched except by the PRI. Parties could cooperate to use scarce resources more effectively, assigning each party responsibility for particular stations in order to increase the number covered. In 1991, the PRD and PPS cooperated to register party poll watchers with the IFE (under the PPS label) in eight states, but only to comply with regulations governing electoral coalitions that restricted them to the same number of representatives due a single party.[83] Outside such coalitions most parties did not coordinate poll watching in the areas targeted by my study, due largely to mistrust and lack of organizational capacity.

CONCLUSIONS

Analysis of the PRD's attempts to construct these networks helps illuminate factors that affect the consolidation of a new party. The emergence of the PRD triggered a series of mechanisms designed to counteract dangerous challenges to the regime. First, the shift from emergence to consolidation—and particularly the shift in time frame from the short-term calculations of emergence to the long-term calculations of consolidation—alters the strategic calculations of actors and uses up resources important to its success during emergence. In eco-

---

83. This applied "for every purpose in the state, even when the political parties have not formed a coalition for other elections in the same electoral process." Mexico, Secretaría de Gobernación, *Código Federal de Instituciones y Procedimientos Electorales* (Mexico City: Secretaría de Gobernación, 1990), 63–64 (Articles 61–62).

nomic terms the present value of the future consolidation of an opposition party may seem quite low compared to the present value of help from the PRI-state, as many popular movements soon realized. Unity around a short-term goal tends to vanish under the pressures and sacrifices required for long-term cooperation.

Second, consolidation tends to force parties to interact more with the institutional arena. The kinds of resources that matter to good performance shift from the ability to command mobilization—where charisma, drama, and enthusiasm matter more than training—to the ability to command institutional and financial resources, and manage them with skill and experience. Thus, new parties may be less prepared to carry out consolidation tasks. The institutional arena can also increase a new party's vulnerability to other actors that may be hostile to its consolidation. Both one-party dominance and the institutional structure of the Mexican state set up a very unequal distribution of resources that allowed the PRI-state to undermine the consolidation of the PRD. This mattered most in the interest network and the administrative network. In essence, presidentialism gave one-party dominance staying power. The breakdown of a one-party dominant regime and the consolidation of new opposition may occur more readily in a decentralized state where opposition parties can use control over local political space to bolster their position. Because municipal governments were not autonomous, the PRD could be allowed to win them but could not do much without some tolerance from the regime. The centralization of the Mexican political system may mean that the threshold for real democratization is winning the presidency, but for that reason the regime will resist acknowledging opposition victory in a presidential election more than in any other.

Third, interaction effects appear. Party performance in one area affects performance in others. Bad government is likely to discourage consolidation of voting support and encourage party divisions. Party unpredictability can block alliances with movements or parties. Choices about rules in one area may affect rules and even performance in others. Internal democracy may affect relations with popular movements. Decisions about modes of incorporating the population in government may lessen or exaggerate the impact of an opposition party's differential access to state resources. And characteristics of the activist network like dependence on charisma or loose organization affect how the party acts as mediator, government, or ally in the party system.

Finally, this analysis highlights some ironies. The economic crisis contributed to the creation of the movement and its early electoral success but also deprived activists of resources to promote its consolidation.

Because Cárdenas drew such sharp contrasts with Salinas, he captured a large protest vote, yet these ideological conflicts and his success encouraged the PRI to use all the means at its disposal to oppose PRD consolidation. Because the movement promoted democracy, it won popular support, but it also adopted democratic procedures that encouraged divisions and weakened party discipline. Because Cárdenas was anti-PRI, social movements trusted and supported him, yet later found it difficult to work with the party. Thus, the party failed to reach escape velocity. It had too much of the wrong ideology for the PRI and the PAN, but not enough to reattach voters and unite activists. And it had too much electoral success for the regime's comfort, but not enough to escape the institutional mechanisms that limit opposition parties by relegating them to positions with little independence from the central executive.

7

Reshaping Electoral Patterns

THE ELECTORAL (MIS)FORTUNES OF THE PRD

Perredistas prepared for the 1991 federal congressional elections with a mixture of dread and determination, anticipating serious setbacks. Nevertheless, the extent of the damage shocked party faithful. While the PAN increased its support slightly over 1988, the PRD's dismal performance left it a distant third, damaged its credibility as a threat to the PRI, and led many to question its very survival. According to official calculations, Cárdenas misplaced more than four million voters between 1988 and 1991—67.9 percent of his original voting base.[1] In Michoacán,

---

1. Silvia Gómez Tagle, *Las estadísticas electorales de la reforma política* (Mexico City: El Colegio de México, 1990), 231; Mexico Instituto Federal Electoral (IFE), *Relación de*

the heart of Cárdenas country, analysts had predicted a fairly even split between the PRI and PRD: five congressional districts to each, with three in doubt;[2] in fact, the PRD lost every district, not only in Michoacán, but in the whole country. The PRI recovered to just over 61 percent of the official national vote and nearly two-thirds of the Congress. In contrast to 1988, electoral fraud did not appear to be the main reason. Even *priistas* seemed stunned by their success, whether they were relieved or dismayed that "the PRI won more than it should, and now the government is going to have to give mouth to mouth respiration to the opposition."[3] Many viewed the "elections of the restoration"[4] as a sign that politics had returned to normal and that "slowly but surely the era of the practically single party that . . . Carlos Salinas de Gortari had declared over was restored. . . . The government managed to neutralize, disarticulate, and shrink the opposition, leaving it at the level of influence it had a decade ago."[5]

In hindsight this evaluation appears premature. In the first place, though often used as a standard, election results are not the same as influence or consolidation. If nothing else, its unification into one party gave the left some advantages in maintaining a constant presence in Mexican politics that the FDN, for all its electoral success, could not ultimately provide. Experience in organizing protests improved its ability to put pressure on the government in postelection situations and influenced the PRI's calculation of the cost of fraud. Despite its reverses, the PRD attracted voter support and contributed significantly to the competitiveness and diversity of the opposition.

In the second place, and perhaps more to the point, rather than a "restoration," 1991 and 1994 electoral patterns reflected the continuing difficulty of reattachment—not only for the PRD but also for the PRI. A 1991 poll found only 28 percent who said they "sympathized" with

---

los 300 distritos federales electorales (Mexico City: IFE, 1991). It is important to remember that in the 1988 and 1991 elections different types of representatives were elected. This vote loss is based on the vote for Cárdenas in 1988 and for PRD candidates in 1991 majority races for Congress. However, PRD losses did not result from decreased participation—in fact, valid votes increased about 20 percent over 1988.

2. Jaime Rivera Velázquez, "Michoacán: Bipartidismo y abstención," *Nexos: Cuadernos* 14, no. 164 (August 1991): 15.

3. Salvador Guerrero Chipres, "Con el PRONASOL Salinas aplicó competencia desleal con los partidos," *La Jornada* (Mexico City), 4 September 1991: 1, 8.

4. Alberto Aziz Nassif, "1991: Las elecciones de la restauración," in *Las elecciones federales de 1991*, ed. Alberto Aziz Nassif and Jacqueline Peschard (Mexico City: UNAM, 1992), 215.

5. Pascál Beltrán del Río, "Mil días bastaron a Salinas para machacar a sus opposi-tores de 1988," *Proceso*, no. 773 (26 August 1991): 6.

the PRI, 6.3 percent who sympathized with the PAN, 5.9 percent who sympathized with the PRD, and an astonishing 52.6 percent who declared they sympathized with no political party.[6] According to these figures, the percentage of nonidentified voters actually grew, and the percentage of PRI sympathizers fell, compared to available 1987 data. Despite its many resources, relatively good economic performance, and the popularity of Salinas, the PRI did not arrest the trend toward independent voting or re-create partisan identifications among many who had abandoned the party. In part as a result the PRI did not repeat in 1994 its 1991 achievement of more than 60 percent of the vote.

In this context the failure of the PRD to consolidate a large, loyal voting base appears less surprising and its limited progress more impressive. Its 1991 vote, though smaller than in 1988, represented a more consolidated, coherent, and committed base. If 1991 polls accurately reflected levels of identification with the PRD (6 percent), nearly three-fourths of its congressional vote (8.2 percent) could be considered consolidated though not immune to erosion. Electoral results from Michoacán confirm this: the PRD lost fewer votes than either the PRI or PAN.[7] As anti-PRI urban voters abandoned the PRD, rural voters without many other opposition options tended to stick with the party longer. The PRD's emerging electoral profile thus included bases in rural areas—a significant advance for a left long limited almost exclusively to large cities.

Nevertheless, the PRD's advances were modest, even when compared to previous left parties instead of the 1988 vote. Why did the left fail to capitalize on its gains? First, and most critically, detachment does not lead inexorably to reattachment. People do not naturally require party loyalties, and they do not drift into them as a matter of course. Indeed, once they define themselves as independent, they may resist new party commitments particularly strongly. As a result, the PRD could not convert sympathy for Cárdenas in 1988 into a reliable voting base. Thus, ironically, the availability of an independent vote encouraged the formation of a new party, as Chapter 4 showed, but did not support its consolidation. Second, as Chapters 5 and 6 suggested, the PRI constantly attempted to interfere with the process of reattachment to the PRD, using institutional and legal resources to undermine the PRD's ability to make payoffs to voters, outbidding them for social support, intimidating and harrassing their activists, and generally raising the costs of alli-

6. Miguel Basañez, "Encuesta electoral 1991," *Este País*, no. 5 (August 1991): 3.

7. For example, the PRD lost 2,587 votes between 1991 (congressional vote) and 1992 (vote for governor), compared to 17,586 (PAN) and 88,561 (PRI). See Ricardo Alemán Alemán and Mireya Cuéllar, "El caso de Michoacán hace indispensable una profunda reforma electoral en el país." *La Jornada* (Mexico City), 31 July 1992: 1, 14.

ance with the PRD. This affected reattachment particularly through the self-interest and social linkages.

Finally, by 1991 the PRD had lost most of the independent swing vote whose support made Cárdenas so successful in 1988. In an electorate with few political loyalties failure to reach independent voters results in disappointing and unpredictable electoral performance. Several factors undercut the PRD's appeal to detached voters. First, PRI electoral strategy aimed above all at independent voters, preferably to mobilize them for the PRI, but at the very least to deprive the PRD of hopelessly anti-PRI votes. This chapter shows how the PRI used control of a centralized state to reposition itself and hurt the PRD: offering state resources to attract voters through payoffs, conducting massive programs for electoral mobilization, manipulating party images through control of the media, accepting selected electoral defeats to channel strategic votes toward the PAN, and seeking international help to improve economic performance and reduce anti-PRI protest.

Second, the limitations of the PRD itself alienated potential supporters. Resource constraints became increasingly relevant as the party lost many first-election advantages, including surprise and novelty. Its fumbling struggles to perform many consolidation tasks did nothing to enhance its image or the reputation of Cárdenas, on which so much depended in 1988. Finally, many party leaders clung reflexively to strategies imposed on them during emergence, delaying the PRD's adaptation to its postemergence situation. There is a logic to this phenomenon, but it is a social movement logic rather than an electoral logic, and the party suffered the electoral punishment. Many of these problems show up in an analysis of PRD electoral strategy, which—in contrast to PRI electoral strategy—tended to mobilize the already convinced rather than appealing to independent voters. Under the relatively optimistic economic optic of 1991, and without Cárdenas as a candidate, this was enough to limit the "satanized" PRD to little more than the historic percentage of the left. Even with Cárdenas as its presidential candidate in 1994, the PRD tended to depend too heavily on the assumption of a loyal voter core that it had not actually consolidated, while other parties won most of the independent strategic vote.

ELECTORAL REFORM AND FRAUD: THE DOG THAT DID NOT BARK

Sometimes the things that do not happen matter as much as the things that do. The PRD's poor (and the PRI's good) performance would have surprised observers less had electoral fraud appeared to account for it. However, the 1991 elections seemed unusually clean. Despite PRD threats that "in the face of the fraudulence and illegality of the elections, we will mobilize the people to demand respect for electoral guarantees," the "people" seemed increasingly skeptical about PRD claims of fraud.[8] In a postelection poll 69.2 percent called the 1991 elections "clean" or "very clean," and only 14.3 percent called them "dirty" or "very dirty."[9] Arguing that fraud corroded the legitimacy and stability of the political system, the Salinas administration tried to make fraud unnecessary, stressing transparent though not fair elections in order to improve credibility. The administration may also have believed that clean elections would improve the chances for U.S. approval of the Free Trade Agreement. By proving that the PRI could win elections without risking fraud and protest, the government guaranteed the continuation of economic policies with stability and met congressional standards for "democracy."[10] The same calculations affected the government's handling of the 1994 presidential election. In a year already filled with violence, including the March assassination of the PRI's first presidential candidate, a wave of kidnappings of prominent businessmen, and a peasant rebellion in Chiapas, Salinas wanted to avoid any further stain that might lead to massive political protests and scare off skittish foreign investors. The 1994 presidential election was perhaps the cleanest and certainly the most thoroughly scrutinized election in Mexican history, with national and foreign observers granted broad access to virtually every aspect of the electoral process for the first time.

Institutional changes in the 1990 Federal Code of Electoral Institutions and Processes do not explain PRD deterioration or PRI recovery in 1991. The PRI did so well that it did not need some safety measures in the law, such as the controversial "governability clause," which guaranteed a majority of Congress to the first-place party if it got at least 35 percent of the vote and assigned it two additional seats for every additional percentage point beyond 35 percent, until it reached 60 percent

8. Quote from Heberto Castillo, 1991 PRD senatorial candidate and party chairman in Mexico City, in Oscar Camacho Guzmán, "Un 'cúmulo de irregularidades' caracterizó los comicios: Cárdenas," *La Jornada* (Mexico City), 19 August 1991: 21.

9. "Encuestalia: Fraude y los votantes," *Nexos* 14, no. 166 (October 1991): 75.

10. During struggles about aid to Central America in the 1980s, certification of progress toward democracy and human rights became a prerequisite for aid approval in the U.S. Congress. The U.S.-educated cabinet of Carlos Salinas knew this precedent, and was sensitive to the possible political consequences of fraud after 1988. PRI president Luis Donaldo Colosio explicitly stated elections would prove the PRI did not need fraud just before the 1991 elections. See José Ureña, "No queremos ni necesitamos el fraude," *La Jornada* (Mexico City), 8 August 1991: 3.

of the vote.[11] Under this rule 40 percent of the vote would suffice to earn the PRI the same number of seats it barely managed with 50.7 percent of the vote in 1988—260.[12] However, since the PRI won more than 60 percent of the vote in 1991, the clause remained inactive. Ironically, PRI overrepresentation in Congress actually increased after the repeal of the governability clause.[13] Another safety measure inhibited the formation of FDN-type coalitions around a single candidate.[14] This measure, which survived to 1994, discouraged a united presidential candidacy. Yet such coalitions seemed unattractive anyway in the 1991 congressional elections, when most successful opposition candidates could expect to win through party lists. Even in 1988 the FDN failed to unite around congressional candidacies.

The 1990 electoral code left intact a number of other safety measures. The 1990 code (and its 1993 and 1994 successors) kept the same three hundred congressional districts drawn for the 1979 election and based them on demographic information from the 1970 census. While convenient for researchers tracking electoral trends over time, the failure to redistrict for nearly twenty years despite major shifts in population location and two national censuses led to significant differences in the

11. Mexico, Secretaría de Gobernación, *Diario oficial* (Mexico City: Secretaría de Gobernación) 3 January 1991: 2.

12. Partido de la Revolución Democrática (PRD), *Comentarios sobre el Código Federal de Instituciones y Procedimientos Electorales* (Mexico City: PRD, 1991), 1.

13. The PRI's ability to win single-member districts gives it a potential 60 percent of the Congress with only a plurality of the vote. Should it lose some plurality seats, the party can make up the difference from the two hundred proportional representation seats. The 1994 electoral code awarded all parties the same percentage of PR seats as their national vote (if 40 percent, then 40 percent of the PR seats), but limiting any party from occupying more than 60 percent of total congressional seats with less than 60 percent of the total vote. In practice, 60 percent of the seats became the floor for the first-place party. Thus, with 50.3 percent of the valid vote, the PRI got 60 percent of the seats in 1994, compared to less than a 3 percent difference in 1991 (64 percent of the seats with 61.5 percent of the vote). See Mexico, Dirección General de Gobierno, *Constitución Política de los Estados Unidos Mexicanos* (Mexico City: Diario Oficial, 1990), especially Articles 51–54. For vote/seat counts see Aziz Nassif, "1991: Las elecciones de la restauración," 231; Mireya Cuéllar and Nestor Martínez, "Profundas inequidades," *La Jornada* (Mexico City), 23 October 1994: 1.

14. The law forbade adoption of any candidate previously registered by another party (as the FDN parties had adopted Cárdenas). Coalitions also could not register more than 30 percent of their plurality candidates within one designated proportional representation region, forcing a broader and more difficult negotiation. Finally, the law limited coalitions to the same number of polling-booth representatives as a single party, even if they proposed their own candidates for a majority of districts and states. Mexico, Secretaría de Gobernación, *Código Federal de Instituciones y Procedimientos Electorales* (Mexico City: Secretaría de Gobernación, 1990), 60–68 (Articles 58–64).

number of voters per seat in different districts. According to the 1991 voter registry, some districts had up to four times the average number of voters per district; others had only a quarter of the average.[15] This tended to overrepresent rural voters, among whom the PRI had strength.

Second, the 1990 code left the PRI with institutional control over the electoral process, creating a potential for fraud as a last resort. Discretionary decisions not to exercise this option sometimes led to democratic results, as when Salinas decided to accept a PAN victory in the 1989 election for governor of Baja California. The perpetrators of fraud did not suddenly become believers in clean elections. It may be true, as the PAN argued, that "the fundamental thing for the democratic transition is not the law but the will to submit to the popular vote," but PRI control of electoral institutions, including voter registration and ratification of electoral results, made it easy to get away with fraud if necessary.[16]

It also imposed one inevitable cost: even when the PRI did not cheat (much), opposition parties often refused to believe it. To improve the credibility of election results, the government accepted some "transparency measures." After 1990 each polling place was required to post results outside on a sheet signed by all party representatives immediately after completing the count. Citizens could see the night of the election how well each party did in their neighborhood. The state also tried to speed up tabulation and reporting of election results through computerization and professionalization of electoral administration. Though some Mexicans—and many *perredistas*—refuse to believe in any election won by the PRI, "transparency measures" prepared popular opinion to believe official results, and thus hurt the PRD's ability to mobilize postelectoral protest.

In keeping with these efforts the 1990 electoral code created a separate Federal Electoral Institute (IFE) and denied any party *qua* party control of the IFE board, though in reality the PRI remained firmly in charge. Mexico's Secretary of Gobernación, a presidential appointee responsible for internal political security, would preside over a board that included two PRI members representing the majority faction in each house as well as six "autonomous" representatives chosen from a

---

15. Guadalupe Pacheco Méndez, "Padrón, credenciales, y distritos en las elecciones de 1991," in *Las elecciones federales de 1991*, ed. Alberto Aziz Nassif and Jacqueline Peschard (Mexico City: UNAM, 1992): 83.

16. Ricardo Alemán Alemán, "No fue ingenuidad del PAN la negociación del Cofipe," *La Jornada* (Mexico City), 26 August 1991: 14.

list presented by the president.[17] The 1994 electoral code strengthened the impartiality of the IFE by eliminating party representatives as voting members and replacing them with six "Citizen Councilors," nominated by the president and approved by a two-thirds vote in the Congress. The PRI has not directly controlled two-thirds of the Congress since 1985. The 1994 "Citizen Councilors" included former PRD and PAN members as well as respected academics. In effect the PRI retained veto power over the selection of the IFE board (and its president—still the Secretary of Gobernación), but ceded direct party control.

Finally, the 1990 reform called for a new voter registry and identification system under the Federal Electoral Registry (RFE), a division of the IFE. For the 1991 election the RFE created a new voter registry from scratch; for 1994 it thoroughly revised the registry and distributed another set of voter registration cards, required as identification to vote, which included the voter's signature, thumbprint, and picture. The PRD accused the PRI of manipulating the registration process to exclude opposition (especially PRD) voters or deliver their cards too late for the election, but it could not conclusively prove its allegations.[18] Its evidence raised only the suspicion of fraud, an easy matter since many half-suspect the PRI on general principles. For example, low registration rates did not seem linked to prior opposition support.[19] Of nine

17. The IFE board gave parties a maximum of four representatives (the number determined by its national vote). The PRI could face a majority of combined opposition votes if only "party" votes counted, but the board also included ten "autonomous" representatives: six from the president's list and four congressmen from the majority party and the largest minority party in each House. Secretaría de Gobernación, *Código Federal de Instituciones y Procedimientos Electorales*, 73–79 (Articles 73–80).

18. The PRD also complained that: (1) the PRI-dominated IFE hired interviewers who neglected opposition areas and intimidated voters by asking about their party preference; (2) a simultaneous house-to-house campaign of the PRI to draw up a membership list gave the RFE information to avoid distributing cards to opposition voters; (3) the requirement of a thumbprint intimidated voters; (4) the RFE duplicated cards for use by PRI "phantom voters." In 1994 the PRD found that one out of every five registered voters in Mexico City had a "homonym"—a person with exactly the same name—elsewhere in the city. After initial denials the IFE accepted this figure but blamed it on cultural tendencies for Mexicans to baptize children with a limited number of Christian names (José, Maria, Juan, etc.). The PRD countered this argument by publishing a state-by-state analysis showing wide variation in the percentage of homonyms on the voter registry, from 2 percent in Quintana Roo to 34 percent in Chiapas. See José Barberán, "Balance de la discusión del padrón," *La Jornada: Perfíl* (Mexico City), 12 August 1994: 1.

19. Pacheco Méndez, "Padrón, credenciales, y distritos en las elecciones de 1991," 63–94. Pacheco Méndez used expected frequency tables to compare districts with low registration and districts won by the opposition in 1988. If 20 percent of electoral districts had lower than average registration, about 20 percent of opposition districts and 20 per-

Mexico City districts that registered more citizens in 1991 than in 1988, Cárdenas had won a majority in seven, though this could also indicate that rapidly growing areas supported the left.[20] The PRD countered that registration rates did not guarantee that the registry counted real people (as opposed to "ghosts" used to pad the PRI vote), nor the accuracy of the RFE's estimates of eligible citizens.[21] In 1991, months after announcing its original count, the RFE changed its mind about the number of eligible voters—a mathematical operation that boosted registration rates by lowering the denominator. A PRD analysis claimed that the RFE modified its estimates in 105 out of 300 districts in 1991, resulting in average increases of 10.8 percent in the registration rates of FDN districts with low rates, without registering one new voter.[22] Overall, the 1991 voter registry shrank by 4.4 percent compared to 1988. Mexico City—where the PRI did exceptionally poorly—shrank by 11.5 percent, accounting for more than a third of the total.[23] As late as four days before the election the RFE removed 4,729 voters from the registration rolls in San Luis Potosí, another expected trouble spot.[24]

Nevertheless, despite a decrease in abstention in 1991, the PRD got more than four million votes less than the FDN in 1988, a loss of 11.2

---

cent of PRI districts should be low registration districts. She found no significant deviation from this pattern.

20. Daniel Cazés, "Situación electoral del D.F.," *La Jornada* (Mexico City), 13 July 1991: 11.

21. Registration rates, of course, reflect a total number of cards issued, divided by eligible voters. The RFE reported both figures, based on estimates from house-to-house surveys, using a census methodology.

22. Jesús Ortega, "El padrón electoral: Viejos vicios, nuevas artimañas," *Coyuntura* (August 1991): 13–15. This was done without modifying total citizens, by transferring them between districts.

23. Daniel Cazés, "El muestreo del 18 de agosto," *La Jornada* (Mexico City), 4 August 1991: 7. Other FDN states, including Michoacán, did not shrink as much. Some accused the government of "fixing" the 1990 census to make the voter registry more plausible (see for example Jerome Monnet, "Las sorpresas del censo," *Nexos* 3, no. 154 [October 1990]: 11–15), but many had trouble believing the population of Mexico City shrank by close to 600,000 between 1980 and 1990, though a change in the criteria for residency may account for the difference. See Mexico, Instituto Nacional de Estadística, Geografía, e Informática (INEGI), *X censo general de población y vivienda, 1980* (Mexico City: INEGI, 1984), 11; *XI censo general de población y vivienda, 1990* (Mexico City: INEGI, 1992), 8. As Octavio Rodríguez Araujo remarked, "If in 1982 there were 4,779,964 registered voters in the D.F., in 1985, 5,074,951, and in 1988, 5,095,462, it does not seem logical that in 1991 there are almost the same as nine years ago: 4,860,721." Octavio Rodríguez Araujo, "Una hipótesis sobre credenciales," *La Jornada* (Mexico City), 21 July 1991: 10.

24. Alejandro Caballero, "Eliminó el Instituto Federal Electoral a 4 mil 729 electores del padrón potosino," *La Jornada* (Mexico City), 14 August 1991: 6.

percent of the total number who received voting cards. That is a lot to lose without being able to document fraud. Nor did PRD problems explain in themselves the PRI's surprising electoral recovery. Thus, in sharp contrast to most statements by the party since 1988, PRD analysis of the 1991 elections admitted that Salinas " 'has overcome' the situation of 'illegitimacy,' " created in 1988.[25] In 1994 Cárdenas claimed that 8 million voters had been "shaved" (illegally removed) from the voter registry.[26] The difference between his vote and the vote of PRI candidate Ernesto Zedillo amounted to more than 11 million. Clearly, voting patterns in the 1991 and 1994 elections demanded a more comprehensive evaluation that would accept a decline in PRD support and look beyond fraud for explanations.

SOMETHING OLD, SOMETHING NEW: PRI STRATEGIES FOR REGIME MAINTENANCE

The FDN's 1988 success galvanized the PRI where the Corriente Democrática had failed. After 1988 the *cardenistas* challenged not just government policies, or the PRI hierarchy, but control of the state. The official PRI interpretation saw 1988 as a "wake-up call" to address popular demands for economic growth, democracy, and attention to pressing social needs.[27] Salinas attempted to respond to those demands, using the institutional and fiscal resources at his disposal to bolster the PRI's position and keep the PRD from recovering the independent swing vote. Salinas immediately attacked perceptions that the government did not care about social welfare by launching the National Solidarity Program amid much media fanfare. In the economic sphere Salinas refused to compromise his economic program but gambled that social spending would buy time for neoliberal reforms to rescue the economy and that recovery would quell enthusiasm for Cárdenas's program of economic nationalism.[28] Within this context Salinas tried to persuade voters of

25. Mireya Cuéllar, "CSG ha remontado la condición de 'desprestigio' de 1988: PRD," *La Jornada* (Mexico City), 10 November 1991: 12.

26. Despite a national appeal, he never produced more than a fraction of the alleged 8 million voters to complain in person.

27. Enrique González Pedrero, *La lección de la elección* (Mexico City: Secretaría de Información y Propaganda, PRI, 1988), 1, 11.

28. Salinas also initiated a crackdown on selected corrupt and antidemocratic sectoral leaders: specifically, his political enemies. While tolerating corrupt leaders that did not oppose him, he arrested and jailed La Quina, the petroleum union leader who advised union members to vote for Cárdenas.

the virtues of neoliberalism. In 1991 a modest recovery gave Salinas "proof" that neoliberalism could succeed and softened anger at the PRI enough for an electoral strategy aimed at independent voters to work. Finally, to satisfy demands for democracy Salinas accepted some highly publicized opposition victories, though real democratic reforms were limited and slow. In a bizarre and sometimes perverted way the fraud of 1988 resulted in more democratic responsiveness than the Mexican PRI had shown in quite some time.

The Electoral Uses of Solidarity: Old Wine in New Bottles

Political parties everywhere use state resources to win support for their candidates. The PRI is no exception. In this respect at least "much of PRONASOL is not new; many of the program's strategies are stream-lined versions of old populist formulas."[29] Certainly, Solidarity's design-ers tried to differentiate it from populist programs of the past, mainly to improve the efficiency of social investment and its potential for winning political support. First, to reduce paternalism in the administration of government projects PRONASOL required the formation of local Soli-darity committees to propose and help carry out projects. Second, to "do more with less" PRONASOL often required copayments from benefi-ciaries as well as state and local governments. Third, to contribute to technocratic efforts to streamline and rationalize administration Soli-darity took money from the old development bureaucracy and put it under Salinas's control.[30] This allowed the federal executive to exercise discretionary control over total costs and the distribution of money.[31] Finally, to avoid market distortions PRONASOL concentrated on social investment that could boost productivity, and targeted recipients rather

29. Denise Dresser, *Neopopulist Solutions to Neoliberal Problems: Mexico's National Solidarity Program* (La Jolla, Calif.: UCSD Center for U.S.-Mexican Studies, 1991), 15.

30. Originally run out of the presidential office, Solidarity moved to its own ministry, the Ministry of Social Development, in 1993.

31. John Bailey, "Centralism and Political Change in Mexico," in *Transforming State-Society Relations in Mexico: The National Solidarity Strategy*, ed. Wayne Cornelius, Ann Craig, and Jonathan Fox (La Jolla, Calif.: UCSD Center for U.S.-Mexican Studies, 1994), 102–3. Bailey makes a useful distinction between "decentralization" as "devolution of decision-making authority to constitutionally authorized bodies separate from the central government line ministries that operate under presidential authority," and "deconcen-tration" as "[delegation of] some degree of decision-making authority from the federal ministries to their own field offices operating in the states and municipalities." He argues that Solidarity's operating logic is one of deconcentration, not decentralization.

than general subsidies that could distort prices or factor inputs. Because of these features many praised Solidarity for trying to meet social needs in a manner "compatible with economic reform . . . [and] politically nonthreatening to Mexico's private sector."[32]

Despite these distinctions, however, PRONASOL clearly shared the political objectives of populist programs: to "divide, buy off, and conquer" the opposition.[33] Indeed, the IMF may have required such a social spending program to accompany economic restructuring.[34] The design for Solidarity developed in part from the Ph.D. dissertation of Carlos Salinas: an investigation of the connection between public expenditure and support for the regime. The dissertation argues that during populist periods "public expenditure does not seem to arouse intense feelings of support for the system among those inhabitants most benefited by it. . . . the fact that the state granted these resources without having been asked for them meant that the public works program . . . could not inspire attitudes of support for the system." Instead, decentralization in spending decisions and activation of the "potential of local-level leadership as an instrument . . . could increase the efficiency of public works and build support for the system."[35]

Even more telling was the timing of Solidarity. The *cardenista* threat and the controversy surrounding the 1988 election contributed to the urgency with which Salinas inaugurated the program on December 2, 1988, in his first official act as president, promising that PRONASOL projects would be under way with the new year. In 1982 Salinas had concluded that "a State which does not permit the participation of its citizens runs the risk of losing not only instrumental efficiency but also its very legitimacy."[36] In 1988, having lost legitimacy in a demonstrably dirty election, his government chose to open new channels for participation in order to recover it.

More controversial were accusations that the *cardenista* vote inspired the targeting of Solidarity, as well as its timing. Government officials denied partisan influence on funding, but the fact that some of

32. M. Delal Baer, "Mexico's Second Revolution: Pathways to Liberalization," in *Political and Economic Liberalization in Mexico: At a Critical Juncture?* ed. Riordan Roett (Boulder, Colo.: Lynne Rienner, 1993), 58.

33. Dresser, *Neopopulist Solutions to Neoliberal Problems*, 19.

34. Peter Ward, "Social Welfare Policy and Political Opening in Mexico," *Journal of Latin American Studies*, no. 25 (October 1993): 628.

35. Carlos Salinas de Gortari, *Political Participation, Public Investment, and Support for the System: A Comparative Study of Rural Communities in Mexico*, Research Report Series, no. 35 (La Jolla, Calif.: UCSD Center for U.S.-Mexican Studies, 1982), 37, 39, 41.

36. Ibid, 42.

the first big recipients of Solidarity money voted overwhelmingly for Cárdenas in 1988 did nothing to discourage suspicion. Statistical analysis tends to confirm the partisan basis of allocations, though results depend on the measure used for the dependent variable, PRONASOL funding. Below the state level there is little evidence to show how PRONASOL spending relates to the vote because the government has refused to release detailed information at the municipal or electoral district level about Solidarity spending. One of the only attempts to measure this, by looking at the use of resources in the education sector, suggests that Solidarity may punish opposition *municipios* while rewarding their PRI neighbors in order to demonstrate the advantages of PRI support.[37]

At the state level of aggregation there are no significant bivariate relationships between PRONASOL allocation per capita and any of the independent variables, whether one looks at measures of partisan support (1988 PRI vote, 1988 Cárdenas vote, and 1988 PAN vote) or economic variables that might plausibly influence allocations in what is officially a poverty alleviation program: per capita GDP (with poorer states expected to receive more money), the state's marginalization rating as calculated by the Coordinación Federal del Plan Nacional de Zonas Deprimidas y Grupos Marginados (COPLAMAR, the measure PRONASOL officials said they used, with greater marginalization resulting in more funding), and the decrease in GDP in the state from 1982 to 1987 (with states harder hit by the crisis expected to receive more funds).

When these same independent variables are tested against another measure of PRONASOL, results improve slightly. The alternative measure, "reorient," is the difference between the amount spent through PRONASOL (1989–90) and the amount spent from 1984 to 1987 under the Ramo XXVI (Development and Social Spending) category of the federal budget by the De la Madrid administration.[38] This measure is re-

37. See Alec Ian Gershberg, "Distributing Resources in the Education Sector," in *Transforming State-Society Relations in Mexico: The National Solidarity Strategy*, ed. Wayne Cornelius, Ann Craig, and Jonathan Fox (La Jolla, Calif.: UCSD Center for U.S.-Mexican Studies, 1994), 233–53.

38. The complexity of Solidarity makes it hard to find an adequate proxy for changes in spending priorities. My measure uses the same comparison (Ramo XXVI to Solidarity) used in Mexican government reports of social development spending. In order to get off to a quick start PRONASOL took over funding already appropriated to the "Ramo XXVI" line of the federal budget, a heterogeneous collection of social development programs run by high-level allies of the president (out of the Secretaría de Programación y Presupuesto, SPP). While the comparison weakens over time with the addition of new programs, shifts in states that got priority should be sharpest in the first year or so of the program. In

lated significantly (at .1) to the 1988 left vote (positively) and GDP per capita (negatively); that is, the higher the left vote and the lower the GDP per capita, the more the federal government reoriented priorities toward that state.

In multivariate models using these same variables partisan vote is the only significant variable. Somewhat surprisingly, the 1988 PRI vote had a significant (.05) positive effect on PRONASOL funding measured as PRONASOL per capita.[39] Although the model as a whole is weak, this suggests that PRONASOL may have helped the PRI reinforce clientelist ties. Juan Molinar Horcasitas and Jeffrey Weldon argue that specific programs within the Solidarity rubric specialize in rewarding PRI loyalists while others try to buy back opposition votes.[40] When "reorient" is used as an alternate measure, 1988 PRI vote becomes insignificant and 1988 left vote (but not the PAN vote) has a significant (.1), positive effect, though again adjusted R^2 is weak. This suggests that the government reacted to the *cardenista* vote, shifting relatively more money to states where Cárdenas did well. In none of these models do economic variables reach significance. Molinar and Weldon (1994) find some economic effects but still conclude that, "besides its specific goals as a poverty alleviation program, PRONASOL is also driven by political and electoral considerations. . . . PRONASOL's allocation decisions are better understood in terms of electoral criteria than poverty indices."[41]

In order to accomplish these electoral ends the Salinas administration made available substantial and increasing funding for the program. The PRONASOL budget more than quadrupled in the first four years, from an initial budget of just over a billion (new) pesos to a 1992 budget

---

addition, the Ramo XXVI and PRONASOL programs, as programs directly controlled by the political elite, may be more flexibly reoriented than most categories of social spending, like education. Two additional caveats apply. First, it is important to remember that both Ramo XXVI and PRONASOL accounted for a small percentage of total government spending on welfare. This measure tries to measure changes in priorities rather than total change in services. Second, Mexico City data are not available for both periods, and it was left out of the statistical analysis.

39. The model using 1988 left vote as its political variable has an R^2 of .08, and the left vote is not statistically significant. Model two, the PAN vote in 1988, shows similar results.

40. Juan Molinar Horcasitas and Jeffrey Weldon, "Electoral Determinants and Consequences of National Solidarity," in *Transforming State-Society Relations in Mexico: The National Solidarity Strategy*, ed. Wayne Cornelius, Ann Craig, and Jonathan Fox (La Jolla, Calif.: UCSD Center for U.S.-Mexican Studies, 1994), 123–41.

41. Ibid., 124. Molinar and Weldon differentiate between two sets of states: those that held local elections as well as congressional elections in 1991 and those that did not. They find few statistical associations for the latter group. Much of their analysis seems driven by the former—a group of only seven, which did not include key *cardenista* states.

of 6.8 billion.[42] Solidarity did not account for a large percentage of either programmable spending or total social spending, which includes such big-ticket items as public education. Nevertheless, its resources were significant, accounting for about half of all public investment in social development.

Perhaps more important, it focused on low-budget items that reached large numbers of people. In the first three years more than 64,000 "Solidarity committees" carried out more than 150,000 projects, bringing drinkable water to 8 million Mexicans, new classrooms to 1.4 million students, and electricity to 11 million in more than 10,000 communities.[43] The number of communities that got electricity equaled 92 percent of the total communities "electrified" in De la Madrid's six-year term.[44] Through Solidarity Salinas issued more than 1.2 million legal land titles, many during a three-day blitz in August 1991, shortly before the congressional elections, when he handed out more land titles than Mexican presidents had issued in ten years.[45] About the same time he announced the opening of 1,000 kilometers of new highway, equaling the kilometers of federal highway built in the previous forty years.[46] Whatever the motives behind it, PRONASOL unquestionably had positive effects on the living conditions of millions of Mexicans.

Moreover, Solidarity became "in terms of social welfare policy, . . . the sectoral 'flagship,' . . . even though in terms of total budget, health and education are far more important."[47] Its political impact probably came as much from this effort to build the National Solidarity Program into a symbol of PRI effectiveness and dedication to social welfare and participation as from its actual achievements. While 92.9 percent of one survey population knew about the Solidarity program, only 25 percent were aware that Solidarity programs operated in their own neighborhoods.[48] The government just did not let Solidarity's achievements

42. Oscar Contreras and Vivienne Bennett, "National Solidarity in the Northern Borderlands: Social Participation and Community Leadership," in *Transforming State-Society Relations in Mexico: The National Solidarity Strategy*, ed. Wayne Cornelius, Ann Craig, and Jonathan Fox (La Jolla, Calif.: UCSD Center for U.S.-Mexican Studies, 1994), 282.

43. Mexico, Secretaría de Gobernación, *Tercer informe de gobierno*, Carlos Salinas de Gortari (Mexico City: Oficina de la Presidencia, 1991), 48–49.

44. Secretaría de Gobernación, *Tercer informe de gobierno: Donde estamos y a donde vamos, solidaridad y bienestar social* (Mexico City: Secretaría de Gobernación, 1991), 2–4.

45. Secretaría de Gobernación, *Tercer informe de gobierno*, 49.

46. Javier Macías, "El 11 estados, CSG entrega más de 800 kms. de autopistas de 4 carriles," *El Nacional* (Mexico City), 10 August 1991: 1.

47. Ward, "Social Welfare Policy and Political Opening in Mexico," 627.

48. Contreras and Bennett, "National Solidarity in the Northern Borderlands," 287.

speak for themselves. A broad publicity campaign began at once, stressing the "new" devotion to social investment exemplified in the "creation" of Solidarity—though existing programs already did many of the same things. However, when 78 percent of the population still could not identify the program by the end of 1990, the government escalated its media campaign.[49] Throughout the 1991 electoral year the ubiquitousness of Solidarity commercials impressed even the casual watcher of Mexican television. In typical commercials one saw happy, hardworking Mexican families who dramatically improved their lives through cooperation with the government, in keeping with the program's new slogan: United to Make Progress. Radio repeated these stories. Some cinemas showed short Solidarity promotional tapes before the main feature. The PRONASOL logo and slogan appeared on walls from Mexico City to remote rural villages. All this propaganda linked Solidarity to Salinas, the PRI, and the state. The Solidarity logo even used the red, white, and green of the PRI and the Mexican flag.

Salinas used state resources and the PRI's privileged position as dominant party to pay for this campaign to convert PRONASOL into an electoral bonanza. Government sources refused to reveal the cost of PRONASOL publicity. Director Carlos Rojas insisted that Solidarity itself paid for "zero" publicity and that "a group of businessmen donated the production" of publicity spots.[50] However, the director of the ad agency hired to do the Solidarity campaign, Oscar Leal, estimated production costs for the ten main television spots alone at more than one billion pesos, about 400,000 dollars.[51] Even more expensive, at least in principle, was the cost of the air time devoted to running ads. In the colorful words of Oscar Leal, "neither Procter and Gamble nor Colgate Palmolive nor all of Bacardí" could actually pay for the air time that PRONASOL used.[52] Again, the government benefited from "freebies." According to PRONASOL director Carlos Rojas, "a good part of what comes out on the television is within the 12.5 percent [of total broadcast time] that the government has a right to, and another [part] is donated by the businesses themselves, the owners of Televisa and other state stations."[53] By July 1991 polls showed 72 percent of Mexicans knew

49. Ciro Gómez Leyva, "Solidaridad gratuita en todas las pantallas," *Este País*, no. 7 (October 1991): 13.
50. Federico Reyes Heroles and René Delgado, "Empleo e ingreso, reto del PRONASOL," *Este País*, no. 7 (October 1991): 6.
51. Ibid.; Gómez Leyva, "Solidaridad gratuita," 16.
52. Gómez Leyva, "Solidaridad gratuita," 15.
53. Reyes Heroles and Delgado,"Empleo e ingreso, reto del PRONASOL," 6.

what Solidarity was, with the majority able to identify it as a partnership between government and society.[54]

But did this awareness translate into votes? Did Solidarity achieve its end of recovering PRI hegemony and "reversing the 1988 electoral victories of the PRD?"[55] Both critics and advocates credit Solidarity with "helping propel the . . . PRI to a stunning victory in the 1991 midterm elections."[56] Some see this as evidence of the PRI's new electoral responsiveness. If "Solidarity has an obvious electoral edge, [t]his is completely legitimate. Society demands a good government, and when that happens, awards it their confidence, . . . that is popular sovereignty."[57] While PRI and government officials deny the partisan basis of allocations, they do not deny the electoral effects of PRONASOL. So what if the PRI intended to benefit electorally from Solidarity? As the director of PRONASOL put it, "I know no party in government in the whole world that works or refrains from working in order to lose."[58]

On the other hand, only the PRI had the power to use state institutions and state resources in this way to win electoral support. If PRONASOL were pork, even "relatively efficient pork,"[59] the PRI owned all the pigs. Thus, PRONASOL constituted "disloyal competition," in the words of one hapless technical secretary in the Secretary of Foreign Relations, whose indiscreet remark cost him his job.[60] Opposition mayors complained that even when they participated in formulating projects and distributing money, PRONASOL's association with the government deprived them of credit. From this point of view, "given the partisan use that the government has made of the program, it is seen as perpetuating the official-party or state-party status of the PRI, and

54. Gómez Leyva, "Solidaridad gratuita," 14.

55. Dresser, *Neopopulist Solutions to Neoliberal Problems*, 23.

56. Ibid., 1.

57. Arturo Martínez Nateras, "Solidaridad y Gobernabilidad," in *Solidaridad a Debate* (Mexico City: Consejo Consultivo del Programa Nacional de Solidaridad, 1991), 195–98. For similar arguments see also Molinar Horcasitas and Weldon, "Electoral Determinants and Consequences of National Solidarity," 140–41; Lourdes Cárdenas, "Las acciones de PRONASOL fueron políticamente favorables al PRI," *La Jornada* (Mexico City), 2 September 1991: 29; Guerrero Chipres, "Con el PRONASOL se aplicó." A humorous interchange between two Mexicans also made this point. One complained that the PRI was simply buying the vote with PRONASOL. To which the other responded, "Well, finally the vote is *worth* something!"

58. Reyes Heroles and Delgado, "Empleo e ingreso, reto del PRONASOL," 6.

59. Molinar Horcasitas and Weldon, "Electoral Determinants and Consequences of National Solidarity," 140.

60. Guerrero Chipres, "Con el PRONASOL Salinas aplicó," 1, 8.

hence undermining any potential move toward free competition among parties on an equal footing."[61]

In fact, both assessments have some truth to them. Solidarity did play a role in the PRI's recovery of support after 1988 (although its importance is sometimes exaggerated), and probably also generally undermined the opposition. Polls suggest an association between approval of Solidarity and intention to vote for the PRI. Of those who said they planned to vote for the PRI, 79.1 percent thought Solidarity was a good program.[62] Only 49.8 percent of those who planned to vote for the opposition approved of Solidarity. At the individual level, analysis based on a *Los Angeles Times* poll suggests a statistically significant, positive association between perceptions of having "personally benefited from PRONASOL" and PRI vote, although other variables had a stronger impact.[63]

Moreover, opposition majorities in 1988 turned to PRI victories in areas that got significant PRONASOL support. In the celebrated case of the Valle de Chalco a massive PRONASOL public works program seemed to contribute to a PRI recovery in the district (see Table 7.1).

However, there is little evidence that PRONASOL "reattached" voters to the PRI. Voters interviewed in Chalco said, "we voted for the PRI,

Table 7.1. Voting in Chalco

	Cárdenas/PRD	PRI	PAN
1988 (pre-PRONASOL)	63.4%	27.7%	7.1%
1991 (post-PRONASOL)	8.8	60.9	11.5
Difference	− 54.6	+ 33.2	+ 4.4

SOURCES: Figures reflect results for District 15 in the state of Mexico, where Chalco is located; from Mexico, Instituto Federal Electoral, *Relación de los 300 distritos federales electorales* (Mexico City: IFE, 1991), and official 1988 results by district provided by the Partido de la Revolución Democrática, in *Elección presidencial* (Mexico City: PRD, 1989), mimeographed electoral results. The former FDN parastatals account for the residual vote.

61. Ruth Berins Collier, *The Contradictory Alliance: State-Labor Relations and Regime Change in Mexico* (Berkeley and Los Angeles: University of California Press, 1992), 165.

62. "Pronasol," *Este País*, no. 7 (October 1991): 11.

63. Alejandro Moreno, "¿Por qué se votó por el PRI?" *Este País*, no. 33 (December 1993): 27–28. More significant variables had to do with party identification and opinion of the PRI. The analysis also found a positive relationship between PRI vote and poverty, and between PRI vote and age, with younger voters less likely to vote for the PRI.

but our vote is for Solidarity. It's better than the PRI."[64] PRONASOL
was renamed shortly after the presidential succession, and even if some
version of it lasts, its medium-term effect on electoral behavior will depend on avoiding bureaucratization and maintaining its funding in an
era of ever-increasing budget cuts. Salinas initially drew on funds from
the proceeds of privatization, the sale of state-owned companies, to expand PRONASOL. These are exhaustible resources. The World Bank
or other organizations may step in to provide continued funding if the
program is seen as a significant contribution to stability, but even these
funds come with strings and may not always be available. In addition,
PRONASOL may not go far enough to guarantee stability. It is not designed to meet demands like those of the Chiapas rebels, which go beyond clean water to democracy, jobs, and equity in income distribution.
And its popularity may work best in contrast to the relative neglect of
the 1980s. Once voters get used to it, demands may escalate and support
drop off.

Statistical analysis also throws doubt on the notion that Solidarity
"saved" the PRI or "doomed" the PRD. At the state level of aggregation
Solidarity expenditure did not have a direct and proportional effect on
left losses.[65] In fact, bivariate correlations show a positive significant
relationship between PRD vote and reorientation; that is, the more the
PRI changed its priorities, the *higher* the PRD vote. Although Solidarity
money had an important impact on the left vote in cases where it disrupted the relationship between the PRD and a popular movement (for
example, the CDP-Durango), neither PRONASOL per capita nor reorientation had a significant, linear effect on either PRD vote or PRD
losses in multivariate models. Although not quite significant, the direc-

64. "El Pronasol atrae más sufragios que el mismo PRI, en Chalco," *La Jornada*
(Mexico City), 19 August 1991: 26.

65. Both PRI gains and left losses are measured as the percentage change in the absolute number of voters supporting the PRI (or the left—that is, the number of votes in
1991 minus the number of votes in 1988 divided by the number of votes in 1988). Because
of the very uneven geographical distribution of the vote in 1988, a simple swing vote
calculation (percentage of the vote in 1991 minus percentage of the vote in 1988) would
distort the meaning of "losses": only states where the left did well in 1988 could produce
high losses. Rankings according to this measure better match intuitive assessments of
how well the PRD did. Subtraction puts Michoacán as a state of greater losses (64.2% −
29.8% = 34.4%) than Baja California Sur (25.9% − 1.4% = 24.5%), largely because the
left did not have 34 percent to lose in Baja California Sur. According to "left loss," Baja
California Sur ranks higher (94 percent of voting base lost) than Michoacán (where Cárdenas kept most of his base). This measure also has the advantage that it takes into account
only a party's own support. Official percentages reflect changes in the PRI's ability to
attract support as well. In both cases calculations rely on congressional vote figures for
1988 and 1991. See Appendix C for statistical tables and sources.

tion of the relationship between increased PRI effort (reorient) and left loss is negative.

At first glance patterns of left loss appear to have a lot to do with socioeconomic structure. The more agricultural and rural a state, the less the left lost, but within that context, higher GDP per capita seemed to benefit the left.[66] The model's performance was quite good, with well over half the variance explained. However, omission of key PRD states (Michoacán, Tabasco, and Chiapas, where the PRD kept most of its votes) causes the model to fall apart. Still, this challenges assumptions that Solidarity killed the left.

Even more surprising, statistical analysis finds little conclusive evidence that Solidarity "saved" the PRI. PRONASOL per capita reaches modest (.1) significance in bivariate correlations, but the sign of the relationship is negative, although this may reflect the original association between PRONASOL funding and PRI vote. In multivariate analysis Solidarity funding does not reach robust significance in any model. Instead, regression to the mean and increases in voter participation have more impact on PRI gains. This suggests that the PRI's intense political effort to win over voters through campaigns may explain PRI gains more effectively than levels of Solidarity spending.

It would be dangerous to read too much significance into the weakness of "Solidarity funding" in statistical analysis. In particular, the use of state-level data, though forced by the government's refusal so far to divulge more specific information, may obscure local trends. Moreover, statistical analysis would not pick up response to Solidarity that is not proportional to the level of funding. Solidarity might improve the general image of the PRI, making voters available for mobilization in a way unrelated to the amount of money spent in a particular area. This fits Oscar Contreras and Vivienne Bennett's findings that most people did not know they were Solidarity beneficiaries. Moreover, whether or not state favoritism cost the left votes, it may well have cost the left elections by helping the PRI enhance its support. Social networks and

66. These models are based on factors found significant in other analyses of Mexican voting, plus Solidarity spending. See, for example, Joseph Klesner, "Modernization, Economic Crisis, and Electoral Alignment in Mexico," *Mexican Studies* 9, no. 2 (Summer 1993): 187–223; Joseph Klesner, "Realignment or Dealignment? Consequences of Economic Crisis and Restructuring for the Mexican Party System," in *The Politics of Economic Restructuring*, ed. Maria Cook, Kevin Middlebrook, and Juan Molinar Horcasitas (La Jolla, Calif.: UCSD Center for U.S.-Mexican Studies, 1994). I omit a separate variable for "rural residence" (defined as the percentage of the population living in towns under 2,500 in size) because of concerns about multicolinearity: agricultural workforce and rural residence are correlated at .88.

other factors of voter reattachment in *cardenista* regions both encouraged PRI spending and helped the PRD survive it. Absent Solidarity, the PRD might have done even better. Most important, Solidarity did not function in isolation but was part of a coordinated strategy to improve the PRI's position. PRI gains may have resulted more from mobilizing previous abstentionists than from winning over lots of leftists, and these political efforts to get out the vote had as much to do with its success as Solidarity expenditures per se.

Economic Policy and Recovery: New Wine in Old Bottles

Nevertheless, the PRI's substantial efforts to win back voters would have met with less success in the absence of some economic recovery and the prospect of more. This was another of the "lessons of 1988." PRI analyses recognized that "the citizen's vote is, among other things, a kind of popular reaction to the concrete circumstances of daily life. The deterioration of income that the majority of the people has suffered in the years of the crisis has affected, without question, their electoral preferences."[67] Salinas believed that even if the Cárdenas vote implied popular support for economic nationalism, significant compromise on economic policy would wreck all hope of recovery. On the other hand, if recovery occurred, voters might change their minds about neoliberalism—especially if helped by government propaganda. Therefore, the Salinas administration continued to deepen neoliberal reforms but also tried to reshape popular opinions and lower inflation in order to provide proof of their effectiveness.

In essence, the PRI under Salinas poured new wine into old bottles, changing the PRI without changing its name, and explaining new policies by employing old labels and rhetoric. In his speeches and public appearances Salinas defined neoliberal policies like privatization and an open economy in terms that traditionally legitimized exactly the opposite approach. In opening remarks to his third State of the Union address, for example, Salinas attempted to take back the banner of nationalism from the economic nationalists on the left, arguing that "modernization is nationalistic," and adding: "We must reject the deformations that see in nationalism a sacred proposal, frozen, composed of yesterday's public policies that no longer work. . . . 'nationalist' is

67. González Pedrero, *La lección de la elección*, 12.

what strengthens the nation . . . not the longing for formulas and characteristics of other times, which, in the present world context, far from strengthening it, weaken it, make it more vulnerable, less viable."[68] Salinas was by no means the first president to redefine the Revolution. It had become a tradition of sorts for PRI presidents to legitimize radically different policies using the same rhetorical heritage and labels. However, Salinas stretched these concepts about as far as anyone in the postrevolutionary period, with the signing of a Free Trade Agreement that more closely resembled the economic policies of the Porfiriato than the 1917 Constitution, and with an agrarian reform, carried out in the name of peasant freedom, that officially ended land redistribution and permitted the legal sale of collectively owned *ejido* land.

More important than this rhetoric, which reached only a minority, was the economic recovery that took place between 1989 and 1992 and soothed resentment against the PRI. Economic recovery brought more hope than real improvement for most Mexicans. According to the 1990 census, more than a quarter of the working population earned less than one minimum salary per month, and 63.2 percent earned two minimum salaries or less.[69] Although GDP per capita grew by 1.5 percent in 1989, and 1.8 percent in 1990,[70] wealthy Mexicans benefited most. Secretary of Finance, Budget, and Programming Pedro Aspe admitted that average salaries had yet to recover significantly.[71] Indeed, the real minimum wage continued to deteriorate.[72] More and more people took refuge in the informal economy, estimated at perhaps as much as 86 percent of

68. Secretaría de Gobernación, *Tercer informe de gobierno*, 4.

69. Mexico, Instituto Nacional de Estadística, Geografía, e Informática (INEGI), *XI censo general de población y vivienda, 1990: Perfíl sociodemográfico* (Mexico City: INEGI, 1992), 63.

70. Mexico, Secretaría de Hacienda y Crédito Público (SHCP), *El nuevo perfíl de la economía mexicana* (Mexico City: SHCP, June 1991), 37.

71. Federico Reyes Heroles and René Delgado, "Pedro Aspe Armella: Una buena noticia . . . y una mala," *Este País*, no. 1 (December 1991), 20.

72. According to one estimate, real minimum wages fell by 14.5 percent in 1990 and 1.2 percent in 1991. See "La economía de este país," *Este País*, no. 10 (December 1991): 24. Francisco Zapata estimates the decline at 10.4 percent in 1990 and 6 percent in 1991. See Francisco Zapata, *El sindicalismo mexicano frente a la restructuración* (Mexico City: El Colegio de México, 1995), 72–73, 80; see also Fernando Pérez Correa, "Modernización y mercado del trabajo: Guión para un diálogo," *Este País*, no. 47 (February 1995): 26–27. However, these authors also suggest that real manufacturing wages rose slightly. A study by the Workshop on Economic Analysis at UNAM found that both minimum real wage and average labor salaries by contract reached their lowest level in Mexican history during 1991. See Sara Lovera, "Durante 1991, los salarios llegaron al nivel más bajo de su historia," *La Jornada* (Mexico City), 26 December 1991: 1.

commerce in Mexico City by 1991 and more than half of all nonagricultural employment by 1985.[73]

However, his government did manage to arrest the brutal speed of deterioration in real wages, mostly by controlling inflation, which fell from a high of 159.2 percent in 1987, to 19.7 percent in Salinas's first year, and to only 14 percent by 1991.[74] The price of basic food staples like rice and tortillas rose faster than either wages or overall inflation; this particularly affected the poor, who spend much of their income on food.[75] Still, lower inflation contributed to dramatic change in evaluations of government performance. In 1991 only 34 percent of Mexico City residents thought the economic situation would worsen—in stark contrast to 1987–88, when 72 percent expected the economic situation to get worse.[76] More than half credited Salinas for the improvement. A Gallup poll done around the same time found that 56 percent thought their economic situation had improved since 1988, and 68 percent felt their economic position would be even better in the next three years—again, a dramatic contrast to 1988, when 88 percent of Mexicans thought the economy was "bad" or "very bad," and 54 percent said it would "never" improve.[77] Despite problems with Mexican polls, the huge difference surely indicates a major decrease in the prevalent sense of crisis.

Polls also suggested that Mexicans responded to the success of Salinas's policies with approval of some, though not all, of the central elements in the neoliberal economic program.[78] Since 1990, polls "consistently found a majority in favor" of the Free Trade Agreement.[79]

73. María de Jesús Espinoza, "Operan en la economía subterránea 86% de comercios del DF: Investigador del ITAM," La Jornada (Mexico City), 15 July 1991: 1; Zapata, El sindicalismo mexicano, 81.

74. SHCP, El nuevo perfil de la economía mexicana, 37.

75. The price of rice, for instance, increased 318 percent between December 1988 and August 1991, the price of black beans by 304 percent, and the price of tortillas by 173 percent. See Juan Antonio Zuñiga and Lourdes Cárdenas, "Veintidós productos básicos han subido más que la inflación en casi tres años," La Jornada (Mexico City), 9 September 1991: 25.

76. "La intuición pluralista en el Distrito Federal," La Jornada: Perfil (Mexico City), 11 August 1991: 1.

77. Mexico, Consejo Nacional de la Publicidad, "Mexico is on the Right Track" (Mexico City: Consejo Nacional de la Publicidad, October 1991), 2; William Stockton, "Mexican Pessimism is Found in Survey," New York Times, vol. 136, 16 November 1988: 16.

78. One key exception was the modification of Article 27 of the Constitution to allow the sale of ejido land and end land redistribution. Sixty-two percent said ejido land should not be sold or privatized; 61 percent said the government ought to continue distributing land. See "El ejido ante la opinión pública," Este País, no. 10 (January 1992): 34–35.

79. Daniel Lund, "El tratado de libre comercio: Los extremos de la confusión," Este País, no. 28 (July 1993): 2.

A 1991 Gallup poll commissioned by the government found that 68 percent supported the president's economic policies in general, 64 percent favored the proposed Free Trade Agreement, and 55 percent supported the privatization of state-owned businesses.[80] Rates of approval increased among Mexicans up to twenty-nine years of age, who constitute the majority of the population. Other polls corroborated these conclusions.[81]

Nevertheless, these figures are soft, not only because of the questionable accuracy of some opinion polls, but also because most Mexicans did not have much information, or had inaccurate information, about the implications of complex policies like the Free Trade Agreement. For example, although the Free Trade Agreement deliberately left out the question of international labor flows (and was supported by some U.S. backers on the premise that it would decrease immigration), 45.8 percent of Mexicans thought that NAFTA would facilitate their getting work in the United States![82] Finally, questions about approval of the Free Trade Agreement may have elicited contingent support of anything to get the economy going, reflecting desperate pragmatism rather than reasoned approval. The PRI's shocking electoral decline since the peso devaluation of December 1994 suggests that support can disappear remarkably quickly if the government fails to provide growth with distribution, though this does not necessarily mean a return to approval of the PRD's economic nationalism. In spite of its preference for economic policies similar to those of the Zedillo government, the PAN has benefited more than the PRD from anti-PRI reaction since the peso crisis, winning landslide victories in gubernatorial elections in Guanajuato and Jalisco, and picking up significant support in the southern state of Yucatán.

Thus, voting could respond more to economic conditions than to specific ideological platforms. In 1991 Salinas's success in lowering the speed of deterioration reduced tensions and convinced the swing vote that he could improve conditions if given time and support, making

80. Consejo Nacional de la Publicidad, "Mexico is on the Right Track," 2, 8.

81. The "World Values Poll" said 57 percent of Mexicans thought Mexico should have closer economic ties to the United States. Another poll found that 59 percent favored becoming part of the United States if it would mean an improvement in the quality of life, and 21 percent favored integration in the United States without any additional conditions. Support for state-owned or employee-owned enterprises decreased from 9 percent in 1981 to 3 percent in 1990. See "Integración económica y nacionalismo: Canadá, Estados Unidos, y México," Este País, no. 1 (April 1991): 5, 7; "Convergencias y divergencias en América del Norte," Este País, no. 2 (May 1991): 7.

82. Lund, "El tratado de libre comercio," 3.

those voters more available for mobilization by the PRI. By 1994 independent voters were less optimistic. Just over 50 percent thought their family could buy fewer things than the previous year, and nearly 70 percent thought getting work was more difficult.[83] More people answered that Mexicans lived worse than six years before (35 percent) than better (less than 25 percent).[84] Though inflation continued in single digits, higher prices for some consumer goods may have influenced people, or the memory of 1987 may have begun to fade. While Salinas's personal popularity remained high, it did not transfer automatically to his chosen successor, especially after the tragic murder of his first choice in March 1994 and the abrupt imposition of classic technocrat Ernesto Zedillo as his successor. In contrast to the assassinated Luis Donaldo Colosio, carefully groomed for the presidency with a series of posts that culminated in his designation as head of the Solidarity Ministry (the Secretaría de Desarrollo Social), Zedillo had little political experience or charisma and was chosen over the protests of important sectors of the PRI. This context diminished the PRI's attractiveness to the flexible swing vote.

The Strategic Uses of Democracy: Bringing the
·   Dinosaurs Up To Date

Last, and certainly least, the Salinas government responded to popular demands for democracy, also expressed in the *cardenista* vote. Official analyses stressed the PRI's dominant role in any future political regime, within the context of a probable preference for more options.[85] Hence, promotion of democracy had to pass a preliminary test: Would it help the PRI recover? There was no sudden capitulation of control and no negotiated transition but rather strategic liberalization intended to stabilize the regime.

Most important, Salinas recognized some opposition victories for important offices. For the first time since the foundation of the ruling party, the PRI accepted defeat in a governor's race, not in a small, mar-

83. "Instantaneas: Pesimismo," *Este País*, no. 39 (June 1994): 2. Similarly, an increasing percentage (29 percent) thought their personal economic situation had worsened since the previous year, though a greater number (37 percent) still thought it had improved. This poll sampled five urban areas, only one (Mexico City) a PRD area. See "Pulsometro," *Este País*, no. 39 (June 1994): 17.

84. "Instantaneas: Hacia las elecciones," *Este País*, no. 40 (July 1994): 2.

85. Thus, "the PRI will have to get used to living with powerful *minorities* that have won popular support." See González Pedrero, *La lección de la elección*, 9, emphasis added.

ginal state, but in Baja California, a well-developed state on the U.S. border, with considerable strategic and economic importance. Two days after the July 1989 election, PRI president Luis Donaldo Colosio formally recognized the victory of the PAN candidate, calling his action a reflection of the PRI's "serious commitment to the democratic modernization of Mexico."[86] Many saw an opposition governorship as a hopeful sign for the future—"the triumph [not] of a political party but of the democracy the Mexican people have chosen."[87]

Nevertheless, even as it passed one test in Baja California, the PRI failed the test posed by local congressional elections held on the same day in the PRD stronghold of Michoacán. In its first election as a registered party, the PRD saw the congressional majority it earned at the polls stolen by methods ranging from intimidation to alteration of vote counts and stealing packets of votes at gunpoint. At the refusal of the PRI to compare documents or accept compromises, the PRD called for the formation of an Independent Citizens Court composed of members of the PRD, the PAN, the PRI's internal Critical Current, and academics. After examining eyewitness testimony and original documents, including carbon copies of official counts kept by polling booth representatives, the court found that the PRD had won in fourteen districts, and in the other four irregularities in more than 50 percent of the polling stations required annulment of the election.[88] But the Independent Citizens Court had no legal authority. Using its control of electoral courts and institutions, the PRI took twelve of the eighteen majority seats.

In the light of Michoacán, Baja California takes on a different appearance. Accepting defeat killed two birds with one stone: winning Salinas national and international credit for defending democracy and, equally important, channeling the democratic opening toward the more reliable PAN, which supported his economic policy. Michoacán was an object lesson designed to convince a national audience that the PRD could not survive a PRI assault. Democracy in Baja California gave Salinas the political space to crush the *cardenistas* in Michoacán and prevented a united opposition coalition. PRI leaders in Baja California fueled speculation about this strategy when they accused national leaders of deliberately throwing the 1989 election to the PAN, starting with the selection of a weak candidate, continuing through the "center's" at-

86. Georgina Saldierna, "Reconocimiento oficial del PRI al triunfo de Ruffo," *La Jornada* (Mexico City), 5 July 1989: 12.

87. José Antonio Román and Victor Cardoso, "Triunfo panista, avance en la vida democrática del país," *La Jornada* (Mexico City), 6 July 1989: 11.

88. Grupo Parliamentario Independiente, *Fraude en Michoacán: Continuidad de una política electoral* (Mexico City: Congreso de la Unión, 1989), 16.

tempt to sow divisions during the campaign, and culminating in its acceptance of defeat.[89] "It was all premeditated," claimed local CTM leaders; but the center had committed "a great stupidity, handing over power to the opposition." What Salinas had done, they argued, amounted to saying that "in the name of modernity, strategies and principles should change, and the Church should be handed over to Luther."[90] The United States encouraged this ideologically selective strategy by accepting PAN victories as evidence of Salinas's commitment to democracy and not strongly criticizing attempts to bury the leftists.[91]

Channeling the vote also involved the intimidation of PRD candidates, voters, and election observers. The contrast between simultaneous 1992 elections for governor in Michoacán and Chihuahua makes this point clearly. The Chihuahua campaign developed in an atmosphere of extraordinary cordiality. Both the PRI candidate Baeza and his PAN opponent Francisco Barrios kept political mudslinging to a minimum, predicted no problems on election day, and publicly promised to respect the results. A similar proposal in Michoacán was quickly frustrated, in part by PRD distrust of the PRI and a strident speech by Cárdenas at a critical point in the discussions. During the campaign, PRI candidates and local journalists warned that the PRD planned to disrupt the election. A poll published one week before the election found 42 percent of *michoacanos* "very" worried about unrest on election day and an additional 28 percent "somewhat" worried.[92] At the governor's request the federal government sent in the army to keep the peace and to monitor and deport any "foreign election observers" caught "interfering" in the Mexican electoral process. Predictions of violence contributed to higher abstention in Michoacán, as well as reluctance to vote for a party who seemed associated with chaos.

The PRI encouraged and capitalized on this fear of what might happen if the opposition in general and the *cardenistas* in particular were to win elections. In the 1994 presidential election many explained sup-

89. Aurelio Garibay, "Los del 'centro vinieron a intrigar y dividirnos,' " *La Jornada* (Mexico City), 5 July 1989: 5.

90. Andrea Becerril, "Ante el resultado en BC, la cúpula obrera plantea crear otro partido," *La Jornada* (Mexico City), 6 July 1989: 3.

91. See for example Cathryn Thorup, "México-E.U.: La democratización y la agenda bilateral," *Nexos* 14, no. 162 (June 1991): 57–60; Christopher Whalen, "Mexico: America's Next Iran?" *New York Times*, 30 July 1990: 40; Andrew Reding, "Mexico: The Crumbling of the 'Perfect Dictatorship': *World Policy Journal* 8 (Spring 1991): 255–84.

92. "Encuesta en Michoacán," *La Jornada: Perfil* (Mexico City), 6 July 1992.

port for the PRI by referring to the Spanish proverb *"más vale malo conocido que bueno por conocer* (better the devil you know . . .)." According to one poll, of Mexicans who thought it would be better for the PRI to win again than for another party to win, 7 percent thought another party would bring instability (political or economic) and 9 percent cited the PRI's experience, compared to 6 percent who thought it would be better for the PRI to win because of programs like PRONASOL.[93] Zedillo beat the PAN by only 23 percent. PRD threats to make the country ungovernable if the PRI perpetrated another fraud (which the PRD constantly predicted) did nothing to relieve this fear. People may well have believed the PRD—a nonprofessional poll by the independent poll-watching group Alianza Cívica found that 66.1 percent expected violence with repression and ungovernability if a fraud occurred in the election—but this would only have encouraged timid voters to vote for *anyone* else, to prevent the PRD from coming within striking distance.[94] Many opponents of the PRI preferred to cast their ballots in favor of the less strident and more socially acceptable PAN, increasing its vote to a record 26 percent.

In addition to a limited democratic opening toward the opposition, many *priistas* argued in 1988 that to reconnect to the electorate it was necessary to "reconstruct the PRI from the base . . . with one step, simple and yet full of difficulties: the democratic selection of leaders and candidates. . . . with this single decision, it will be possible to . . . revitalize internal consensus and above all recover undeniable leadership in each state and in the whole country."[95] Reversing their stance on the Corriente, PRI leaders encouraged such proposals. At a September 26 meeting the PRI's National Executive Committee concluded that the PRI had to become a modern political party and should support experienced politicians in order to recover—an implicit criticism of De la Madrid's reliance on *técnicos*.[96] They selected as head of the Chamber of Deputies a *priista* who called for more participation in candidate selec-

93. "La moneda en el aire," *Voz y Voto*, no. 17 (July 1994): 35. A total of 46 percent thought it would be better if the PRI won, and 39 percent thought another party would be better.

94. "Los ciudadanos y las elecciones," *La Jornada* (Mexico City), 30 July 1994: 15.

95. González Pedrero, *La lección de la elección*, 13, 15, 17.

96. This information was publicized in an ad paid for by a group of *priistas* who responded to the "invitation" by proposing fifteen internal reforms. Eight reforms stressed the urgent need for the "elimination of authoritarianism and of the distance between some public functionaries and the base." See "Transformar al PRI," *La Jornada* (Mexico City), 3 October 1988: 12.

tion, and criticized "attitudes that hurt the party: corruption, arrogance, but above all decisions by the select few at the top."[97]

Yet by the time the PRI held its triennial National Assembly in September 1990 much of the original post-'88 sense of crisis had passed. The PRD was already struggling. In part as a result, internal reforms passed by the 1990 assembly did not go nearly as far as early proposals suggested. Still, changes affected the internal balance of power and procedures for choosing leaders and candidates. First, without abandoning the sectoral structure established in the thirties the assembly added a parallel territorial structure that members would join as individuals according to their districts of residence. The territorial and structural organizations would have "equal representation" in party organs. Second, the new statutes permitted election of party leaders and candidates by convention or primary, ruling out primaries only for proportional representation lists and presidential candidates.[98] These changes expanded the limits of the "direct consultation of the base" used previously for local elections, but party leaders retained discretionary control over the type of election used in specific cases. Similar procedures governed the election of leaders, with the selection of each new CEN firmly controlled by the previous CEN, and progressively more reliance on direct elections toward the local level.

In practice, little changed, especially in candidate selection. The PRI used elections for propaganda purposes in regions of strong opposition, but in only one or two token districts, and generally not the most competitive ones. PRI leaders rarely wanted to risk a direct primary, leaving conventions to ratify selections made by *dedazo* and top-level negotiation. In 1991 the PRI chose all senatorial candidates and all but twenty-two of its three hundred candidates for majority election to Congress as "unity candidates," meaning that only one precandidate registered for election by convention.[99] The PRI did make an effort to select more popular candidates but did not use internal elections to choose them. In part because of the poor performance of many sectoral candidates in 1988 the labor sector lost twenty candidacies between 1988 and 1991 (from seventy-five to fifty-four) and the agrarian sector lost ten (from

97. "El PRI debe enfrentar la nueva realidad o hacerse a un lado: Vargas Saldaña," *La Jornada* (Mexico City), 30 September 1988: 3.

98. Partido Revolucionario Institucional (PRI), *Documentos básicos* (Mexico City: PRI, 1990), 59, 86–87.

99. José Ureña, "Reclamos tras conocerse la lista de aspirantes priistas," *La Jornada* (Mexico City), 9 May 1991: 5; José Ureña, "Pide el PRI a sus miembros que aporten 1% de sus ingresos," *La Jornada* (Mexico City), 16 May 1991: 5.

fifty-eight to forty-eight).[100] Within the popular sector the official teachers' union (−8) lost ground, while local officials (+20) and federal officials (+14) picked up candidacies. Six senators and more than seventy elected congressmen—respectively 19 percent and 24 percent of the PRI total—came from positions as administrators of PRONASOL, evidently to tap into the program's popularity.[101] Ironically, the attempt to be more competitive contributed to a 67 percent drop in the number of women candidates (−6), to only 1 percent of the total.[102]

Those who sought democratic reforms and those who rejected internal democracy disagreed only on whether internal elections would give the PRI a competitive advantage or handicap it in the general election. Reformers argued that competitiveness came from having popular candidates, and that internal elections more frequently selected popular candidates. Antireformers argued that electoral competitiveness came from a united effort, and internal elections tended to divide the party. The second argument dominated. *Priistas* in positions to choose the format of candidate selection affirmed in interviews that rational nondemocratic procedures resulted more consistently in good candidates than internal elections, something PRD internal reports ironically echoed. In addition, primaries could turn into a civil war that would weaken the party. Thus, they preferred to maintain party unity by designating a candidate or working out a compromise behind the scenes, especially in large districts (which tended to have more aspiring candidates) and districts with existing conflicts (which primaries might worsen).[103]

Instead of using primaries to improve electoral competitiveness, the PRI relied on intelligent, ruthless, and lavish campaigns, led by a professional, well-organized, and well-financed staff. PRI strategists

100. Of forty-eight candidates nominated by the CTM in 1988, fifteen (31 percent) lost. See Juan Reyes del Campillo, "La selección de los candidatos del Partido Revolucionario Institucional," in *Las elecciones federales de 1988 en México,* ed. Juan Felipe Leal, Jacqueline Peschard, and Concepción Rivera (Mexico City: UNAM, 1988), 96; Juan Reyes del Campillo, "Candidatos: Hacia una nueva cámara," *Nexos* 14, no. 164 (August 1991): 56–57. A different perspective saw internal elections as an excuse to abandon sectoral quotas and undermine the power of entrenched sectoral leaders. The argument assumes that labor threatened the neoliberal project, a questionable assumption given labor's cooperation in implementing neoliberal programs, but in any case, since internal elections did not select candidates, territorial structure appears a more plausible tool for balancing the sectors. See Rogelio Hernández Rodríguez, "La reforma interna y los conflictos en el PRI," *Foro Internacional* 32, no. 126 (October–December 1991): 222–49.

101. José Ureña, "Clase política, *La Jornada* (Mexico City), 15 September 1991: 6.

102. Reyes del Campillo, "Candidatos: Hacia una nueva cámara," 57.

103. Confidential interview BE, September 1991. Confirmed by confidential interviews AW, August 1991; C, April 1991.

adopted many features of U.S. campaigns, including an aggressive media effort and precise, private polls to identify targets and track responses to its campaigns.[104] In addition to paid advertisements, the PRI took advantage of its position as the party of the state to get free coverage on television and radio stations. The head of one of the main "private" TV networks, Televisa, contributes to PRI causes, in part because state-awarded concessions of new stations made him rich.[105] Televisa donated time for PRONASOL commercials, and its news programs gave priority to favorable coverage of the PRI. According to an independent study of Mexico's most-watched news program, Televisa's "24 Horas," between January and April 1994 the PRI candidate received forty-six times as much coverage as the other candidates; 91 percent of the electoral news presented in the first ten minutes of each show referred to the PRI.[106] In part as a result of this report Televisa balanced its coverage more. However, a second analysis in May 1994 found that while the proportion devoted to the PRI declined, the slant of news still favored the PRI: 30 percent of the positive notices discussed the PRI as a party (compared to 17 percent each for the PAN and PRD), and 43 percent discussed Zedillo as a candidate (compared to 17.8 percent for the PAN candidate and 10.7 percent for the PRD candidate); Televisa singled out the PRD for 41.1 percent of the total negative notices.[107] The national printed media also favored the PRI. One analysis of seven national newspapers from March 1 to March 23, 1994 (before the murder of PRI candidate Colosio) found 61 percent of the coverage of the main presidential candidates talked about the PRI candidate; of the 22 percent that mentioned Cárdenas, 35 percent criticized him.[108]

104. Confidential interview BE (*priista*), September 1991.

105. One of twenty-nine Mexican millionaires asked by Salinas at a now infamous private dinner in March 1993 to contribute 75 million new pesos to the PRI in gratitude, he allegedly responded, "I have earned so much money in these years that I commit myself to a greater amount." The government rewarded him with sixty-two new television channels in 1993. Salvador Corro, "De los gobiernos priistas, Emilio Azcárraga ha recibido todos los favores y, como priista confeso, sabe ser agradecido," *Proceso*, no. 922 (4 July 1994): 6.

106. The study was conducted by the Mexican Academy of Human Rights. See Gerardo Albarrán de Alba, "Zabludovsky pone a '24 Horas' al servicio de la 'promoción acelerada' de la imagen de Zedillo," *Proceso*, no. 922 (4 July 1994): 13.

107. Ibid., 15. This study was also conducted by the Mexican Academy of Human Rights.

108. *La Jornada* published relatively more mentions of the PRD candidate (27 percent) and was relatively less critical (17 percent negative mentions); *Excelsior* published the fewest mentions of the PRD candidate (19 percent) and was the second most critical paper (45 percent negative). *El Nacional* published more about the PRD (26 percent), but

Second, the PRI spent lavishly on electoral campaigns. PRI candidates, especially in key districts, received a party platform, a stipend to cover expenses, preprinted propaganda, and other electoral trinkets. The PRI senatorial candidate in Mexico City, for instance, had hot air balloons and live bands in addition to the usual deluge of hats, shirts, key chains, stickers, and calendars. He distributed a free board game entitled "Electoral Lotto," offering cards with questions and answers about elections, such as how one goes about voting and what a senator does, but that also identified the PRI candidate as the answer to the questions "the candidate" and "the best choice" and that omitted any mention of the opposition.[109] PRI propaganda invited the inhabitants of at least one community to a "Free Medical Assistance" day, which offered services from free haircuts and repair of home appliances to legal or medical advice, as gifts from the PRI.

Third, supplementing traditional dependence on official unions for electoral mobilization, the PRI launched the "promoters of the vote" program, to mobilize voters *"de la casa a la casilla,"* from home to the polls. Its work began several months before election day. Each promoter assumed responsibility for a territory, which could be as small as a block, and went house-to-house to get voters to make a commitment to support the PRI. Methods of persuasion allegedly included everything from bribes to more plausible offers of assistance with legal problems and benefits from government programs. Once the voter made a commitment, the promoter made sure that he/she registered to vote and received a voter card. On election day promoters escorted voters on their lists to the polls and watched them vote.[110] Only the last step—actually escorting voters to the polls—was made illegal by the 1994 electoral reform package.

Because of its intensity, thoroughness, and duration, the mobiliza-

---

66 percent was negative (only 7 percent of its mentions of the PRI candidate were critical). See Felipe Chao, "La marcha de las campañas," *Este País*, no. 39 (June 1994): 19–21.

109. Manuel Robles, "Manuel Aguilera y Luz Lajous juegan a la lotería . . . electoral," *Proceso*, no. 770 (5 August 1991): 7.

110. In Mexico City the process was so systematic that promoters filled out hourly reports on forms that the PRI distributed, indicating how many people he/she had watched vote. Every hour polling-booth representatives counted how many people had voted overall, and filled out a parallel form. The PRI district headquarters thus received a running hourly count of the approximate "PRI" vote (from the promoters) over the total vote (from its representatives). Red, green, and yellow stickers attached to the pads were used to flag stations where the PRI was clearly winning (green), in a close fight (yellow), or losing (red), so party workers could redouble their efforts where the outcome was in doubt.

tion plan required a staggering number of vote promoters. In 1991 informed sources within Michoacán estimated some 48,000 promoters for that state alone; Mexico City sources indicated that the PRI recruited 900–1,200 promoters for each district—approximately 36,000–48,000 overall.[111] It was also potentially quite costly. One of the more controversial tactics used by vote promoters in 1991 involved taking voters to breakfast before escorting them to the polls. PRD critics called "Operation Tamale," as PRI organizers dubbed it, "the worst torment that could be applied to a people . . . with one deliberate policy to provoke misery and the stagnation of the country, and with another to give them some carrots if they agree to vote for the PRI."[112] The PRI argued that it was ridiculous to suppose that one breakfast could buy a vote, and stressed that the vote is secret.[113] Yet the autonomous Human Rights Academy of Jalisco found that in 17.9 percent of polling places it surveyed, "it was not possible to vote in secret."[114] In 1994 observers from the critical Alianza Cívica charged that the secrecy of the vote had been violated in 34 percent of polling stations they observed.[115] Even when a PRI promoter could not see how individuals marked their ballots, the fact that he took them to the polls, watched them vote, and crossed their names off a list may have created pressure to vote for the PRI.

The specific techniques of the 1991 mobilization were not new. One PRI congresswoman defended Operation Tamale as simply an "old practice in my party."[116] However, two particular features of the 1991 operation made it in some sense a new development. First, the scale of the operation—the number of promoters, the length of time they worked, the specific information they gathered, and the penetration of society they achieved in key areas—seemed different from the style of PRI mobilizing in at least the last twenty years. PRI activists spoke of the 1991 operation as "a tremendous organizational effort" and a "ti-

111. Information came from multiple interviews with *priista* participants and Jorge Castañeda, "El fraude 'moderno,' " *Proceso*, no. 773 (26 August 1991): 34, 36.
112. Néstor Martínez, "Se ha roto la transición democrática, señala la oposición en la permanente," *La Jornada* (Mexico City), 22 August 1991: 15.
113. José Ureña, "A la gente no se le compra con un desayuno: Augusto Santiago," *La Jornada* (Mexico City), 22 August 1991: 16.
114. Manuel González Oropeza, "Los tribunales electorales," in *Las elecciones federales de 1991*, ed. Alberto Aziz Nassif and Jacqueline Peschard (Mexico City: UNAM, 1992), 175. The academy also found that in 44 percent of the polling stations some could not vote because they did not appear on the list and that 89.5 percent of polls did not open on time.
115. "Alianza Cívica/Observación 94: Informe de la muestra estratificada," *La Jornada: Perfil* (Mexico City), 24 August 1994.
116. Martínez, "Se ha roto la transición democrática."

tanic, exhausting" labor.[117] They attributed the adoption of the "promoters'" approach to the lesson of 1988, "that the traditional
organization of the PRI wasn't working."[118] It was time to modernize
mobilization.

Second, like advertising on television, this canvassing system reached
out to voters who might not be part of traditional PRI structures, voters
who were independent but persuadable. Promoters worked primarily
through the territorial structure of the PRI, coordinated by district
committees, instead of through official sectoral unions. Thus, despite
the claims of CTM spokespersons that labor still does the bulk of political work, the territorial structure took over crucial mobilization tasks
and targeted those outside the official PRI umbrella.[119] The promoters
of the vote seemed quite effective. In Michoacán, one of the targeted
states, PRI support in 1991 increased more than in any other state.
Perhaps the best evidence of the program's effectiveness is the PRI's
decision to resurrect it in later elections and extend it to new regions.
In Michoacán, estimates indicate that the PRI recruited about 72,000
promoters for the 1992 governor's election—an increase of about 50
percent over the number of promoters used in 1991.[120]

This kind of intensive campaigning and mobilization cost a lot of
money. Exactly how much remains unclear. Estimates usually only
cover one election or one program. After the 1994 presidential election
parties submitted financial statements to the IFE for the first time. Because the IFE relied entirely on honest self-reporting, statements certainly underestimate actual expenditures.[121] Even so, the PRI admitted
spending approximately $105 million on its 1994 campaigns, and the
equivalent of about three dollars for each Zedillo vote.[122] Spending limits

117. Confidential interviews BG, September 1991; BF, August 1991.
118. Confidential interview BE, September 1991.
119. "No ha funcionado la territorialización que promovió el PRI," *El Universal* (Mexico City), 10 September 1991: 5.
120. Oscar Camacho Guzmán, "No podrán votar 211 mil ciudadanos en los comicios
de Michoacán: CFE," *La Jornada* (Mexico City), 2 July 1992: 3.
121. In the case of the 1994 gubernatorial race in Tabasco, for example, the PRD
acquired several boxes of checks and invoices allegedly documenting that the PRI spent
sixty times the legal limit—an amount equivalant to nearly 10 percent of the state's annual budget, and four hundred times what the candidate of the PRD spent—to elect its
candidate, Roberto Madrazo. The PRD sought criminal charges, which Madrazo fought
by claiming the investigation was state and not federal business. See Gerardo Albarrán
de Alba, "De Zedillo a Madrazo: En documentos, el derroche, el acarreo, la compra de
voluntades y el soborno a la prensa, durante las campañas del PRI," *Proceso*, no. 971 (12
June 1995): 18–21.
122. Mireya Cuéllar, "Gastaron partidos N$414.78 millones en las elecciones de 1994;
78.28% lo erogó el PRI," *La Jornada* (Mexico City), 6 April 1995: 8. The calculation of

set by the IFE proved ridiculously irrelevant. The campaign expenses of all the parties put together totaled less than half the amount allowed for *one* party. In addition to these "official" campaign expenses, charges continued that the PRI used state resources to buy votes, by distributing PRONASOL checks shortly before the election or leaving the interest rates on loans blank until after the vote count confirmed a PRI victory. The PRI—and only the PRI—had the resources to adopt an electoral strategy that required this kind of campaign.

PRD LIMITATIONS: RESOURCES, ELECTORAL STRATEGY, AND CONSOLIDATION

This resource imbalance put the PRD at a significant disadvantage in the competition for votes. In the 1992 election for governor of Michoacan, for example, the PRI spent an estimated 33 million dollars—about three times the annual municipal budget of the state capital and fifty times as much as estimated PRD expenditures.[123] According to IFE financial statements, the PRI spent more than 78 percent of the total reported in 1994: 7.5 times as much as the PAN and 16.5 times as much as the PRD.[124] Even underreporting of expenditures by all parties could not diminish the huge disparity; actually, it is likely that the PRI more significantly underreported its expenditures than any of the other parties, if only because the PRI more likely received and could cover up large unreported income. Moreover, the Mexican state distributes subsidies to all parties for normal party operations and electoral campaigns

cost per Zedillo vote is based exclusively on the presidential campaign. Total figures include the cost of senatorial and congressional campaigns as well. See also Alejandro Caballero, "La desigualdad electoral en cifras: En la campaña del 94 el PRI gastó 78% del costo total; el PAN, 10.38%; el PRD, 4.58%," *Proceso*, no. 951 (23 January 1995).

123. Elías Chávez, "Michoacán: Cada voto del PRI costó 239,188 pesos; cada voto del PRD costó 6,916 pesos," *Proceso*, no. 821 (27 July 1992): 22. Teresa Gurza, "No se cumplen en Michoacán . . . ," *La Jornada* (Mexico City), 30 June 1992. In another case opposition candidates in District 32 of Mexico City estimated the amount spent by each party compared to the votes it received. Though the PRI won more votes than any other party, its cost of 223,000 (old) pesos per vote still dwarfed the cost-per-vote of other parties: 2,200 pesos for the PAN, 2,100 for the PRD, 2,500 for the PARM, and 2,400 for the PRT. Alberto Prieto Madero et al., "Sobre las elecciones en el Distrito XXXII," *La Jornada* (Mexico City), 9 September 1991.

124. Cuéllar, "Gastaron partidos N$414.78 millones en las elecciones de 1994," 8. See also Alejandro Caballero, "La desigualdad electoral en cifras," 29–35.

in proportion to the percentage of the vote obtained by each party in the previous national election.[125] Until 1991, since the PRD took the PMS registry, its subsidy reflected the 1988 PMS vote: the smallest of any party in the FDN. As a result, its resources were initially extremely limited.

Resource constraints affected PRD campaigns and electoral strategy. A comparison of PRI and PRD campaigns clarifies this problem. Lack of resources limited the PRD's ability to call on tools like private polls and television advertising, for example, compared to the PRI or even the PAN. In 1991 the PRD's government subsidy in Mexico City could have paid for about two minutes of prime television time.[126] Free time allotted to registered parties by the electoral code accounted for most PRD television exposure, but even there, the PRI advantage continued. In 1991 the PRI used 19 percent more air time (radio and TV) than the PRD, a difference of approximately seven and a half hours.[127] Opposition parties also complained that the free political party programs were relegated to low viewing times on channels rarely watched by most people.

Moreover, compared to the relatively well organized, professional PRI campaigns, the PRD's lack of resources encouraged campaigns that were highly personalized—even idiosyncratic—often unprofessional, and frequently uncoordinated with overall party strategy. To encourage coordination with the party PRD statutes called for the formation of District Electoral Commissions, composed of a representative of the candidate, representatives chosen by municipal committees in the district (or, in municipal elections, by base committees), and a representative of the State Executive Committee. The commission was charged with key electoral tasks, to "verify the voter registry list, . . . propose names of party representatives in polling stations, . . . and electoral commissions, . . . formulate and carry out the propaganda program, . . . train party representatives, . . . establish citizen organizations to ob-

125. This subsidy was supposed to be distributed in three annual allotments, with 20 percent of the financing arriving in the first year, 30 percent in the second year, and 50 percent in the third year, when new national elections would occur. See Mexico, Instituto Federal Electoral (IFE), *Memorias del proceso electoral federal de 1991* (Mexico City: IFE, 1993), vol. 3, pt. 1, p. 26.

126. Heberto Castillo, interview by author, Mexico City, 22 August 1991. According to Castillo—at the time, head of the PRD committee in Mexico City—the government subsidy came to about 640 million pesos, approximately $213,000, for forty majority district congressional campaigns, one senator's race, and spots on the Mexico City Assembly. One minute of television time cost between 39 million pesos (for the least desirable time) and 321 million pesos (for the most desirable).

127. IFE, *Memorias del proceso electoral federal de 1991*, 40.

serve, impartially, the electoral process, . . . formulate and carry out the program of defense of the vote, . . . [and] formulate and carry out the campaign plan."[128] Like other PRD statutes, this one was observed mostly in the breach. While candidates drew heavily on party activists and municipal committee members, they usually recruited their campaign teams personally, choosing loyal clients whom they trusted to carry out vital electoral tasks.

Candidates also provided most of the resources for their campaigns. In 1991 the National Executive Committee decided that dividing the limited PRD subsidy into three hundred congressional pieces and thirty-two senatorial pieces would leave just a token contribution. Instead, they invested in general publicity (such as PRD posters) and selected critical campaigns. In 1994 the CEN offered state committees a choice: either 3,000 pesos per congressional candidate and 7,000 pesos per senatorial candidate, distributed through the state party leadership, or electoral propaganda. Most states chose the propaganda, which kept the focus on Cárdenas and saved them some effort. All other campaign resources came from each candidate's personal funds, donations from friends, fundraising events, or municipal committees. The latter often took responsibility for posting flyers, buying paint, and painting local walls and hillsides with propaganda. Candidates usually took responsibility for printing flyers and promotional items, like bumper stickers or small calendars. They also paid food and transportation costs, a particularly heavy burden for those running in large rural districts. PRI candidates rarely had to scrounge trucks or gas money to get to their rallies.

This burden may have affected the kind of candidates the PRD could nominate. Not only did candidates have to leave work in order to campaign hard, but only those with savings or resources from family and friends could afford to forgo their salary and pay campaign costs. Others simply could not spend much time or money campaigning.

In addition, since candidates themselves shouldered much of the burden of campaign costs and organization, the effectiveness of campaigns varied widely. An internal PRD analysis blamed much of the party's disastrous performance in local elections in Morelos—a state Cárdenas won in 1988—on the fact that "electoral campaigns . . . were left entirely up to the candidates. This explains in good part the fact that the most minimum requirements of campaigning were not reached in some *municipios*. In those places visited by Ing. Cuauhtémoc Cárdenas it was observed that the campaigns rested principally on the rally held for that

---

128. Partido de la Revolución Democrática (PRD), *Documentos básicos* (Mexico City: PRD, 1990), 55.

visit." Candidates ran "without specific policy proposals" and distributed propaganda of low quality or containing misleading information, such as the wrong party colors, an error that could lead less literate voters to choose another party's symbol on the ballot.[129]

Lack of coordination and uneven advance publicity clearly undermined the PRD's ability to convince uncommitted voters. Often a candidate would arrive in a village for a scheduled campaign stop and find only a handful of people from the municipal committee. Occasionally, even the local committee seemed unaware of planned rallies. The candidate then had to drive around with loudspeakers announcing his arrival until a larger crowd gathered. Smart candidates planned crucial rallies for Sunday evenings outside a church (when mass let out) in order to capture more casual attendance, but often voters were not home to take advantage of an impromptu rally. Candidates sometimes found themselves going door-to-door in order to reach voters, any voters. While PRI armies of trained promoters of the vote could use such tactics, house-to-house canvassing is not an efficient way for a candidate with limited resources to reach a wide audience. Candidates outside urban areas found it hard to cover even every municipal seat in their district, much less all the small *ranchos* and *ejidos*.

Finally, bitter experience of past electoral fraud forced the PRD to spend precious energy and resources to monitor the polls. Much of the fraud in 1988 apparently occurred at polling stations not covered by opposition representatives. Yet the opposition has a lot of trouble organizing poll watching. According to IFE information, PRD coverage in 1991 ranged from a low of 1 percent of potential poll watchers in Yucatán to a high of 67 percent of potential poll watchers in Michoacán.[130] The PRI registered more than three times as many representatives as

129. Partido de la Revolución Democrática (PRD), *Informe sobre las elecciones en Morelos* (Mexico City: PRD, Comisión para la Defensa del Voto, 1991), 7.

130. Electoral law allowed each party up to three representatives per polling station, or *casilla*. Thus, total registered representatives overestimates coverage, since parties might register more than one for some *casillas*. But even if the PRD had registered only one representative per *casilla*, a highly unlikely assumption, it could have covered no more than 80 percent of the total. The PRD registered at least as many poll watchers as *casillas* in only eight states. This calculation includes 35,774 representatives registered under the PPS label as part of their 1991 alliance as well as the 35,136 representatives registered under the PRD label. It does not include the PRD's 2,443 registered "general representatives," who have the right to check up on many *casillas*. These representatives, since they are not present in any one *casilla* all day, have a limited ability to detect fraud. Based on Jacqueline Peschard, "La organización de las elecciones de 1991: En deuda con la imparcialidad," in *Las elecciones federales de 1991*, ed. Alberto Aziz Nassif and Jacqueline Peschard (Mexico City: UNAM, 1992), 122–23.

the PRD. If estimates are accurate, the PRI had more promoters of the vote than the PRD had poll watchers. In 1994 opposition poll coverage reached unprecedented heights. Opposition parties claimed to have covered 80–90 percent of the polls, an exaggeration, but an independent teachers' electoral observation team found accredited PRD representatives on election day in 67 percent of their sample of more than 7,500 polling places, compared to 66 percent for the PAN, and 91 percent for the PRI.[131] While limiting fraudulent manipulation, none of this massive effort convinced new voters to vote for the PRD.

The shift from emergence to consolidation substantially increases the relevance of such resource constraints. First, resources may become more important for effective campaigns in the typical postemergence context of a detached electorate that cannot be mobilized through traditional structures or counted on to vote party loyalties. Second, new parties lose some first-election advantages that initially compensate to some extent for poverty and disorganization. The advantage of surprise, for example, lets weaker opponents magnify the effect of their forces. Because they had surprise, the FDN's small, uncoordinated teams of organizers could use their flexibility to take advantage of local weaknesses. Once the PRI knew exactly who supported the PRD and where they could focus on wiping out these uncoordinated opposition pockets. Since 1988, voting results and polls commissioned by the PRI gave the party increasingly sophisticated and precise information, indicating not only which districts but even which polling stations tended to go to the PRD. It could bring all its resources to bear on specific areas, down to the fine details of placing polling stations in PRI areas rather than PRD areas of *municipios* to make it harder for *perredistas* to get to the polls. Thus, the loose, flexible structure of the FDN coalition in 1988 worked adequately for a simple, offensive task with a short-term payoff and a confused rival but could not withstand a long-term siege by a well-organized and determined opponent.

Similarly, a new party has no record to defend. Voters can see in it what they choose to see. Over time, the party acquires a history that some will find less attractive than the limitless possibilities presented at first. Party performance on consolidation tasks begins to affect its image. Any internal problems become public and spill over into other areas of activity, affecting its ability to deliver results and win elections. The PRI helped this process along by using its resources to undermine

---

131. Organización Nacional de Observación Electoral del Magisterio (ONOEM), *Informe de la observación del proceso electoral de la ONOEM* (Mexico City: ONOEM, 1994), mimeographed report.

the PRD's performance of tasks like mediation and governing. Ultimately, people notice whether or not a party provides useful services as well as opportunities for participation and self-expression. And in a strictly electoral sense the FDN's first consolidation failure, its inability to compel a political transition in 1988, damaged the PRD's standing among strategic voters. Subsequent losses at the polls discouraged (as the PRI intended) the population's sense that a PRD vote would not be wasted. By 1991 most PRD leaders sought sure seats through proportional representation rather than gambling on winning a majority in any district. If the PRD could not keep its leaders from suspecting they could not get a majority, it could hardly expect to convince strategic voters.

Other factors that contributed to the formation of a successful new party actually changed because of the threat the PRD now posed. For example, the PRI's perceived indifference to social suffering contributed to both the decision by dissident elites to create a new leftist coalition that denounced austerity and to their initial electoral success. Yet the size and orientation of the Cárdenas vote forced some changes in rigid austerity. The National Solidarity Program implicitly responded to voter demands for state services and attention, while driving a wedge between the PRD and popular movements. At the same time the PRI accepted some political liberalization, but in a way that channeled protest votes toward the PAN. The elite disunity that created political space for the new left gave way initially to a closing of ranks within the PRI, against the common enemy. Finally, the United States and international banking, concerned by the prospect of a president who opposed repayment, showed greater flexibility with respect to the debt. Shortly after the election the United States extended a large emergency bridge loan to Mexico. Within six months of his inauguration Salinas was able to announce a major debt renegotiation that saved Mexico more than two billion dollars in external transfer payments in 1990 alone.[132] Combined with a negotiated trade opening, this helped the government get inflation under control and freed up money for spending on programs to win voters back. All these developments improved the PRI's electoral position and limited the support available to the PRD.

Finally, some of the factors that encouraged emergence contributed to the PRD's trouble in consolidation. The FDN's vaguely leftist ideology and its apparent prospects for success attracted voters alienated by neoliberal austerity programs but provoked a strong and selective PRI-state response aimed at neutralizing its influence. Likewise, reliance on

132. SHCP, *El nuevo perfil de la economía mexicana*, 20.

charisma compensated for disorganization and lack of resources initially but does not necessarily help a new party in later elections. Charisma is not interchangeable. No matter how hard Cárdenas campaigned, he could not transfer his peculiar charisma to other candidates. In addition, if charisma hinders party institutionalization, it may indirectly damage party performance and appeal, particularly to independent voters. Last, but not least, charisma is fragile. Cárdenas's image was tarnished by his failures to defend the vote in 1988, keep the FDN together, or make the PRD harmonious, as well as by the PRI media campaign against him. By 1994 an astonishing 36 percent in national polls cited Cárdenas as someone for whom they would "never" vote—more than three times as many as any other national candidate and twice as many as supported the PRD.[133] Within the PRD he suffered the common fate of incumbents: accumulating discontented followers who blame the leader for reverses or their own failure to advance. Paradoxically, a new party may die stillborn without charisma to unify elites and attract attention and support. But the relative rarity of charisma makes it an unreliable foundation for consolidation. When charisma fades or a charismatic leader dies, the party may have trouble surviving.

These differences between emergence and consolidation may explain more electoral loss than many assume. Much of the decline in left support appeared almost immediately in local election results, often *before* the economy improved and *before* the full implementation of many PRI measures aimed at recovering voters. In fourteen local elections during 1989 the PRD vote fell by an average of 19.4 percent with respect to the 1988 *cardenista* vote in the same states. In eight local elections in 1990 the PRD lost an average of 19.23 percent.[134] The PRD actually improved its percentage of the vote in ten states in 1991 congressional elections compared to the *first* local election between July 1988 and December 1990; in the remaining fifteen, average additional loss amounted to only 3.2 percent of the vote.[135] This suggests that the transition from emer-

133. "La moneda en el aire," 37.

134. Calculations based on official 1988 results, in Gómez Tagle, *Las estadísticas electorales de la reforma política*, 228–31; official local results from the Comisión Federal Electoral, in Leonardo Valdés, "Partido de la Revolución Democrática: The Third Option in Mexico," in *Party Politics in 'an Uncommon Democracy': Political Parties and Elections in Mexico*, ed. Neil Harvey and Mónica Serrano (London: Institute of Latin American Studies, 1994), 68–70; for the 1989 election in Tamaulipas, not covered by Valdés, I rely on official results provided by the PRD. Otherwise, PRD sources and Valdés come up with the same number (and location) of 1989 elections.

135. Ibid.; in addition, 1991 results from IFE, *Relación de los 300 distritos federales electorales*. Some states held more than one local election between July 1988 and December 1990; only the first election was used to calculate losses. At least one local election—in

gence to consolidation had an immediate effect on the electoral support of the new party. In contrast, PRI support did not return as quickly as the PRD support fell, but grew over time, as policy changes took effect. By 1990 the PRI gain had increased to an average of 10.7 percent. But in 1989 the PRI gained an average of only 8.6 percent, less than half of PRD losses. A continuing anti-PRI vote distributed itself differently among opposition parties. Established parties like the PAN gained at the expense of the new party, especially in developed urban areas where the anti-PRI middle class that defected to the FDN in 1988 recalculated its strategic options. The clearest case is Baja California (see Table 7.2). Before 1988 the anti-PRI vote went to the conservative PAN; in 1988 an augmented opposition vote supported the leftism of Cárdenas; and in 1989 most of the 1988 opposition elected a *panista* governor.

However, it must be admitted that the PRD did not respond as effectively as it might have to the altered circumstances it faced after 1988. PRD errors and strategic inflexibility exaggerated the already difficult conditions for competition and undermined its appeal to independent voters. In addition to performance problems already discussed, especially internal division, three strategic problems stand out: (1) a confrontational approach toward the government that included nearly constant denunciations of fraud; (2) public support for the most radical and combative social groups; and (3) an electoral strategy built around rallies. Confrontation not only proved ineffective as a strategy for deliv-

Table 7.2. Opposition voting in Baja California, 1982–1991

	1982	1985	1988	1989	1991
PAN	32.5%	26.0%	26.0%	46.4%	43.0%
Independent left	5.9	4.8	31.9	3.6	2.9
Other opposition	8.1	10.7	1.0	9.8	6.2
PRI	53.5	46.6	41.1	40.2	43.9
Total Opposition Vote	46.5	41.5	58.9	55.9	52.1

SOURCES: Figures on the 1982, 1985, and 1988 federal elections (congressional vote) found in Silvia Gómez Tagle, *Las estadísticas electorales de la reforma política* (Mexico City: El Colegio de México, 1990), 176, 192, 220. In 1985 the remaining 11.9 percent represents annulled votes. 1989 figures (governor's election) from Leonardo Valdés, "Partido de la Revolución Democrática: The Third Option in Mexico," in *Party Politics in 'an Uncommon Democracy': Political Parties and Elections in Mexico,* ed. Neil Harvey and Mónica Serrano (London: Institute of Latin American Studies, 1994), 68. The category "other opposition" is derived by subtraction from 100 percent, as Valdés does not report directly. 1991 figures (congressional vote) from Mexico, Instituto Federal Electoral, *Relación de los 300 distritos federales electorales* (Mexico City: IFE, 1991).

Veracruz in the fall of 1988—is not covered in available sources. Based on valid vote in 1991.

ering payoffs but tended to frighten and annoy undecided voters. Those who managed to avoid classifying the PRD as a dangerous group of agitators still saw them as unruly troublemakers who blocked traffic and disrupted business at the drop of a hat. Denunciations of fraud in virtually every election both discouraged voting among those who believed the fix was in and undermined PRD credibility among voters who could see that not all elections were equally fraudulent. Second, PRD overtures to radical, even violent, social organizations tied them to violence in the minds of some middle-class voters. Most damaging was the visit that Cárdenas paid to Subcomandante Marcos and the Zapatista guerrillas in Chiapas while campaigning for the presidency in 1994. Finally, PRD campaigns tended to rely on mobilization through a series of rallies, in contrast to the PAN or the PRI, which put more effort into media campaigns. According to one count, nearly 70 percent of PRD "campaign acts" were rallies, compared to just over 50 percent of PRI "campaign acts" and 42 percent of PAN "campaign acts."[136] Since most of those who bothered to attend rallies already supported the PRD, this "plazismo," or plaza-centered strategy ended up preaching to the converted rather than reaching out to independent voters.

From a rational choice point of view it is difficult to understand how PRD leaders could remain unaware of the negative effect of their actions after repeated electoral disappointments. In fact, many critics within the PRD pointed out the dangers within the first year of the party's existence. Yet if aware, why would PRD leaders keep making the same mistakes? Errors, miscalculation, and wishful thinking unquestionably played a part in the decisions of PRD leaders, some of whom— and particularly Cárdenas—continued to promote unsuccessful strategies against the advice of growing factions in the PRD. It is unfortunately impossible to rid theoretical explanations of this human element. Yet one possibility, which deserves further research, is that PRD leaders reacted according to a social movement logic rather than a party logic to preserve PRD identity even at the cost of some electoral reverses. Indeed, the farther away actual success seemed, the less they would have to lose by investing in sources of PRD cohesion. This raises the likelihood that characteristics created by the process of emergence may persist and affect the party well into its consolidation period, like

136. Other campaign acts included private meetings and press conferences. In absolute figures the PRD held almost twice as many rallies as the PRI and almost four times as many rallies as the PAN. The count was based on a survey of articles printed in *La Jornada* and should therefore be considered "only indicative figures." See Enrique Calderón and Daniel Cazés, *Informe: Las elecciones presidenciales de 1994* (Mexico City: Fundación Arturo Rosenblueth, 1995), sec. 6.5, 13–20.

the "birth defects" that Terry Karl and Philippe Schmitter suggest may affect democracies long after a democratic transition.[137]

The single most important formative experience of the PRD was the fraudulent election of 1988. The PRD often referred to itself, especially in the early years, as the "party of the sixth of July." In this experience party identity became mixed up with intransigent resistance to the government, denunciations of fraud, rejection of negotiation (of electoral results in particular), and public protest. The PRD was the party of those who would never sell out to an unjust government, the party of the usually silent majority. If it negotiated with the government, or admitted losing fairly, it would compromise these elements of party identity, perhaps alienating consolidated voters for the risky hope of attracting voters it did not yet have. Even when the PRD's own records of polling-place counts confirmed the official result, some continued to insist that somehow the PRI must have cheated. Those who privately acknowledged defeats avoided the word in public, while those that supported negotiation only recently received authorization to conduct a dialogue, but with a long list of demands that may block successful negotiation.

Similarly, the PRD's self-image as the party of the oppressed majority led it to adopt with little hesitation the banner of groups like the *zapatista* rebels in Chiapas. Although the PRD rejects the use of violence, it could not bear to dissociate itself from the *zapatistas*, despite rather public *zapatista* distaste for most of the PRD. Instead of positioning the PRD as an *alternative* to *zapatista* violence, the PRD embraced its agenda. Only days after his disastrous performance in Mexico's first national televised presidential debate, Cárdenas headed off for the jungles of Chiapas at the invitation of the rebel leader Subcomandante Marcos. The rebels controlled all the circumstances of the meeting, from its time and place to its agenda. Marcos let the press in before his guests, so they could take good pictures.[138] Cárdenas looked like another Marcos groupie, not a statesman negotiating their surrender. Even worse, he and his entourage endured a public attack on PRD defects by Marcos himself. The entire national leadership showed up for this circus, including PRD president Muñoz Ledo, identified with the moderate,

137. Terry Karl and Philippe Schmitter, "Modes of Transition in Latin America, Southern and Eastern Europe," *International Social Science Journal*, no. 128 (May 1991): 273.

138. I rely on the description of Adolfo Aguilar Zínser, media spokesman for the Cárdenas campaign, who witnessed this encounter. See Adolfo Aguilar Zínser, *¡Vamos a ganar!: La pugna de Cuauhtémoc Cárdenas por el poder* (Mexico City: Editorial Oceano, 1995), especially 395–416.

pronegotiation line in the PRI. Too many PRD activists saw themselves and their goals in Marcos. As one member of the inner circle put it, although it is an "enormous problem" to "extend bridges" to the extreme left while also reaching out to the middle class, ultimately no left party could renounce the extreme left without ceasing to be a "party of masses."[139]

Finally, the strategy of *plazismo*, while encouraged by resource constraints, also reflected lessons of 1988. In 1988 the massive crowds attracted by Cárdenas had a profound public impact, convincing voters that the PRI could be beaten, and by Cárdenas. Through 1994 rallies were often seen by the PRD as publicity tools to prove that the PRD could win by demonstrating that it could gather more people than PRI or PAN rallies. Efforts were made to bring part of the crowd with the candidate and to organize bus caravans to rallies in key cities. PRD activists never quite understood the difference between large rallies and large votes. In 1988 big rallies had foreshadowed even more votes. In 1994, despite pitifully small and unenthusiastic rallies, even the PAN won more votes than the PRD. *Plazismo* expressed the PRD's sense that it was a party of the forgotten and neglected, whom no one else bothered to visit. It was also a familiar strategy, particularly to Cuauhtémoc Cárdenas, who learned it from his father, another inveterate "plazista." According to Adolfo Aguilar Zínser, media coordinator for the Cárdenas campaign, Cárdenas at first agreed to investigate such modern techniques as polls, private meetings with focus groups, and media consultants, but he later reverted to a more comfortable style, particularly after his dismal performance in the 1994 presidential debate. Cárdenas has never been a remarkable speaker; Aguilar Zínser adds that he disliked the notion of tailoring his speeches to what polls suggested the public wanted to hear, and was uncomfortable on television.[140] Thus, in a debate watched by most of the nation he appeared wooden, unconvincing, and at a loss to counter attacks on his character and record in the PRI by the charismatic and articulate PAN candidate Diego Fernández. Overnight Cárdenas fell from second place in the polls to a distant third. Afterward Cárdenas increasingly took refuge in small-town rallies, where he was received and adored like a savior—his "bet" that going "full out [to mobilize] his fundamental base of support" would—as in 1988—bring success.[141] Unfortunately, this base was too small to win.

139. Confidential interview with PRD leader, September 1994.
140. Aguilar Zínser, *¡Vamos a ganar!* especially chapter 4.
141. Ibid., 345.

PATTERNS OF ELECTORAL RESPONSE TO THE PRD

What did that loyal base look like? First of all, the PRD maintained areas of regional strength on idiosyncratic grounds that did not always reflect the region's socioeconomic structure. When key *cardenista* states are omitted from multivariate analysis as potential outliers, socioeconomic findings become weaker or disappear, suggesting that models may be driven in large part by the impact of these key states. In addition, regional patterns of support increasingly developed the PAN and PRD as complementary opposition alternatives to the PRI. The 1994 PRD vote is correlated with the PAN vote at $r = -.84$ (significance of .001) and with the PRI vote at just $r = -.30$ (significance of .1), in direct contrast to the 1988 pattern.

Second, in models based on voting results the strongest and most consistent socioeconomic predictors of PRD support on a national level are a low level of education, large agricultural workforce, and high GDP per capita, depending on the model and data used. Thus, in comparison to the PAN and PRI, the PRD remains relatively weakly linked to socioeconomic structure. In 1991 voting results my own analysis of state-level data found that lack of primary school came closest to statistical significance in models that included as variables PRONASOL spending, agricultural population, GDP per capita, and abstention rate (see Appendix C for additional statistical sources and tables). Joseph Klesner's analysis finds only low industrialization as a significant variable in models that included urbanization, no school, participation, and four "regional" dummy variables,[142] and low industrialization, outmigration, and no school significant in models that included participation but no regional dummy variables.[143] Models based on 1994 state-level data find high agricultural population, high GDP per capita, and no primary school significant at .1 or better, with an adjusted r-squared of .44 (see Table 7.3). The association with agricultural population represents a departure for the Mexican left, which was always strongly urban, but the significance of GDP per capita may indicate that once the effect of rural residence is taken into account, the PRD has kept traditional left influence in richer, urbanized states. Omitting the key PRD state of Michoacán as a probable outlier, these socioeconomic associations become stronger.

142. Klesner, "Modernization, Economic Crisis, and Electoral Alignment in Mexico," 206. Variables measured at the federal electoral district level.
143. Klesner, "Realignment or Dealignment?" 172.

Table 7.3. PRD vote, 1994

	PRD Vote	Minus Michoacán
Agricultural population	.39*	.44**
GDP/capita	.52***	.62***
No primary school	.58***	.59***
r-squared	.50	.57
Adjusted r-squared	.44	.52
	N = 32	N = 31

Significant levels: * = <.10   ** = <.05   *** = <.01
Each cell reports Beta coefficient.

Individual-level data suggest that the most significant predictors of PRD vote include previous *cardenista* support—a sign of consolidation—disapproval of the president (Salinas), and prospective evaluations of the future (see Table 7.4). Those who thought the national economy would improve if another party won, and those who thought the PRI would be weaker in ten years were more likely to support the PRD but also more likely to support the PAN.[144] Likewise, residents of

Table 7.4. Individual support for the PRD: A summary of significant variables

	PRD–1988	PRD–1991
Female	−.21	−.52*
North	−.87**	.48
Federal District	.04	1.04**
Professional class	−.68**	−.23
Church attendance	−.17**	−.11
State industries	.18*	NA
Environmentalism	NA	.31*
Previous PRI supporter	−1.20	−2.14**
Previous PAN supporter	1.12**	.63
Previous *cardenista*	NA	1.62**
PRI getting stronger	−.52**	−.53
Economy—other party	1.20**	.71
Unrest—other party	.30*	.19
Presidential approval	−.15**	−.23**

SOURCE: Jorge Domínguez and James McCann, "Shaping Mexico's Electoral Arena: The Construction of Partisan Cleavages in the 1988 and 1991 National Elections," *American Political Science Review* 89 (March 1995): 42.
NOTE: This table includes all significant variables, but not all variables in their models.
Significance levels: * = <.05   ** = <.01

144. Men were also significantly more likely to support the PRD. See Jorge Domínguez and James McCann, "Shaping Mexico's Electoral Arena: The Construction of Partisan Cleavages in the 1988 and 1991 National Elections," *American Political Science Review* 89 (March 1995): 42.

the Federal District (Mexico City) tended to support both opposition parties. Within this general context of a predisposition to vote for the opposition, Jorge Domínguez and James McCann suggest that voters with right-wing inclinations tended to vote for the PAN, while voters with left-wing inclinations tended to vote for the PRD. While Cárdenas managed to pick up many right-wing voters in 1988, the PRD lost "more than half [this] vote among right-wing voters" by 1991. Strategic but right-leaning voters were no longer prepared to take the risk of actually electing a leftist, especially given the improved prospects of the PAN.

These national results find confirmation in analysis of municipal-level voting patterns in Michoacán.[145] Overall, 1991 PRD vote is significantly correlated to agricultural population, illiteracy, and smaller municipal size. Controlling for previous experience of PRD municipal government by using only the subset of PRD-held towns, bivariate associations with socioeconomic variables improve (see Table 7.5). In multivariate regression, illiteracy and smaller size remain significant, as well as a dummy variable indicating that the town had been governed by the PRD from 1989 to 1991.[146]

Finally, exit polls taken during the 1992 race for governor of Michoacán confirm a relationship between PRD vote and marginality at the individual level. Within each socioeconomic category (type of employment, income, age, etc.), PRD vote was highest among those engaged in agriculture, those making the equivalent of one or less than one mini-

Table 7.5. Correlates of the 1991 PRD vote

	Municipal Population	Agricultural Population	Illiteracy
PRD 1991 (overall)	−.24***	.28***	.26***
PRD-held towns	−.40***	.41***	.29***
Non-PRD towns	−.31***	.23*	.47***

Significance levels: * = <.10   ** = <.05   *** = <.01
Each cell reports Pearson's *r*.

145. The government generally does not release voting results by *municipio*. These figures come from an internal PRD report, elaborated for the 1992 governor's race, and based on official figures calculated by *municipio*. See Partido de la Revolución Democrática (PRD), *Tablas comparativas de los resultados electorales* (Mexico City: PRD, Secretaría de Defensa del Voto, 1992). Sociodemographic data from Mexico, Instituto Nacional de Estadística, Geografía, e Informática (INEGI), *Michoacán: Resultados definitivos, tabulados básicos del XI censo general* (Mexico City: INEGI, 1992), vols. 1 and 2. Municipal population is calculated as the natural log of population due to kurtosis if raw data are used. Four towns were omitted from the analysis due to incomplete or unclear data. See Appendix C for additional results.

146. However, multivariate analysis may be misspecified because of a lack of municipal data on incomes and PRONASOL spending.

mum salary, those working independently, unsalaried workers, those with no education, and those older than sixty-one. The PRD depended heavily on voters from these socioeconomic categories for its overall results.[147] While to some extent a reflection of the distribution of voters in these categories (that is, there are more poor, agricultural, and uneducated voters in Michoacán than wealthy, industrial, and educated ones), the PRD depended more heavily than the PRI on agricultural workers and less heavily on women.

THE PRD AND THE ELECTORAL NETWORK

The PRD's experience in the electoral arena since 1988 illustrates a number of hypotheses about the emergence of new parties and the process of party system change. First, a new party facing successive elections may find it difficult to design a flexible electoral strategy while trying to consolidate internal activist relations and alliances. Changes in party strategy, program clarification, or moderation may threaten the construction of a stable party identity and the survival of fragile new relationships.

Second, new parties seem especially likely to attract the kind of voter that is most difficult to keep: independent, strategic voters. The sheer scarcity of viable options for these voters in rural areas helps explain why the PRD apparently kept more rural voters than urban voters, despite traditional support for the independent left in large cities. In addition, because of its reliance on the swing vote, any new party depends as much on the mistakes of the incumbent as on its own ability to mobilize support. This principle may continue to apply to opposition parties even after initial consolidation, particularly in one-party dominant systems (where the relevant reference is always support or rejection of the ruling party), and particularly where a pool of detached voters has become the winning margin in elections. Opposition electoral performance in Mexico varies more consistently with the policy performance of the government and the seriousness of internal divisions in the PRI than with changes in opposition strategy or effort.

Finally, the transition from electoral to consolidation tasks adversely affects the appeal of new parties, especially if they do not win their first

147. "Encuestalia: El voto en Michoacán," *Nexos* 15, no. 176 (August 1992): 84–85. Percentages overlap because responses are catalogued separately within each category. Hence, 43 percent of the PRD vote among those listing an "occupation" comes from agricultural workers, etc. For a more complete table of this poll see Appendix D.

election. Paradoxically, new parties are most likely to emerge and experience early success if they present a radically different alternative to incumbent policies, but this provokes a strong reaction. After 1988 the PRD faced opposition from a PRI-PAN coalition that undermined its attractiveness to the independent swing vote. The state used its superior resources to mobilize these voters for the PRI, or at least to channel them away from the left. Cárdenas's inability to compel acceptance of victory in 1988 loomed larger over time.

In contrast, winning can help consolidate electoral strength. After the PAN won the 1989 governor's race, the PRI in Baja California lost institutional resources and state authority, disarticulating its clientelist network. Meanwhile, the governorship gave the PAN an institutional position to combat the advantages of the PRI and keep more of the 1989 protest vote. In 1991 the Baja California PAN won several congressional seats and the only senate seat to go to the opposition. Agreement with PRI economic policies also bought the PAN some tolerance, including acceptance of its victory in the first place. In contrast, aggression and confrontation characterized the PRI-state's response to the PRD. The PAN's experience thus serves to highlight the handicap imposed by the position of the PRD as a left party confronting a neoliberal state.

8

New Parties and the Dynamics of Democratization

Mexico is a country of solid institutions, in which political stability has been a real, impressive fact for over sixty years, and which right now is more solid and firmly rooted than ever. The PRI must play the role that belongs to it as the majority party, as the party that has been and remains the legitimate heir of the most authentic struggles of the Mexican people.
— PRI senator; member of the CEN of the PRI in 1987[1]

The PRD proposes to the nation a pacted, peaceful, and constitutional transition toward democracy. . . . The more the government resists a democratic solution, the more stormy and costly will be the accord that they will, in the end, have to negotiate. . . . [And] the greater the capacity of . . . organization of the democratic movement, the less costly will be the beginning of the transition. . . . [We] call on society and its organizations to debate and support this alternative, so that with the broadest popular consensus we may establish a national dialogue among the political, social, and governmental forces . . . that gives rise to a profound democratic reform.
— Resolution of the Third National Congress of the PRD, 1995[2]

There won't be democracy in Mexico because they kill those that try to bring it. . . . Cárdenas faces the same danger, but if it weren't for him, the PRI would not send any help to us.
— PRD *comité de base*, rural indigenous community, Michoacán[3]

In gradual processes of political change, like that of Mexico, it is often difficult to draw a clear line marking "transition" or to indicate in advance which events will prove to be the "turning point." Both democratization and party system change are reversible. Yet while full democracy remained unrealized, clearly Mexico was by 1994 a more

1. Confidential interview with former PRI member (written questions and responses), September 1991.
2. "Resolutivo del III Congreso Nacional del Partido de la Revolución Democrática sobre linea política," *La Jornada* (Mexico City), 31 August 1995: 38–39 (paid advertisement).
3. Confidential interview AS, July 1991.

open system with more competitive politics than at virtually any time in the country's past. Regardless of its individual fate, the PRD contributed significantly to these changes. Its creation was in part a consequence and in part a contributing cause of the broader processes of party system change and democratization. Its experience provides clues to the role of new parties in party system change and the factors that may make particular paths of democratization more or less likely. Finally, by throwing a spotlight on the mechanisms of regime maintenance, the experience of the PRD demonstrates how one-party regimes may shape democratization and party system change, even if—one hopes—they cannot ultimately prevent it.

DEALIGNMENT, REALIGNMENT, OR THE RETURN OF HEGEMONY?

The central characteristics of the Mexican party system since 1988 are consistent with a hypothesis of continuing dealignment and weakened party loyalties. The PRD both resulted from and contributed to this process. On the one hand, the detachment of voters and elites from traditional party identifications encouraged the creation of a new party, by bringing together an opposition coalition and making possible its initial electoral success. This led optimistic leaders to predict a bright future and formalize their movement in a new party. On the other hand, its emergence promoted detachment. In the first place, by giving voters an attractive option for protest, the Cárdenas candidacy moved many from passive to active detachment, leading them across a psychological Rubicon that may inhibit return to previous loyalties. Second, the PRD's disappointing consolidation performance and electoral failures— themselves in part the result of voter detachment as well as differences between emergence and consolidation—added to disillusionment with parties and the political system and further discouraged the consolidation of new loyalties.

Patterns of electoral competitiveness confirm this secular trend toward declining PRI hegemony. Mexico's authoritarian one-party system has repeatedly proved itself extraordinarily resilient. The PRI has survived crisis after crisis, with more lives than a cat, stubbornly defying predictions that it had no future. Nevertheless, survival is not hegemony. The case for recovered hegemony rested largely on the PRI's electoral performance in 1991. For many, like the PRI senator quoted above, 1991 vividly demonstrated the "real, impressive fact" of PRI stability, so solidly rooted in Mexican institutions that not even 1988 could destroy it. The 1994 presidential race threw this conclusion into question. Although the PRI won, it was severely tested in a difficult campaign. No one watching the 1994 election could conclude—as in pre-1988 elections—that the PRI presidential campaign amounted to little more than a triumphal tour before the fact. Moreover, comparison of 1991 election results to the anomalies of 1988 obscures the continuation of pre-1988 trends toward expanded competitiveness (see Table 8.1). If the opposition made little headway in the critical area of beating the PRI, it significantly reduced the areas where the PRI ruled without opposition. By 1991 the PRI could no longer claim any districts by more than 95 percent, and faced meaningful competition from at least one opposition party in more than half of all districts. By 1994 the number of districts in which the PRI won more than 70 percent of the vote had declined to less than 3 percent of the total.

Table 8.1. Electoral competitiveness, 1964–1994 (percentage of electoral districts—N = 300)

Year	Monopoly	Strong Hegemony	Type of Competitiveness Weak Hegemony	Two-Party	Multiparty	Opposition Victory
1964	28.1%	52.2%	4.5%	14.0%	0%	1.1%
1967	24.2	61.2	3.6	9.7	0	1.2
1970	27.0	53.9	1.7	17.4	0	0
1973	18.7	51.3	4.1	21.8	1.0	3.1
1976	35.8	44.6	6.7	11.9	.5	.5
1979	9.4	48.0	12.3	6.3	22.7	1.3
1982	1.3	51.7	6.3	26.1	14.0	.3
1985	3.3	41.7	9.0	21.0	21.3	3.7
1988	1.0	19.0	15.0	8.3	34.0	22.7
1991	0	31.0	17.0	23.3	25.3	3.3
1994	0	2.3	8.3	26.0	55.3	8.0

SOURCES: Classifications and figures for 1964–88 are from Leopoldo Gómez and John Bailey, "La transición política y los dilemas del PRI," *Foro Internacional* 31, no. 121 (July–September 1990): 69, determined as follows: monopoly if PRI > 95%; strong hegemony if PRI < 95% but > 70%; weak hegemony if the PRI < 70% but the difference between the PRI and the second party is > 40 percentage points; two-party if the PRI < 70%, the difference between the PRI and the second party is < 40 percentage points, the second party > 25%, *and* the third party < 10%; multiparty if the PRI < 70%, the difference between the PRI and the second party is < 40 percentage points, but the second party < 25%, *or* the third party > 10%. For 1988 opposition victories sum the votes of coalitions. 1991 and 1994 figures calculated by author from Mexico, Instituto Federal Electoral, *Relación de los 300 distritos federales electorales* (Mexico City: IFE, 1991); and Mexico, Instituto Federal Electoral, *Elecciones federales 1994: Resultados definitivos según los cómputos distritales* (Mexico City: IFE, 1994).

Moreover, partisan loyalties declined overall. From 55.3 percent of the population in 1983, PRI sympathizers fell to only 28 percent by 1991—far fewer than the 52.6 percent who declared they sympathized with no political party.[4] Instead, more voters made contingent calculations about which party or candidate to support in each election. This meant, above all, that electoral success would depend much more on the PRI's ability to maintain economic stability, provide payoffs to losers in the modernization process, and mobilize uncommitted voters in its favor.

New party formation is often part of this process of detachment. It is at once a common symptom and an obstacle to its elimination, in part because new parties characteristically have trouble reattaching voters and in part because increased competitiveness offers voters more options. The PRD contributed to competition by introducing or enhancing opposition presence in areas that the PAN had not successfully penetrated, such as Michoacán. The regionalization of electoral patterns helped preserve the PRI's national predominance by dispersing opposition efforts and encouraging specialization in complementary areas of regional strength. However, regionalization also gave voters viable options in areas where the PRI had previously governed uncontested. Opposition parties, meanwhile, relied on these strongholds to survive as national electoral actors. Just as the PAN found refuge in the north, the PRD found support in the center and some southern states—most notably, Tabasco (based on PRI splits and alliance with disgruntled petroleum workers) and Chiapas (based on an intermittent alliance with the *zapatista* rebels, who have at times supported PRD candidates and run their cadres under the PRD label). Areas formerly "safe" for the PRI became minefields in which any election, no matter how insignificant, could turn into a public relations disaster, electoral loss, or worse. In Chiapas, for example, Salinas won nearly 90 percent of the vote in the highly contested 1988 election. But in December 1994 conflict over alleged fraud in the August gubernatorial race probably contributed to the calamitous devaluation of the peso. The PRD candidate for governor, supported by the *zapatista* rebel forces, claimed victory in the race and demanded the resignation of the PRI candidate. If he did not resign before his scheduled inauguration in early December, the *zapatistas* threatened to renew military action. The threat—coupled with PRI refusal to capitulate—heightened investor nervousness about the stability

---

4. Miguel Basañez, "Elections and Political Culture in Mexico," in *Mexican Politics in Transition*, ed. Judith Gentleman (Boulder, Colo.: Westview Press, 1987), 197–98; Miguel Basañez, "Encuesta electoral 1991," *Este País*, no. 5 (August 1991): 3.

of their investments, motivating a run on the stock market that contributed to the exhaustion of Mexico's financial reserves and a forced devaluation in mid-December.

The PRD's appearance also diversified the ideological content of opposition support. An analysis of the order in which parties finished in 1985, 1991, and 1994 (Table 8.2) suggests that a more widespread left presence expanded the political spectrum, mostly at the expense of smaller parastatal parties allied to the PRI. In essence, the concentration of leftist opposition in a single, independent left party slowed Mexico's rush toward a de facto two-party system at the national level. These figures may even underestimate improvement in left presence: since the PRD did not exist in 1985, the "left vote" for that year represents the sum of the votes of two separate left parties (PSUM and PMT). Unification into a single party made it possible for the left to act more coherently and with greater coordination, as well as to project a simpler profile, though this potential is not fully realized.

Table 8.2. Win, place, and show: Party order in electoral districts (percentage of total districts in which the party finished in a given rank)

	PRI	PAN	PRD/Left	Other
Win 1985	97.7%	1.7%	0.0%	.7%
Win 1991	97.0	3.0	0.0	0.0
Win 1994	92.3	6.0	1.7	0.0
1985–94	−5.4	+4.3	+1.7	−.7
Place 1985	2.3	76.0	5.3	16.2
Place 1991	3.0	62.3	25.7	8.7
Place 1994	7.7	64.0	28.3	0.0
1985–94	+5.4	−12.0	+23.0	−16.2
Show 1985	0.0	10.7	51.0	38.3
Show 1991	0.0	18.7	39.0	42.3
Show 1994	0.0	29.0	63.7	7.3
1985–94	—	+18.3	+12.7	−31.0
Top 3 1985	100.0	88.3	56.3	55.2
Top 3 1991	100.0	84.3	64.7	51.0
Top 3 1994	100.0	99.0	93.7	7.3
1985–94	—	+10.7	+37.4	−47.9

SOURCES: All data represent official vote totals from: Mexico, Registro Nacional de Electorales, computer printout furnished by Juan Molinar Horcasitas; Mexico, Instituto Federal Electoral, *Relación de los 300 distritos federales electorales* (Mexico City: IFE, 1991); Mexico, Instituto Federal Electoral, *Elecciones federales 1994: Resultados definitivos según los cómputos distritales* (Mexico City: IFE, 1994).

In addition, though the PRD's direct effect on policy was limited, due in part to its relegation to the legislature and its lack of a coherent economic policy alternative, the PRD became more like a party that "counts," in Giovanni Sartori's terms, than previous left parties.[5] First, the PRD demonstrated "governing potential"—hypothetically at the national level in 1988 and at the local level in its regional strongholds. The shadow of 1988, together with its local strength, invested the PRD with a weight in political debates that its national electoral base after 1988 might not otherwise have warranted.

Second, the PRD—like the PAN—demonstrated limited veto power within its regions of influence. The combative PRD could not compel the state to recognize all of its electoral victories (real and illusory), but it *could* compel the state to remove particular targets of protest and convert "successful" PRI electoral efforts into Pyrrhic victories. Between 1988 and 1993 Salinas asked for the resignations of PRI governors in more than a third of the states of Mexico, many of them—including the governors of San Luis Potosí, Guanajuato, and Michoacán (twice)—as a direct result of electoral conflicts in which the PRD became involved. For example, the PRD forced the resignation of Eduardo Villaseñor, officially elected governor of Michoacán in 1992. Though the PRD candidate Cristóbal Arias lost the official vote by nearly two to one, he held a victory party on election night, later alleging that PRI fraud in key districts and polling sections accounted for the official results.[6] He vowed that Villaseñor would never govern Michoacán. President Salinas put all his prestige behind the official results: formally congratulating Villaseñor on his victory, unconditionally backing his government, and personally attending his taking the oath of office. However, due to a PRD demonstration blocking the doors of the state house, Villaseñor had to hold his inauguration secretly in Morelia's convention center so that *perredistas* would not disrupt it— presaging a pattern of PRD disruption that forced him to continually relocate his state offices. After only a matter of weeks he admitted defeat and asked the local legislature for a "leave of absence," having never set foot in the statehouse as governor. The PRD's victory was more moral than substantive—and costly in terms of its reputation as a party of confrontation, insecurity, and disorder. Salinas named as interim governor another *priista*, well placed in the local PRI network and

5. See Giovanni Sartori, *Parties and Party Systems: A Framework for Analysis* (New York: Cambridge University Press, 1976).

6. Arias claimed victory on the basis of preliminary vote returns. He reached his final calculations by annulling polling stations where alleged irregularities occurred. The electoral court denied that these irregularities warranted annulment.

a more formidable enemy to the PRD than the uneducated and politically isolated Villaseñor, to whom state PRI leaders had always objected. Still, the PRD had made an important point just two years before the 1994 presidential election: despite electoral reverses and internal conflicts, the PRD could impose heavy costs on the PRI, with or without clear evidence of fraud. Significant fraud would come with an even steeper price.

Third, the PRD influenced the ideological dynamics of competition. Its emergence pushed the PAN toward closer cooperation with the PRI, encouraged democratic concessions by the PRI to the PAN, and thus ultimately contributed to the PAN's electoral advances in the 1990s. Moreover, it pulled the PRI itself toward the left in terms of social policies. There is a grain of truth in the perception that "if it weren't for [Cárdenas], the PRI would not send any help to us." After 1988 President Salinas initiated a vigorous and multifaceted program to reach alienated voters, responding to demands made by Cárdenas. He included more *políticos* in his cabinet than his predecessor De la Madrid, in part to deal with problems of stability and governability raised by the emergence of the *cardenista* opposition.[7] Though it is impossible to prove that the PRD caused specific concessions, PRD demands—for the closing of a major oil refinery in Mexico City, for a public debate on free trade, for legal restrictions on campaign finance, or for the resignation of Mexico's attorney general—often became "PRI initiatives" after a suitable delay. Other programs, like PRONASOL, were clearly intended to improve the PRI's electoral position. Regardless of fluctuations in the electoral performance of the opposition, the regime had to behave more as if it faced competition, whether actual or potential.

Finally, the creation of the PRD purged the PRI of some dissident elites and hence contributed to the recomposition of the ruling coalition begun nearly twenty years earlier under Echeverría. Judging by the dramatic changes carried out by Salinas, including NAFTA and reform of some of the most radical clauses of the 1917 Constitution, the 1988 election could mark a definitive break with Mexico's revolutionary past. Though today's ruling party uses the same name, it behaves less like the old PRI. If critical elections "decide substantive issues in a more clear-cut way, . . . involve constitutional readjustments, . . . [and produce] transformations in large clusters of policy," then 1988 may indeed prove a critical election in at least this sense.[8]

7. Miguel Ángel Centeno, *Democracy Within Reason: Technocratic Revolution in Mexico* (University Park: The Pennsylvania State University Press, 1994), 142–43.

8. Walter Burnham, *Critical Elections and the Mainsprings of American Politics* (New York: Norton, 1976), 1, 8.

THE DYNAMICS OF DEMOCRATIZATION

Nevertheless, its success in holding on to the presidency in 1988 laid the bases for the PRI to reassert control over democratization. Instead of a sweeping transformation of party system and political regime, Mexico experienced limited, gradual democratization from above. Many advances in liberalization reflected choices by those at the top of the system to selectively recognize victories by some parties and groups while undermining others. As a result, though it failed to eliminate the PRD, the PRI-state shaped the conditions for competition in such a way as to reduce the PRD threat, salvage the PRI's electoral dominance, and ensure the implementation of the Salinas economic program.

Thus, in Terry Karl's useful typology of transitions, as of 1994 Mexico came closest to the "imposition" form.[9] Her typology sorts transitions according to two factors: the ascendancy of elite versus mass actors and the dominant strategy (force or compromise). "Imposition" combines elite ascendancy and unilateral force—except that in Mexico elites did not intend to make a transition to full democracy in the short term. Rather, they accepted limited, channeled liberalization to substitute for, and thus prevent, the development of a competitive democracy in which opposition parties could effectively challenge the predominance of the PRI at the national level.

Mexico evolved toward this route after beginning a tentative transition through other paths (see Figure 8.1). In 1986 the Corriente Demo-

Fig. 8.1. The (incomplete) Mexican "transition"

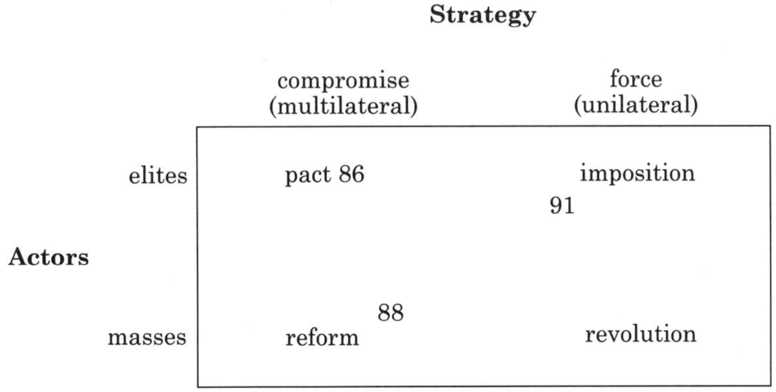

Strategy

	compromise (multilateral)	force (unilateral)
elites	pact 86	imposition 91
masses	88 reform	revolution

Actors

9. Terry Karl, "Dilemmas of Democratization in Latin America," *Comparative Politics* 23 (October 1990): 9.

crática attempted to democratize Mexico by democratizing the PRI. This required at a minimum that the PRI accept democratization de facto if not de jure. Whether or not the rules changed to permit internal election of the PRI presidential candidate, the Corriente hoped to force the PRI to acknowledge popular support for compromise on economic policy by selecting a candidate less committed to "pure" neoliberalism. Meeting with resistance, the CD escalated by mobilizing the masses, first within the PRI, and later from outside, using the candidacy of Cárdenas. By election day 1988 mass mobilization reached unprecedented heights, nearly escaping the control of those who had invoked it. Yet instead of either reform or a pacted transition, the FDN broke apart, mobilization died down, the PRI reasserted its hold on the presidency, and (at least until the Chiapas rebellion) controlled the pace and direction of liberalization.

Why did Mexico end up in this path? Are there lessons in the Mexican experience that apply to other cases? I have argued that three key characteristics of the PRD help explain its fate: it is a *new* party, a *left* party, and an *opposition party in a hegemonic one-party regime*. Each of these characteristics points to dynamics that not only blocked consolidation of the PRD but also tended to steer Mexico toward democratization from above. Analysis of the PRD therefore suggests a series of arguments about the relationship between party formation and party systems on the one hand, and party systems and democratization on the other. While tentative, these hypotheses offer some starting points for future comparative research.

First of all, adding Mexico as a case of failed pacting to the case classifications of Terry Karl (1990) and Terry Karl and Philippe Schmitter (1991), no one-party regime with the possible exception of Poland has yet made a transition through the "pact" mode that Karl and Schmitter single out as the most likely to result in stable democracy.[10] Most of these cases fall into the imposition or reform modes, with at least one (Romania) edging toward revolution because of the significance of mass violence. One-party regimes resist multilateral compromise to negotiate themselves out of power. Compared with a military authoritarian government, a party in power may behave differently because *as* a party it expects to participate in any future democracy. The guarantees a party requires for a pacted "transition" may differ substantially from guarantees demanded by a military government, probably including electoral

10. Ibid., 1–21; Terry Karl and Philippe Schmitter, "Modes of Transition in Latin America, Southern and Eastern Europe," *International Social Science Journal*, no. 128 (May 1991): 276.

rules that favor its continued influence. In negotiating, one-party regimes may also have access to resources generally denied to military governments, especially connections to a mass base. Full transition in such cases may require more mass mobilization. The contribution of the guerrilla rebellion in softening PRI resistance to significant electoral reform tends to confirm this prediction.

In 1988, as the only opposition force that could credibly claim the support of a significant mass base, the FDN was a critical element in any hypothetical transition—as a key participant in a pact, and as the only agent able to mobilize enough people nationally to force concessions from the regime. The FDN neither pacted nor escalated mobilization, and Mexico fell into the imposition mode. Why did the FDN fail to act? One key reason was its newness as a political force. It is telling that in the four "classic pact" cases identified by Karl and Schmitter—Venezuela, Colombia, Uruguay, and Spain—the construction of a pact was facilitated by the presence of at least one relatively consolidated party able to count on the loyalty of a mass base and committed to democratization. But the FDN was not a consolidated party. Its leaders thought they would lose their fragile, new support if they compromised in a pact, especially the kind of pact they were likely to get from the PRI. Their rejection of negotiation had something to do with anger at the PRI, but it also had a lot to do with their conviction that they could not afford to look like sellouts. Second, the leaders of the amorphous FDN had not reached consensus on basic goals or strategy. While convenient for bringing together an opposition challenge, the FDN's loose structure did not facilitate bargaining with more organized opponents.[11] At least some of the parastatals probably did not prefer full democratization; even more elusive was consensus on the most desirable type of transition or the best transition strategy. Even had he been prepared to negotiate, Cárdenas lacked the organization to compel or concert a consistent strategy with his new allies.

For similar reasons FDN leaders did not call for more aggressive mass protests to force the regime to turn over power or grant significant concessions. Their hesitance reflected their assessment that they lacked the organization to control mass mobilization and their fear that uncontrolled mobilization would lead to state repression that would abort the

11. It is worth noting that despite its weaker electoral performance in 1988, the PAN managed to profit more from the 1988 scare than the PRD itself, even winning PRI acceptance of PAN governorships in several states. One reason was the PAN's more consolidated party organization, product of almost fifty years of party activity, which gave it the ability to bargain effectively and bind members to the results, and thus put it in a much better position to take advantage of the PRI's temporary weakness to strike a deal.

transition. There was no reliable communication structure, "no organized base, . . . [and] no form of discipline so that the leadership might make its position clear."[12] If it came to violence, the *cardenistas* would be completely outmatched by a PRI-state that controlled the institutional means of force. Thus, Cárdenas argued, "[the PRI] would like us to provoke a confrontation . . . in a disorganized and unprepared fashion, so they could respond with a bloodbath."[13] At the time, the *cardenistas* had as examples the transitions in Latin America and Spain, where pacting played a prominent role, not the later transitions in Eastern Europe, which stemmed largely from virtually uncoordinated mobilization against apparently overwhelming odds. However, their tactics also implied a recognition of the Mexican regime's determination to stay in power and its international support, in dramatic contrast to the situation of the Eastern European regimes. Their own prospects as well as the prospects for democracy looked better on the slow road than the fast one. Yet when the FDN tried to organize to play a more effective role in a gradual transition the differences between emergence and consolidation soon affected its ability to challenge the PRI and speak for a significant mass base.

A second key factor in the explanation of the PRI's ability to influence the pace and extent of liberalization is the institutional context. As mobilization declined, institutional tools available to the PRI as a state-party alliance allowed it to veto some outcomes (like the assumption of power by Cárdenas) and to shape relative actor resources over time. Two sets of institutional constraints seem particularly important, deriving from the centralization of power and resources in the national state and in the federal executive.

Centralization hampers democratic competition, especially in state-party regimes. First, it tends to undermine the consolidation of effective opposition parties by relegating them to mostly marginal offices. It is hard for an opposition party to build up a record of good government when the positions they win have little independent authority. Second, when combined with a state-party identity, centralization makes party competition extremely unequal. The PRI-state used the resources and authority of the state to exacerbate the normal difficulties of party consolidation for the PRD by dividing the PRD from sympathetic organizations in civil society, by preventing PRD representatives from delivering payoffs to constituents, by winning back voters through costly social

12. Arnoldo Martínez Verdugo, interview by author, Mexico City, 23 April 1991.
13. Cuauhtémoc Cárdenas Solórzano, *Nuestra lucha apenas comienza* (Mexico City: Editorial Nuestro Tiempo, 1988), 154.

programs, by controlling elections and certifying results, and by portraying the PRD as an isolated, ineffective, and dangerous party. The PRI-state also reproduced its electoral dominance by attracting resources from private donors as the most likely winner of elections and by mounting elaborate campaigns. Opposition parties could not match this strategy. They had to compete not with a party but with the state itself.

Presidentialism compounded this problem. The system had few mechanisms for translating dissent into influence when it challenged the authority of the president. On the one hand, this contributed to the stress that led to the formation of new opposition. On the other hand, it castrated the few institutional bodies open to opposition influence, like the Congress. In addition, centralization and presidentialism hurt democratization by raising the stakes of the presidential election to the point that even costly fraud seemed worth the risks. In a centralized presidential system there is no consolation prize, especially for a ruling party with sixty-odd years of skeletons to hide.[14] Losing the presidency meant losing control of the federal budget and appointment powers, which funded the network of patron-client ties that kept the PRI together as a party. The identity of state and party reinforced this problem because it led even some opposition leaders to fear that chaos—the loss of *state* control and order—would follow loss of *party* control of the presidency. Therefore, the PRI-state accepted the cost of fraud to ensure that the state did not fall into the hands of the opposition in 1988.

While new parties would still face difficult challenges in confronting consolidation under any conceivable reform, the lowering of some of these institutional barriers would improve the balance of power considerably. The experience of the PRD suggests that electoral reform, though certainly vital, does not exhaust the list of necessary targets for democratic reformers. Decentralization and the construction of checks on the power of the executive would deprive the PRI of some tools for undermining opposition parties and improve the chances of democratization. The problem is that the governing elite also recognizes this and therefore has only conceded such reforms after considerable pressure.

For this reason more effective opposition organization becomes vital. In the first place, opposition organization—through nonpartisan monitoring as well as parties—raises the costs of fraud and repression by

14. If an opposition party took over the presidency, it would probably have to count on cooperation from *priista* state officials in order to govern. Neither of the main opposition parties has enough activists (let alone trained activists familiar with administration) to manage a polity as complex as modern Mexico. However, even this favorable scenario would deprive the PRI of much of its power.

making it harder to decapitate the opposition and by giving civil society tools to punish either repression or fraud. Modern communication networks increase the difficulty of hiding fraud and lower the cost of constructing national and even international alliances, expanding the possibility of such alliances to many more nonstate actors: appeals through media and computer networks like the Internet played an important role in limiting the government's response to the Chiapas rebels, for example.[15] The need to bolster the confidence of investors in Mexican stability makes the regime vulnerable to opposition threats to protest and to publicize human rights violations or fraud. All these developments make fraud and repression more costly, encouraging the PRI to rely more on responsiveness to voters in order to remain in power. Opposition parties and independent organizations supply the energy for democratization, even democratization from above. In Mexico elites would have had little incentive to initiate a transition from above without the threat of transition from below. If the threat of a transition from below rises, the government may even feel compelled to begin some decentralization in order to retain for their faction some power in a posttransition setting.

In the second place, organized opposition presents the potential for a more orderly, more consensual, and at least partly negotiated transition. Should a scenario similar to 1988 recur, perhaps in the presidential election of 2000, it would be harder for the PRI to get away with fraud and easier for opposition parties to place conditions on the PRI that could transform the political system. The assumption of power by any opposition party, even the PAN, would require a fundamental renegotiation of the rules of the game in Mexico, including extensive changes in executive powers and a reorganization of alliances at the national and local level. The result could be *ruptura* by way of *reforma*, which by leading to a gradual shift in the balance of power in Mexico makes possible a profound renegotiation of the rules.

External opposition should also be taken into account. International lending agencies and the United States often expect at least an appear-

---

15. The Chiapas rebels posed little military threat. Fighting ended relatively soon after the January 1994 rebellion began. Nevertheless, on at least two occasions (January–February 1994 and February 1995) the government pulled back from attempts to eliminate the *zapatistas* militarily. Unprecedented national and international coverage of the *zapatistas* helps explain this uncharacteristically restrained reaction. *Zapatista* allegations of human rights abuses were matched by urban protest marches and international negative publicity. The threat that an armed response would spread domestic protest and frighten international investors added to political-electoral motives for not shooting a lot of peasants, especially in the presidential election year.

ance of democracy from aid recipients. While the United States seems willing to overlook substantial imperfections in Mexican democracy, its pressure has checked repressive policies and undemocratic practices.[16] More important, the demonstration effect of democratic transitions in virtually every Latin American country, Eastern Europe, and even the former Soviet Union have inspired the Mexican opposition and made it harder for the PRI-state to justify one-party rule. *Priistas* may believe in private that democracy jeopardizes economic and political stability, but in public, policy must conform to a democratic justification—a weakness already discovered and exploited by opposition leaders, who paint policies they dislike in antidemocratic terms. In addition, Mexican opposition, both parties and popular movements, have begun to construct alliances with counterparts in the United States, Canada, and Europe. These transnational networks transfer resources, expertise, information, and support for such issues as mutual resistance to NAFTA, international denunciation of human rights abuses and electoral fraud, and building up organizational infrastructure. To cite only one obvious example, civic election-monitoring groups like Alianza Cívica have received resources from the NED, the UN, and private organizations in the United States for their activity. They publicized their findings through these same networks, as well as on electronic bulletin boards. Without these resources it is highly doubtful that Alianza Cívica could have afforded to mount the substantial poll-watching effort in 1994, if it organized at all. This organization building has already had repercussions beyond its effect in raising the credibility of the 1994 results: Alianza Cívica provided critical logistic aid for the *"Consulta Nacional"* sponsored by the *zapatista* rebels in August 1995, which attracted about a million "voters" in overwhelming support of *zapatista* demands and probably contributed to the government's concession to admit the *zapatistas* to any national dialogue on political reform on an equal footing with the political parties.

Finally, internal regime divisions lower the effective concentration of

16. In 1991 in Guanajuato, for instance, Salinas seemed quite prepared to condone fraud by the PRI gubernatorial candidate until an article appeared in the *New York Times* urging him to "correct" the mistake made in Guanajuato. Within days he forced Aguirre to resign and appointed a PAN interim governor. Similarly, in early 1993 news leaked that Salinas had invited twenty to thirty Mexican millionaires to dinner and asked each to contribute a substantial sum to the PRI. An unrepentant Salinas defended his action to the Mexican press, but a critical article in the *New York Times* was followed by a change of heart and the announcement that no such contributions would be solicited in the future. Mexican opposition leaders openly speculated that the key to influencing the president lay in access to the *New York Times*.

power. Divisions provide space for the growth of opposition, and often its leadership as well. Evidence of continuing internal conflict abounds, in the assassination of the PRI's first 1994 presidential candidate, widely attributed to PRI enemies; the murder of PRI congressman Francisco Ruíz Massieu, for which the brother of former president Salinas was indicted; public calls for the trial of Salinas for crimes against Mexico; and unbridled criticism within the party of sitting president Ernesto Zedillo. Such indications of splits and even homicidal feuds within the PRI contribute both to public doubts that the PRI can ensure social peace and private sedition that lowers PRI defenses. The PRD's mysterious acquisition of PRI checking account records and invoices, allegedly documenting violation of legal limits on electoral spending in Tabasco, can only have come from sources within the PRI, opposed to the (PRI) Tabasco governor.

The third major key to the PRI's reassertion of control over liberalization reflects special problems faced by left parties in the post–Cold War international system. In general, economic policy often holds democratization hostage. Conflict over economic policy can contribute to democratization by unifying opposition to the regime and by causing internal divisions. The willingness of the governing coalition to liberalize politically may depend in part on ideological agreement with the opposition that seems most likely to benefit from democracy, particularly on economic policy. If its strongest competitor shares a basic policy consensus, threatening fewer goals of the dominant coalition, it should be easier for even "hard-liners" to accept liberalization. Because *new* opposition often springs from deep conflicts over policy, it may not meet this condition. In 1988, though conflict over economic policy created an opposition with the potential to push for democracy, the Mexican transition took a detour in part because polarization on the substantive demands of Cárdenas impeded negotiation over the broader rules of the game. The PRI and PAN, agreeing that a Cárdenas presidency meant economic disaster, embraced reforms that reinforced PRI dominance and channeled democratization toward parties that did not threaten economic policy. Ironically, democratization may benefit from the weakening of the ideologically incompatible opposition.

The dominance of neoliberal economic policies complicates matters for left opposition parties in particular as agents of democratization. The costs of neoliberal adjustment create potential supporters for left opposition and at the same time undermine their capacity to act. First, left parties may find consolidation of partisan loyalties especially difficult in the post–Cold War, pro-market context. The left has lost some traditional tools for establishing solid political alliances. Greater workforce mobility and the globalization of production have tended to weaken unions, handicapping socialist and labor parties around the world. For the Mexican left these trends raised barriers to the task of organizing unions independent of the PRI, just at the moment when PRI unions seemed most vulnerable. Alliance with civil society organizations has been complicated for a number of reasons, including their diversity, size, and organizational autonomy. Second, in an age of neoliberalism, debt, and austerity, states have trouble funding extensive welfare programs to compensate market losers or make clientelistic payoffs. The left cannot expect to protect losers from markets. At best, the price of buying support will fall, but if left parties cannot claim a stable share of shrinking resources, losers who might want to protest may be more vulnerable to conservative efforts to buy support. Finally, in the post–Cold War world, old ideological categories no longer provide coherent, compelling sources of identification separating "them" and "us." Ideological confusion on the left, and especially its lack of a plausible alternative to neoliberalism, limits its appeal to inconstant protest voters. Thus, left parties have some advantages in attracting voters who respond to the costs of neoliberal restructuring but face tough problems consolidating stable and loyal bases. This may make it difficult for them to participate effectively in negotiating a democratic transition; ideological opponents can always wait and hope that protest will die down and exempt them from any serious sacrifice of their position.

Indeed, the kind of enemies attracted by left parties' rejection of neoliberalism may matter almost as much as the support they might win. Unless left opposition accepts basic principles of the neoliberal model (which may blur its appeal to the losers), it comes under attack from the winners, both national and international. This marks a potentially critical difference in the international context for democratization between Eastern European transitions and transitions elsewhere in the Third World. While Eastern European reformers shared many economic proposals with powerful international allies in the Western world, those who confronted capitalist authoritarian governments were often seen as potential threats. This could buy time and support for authoritarian governments.

Overall, however, the effect of neoliberalism on the chances of democratization is probably indeterminate. Neoliberal policies guarantee neither a transition nor recovery of one-party dominance. Political outcomes depend in part on the effect of neoliberal policies on growth and patterns of distribution. If neoliberal policies result in growth with some distribution, for example, the political outcome may be stabilization of whatever political system the adopting country has, including authoritarian rule, though over time the spread of education and wealth should create the potential for more sustained competition. In 1991 trade opening helped Mexico bring in new investment, hold down inflation (by holding down consumer prices), and resume growth. Economic success helped the PRI repair internal divisions, soften opposition, and shape democratization.

If neoliberal policies result in no growth, but prolonged economic crisis, popular protest and elite divisions should increase, possibly creating the space for democratization but also for state repression. Economic liberalization builds in vulnerability to sudden changes in the international economy, outside the control of national planners. Rapid changes—like high inflation or a sudden devaluation—may have more destabilizing potential than gradual change, including the potential to bring down a regime. Just as the opposition's fate depends significantly on the mistakes, tolerance, and internal divisions of the PRI-state, the PRI's own fortunes may increasingly depend on circumstances beyond its or any national government's power to alter.

Finally, if neoliberal policies result in growth *without* distribution, one might expect a polarization of legitimacy—popular protest but little elite division—which favors increased repression. However, in each scenario the prognosis depends on the size and organization of political actors (especially parties) and their strategic choices. It matters which opposition benefits from protest votes, whether opposition movements can make binding agreements on behalf of supporters and allies, and whether opposition parties can unite with movements and each other on specific institutional reforms.

TAKING ON GOLIATH: A FINAL WORD

The biblical story of David and Goliath presents a dramatic picture of an unequal contest. David, a young shepherd boy, is chosen as the champion of the Jewish people in single combat against the powerful and experienced warrior Goliath of the Philistines, largely because no one else wants to take such a suicidal job. David is woefully unprepared. Inexperienced in war, and too small to wear the armor of a grown man or wield a sword, he goes armed only with a slingshot and some stones—ludicrous weapons against the heavily mailed Goliath. Nevertheless, David takes advantage of Goliath's initial underestimation of the threat to strike the first blow and kills Goliath instantly with a single stone.

Modern writers use this story as a metaphor for the power of the underdog.

One can also use this story to understand another unequal contest, between the powerful PRI-state and the opposition in Mexico. Such a retelling might cast Cárdenas in the role of David—confronting the champion of the Philistines as the defender of his people, and despite his unpreparedness taking a remarkably successful shot that reveals the giant's vulnerability. Yet here the story diverges from the biblical tale. Unlike David, Cárdenas did not fell his opponent with the first blow. One can only imagine what an enraged and bruised Goliath might have done to David if David had missed, but it seems likely that the real inequality between the two would eventually have determined the outcome in a long confrontation. Thus, the basic lesson of the PRD experience can be drawn in these fanciful terms: when David challenges Goliath, he had better aim well with the first stone or Goliath may end up dictating the terms of surrender.

Appendixes

APPENDIX A
A PRD FAMILY TREE

Acronym Guide

ACHR **Asociación Civil-Hombres de la Revolución—founded 1948**
After the PRI dissolved its military sector, disgruntled veterans of the Revolution formed the ACHR, which evolved into the PARM in 1954.

ACNR **Asociación Cívica Nacional Revolucionaria**
Supportive of the guerrilla movement of the early 1970s, this group later ended up in the PMS and then the PRD.

ASU **Acción Socialista Unificada—founded 1940**
Valentin Campa and Hernan Laborde formed this small group when expelled from the PCM in 1940. It returned to the PCM after participating in the POCM.

CD **Corriente Democrática—founded 1986**
Led by prominent *priistas*, including Porfirio Muñoz Ledo (ex-president of the PRI and ex-ambassador to the UN), Cuauhtémoc Cárdenas (governor of Michoacán), Ifigenia Martínez (economist and ex-congresswoman), and Rodolfo González Guevara (then Mexico's ambassador to Spain), the CD wanted to reform the PRI. Its main demands—democratization of candidate selection and changes in economic policy—were rejected at the 13th National Assembly of the PRI in March 1987. The CD's isolation in the PRI led to the decision of Cárdenas and some Corriente activists to resign from the PRI and support Cárdenas for president.

CNAO **Comité Nacional de Auscultación y Organización—founded 1971**
Originally called the Comité Nacional de Auscultación y Coordinación, this group proved a fertile source of new party organization in the seventies. Its leadership derived from the MLN and the Student Movement of 1968.

FEP **Frente Electoral del Pueblo—founded 1964**
MLN activists formed the People's Electoral Front to contest the

1964 presidential election. The FEP nominated Ramón Danzós Palomino, a peasant organizer of the MLN's recently founded Central Campesina Independiente (Independent Peasant Union), for president. It failed to win legal registry to participate in the election, and so it conducted a largely symbolic campaign, nominating many political prisoners as candidates. Conflict over whether or not the MLN should offer the FEP electoral support created rifts in the MLN, whose disintegration began about this time.

Movimiento Estudiantil—1968

Student protests over police incursions into Mexico City preparatory schools and the National University were crushed in the Plaza of Three Cultures in Mexico City on October 2, 1968, when police snipers opened fire on demonstrating students, killing hundreds. Student leaders and teachers were jailed. The massacre inspired a decade of organization, from social movements and democratic currents in official unions to parties and guerrilla insurgency.

MAP   Movimiento de Acción Popular—founded 1980

This movement enjoyed only a few months of official existence before joining the PSUM, but many of its members had formed an unofficial cohesive group for years. It stressed the benefits of dialogue with the PRI-state. Many ex-members of this group (including José Woldenberg, Pablo Pascual Montoya, Rolando Cordera, Adolfo Sánchez Rebolledo, and Arnaldo Córdova) later defected from the PRD.

MAS   Movimiento al Socialismo—founded 1987

MAS started as a group within the PRT that disagreed with the PRT policy of rejecting alliance with Cárdenas. MAS broke with the PRT and joined the Cárdenas campaign.

MAUS   Movimiento de Acción y Unidad Socialista—founded 1972

Miguel Arroche Parra and Carlos Sánchez Cárdenas, expelled from the Communist Party in 1948, passed through the MRPC, POCM, and CNAO on their way to form this small movement. MAUS joined the PCM and other CNAO veterans in PSUM.

MLN   Movimiento de Liberación Nacional—founded 1961

This movement was a public pressure group founded by Lázaro Cárdenas to support the Cuban revolution. Much of the *cardenista* wing of the PRI participated, including Cuauhtémoc Cárdenas, who served on its board of directors with popular movement leaders, PCM members, leftist intellectuals, and the PPS (from 1961 to 1963). The MLN disbanded when its leaders were jailed for participation in the 1968 student movement.

MRP   Movimiento Revolucionario Popular—founded 1981

At first against electoral participation, this maoist group joined the PMS in 1987.

MRPC   Movimiento de Reivindicación del Partido Comunista—founded 1948

Miguel Arroche Parra and Carlos Sánchez Cárdenas (leaders in MAUS, CNAO, and PSUM) formed MRPC after their expulsion from the PCM.

MRT   Movimiento Revolucionario de los Trabajadores—founded 1979

After breaking with the PMT, the founders of the MRT quickly joined MAP, and equally quickly dissolved the MAP in favor of the PSUM.

Punto Crítico—founded 1971

Punto Crítico grew out of a journal of the same name run by intellectuals at the National University UNAM. Collaborators helped organize the UNAM union, STUNAM. Punto Crítico included, among others, Rolando Cordera, José Woldenberg, and Pablo Pascual Montoya. See MAP.

PAN   Partido Acción Nacional—founded 1939

The only major independent opposition party before 1979, the National Action Party was formed by conservative businessmen unhappy with the leftward drift of the Revolution during the presidency of Lázaro Cárdenas (1934–40). The PAN traditionally favored pro-Catholic, prodemocracy, and probusiness policies. It is strongest in the north and in Mexico City.

PARM   Partido Auténtico de la Revolución Mexicana—founded 1954

Outgrowth of the ACHR, the PARM was traditionally one of the parastatal parties, which though nominally "opposition" parties, consistently supported PRI policies and candidates for president. The PARM is a moderate, anticommunist party with no strong ideology.

PCM   Partido Comunista Mexicano—founded 1919

The only communist party in Latin America to condemn the 1968 invasion of Czechoslovakia, the Mexican Communist Party maintained an unusually independent line from the PRI and the Soviet Union. It advocated cooperation and alliance within the left for thirty years, and instigated negotiations leading to its voluntary dissolution in 1981 to form the PSUM.

PFCRN   Partido Frente Cardenista de Reconstrucción Nacional—founded 1987

Formerly the PST, the PFCRN officially changed its name upon nominating Cárdenas as its presidential candidate in 1987. Afterward the PFCRN left the FDN and returned to cooperation with the PRI. See also PST.

PMS   Partido Mexicano Socialista—founded 1987

The PMS resulted from an attempt to finish the unification project left incomplete in 1981 when the PMT and PRT withdrew from the PSUM. Its largest components were the PSUM and PMT. The party lasted barely a year before voluntarily dissolving in order to give legal registry to the PRD.

PMT   Partido Mexicano de los Trabajadores—founded 1974

With the PST, the PMT was one of two parties formed from the CNAO that gained legal registry. Led by Heberto Castillo and railroad organizer Demetrio Vallejo, former political prisoners, the PMT remained skeptical about elections and did not participate with registry until 1985.

POCM   **Partido Obrero-Campesino Mexicano—founded 1950**
Formed by ex-communists in 1950, the POCM enjoyed a short institutional life before disintegrating after the repression of the 1959 railroad workers' strike. One group (the ASU) returned to the PCM; members of another (led by railroad union head Demetrio Vallejo) were jailed; the largest group (originally the MRPC) joined the PPS but was expelled from the PPS in 1969 after the death of Vicente Lombardo Toledano.

PPM   **Partido del Pueblo Mexicano—founded 1977**
A popular Nayarit politician, PPM founder Alejandro Gascón Mercado ran in 1976 as the PPS candidate for governor of Nayarit. Convinced he had won, he pressed the PRI-state to accept his victory. Instead, PRI president Porfirio Muñoz Ledo made a deal with the president of the PPS, Jorge Cruikshank García. The PPS publicly accepted defeat in Nayarit; in return the PRI allowed Cruikshank to run unopposed for senator in another state. Gascón Mercado, outraged at this betrayal, left the PPS to form the PPM.

PPR   **Partido Patriótico Revolucionario**
The PPR maintained a small local presence in certain *municipios* of the Estado de México and the Distrito Federal, and joined the PMS in 1987.

PPS   **Partido Popular Socialista—founded 1948 (as Partido Popular)**
Vicente Lombardo Toledano, a collaborator of President Lázaro Cárdenas in the formation of the CTM, created the Partido Popular after he lost his position at the head of the CTM to Fidel Velázquez. The Partido Popular changed its name to Partido Popular Socialista in 1962 and declared itself marxist-leninist, an identity it maintained through 1994. As part of its "anti-imperialist strategy" it supported the PRI "against international capital" until 1988, when it nominated Cárdenas for president.

PRD   **Partido de la Revolución Democrática—founded 1989**
The PRD defined itself as the party "born on the sixth of July," date of the 1988 presidential election, though it contains only one of four registered parties that supported Cárdenas. This party, the PMS, gave its registry to the PRD to avoid expected government refusal to register a Cárdenas party. The PRD's basic program includes economic nationalism, democracy, and social equity.

PRI   **Partido Revolucionario Institucional—founded 1929**
President Plutarco Calles organized the PRI to contain conflicts among the ruling elite and to exercise power. Founded as the National Revolutionary Party, it became the Mexican Revolutionary

Party under President Lázaro Cárdenas (when it acquired its corporatist sectoral structure) and adopted its current name under President Alemán when it eliminated the military sector, leaving peasant, worker, and popular sectors.

PRT   **Partido Revolucionario de los Trabajadores—founded 1976**
Though officially constituted in 1976, the PRT has much older roots within the trotskyite Fourth International. Its major distinctions were its insistence on a new revolution in Mexico, its respected leader (human rights activist Rosario Ibarra), and its refusal to support Cárdenas in 1988. Its growing isolation on the left contributed to its loss of registry.

PSD   **Partido Social Democrata—founded 1980**
Ex-*priistas* formed the Social Democratic Party, which lost its registry in its first election. Founder Manuel Moreno Sánchez was the *priista* president of the Senate under President Lopez Mateos. The PSD supported Cárdenas in 1988, and many PSD members belong to the PRD.

PSR   **Partido Socialista Revolucionaria—founded 1974**
The Movement of Socialist Organization (MOS) changed its name to PSR.

PST   **Partido Socialista de los Trabajadores—founded 1973**
Believing the CNAO was moving too slowly to organize a party, Rafael Aguilar Talamantes and a handful of others formed the PST. Once registered, the PST cooperated with the PRI as a parastatal party. The PST changed its name to the Cardenista Front of National Reconstruction (PFCRN) in 1987, and adopted Cárdenas as its candidate.

PSUM   **Partido Socialista Unificado Mexicano—founded 1981**
The PSUM, incorporating five major and several minor organizations of the independent left, was the first significant attempt to unify the left in one electoral party. The PCM and its general secretary Arnoldo Martínez Verdugo led the drive for unification and dominated the new party.

SUTIN   **Sindicato Unico de Trabajadores de la Industria Nuclear**
SUTIN was one of the unions in the early 1970s that attempted to democratize and break away from the corporatist control of the PRI.

TD   **Tendencia Democrática**
The Tendencia Democrática was a movement to democratize the electrical workers' union (SUTERM) and make it more independent of the government. The state succeeded in eliminating the movement in 1976.

UIC   **Unidad de Izquierda Comunista—founded 1976**
Split from the PCM over the question of participation in electoral alliances, UIC eventually joined in the formation of the PMS.

A PRD Family Tree

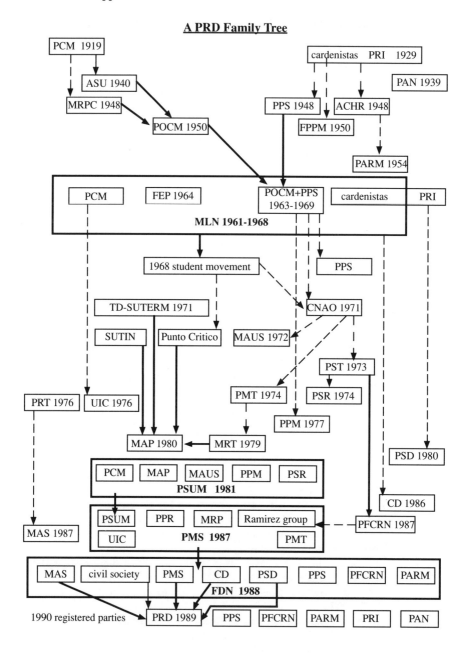

Interpretive notes to "Family Tree" chart

1. Double lines indicate a fusion; single lines with an arrow indicate a split from a party.
2. Foundation dates relate to the appearance of the group as a recognizable entity with goals, not necessarily its first appearance under its current name or the date of legal recognition.
3. Parties may appear more than once on the chart.
4. The left-right placement of parties on the chart is not intended to give a precise evaluation of the ideological stance of these parties.
5. This is not an exhaustive listing of opposition movements by any means, or even of all movements who supported Cárdenas and the PRD. I have only tried to give an indication of the main institutional antecedents of the PRD (concentrating on parties and explicitly political groups) and its principal opponents.

APPENDIX B
CHRONOLOGY OF THE PRD, 1985–1989

The Corriente Democrática Period

1985

July 7	Mid-term congressional elections; especially dirty in the north against the PAN.
Aug. 30	Governor Cárdenas speaks of need to "recover the path" of the Revolution.
Oct. 19	Muñoz Ledo leaves post as ambassador to UN, returns to Mexico.
Oct.–Nov.	Muñoz Ledo discusses plans for democratization of PRI with González Guevara in Spain; González Guevara proposes internal current.

1986

Mar. 4	Meeting of PRI leaders in Queretaro to celebrate anniversary of PRI.
May	González Guevara talks about internal current with Cárdenas, who approves.
May	Muñoz Ledo returns to Madrid.
May 21	Future Corriente members join March for National Sovereignty in Mexico City.

May 22–23	Muñoz Ledo and Cárdenas attend PRI National Council in Mexico City.
	Muñoz Ledo and Cárdenas make plans to talk privately.
May 28	Cárdenas calls for precandidates to presidency to announce themselves.
May 29	Muñoz Ledo asks for open debate among potential PRI candidates.
days later	Muñoz Ledo and Cárdenas meet for dinner at La Cava in Mexico City.
days later	As agreed with Cárdenas, Muñoz Ledo asks Ifigenia Martínez to host a dinner for those interested in forming a new current.
June 17	Jesús Silva Herzog, treasury minister, resigns after arguing for aggressive renegotiation of debt, debt forgiveness, but losing to Salinas faction.
late June/early July	Fifteen to twenty *priistas* meet at home of Ifigenia Martínez to discuss current; González Guevara suggests Cárdenas run as "precandidate of sacrifice."
July 9	Cárdenas publicly says PRI needs to recover revolutionary principles.
July 10	Cárdenas says precandidates should begin precampaign to strengthen party.
July 11	Muñoz Ledo leaves the country.
July	Group of *priistas* meets in home of Gonzalo Martínez Corbalá to discuss the elaboration of a policy proposal to be issued April/May of 1987.
Aug. 14	*Unomásuno* reports existence of "Corriente Democratizadora" (CD) in the PRI; names Muñoz Ledo, Cárdenas, González Guevara as members.
Aug. 16	*Unomásuno* publishes positive opinions on CD from some PRI officials.
Aug. 18	Muñoz Ledo and Ifigenia Martínez confirm existence of Corriente.
Aug. 19	Martínez Corbalá denies González Guevara's involvement (at latter's request).
Aug. 22	Muñoz Ledo meets with PRI president Adolfo Lugo Verduzco for two hours.
	In press conference Muñoz Ledo defends statutory basis of CD.
	In speech to Politécnico Cárdenas criticizes use of oil money to pay debt.
	Later Cárdenas launches the CD-Michoacán, with presence of campesinos.
Aug. 24	CNC calls the CD a serious and valid attempt to address problems in the PRI.

Aug. 30	Fidel Velázquez says the group endangers the unity of the PRI.
Sept.	Meetings between members of the CD and Lugo Verduzco.
Sept. 5	Cristóbal Arias removed as president of State Committee of PRI-Michoacán.
Sept. 15	Cárdenas ends term as governor of Michoacán; *Little Cárdenas* published.
Sept. 20	Miguel De la Madrid declares in *Le Monde* that the CD is nothing new.
late Sept.	Meeting between Lugo Verduzco and CD; decision to publish Document #1.
Oct. 1	CD presents Working Document Number One in Morelia. Electoral reform initiative to enlarge Congress discussed by executive.
Oct. 8	Lugo Verduzco resigns as president of PRI to run for governor of Hidalgo. Jorge De la Vega Domínguez announced as new PRI president.
Oct. 9	Twelve hundred ninety *priistas* in Michoacán sign petition of support for CD.
Oct. 21	Muñoz Ledo speech at PRI Center of Political Studies (IEPES).
Oct. 24	Martínez Corbalá says he left CD because he disagreed with publishing Document #1.
Nov. 1	PMT and PSUM announce fusion into PMS will take place February 1987.
Nov. 4	Denunciation of CD by Irma Cue, secretary-general of PRI, in Morelia. De la Madrid sends 1986 Electoral Reform to Congress.
Nov. 5	Cárdenas, Muñoz Ledo, Ifigenia Martínez, Jorge De la Vega in high-level talks. IEPES criticizes the CD.
Nov. 7	Graco Ramírez removed as head of PST *diputados*. Jorge De la Vega meets with all PRI congressmen to discuss action on CD.
Nov. 9	Muñoz Ledo, Carlos Tello, Cárdenas will travel outside Mexico in November.
Nov. 10	First (known) time Fidel Velázquez consigns CD to "history."
Nov. 28	Pablo Gomez predicts split in PRI.
Dec. 19	1986 Electoral Reform approved.

1987

Jan.	Members of CD on tours throughout Mexico.

Jan. 5	PST publicly proposes name change to Cardenista Party of Mexican Workers.
Jan. 6	Irma Cué resigns as secretary-general of PRI.
Jan. 8	Extraordinary Council makes changes in PRI's National Executive Committee.
	Talks break down between CEU (student union at UNAM) and UNAM rector.
Jan. 12	CEU sets strike date for January 29.
Jan. 24	PSUM votes to join the PMS.
Jan. 29	Students go on strike at the National University.
Feb.	CD continues tours throughout Mexico.
Feb. 1	Leadership of PPS decides not to support any PRI candidate for president.
Feb. 17	UNAM strike officially ends.
Mar. 2	Inauguration of the 13th National Assembly of the PRI.
Mar. 3	Working Group on Democratization votes to reject presentation of Cárdenas.
Mar. 4	Jorge De la Vega attacks CD during closing ceremonies of the 13th Assembly.
Mar. 9	Cárdenas letter published, denounces authoritarian attitude of PRI leadership.
Mar. 10	PRI National Executive Committee "expels" Cárdenas from the PRI.
Mar. 12	Muñoz Ledo sends open letter in support of Cárdenas's position.
	PSUM, PMT, PRT, PPR, UIC, MRP form Front for Estado de Mexico election.
Mar. 13	Jorge De la Vega says CD is "finished."
	Two leaders of PRI Youth reject conclusions of 13th Assembly, announce march to demand democracy in PRI.
Mar. 18	Cárdenas hints that the CD might present a precandidate for presidency.
	PRT announces it will not join the fusion of the left in the PMS.
Mar. 25	De la Vega leaves on a tour to improve "party communication."
Mar. 28	PMT finally approves fusion with PMS.
Mar. 29	Left parties sign agreement to form PMS.
Apr. 6	De la Vega says "destape" will take place after September to shorten campaign.
Apr. 10	PST expels Graco Ramírez; he refuses to recognize the action.
Apr. 14	CROC, COR leaders walk out on Michoacán assembly, allege marginalization.
Apr. 23	PARM announces it will not support any PRI presidential candidate.

Apr. 25	Dinner at "Los Barandales"; Cárdenas declines proposed precandidacy.
Apr. 26	Manuel Stephens of PMS says PMS might support a Cárdenas candidacy.
May 5	PMS registers precandidates for presidency; PPS suggests unified candidacy.
May 6	Cárdenas and Janitzio Múgica present Document #2 in Chihuahua.
May 14	Cárdenas does not deny he could be candidate of the left.
May 16	Janitzio Múgica says Carlos Tello out of the CD; Tello thinks CD went too far.
May 20	Cárdenas says he would like to be president.
May 24	Graco Ramírez group expels Aguilar Talamantes.
May 25	Graco Ramírez group elects Jesús Ortega president of PST.
May 29	Cárdenas "destapado" by Muñoz Ledo as precandidate of PRI.
May 30	Cárdenas denies he is precandidate of CD.
June 9	Heberto Castillo registered as precandidate of PMS.
June 21	Labra, Fuentes Díaz, Tello do not sign letter protesting "satanization" of CD.
June 24	Castillo proposes Cárdenas as PMS candidate; Cárdenas claims PRI loyalties.
June 25	González Guevara back from Spain.
July 3	Three thousand militants "nominate" Cárdenas as precandidate at his Mexico City home.
July 9	Graco Ramírez group joins PMS after nine months of dissidence in the PST.
July 30	Dissident young *priistas* occupy PRI building, demand democracy.
Aug. 12	More than 1,750 "CD sympathizers" demand convocation of preregistry in advertisement.
Aug. 13	Working Document #3 presented.
Aug. 14	PRI announces names of six precandidates to appear before PRI councils.
Sept.	CD members talk privately about leaving the PRI.
Sept. 3	Manuel Clouthier registers as PAN candidate for the presidency.
Sept. 6	PMS holds primary elections to choose its presidential candidate.
Sept. 10	CD presents proposal for inclusion in campaign platform of the PRI.
Sept. 14	Young *priistas* deny CD affiliation, do not support Cárdenas for president.
Sept. 30	PRI sets Extraordinary Congress to nominate presidential candidate for October 3.

Oct. 3	Extraordinary Congress meets.
Oct. 4	De la Vega announces Salinas as PRI candidate.
Oct. 11	PARM offers Cárdenas their candidacy; he accepts.
Oct. 12	PARM leadership announces Cárdenas is the PARM candidate.

The Coalition Assembles

Oct. 14	PARM Assembly makes Cárdenas its official candidate; he joins PARM.
Oct. 16	PRI says Cárdenas automatically no longer PRI member by this act.
Oct. 24	Janitzio Múgica, founding member of the CD, declares support for Salinas.
Oct. 27	Cárdenas accepts in principle new primary elections with PMS if enacted soon.
Oct. 29	PMS accepts primaries *if* all left parties participate; PARM rejects primaries.
Nov. 6	PARM, PST, PSD accept primaries, but PMS says PPS, PRT, too, or no dice.
Nov. 11	Popular Defense Committee of Durango backs Cárdenas.
Nov. 19	Government devalues peso, forced by October Wall Street stock market crash.
Nov. 22	Asamblea de Barrios (union of popular movements) nominates "Superbarrio."
	PST becomes Cardenista Front for National Reconstruction, nominates Cárdenas.
Dec. 6	PSD nominates Cárdenas.
Dec. 9	Partido Verde (an ecology party) nominates Cárdenas.
Dec. 12	Unidad Democrática nominates Cárdenas.
Dec. 14	PPS Assembly formally nominates Cárdenas.
Dec. 16	Muñoz Ledo officially resigns from PRI.

The FDN Period

1988

Jan. 12	FDN (National Democratic Front) constituted, signs electoral platform.
Feb. 4	Ricardo Valero, CD sympathizer (not member), named ambassador to USSR.
Feb. 6	OIR-LM separates from PRT to join PMS.
Feb. 11	Cárdenas visits La Laguna; trip lasts 5 days, evokes massive public response.

Feb. 22	Five presidential candidates debate in the press—Salinas abstains.
Feb. 25	Pedro Peñaloza, Ricardo Pascoe, Adolfo Gilly "outside PMS" for supporting Cárdenas campaign.
Mar. 16	Muñoz Ledo and Ifigenia Martínez announced as candidates for Senate.
Mar. 18	Cárdenas leads rally for fiftieth anniversary of oil expropriation; 70,000 attend.
	Official rally to honor expropriation falls flat.
	MAS offers support to Cárdenas.
Mar. 30	Miguel De la Madrid removes Ricardo Valero as ambassador to USSR.
May 2	Carpizo (rector of UNAM) speaks against "political proselytism" in UNAM.
May 3	MAS publicly asks Cárdenas to come to UNAM.
May 11	CEU and STUNAM formally invite Cárdenas to speak at UNAM.
May 21	Largest rally yet in Apatzingan, Michoacán, on Lázaro Cárdenas's birthday.
May 22	Even larger Cárdenas rally in Uruapan, Michoacán.
May 26	Cárdenas speaks at UNAM to large and attentive crowd.
May 28	Graco Ramírez and Cárdenas meet to discuss defense of vote.
	Heberto Castillo says he could withdraw candidacy at June PMS meeting.
June 3	Castillo offers to withdraw if Cárdenas accepts twelve-point platform; he does.
	PMS candidate for Senate, Gilberto Rincón Gallardo, resigns in favor of CD.
June 4	Police beat up Cárdenas supporters at a rally in Oaxaca (Cárdenas absent).
June 5	PMS and CD approve common program.
June 7	Cárdenas and Castillo sign agreement on common program.
	Rosario Ibarra of the PRT refuses to withdraw for Cárdenas.
June 14	ACNR withdraws support from Rosario Ibarra, supports Cárdenas.
June 21	Cárdenas proposes creation of new political party after July 6.
June 25	Cárdenas fills the Zócalo in his close of campaign rally.
July 2	Murders of Román Gil and Francisco Xavier Ovando, top Cárdenas aides.
July 6	Presidential election.
	Jorge De la Vega announces PRI victory.
	PAN, FDN, PRT present "Call to Legality."

July 10	Cárdenas claims victory in the presidential election.
July 11	CFE (Federal Electoral Commission) releases results of ninety-five electoral districts, claims Salinas lost only in Mexico City and Michoacán.
July 12	CFE says Salinas official winner; FDN issues "Declaration for Sovereignty."
July 13	CFE gives official vote: 17.07 percent PAN, 50.36 percent PRI, 31.12 percent FDN.
July 16	March in Defense of the Vote in Zócalo.
July–Aug.	CFE issues certificates of victory for majority districts.
Aug. 3	Top PRI leader in Tabasco (Manuel López Obrador) resigns from PRI.
Aug. 4	Head of CNC in Tabasco resigns.
early Aug.	PAN, PRT, FDN issue Declaration for Democracy, call for annulling election.
Aug. 14	CFE resolves all but thirteen pending cases of congressmen-elect.
Aug. 15	Electoral College of the Chamber of Deputies installed from resolved cases.
Aug. 28	All FDN parties except PMS approve cases of eighty-three disputed *diputados* in Electoral College to install Congress by September 1 deadline.
Sept. 4	Fidel Velázquez demands greater democratization of the PRI (!)
	PRI announces shakeup in leaderships of party in Tabasco and Michoacán.
	Three FDN congressmen join PRI; one PRI congressman joins FDN.
Sept. 6	Cárdenas says FDN won't mobilize unless presidential election ratified.
Sept. 10	Salinas declared president-elect by Congress; decree signed only by *priistas*.
Sept. 14	Cárdenas calls for continued unity of FDN forces in permanent organization.
Sept. 17	PMS officially offers its registry to new party.
Sept. 19	PARM says it is unlikely to join new party.
Sept. 23	*La Jornada* quotes other FDN parties rejecting participation in the new party.
Sept. 26	Samuel Del Villar starts series of articles criticizing election; later quits PRI.
Oct. 3	*Priistas* take out ad in national press supporting internal reform in the PRI.
Oct. 18	González Guevara resigns PRI Modernization Commission to form new Corriente Crítica.
Oct. 21	Cárdenas issues "Call to the Mexican People" to form PRD.

| Oct. 24 | PRI replaces State Committee of the Estado de México. |

1989

Jan./Feb.	PMS and CD discuss proposed statutes and program of new party.
Mar. 18	PFCRN/PPS oil expropriation rally invites PRI speaker—death knell of FDN.
May 14	Party of the Democratic Revolution takes PMS registry; formally registered.

APPENDIX C
STATISTICAL NOTES AND SOURCES

General Comments on Methodology

Statistical analyses of voting results arrived only quite recently in scholarship on Mexico for three main reasons. First, since one party won every election, many scholars questioned the usefulness of the effort to construct "models" of the vote. Second, most analysts believed that pervasive fraud marked Mexican elections, inflating vote results even when the outcome would have been the same with or without manipulation. Therefore, the dependent variable—official election results—did not measure voter preferences. Third, the limitations of demographic data made the validity of independent variables questionable. Often demographic data were ten years out of date, covered a population that is difficult to count (informal, not documented, and/or rural), and did not exist at a level of aggregation that permitted large statistical comparisons or that reflected intrastate differences.

Nevertheless, statistical techniques are becoming increasingly significant in analyses of party support in Mexico, partly because data have become more reliable and timely, partly because competition has dramatically increased. Not only does the opposition win occasionally, but the margin of victory of the PRI varies considerably, making it possible to discern associations between high/low margins of victory and demographic variables. At a minimum, even if they do not give an exact reflection of voter preferences, voting results say something about party strength and the opposition's ability to prevent fraud. Opposition vote may therefore be more accurate than the PRI vote. Second, data problems principally apply to the interpretation of null hypotheses—no statistical relationship between variables. If a statistical relationship is found despite data problems it should be taken seriously. Some analyses find significant relationships even using the tainted 1988 voting results. Finally, to explain government decisions like PRONASOL funding, one should use the information available to the government. Whatever the level of fraud in 1988, it seems likely that Salinas himself does not really know what the results would have been since most fraud occurred at a local level.

Some precautions were taken to make statistical modeling as useful as could be expected. First, where possible several estimates of the same variable were used in alternative models to make sure that results did not simply reflect the imperfections of one estimate. Since the 1988 election results were contested, I constructed separate models using the official vote and unofficial (PRD) estimates (Maldonado, 1989). In every case, models constructed on the basis of the unofficial vote performed slightly worse than models constructed on the basis of the official vote, but showed the same general tendencies. The fact that PRD estimates had a lot of missing information (and hence fewer cases) may account for their poor performance. For the 1991 race, since the PRD offered no estimates of its own, I used only official results. Finally, models of voting strength and swing vote reflect variables found important in other analyses of Mexican voting (particularly Klesner, 1993 and 1994). However, I do not include both agricultural EAP and rural population because high intercorrelation (.88) poses a multicollearity problem. When rural population was included, the significance of agricultural population decreased slightly, the R-squared of the model increased, and rural population was not significant.

Data were derived from or cross-checked in the following sources:

Alcocer, Jorge, and Rodrigo Morales. "Mitología y realidad del fraude electoral." *Nexos* 14, no. 166 (October 1991): 27–40.

Gómez Tagle, Silvia. *Las estadísticas electorales de la reforma política.* Mexico City: El Colegio de México, 1990.

González Graf, Jaime, ed. *Las elecciones de 1988 y la crisis del sistema político.* Mexico City: Editorial Diana, 1989.

Guevara N., Alfonso, and Gregorio Santibañez. "Los grupos étnicos autóctonos como motivo de marginación." In *Marginalidad urbana y pobreza rural,* edited by Fernando Serrano Migallón. Mexico City: Editorial Diana, 1990.

Maldonado B., Samuel. *Origines del Partido de la Revolución Democrática.* Morelia, Michoacán: published by author, 1989.

Mexico. *Elecciones federales 1994: Resultados definitivos según los cómputos distritales.* Mexico City: IFE, 1994.

———. Instituto Federal Electoral. *Relación de los 300 distritos federales electorales.* Mexico City: IFE, 1991.

Mexico. Instituto Nacional de Estadística, Geografía, e Informática. *XI censo general de población y vivienda, 1990.* Mexico City: INEGI, 1992.

———. *XI censo general de población y vivienda, 1990: Perfíl sociodemográfico.* Mexico City: INEGI, 1992.

———. *Michoacán: Resultados definitivos, tabulados básicos del XI censo general.* Vols. 1 and 2. Mexico City: INEGI, 1992.

Mexico. Presidencia de la República. *Geografía de la marginación.* Mexico City: COPLAMAR/Siglo Veintiuno, 1982.

Mexico. Secretaría de Gobernación. *Tercer informe de gobierno: Anexo.* Mexico City: Presidencia de la República, November 1991.

Partido de la Revolución Democrática. *Tablas comparativas de los resultados electorales*. Mexico City: PRD, Secretaría de Defensa del Voto, 1992.
Puig Escudero, Antonio, and Jesús Hernández Rivas. "Un modelo de desagregación geográfica: Estimación del PIB por entidad federativa, 1970–1988." Serie de Documentos de Investigación, no. 1. Mexico, D.F.: INEGI, 1989.
Silvestre Méndez, José, and Santiago Zorrilla. *Mexico por entidades federativas*. Mexico City: Ediciones Oceano, 1986.

Basic Variables

Abstention, 1988	percentage of registered population that abstained in 1988
Abstention, 1991	percentage of registered population that abstained in 1991
Agricultural population	percentage of EAP in agriculture
Decrease in GDP	percentage decrease in GDP per state, 1980–88
Illiteracy	percentage of adults (over 15) that are illiterate
GDP/capita	GDP per capita
Left losses	percentage decrease in number of votes, 1988–91
Marginalization	COPLAMAR marginalization index
No primary school	percentage with incomplete primary education
Participation increase	percentage increase in participation rate, 1988–91
Population (municipal models only)	natural log of municipal population (a necessary adjustment to avoid kurtosis and skewness problems)
PRD government	dummy variable, = 1 if governed by PRD 1989–91; = 0 if not
PAN, 1988	PAN congressional vote, 1988, in percentage
PAN, 1991	PAN congressional vote, 1991, in percentage
PRI, 1988	PRI congressional vote, 1988, in percentage
PRI, 1991	PRI congressional vote, 1991, in percentage
PRI, 1994	PRI congressional vote, 1994, in percentage
PRD, 1994	PRD congressional vote, 1994, in percentage
PRI gains	percentage increase in number of votes, 1988–91
PRONASOL per capita	PRONASOL per capita budget per state, 1989–90 total
Regression to the mean	difference between 1988 state vote and national vote
Reorientation	percentage increase, from Ramo XXVI (1984–87) to PRONASOL budget (1989–90), per state
Rural population	percentage of population in communities of 2,500 or less
Left vote, 1988	FDN vote, 1988 (presidential)
Left vote, 1991	PRD congressional vote, 1991, in percentage

ADDITIONAL STATISTICAL TABLES

Voting Correlation Matrix—Selected Variables

	FDN 1988	PRD 1991	PRD 1994
agricultural population	−.16	.26	.53***
no primary school	−.02	.33*	.56***
GDP/capita	.01	−.07	−.06
reorient	.34*	.34*	.34*
PRONASOL/capita	−.14	−.19	−.17
PRI vote	−.78***	−.17	−.30*
PAN vote	−.38**	−.57***	−.84***

Significance levels: * = <.10 ** = <.05 *** = <.01
Each cell reports Pearson's R.
N = 32, except reorient and PRONASOL/capita, where N = 31.

PRONASOL Funding Correlations

	PRONASOL/Capita	Reorientation
PRI vote 1988	.27	−.18
Left vote 1988	−.14	.34*
PAN vote 1988	−.07	−.22
PRI vote 1991	.33*	−.16
PRD vote 1991	−.19	.34*
Marginalization index	−.02	.21
GDP/capita	−.05	−.35*
Change in GDP/capita	.22	.04

Significance levels: * = <.10 ** = <.05 *** = <.01
Each cell reports Pearson's R.
N = 31

Muncipal Voting Correlations—Michoacán

	PRD 1991	PRD 1989–91	PRI 1991	PRI 1989–91
Agricultural population	.28***	−.13	−.11	−.27***
Illiteracy	.26***	−.01	−.14	−.32***
Municipal population	−.24***	.28***	.04	.48***

Significance levels: * = <.10 ** = <.05 *** = <.01
Each cell reports Pearson's R.
N = 109

Vote Swing, 1988–1991: Selected Correlations

	PRI Gain	Left Loss
Reorientation	.25	−.20
PRONASOL/capita	−.31*	.18
Agricultural population	−.23	−.50***
No primary school	−.03	−.36**
GDP/capita	−.07	−.14
Change in participation	.60***	−.11
Abstention 1991	−.51***	−.21
Left loss	−.001	1.00
PRI gain	1.00	—
1991 PRD vote	—	—

Significance levels: * = <.10   ** = <.05   *** = <.01
Each cell reports Pearson's R.
$N = 31$

PRONASOL Spending

	PRONASOL Per Capita	Reorientation of Priorities
PRI vote 1988	.47**	−.26
Marginalization index	−.26	.20
GDP/capita	−.16	−.23
Change in GDP/capita	.23	−.05
R-squared	.19	.17
Adjusted R-squared	.07	.04
Left vote 1988	−.15	.31*
Marginalization index	.04	.10
GDP/capita	.02	−.26
Change in GDP/capita	.24	−.02
R-squared	.07	.21
Adjusted R-squared	−.07	.09

Significance levels: * = <.10   ** = <.05   *** = <.01
Each cell reports Beta coefficient.
$N = 31$

Vote Swing, 1988–1991

	PRI Gain	Left Loss	PRI Gain— Minus Key States (a)	Left Loss— Minus Key States (b)
Reorientation	.11	−.22	−.06	−.32
Agricultural population	−.07	−.70***	−.24	−.32
GDP/capita	−.12	−.71***	−.21	−.03
No primary school	.18	−.23	.27	−.01
Participation increase	.40***	−.26**	.52***	−.07
Regression to the mean	−.49***	.04	−.39**	.25
R-squared	.64	.66	.56	.23
Adjusted R-squared	.56	.57	.44	.00
PRONASOL/capita	−.03	.10	−.04	.19
Agricultural population	−.37	−.74***	−.25	−.42
GDP/capita	−.13	−.66***	−.21	−.04
No primary school	.18	−.22	.22	.06
Participation increase	.38***	−.22	.45***	.03
Regression to the mean	−.53***	−.01	−.37*	.19
R-squared	.64	.63	.56	.16
Adjusted R-squared	.54	.55	.44	−.07

Significance levels: * = <.10   ** = <.05   *** = <.01
Each cell reports Beta coefficient.
$N = 31$
(a) $N = 29$ (PRI model); if two most improved performances subtracted as outliers.
(b) $N = 28$ (PRD model); if three least damaging performances subtracted as outliers.

1988 Presidential Vote

	Salinas	Clouthier	Cárdenas
Decrease in GDP	−.03	.05	−.03
Agricultural population	.76***	−.45	−.42
GDP/capita	.24	−.20	−.10
No primary school	−.12	−.26	.24
Abstention	−.12	.06	.08
R-squared	.36	.36	.07
Adjusted R-squared	.23	.24	−.11

Significance levels: * = <.10   ** = <.05   *** = <.01
Each cell reports Beta coefficient.
$N = 32$

Voting Support, 1991

	PRI	PRD
Reorientation	− .37**	.23
Agricultural population	.67***	.07
GDP/capita	− .10	.10
No primary school	− .22	− .30
Abstention 1991	.39**	.15
R-squared	.51	.23
Adjusted R-squared	.41	.08
PRONASOL/capita	.25	− .20
Agricultural population	.63***	.11
GDP/capita	.05	− .01
No primary school	− .19	.27
Abstention 1991	.28*	.22
R-squared	.46	.23
Adjusted R-squared	.35	.07

Significance levels: * = <.10   ** = <.05   *** = <.01
Each cell reports Beta coefficient.
$N = 31$

PRD Vote 1994

	PRD Vote	Minus Michoacán	Minus Top 4	Minus Lowest 3
Agricultural population	.39*	.44**	.59*	.18
GDP/capita	.52***	.62***	.38	.57***
No primary school	.58***	.59***	.61*	.80***
R-squared	.50	.57	.28	.58
Adjusted R-squared	.44	.52	.19	.53
	$N = 32$	$N = 31$	$N = 28$	$N = 29$

Significance levels: * = <.10   ** = <.05   *** = <.01
Each cell reports Beta coefficient.

Congressional Vote in Michoacán, by municipio, 1991

	PRD Vote	PRI Vote
Agricultural population	.08	−.01
Illiteracy	.22***	−.16**
Municipal population	−.16*	.02
PRD government	.64***	−.61***
R-squared	.52	.39
Adjusted R-squared	.51	.37

Significance levels: * = <.10   ** = <.05   *** = <.01
Each cell reports Beta coefficient.
$N = 109$

Municipal Vote Swing (Michoacán), 1989–1991

	PRD Loss	PRI Gain
Agricultural population	.01	.01
Illiteracy	.09	−.17**
Municipal population	.31***	.41***
PRD government	.11	.27***
R-squared	.10	.33
Adjusted R-squared	.06	.31

Significance levels: * = <.10   ** = <.05   *** = <.01
Each cell reports Beta coefficient.
$N = 109$

APPENDIX D
A SOCIOECONOMIC PROFILE OF THE PRD

	Population	PRD	$N =$
Sex			
male	36.7%	54.6%	2,880
female	29.2	45.4	2,969
Age			
18–25	33.2	20.7	1,177
26–40	30.4	33.6	2,120
41–60	31.7	29.1	1,769
61 or more	41.6	16.6	772
Income			
0–1 minimum wage	34.4	49.0	2,725
1–3 minimum wage	31.7	36.3	2,176
3–5 minimum wage	29.7	6.2	436
5–7 minimum wage	31.1	2.9	203
7–10 minimum wage	27.3	1.3	110
10–minimum wage	20.4	1.3	126
Education			
none	37.7	20.9	1,092
incomplete primary	34.2	31.1	1,688
primary	28.6	13.1	890
secondary	33.2	10.2	562
university	26.5	5.2	428
Occupation			
agriculture	42.1	43.0	1,073
industry	26.9	5.0	217
commerce	26.7	14.7	641
construction	40.9	7.2	197
education	36.4	7.1	226
Nonsalaried			
housewives	30.4	82.5	2,188
students	36.2	6.4	160
retired	35.7	2.9	78
unemployed	38.5	3.7	85

Column A (Population) indicates the percentage of this group that preferred the PRD.
Column B (PRD) indicates the percentage of PRD voters that belonged to this group.
SOURCE: Adapted from "Encuestalia: El voto en Michoacán," *Nexos* 15, no. 176 (August 1992): 81–85. A more extensive breakdown of the socioeconomic profile of the PRD (including the categories "position in workplace" and "type of workplace") appears in this article, together with a direct comparison to the PRI vote in each category.

Selected Bibliography

Primary Sources

Public Documents

Mexico. Comisión Federal Electoral. *La evolución electoral del México contemporaneo.* Edited by Luis Medina. Mexico City: Comisión Federal Electoral, 1979.

Mexico. Consejo Nacional de la Publicidad. "Mexico is on the Right Track." Mexico City: Consejo Nacional de la Publicidad, October 1991.

Mexico. Dirección General de Gobierno. *Constitución Política de los Estados Unidos Mexicanos.* Mexico City: Diario Oficial, 1990.

Mexico. Instituto Federal Electoral (IFE). *Contienda electoral en las elecciones de diputados federales.* Edited by Jenny Saltiel Cohen. Mexico City: IFE, 1991.

———. *Contienda electoral en las elecciones presidenciales.* Edited by Jenny Saltiel Cohen. Mexico City: IFE, 1991.

———. *Elecciones federales 1994: Resultados definitivos según los cómputos distritales.* Mexico City: IFE, 1994.

———. *Memorias del proceso electoral federal de 1991.* Mexico City: IFE, 1993.

———. *Relación de los 300 distritos federales electorales.* Mexico City: IFE, 1991.

———. "Reporte general de candidatos a diputados de representación proporcional por partido." Mexico City: IFE, Dirección Ejecutiva de Prerrogativas y Partidos Políticos, 1994. Computer printout.

Mexico. Instituto Nacional de Estadística, Geografía, e Informática (INEGI). *Anuario de estadísticas estatales, 1985.* Mexico City: INEGI, 1986.

———. *X censo general de población y vivienda, 1980.* Mexico City: INEGI, 1984.

———. *XI censo general de población y vivienda, 1990.* Mexico City: INEGI, 1992.

———. *XI censo general de población y vivienda, 1990: Perfíl sociodemográfico.* Mexico City: INEGI, 1992.

———. *Michoacán: Resultados definitivos, tabulados básicos del XI censo general.* Vols. 1 and 2. Mexico City: INEGI, 1992.

Mexico. Municipal budget reports from eight municipios in Michoacán, 1991.

Mexico. Presidencia de la República. *Geografía de la marginación.* Mexico City: COPLAMAR/Siglo Veintiuno, 1982.
Mexico. Registro Federal de Electores. "Cobertura estatal del proyecto." Mexico City, 21 July 1991.
Mexico. Secretaría de Gobernación. *Código Federal de Instituciones y Procedimientos Electorales.* Mexico City: Secretaría de Gobernación, 1990.
———. *Diario oficial.* 3 January 1991: 2–3. Mexico City: Secretaría de Gobernación.
———. *Diario oficial.* 18 May 1994: 2–10. Mexico City: Secretaría de Gobernación.
———. *Legislación electoral mexicana: 1812–1988.* 3d ed. Edited by Antonio García Orozco. Mexico City: Secretaría de Gobernación, 1990.
———. *Tercer informe de gobierno.* Carlos Salinas de Gortari. Mexico City: Oficina de la Presidencia, 1991.
———. *Tercer informe de gobierno: Anexo.* Mexico City: Presidencia de la República, November 1991.
———. *Tercer informe de gobierno: Donde estamos y a donde vamos, solidaridad y bienestar social.* Mexico City: Secretaría de Gobernación, 1991.
Mexico. Secretaría de Hacienda y Crédito Público (SHCP). *El nuevo perfíl de la economía mexicana.* Mexico City: SHCP, June 1991.

Party and Movement Documents

Grupo Parlamentario Independiente. *Fraude en Michoacán: Continuidad de una política electoral.* Mexico City: Congreso de la Unión, 1989.
Organización Nacional de Observación Electoral del Magisterio (ONOEM). *Informe de la observación del proceso electoral de la ONOEM.* Mexico City: ONOEM, 1994. Mimeographed.
Partido Mexicano Socialista (PMS). "Resoluciones de la mesa de movimientos sociales." *La Unidad.* Mexico City, 26 February 1989.
———. *La situación nacional y la construcción del Partido de la Revolución Democrática.* Mexico City: PMS, 1989.
Partido Popular Socialista (PPS). *Denunciar y derrotar la negativa política económica.* 82d Pleno del Comité Central. Mexico City: PPS, 1986.
———. *Es necesario y urgente poner otra vez en marcha a la revolución mexicana.* 84th Pleno del Comité Central. Mexico City: PPS, 1987.
———. *Nos empeñamos en manejar con certeza la ciencia de la sociedad, el marxismo-leninismo.* 83d Pleno del Comité Central. Mexico City: PPS, 1987.
———. *Plataforma común del Frente Democrático Nacional.* Mexico City: PPS, 1988.
Partido de la Revolución Democrática (PRD). *Comentarios sobre el Código Federal de Instituciones y Procedimientos Electorales.* Mexico City: PRD, 1991.

———. "Conclusiones de la primera reunión estatal." Morelia, Michoacán: PRD, 1991. Mimeographed minutes.

———. *Cuadernos del Tercer Congreso Nacional*. Mexico City: PRD, 1995.

———. *Documentos básicos*. Mexico City: PRD, 1990.

———. *Documentos básicos: Anteproyectos*. Mexico City: PRD, 1989.

———. *Documentos básicos: Proyectos*. Mexico City: PRD, 1989.

———. *Elección presidencial*. Mexico City: PRD, 1989. Mimeographed electoral results.

———. *En defensa de los derechos humanos*. Mexico City: Secretaría de Derechos Humanos, Grupo Parlamentario del PRD, 1994.

———. *Informe sobre las elecciones en Morelos*. Mexico City: PRD, Comisión para la Defensa del Voto, 1991.

———. *Plataforma electoral para las elecciones federales de 1991*. Mexico City: PRD, 1991.

———. "Relatoría de la mesa de trabajo III: Situación de los movimientos sociales y las tareas del partido." Mexico City: PRD, 1995. Mimeographed copy.

———. *Tablas comparativas de los resultados electorales*. Mexico City: PRD, Secretaría de Defensa del Voto, 1992.

———. *Tres años de represión política en México*. Mexico City: PRD, Comisión de Derechos Humanos, 1991.

———. *La violencia política en México: Un asunto de derechos humanos*. Mexico City: PRD, Comisión de Derechos Humanos, 1992.

Partido Revolucionario Institucional (PRI). *Documentos básicos*. Mexico City: PRI, 1987.

———. *Documentos básicos*. Mexico City: PRI, 1990.

Interviews by Author

Alcocer, Jorge. Mexico City, 19 February 1991.

Buenrostro, César. Mexico City, 19 April 1991.

Cárdenas, Cuauhtémoc. Morelos, 3 May 1991.

Castillo Martínez, Heberto. Mexico City. 22 August 1991.

Confidential interviews, randomly marked with letters A–Z, AA–AZ, BA–BZ, etc.

Del Villar, Samuel. Mexico City, 11 April 1991.

Durán, Leonel. Mexico City, 19 April 1991.

González Guevara, Rodolfo. Mexico City, 22 September 1991.

Labra, Armando. Mexico City, 26 April 1991.

Martínez, Ifigenia. Mexico City, 19 April 1991.

Martínez Verdugo, Arnoldo. Mexico City, 23 April 1991.

Múgica, Janitzio. Mexico City, 2 May 1991.

Muñoz Ledo, Porfirio. Guanajuato, March 1991.

Rascón, Marco. Mexico City. September 1994.

Ramírez Garrido Abreu, Graco. Mexico City, 6 March 1991.

Rincón Gallardo, Gilberto. Mexico City, 23 August 1991.
Robles Gárnica, Roberto. Mexico City, 4 April 1991.
Valero, Ricardo. Mexico City, 3 April 1991.

Secondary Sources

Aguilar, Alonso. "El MLN y la sucesión presidencial." *Política* 4 (15 August 1963): special documents section.
Aguilar Camín, Hector. "The Mexican Transition." *Voices of Mexico* (June–November 1988): 3–10.
———. *Saldos de la Revolución*. Mexico City: Ediciones Oceano, 1984.
Aguilar Zínser, Adolfo. *¡Vamos a ganar!: La pugna de Cuauhtémoc Cárdenas por el poder*. Mexico City: Editorial Oceano, 1995.
Albarrán de Alba, Gerardo. "De Zedillo a Madrazo: En documentos, el derroche, el acarreo, la compra de voluntades y el soborno a la prensa, durante las campañas del PRI," *Proceso*, no. 971 (12 June 1995): 18–21.
———. "Zabludovsky pone a '24 Horas' al servicio de la 'promoción acelerada' de la imagen de Zedillo." *Proceso*, no. 922 (4 July 1994): 7–16.
Alcocer, Jorge. "IFE: Legalidad y conflicto." *Nexos* 14, no. 164 (August 1991): 11–26.
———. "PRD: La hora del Congreso." *Nexos* 13, no. 155 (November 1990): 53–58.
Alcocer, Jorge, and Rodrigo Morales. "Mitología y realidad del fraude electoral." *Nexos* 14, no. 166 (October 1991): 27–40.
Alisedo, Pedro José, and Homero Campa. "El PRI resultó un partido rural, desairado en las capitales." *Proceso*, no. 611 (18 July 1988): 22–25.
Almond, Gabriel, and Sidney Verba. *The Civic Culture: Political Attitudes and Democracy in Five Nations*. Princeton: Princeton University Press, 1963.
———, eds. *The Civic Culture Revisited*. Boston: Little, Brown, 1980.
Alvarado, Arturo, ed. *Electoral Patterns and Perspectives in Mexico*. La Jolla, Calif.: UCSD Center for U.S.-Mexican Studies, 1987.
Alvarado Mendoza, Arturo. "La fundación del PNR." In *El partido en el poder: Seis ensayos*. Mexico City: Partido Revolucionario Institucional, IEPES, 1990.
Ávila García, Patricia. "Estudio preliminar sobre el deterioro socioambiental en la ciudad de Morelia: El caso del água." In *Urbanización y desarrollo en Michoacán*, edited by Gustavo López Castro. Zamora, Michoacán: El Colegio de Michoacán, 1991.
Avramow Gutiérrez, Jacqueline. "Los partidos contendientes en 1988." In *Las elecciones de 1988 y la crisis del sistema político*, edited by Jaime González Graf. Mexico City: Editorial Diana, 1989.
Aziz Nassif, Alberto. "1991: Las elecciones de la restauración." In *Las elecciones*

federales de 1991, edited by Alberto Aziz Nassif and Jacqueline Peschard. Mexico City: UNAM, 1992.

Baer, M. Delal. "Mexico's Second Revolution: Pathways to Liberalization." In *Political and Economic Liberalization in Mexico: At a Critical Juncture?* edited by Riordan Roett. Boulder, Colo.: Lynne Rienner, 1993.

Bailey, John. "Centralism and Political Change in Mexico." In *Transforming State-Society Relations in Mexico: The National Solidarity Strategy*, edited by Wayne Cornelius, Ann Craig, and Jonathan Fox. La Jolla, Calif.: UCSD Center for U.S.-Mexican Studies, 1994.

Bailey, John, and Jennifer Boone. "National Solidarity: A Summary of Program Elements." In *Transforming State-Society Relations in Mexico: The National Solidarity Strategy*, edited by Wayne Cornelius, Ann Craig, and Jonathan Fox. La Jolla, Calif.: UCSD Center for U.S.-Mexican Studies, 1994.

Barberán, José, et al. *Radiografía del fraude: Analisis de los datos oficiales del 6 de julio*. Mexico City: Editorial Nuestro Tiempo, 1988.

Basañez, Miguel. "Elections and Political Culture in Mexico." In *Mexican Politics in Transition*, edited by Judith Gentleman. Boulder, Colo.: Westview Press, 1987.

————. "Encuesta electoral 1991." *Este País*, no. 5 (August 1991): 3–6.

————. *El pulso de los sexenios: 20 años de crisis en México*. Mexico City: Siglo Veintiuno, 1990.

Beltrán del Río, Pascal. "Afloran las diferencias internas: Resbalón perredista en el día y el lugar de la apoteosis de Cárdenas en 1988." *Proceso*, no. 907 (21 March 1994): 6–11.

————. *Michoacán, ni un paso atrás: La política como intransigencia*. Mexico City: Proceso, 1993.

————. "Mil días bastaron a Salinas para machacar a sus opositores de 1988." *Proceso*, no. 773 (26 August 1991): 6–13.

————. "El PRD se dividió en dos grupos y extravió el camino a la democracia: Jorge Alcocer." *Proceso*, no. 740 (7 January 1991): 6–11.

Bennett, Vivienne. "The Evolution of Urban Popular Movements in Mexico Between 1968 and 1988." In *The Making of Social Movements in Latin America: Identity, Strategy, and Democracy*, edited by Arturo Escobar and Sonia Álvarez. Boulder, Colo.: Westview Press, 1992.

Berger, Peter. *The Capitalist Revolution: Fifty Propositions About Prosperity, Equality, and Liberty*. New York: Basic Books, 1986.

Bobbio, Norberto. *Which Socialism? Marxism, Socialism, and Democracy*. Translated by Roger Griffin. Cambridge: Polity Press, 1987.

Brandenburg, Frank. *The Making of Modern Mexico*. Englewood Cliffs, N.J.: Prentice-Hall, 1964.

Bruhn, Kathleen, and Keith Yanner. "Governing Under the Enemy: The PRD in Michoacán." In *Opposition Government in Mexico*, edited by Victoria Rodríguez and Peter Ward. Albuquerque: University of New Mexico Press, 1995.

Buendía Laredo, Jorge, and Leo Zuckermann Behar. "Agosto de 91: Los pronósticos y las urnas." *Nexos* 14, no. 164 (August 1991): 75–81.
Burnham, Walter. *Critical Elections and the Mainsprings of American Politics.* New York: Norton, 1976.
Caballero, Alejandro. "La desigualdad electoral en cifras: En la campaña del 94 el PRI gastó 78% del costo total; el PAN, 10.38%; el PRD, 4.58%." *Proceso*, no. 951 (23 January 1995): 29–35.
Calderón, Enrique, and Daniel Cazés. *Informe: Las elecciones presidenciales de 1994.* Mexico City: Fundación Arturo Rosenblueth, 1995.
Camp, Roderic. *Mexico's Leaders: Their Education and Recruitment.* Tucson: University of Arizona Press, 1980.
———. "The Political Technocrat in Mexico and the Survival of the Political System." *Latin American Research Review* 20, no. 1 (1985): 97–118.
Campbell, Angus. *Elections and the Political Order.* New York: John Wiley, 1966.
Campuzano Montoya, Irma. "Una novedad: Las encuestas pre-electorales." In *Las elecciones de 1988 y la crisis del sistema político*, edited by Jaime González Graf. Mexico City: Editorial Diana, 1989.
Cándano Fierro, Mónica. "Las campañas electorales." In *Las elecciones de 1988 y la crisis del sistema político*, edited by Jaime González Graf. Mexico City: Editorial Diana, 1989.
Cárdenas Solórzano, Cuauhtémoc. *Llamamiento al pueblo de México.* Mexico City: PRD, 1988.
———. *Nuestra lucha apenas comienza.* Mexico City: Editorial Nuestro Tiempo, 1988.
———. *La revolución a futuro.* Jiquilpan, Michoacán: Centro de Estudios de la Revolución Mexicana "Lázaro Cárdenas," 1985.
———, et al. *Corriente Democrática: Alternativa frente a la crisis.* Mexico City: Editores Costa-Amic, 1987.
Carr, Barry. "The Left and Its Potential Role in Political Change." In *Mexico's Alternative Political Futures*, edited by Wayne Cornelius, Judith Gentleman, and Peter Smith. La Jolla, Calif.: UCSD Center for U.S.-Mexican Studies, 1989.
———. *Mexican Communism, 1968–1983: Eurocommunism in the Americas?* La Jolla, Calif.: UCSD Center for U.S.-Mexican Studies, 1985.
———. *El movimiento obrero y la política en México, 1910–1929.* Translated by Roberto Gómez Ciriza. Mexico City: Ediciones Era, 1981.
Castañeda, Jorge. "El fraude 'moderno.' " *Proceso*, no. 773 (26 August 1991): 34, 36.
———. "Latin America and the End of the Cold War: A Mixed Blessing for the Left." *World Policy Journal* 7 (Summer 1990): 469–92.
———. "La manera como el PRI conservó el poder puede impedir que lo use como quisiera." *Proceso*, no. 617 (29 August 1988): 14–15.
———. "Salinas's International Relations Gamble." *Journal of International Affairs* 43 (Winter 1990): 407–22.

————. "Urnas cruzadas." *Nexos: Cuadernos* 11, no. 128 (August 1988): 11–12.

————. *Utopia Unarmed: The Latin American Left After the Cold War.* New York: Alfred A. Knopf, 1993.

Castillo, Heberto. "Lázaro Cárdenas y el Movimiento de Liberación Nacional." In *Lázaro Cárdenas*, edited by Gilberto Bosques et al. Mexico City: Fondo de Cultura Económica, 1975.

Centeno, Miguel Ángel. *Democracy Within Reason: Technocratic Revolution in Mexico.* University Park: The Pennsylvania State University Press, 1994.

Centro de Estudios Sociológicos. *México en el umbral del milenio.* Mexico City: El Colegio de México, 1990.

Chao, Felipe. "La marcha de las campañas." *Este País*, no. 39 (June 1994): 19–21.

Chávez, Elías. "Michoacán: Cada voto del PRI costó 239,188 pesos; cada voto del PRD costó 6,916 pesos." *Proceso*, no. 821 (27 July 1992): 22–27.

————. *Los priistas.* Mexico City: Proceso, 1980.

Collier, Ruth Berins. *The Contradictory Alliance: State-Labor Relations and Regime Change in Mexico.* Berkeley and Los Angeles: University of California Press, 1992.

Collier, Ruth Berins, and David Collier. *Shaping the Political Arena: Critical Junctures, the Labor Movement, and Regime Dynamics in Latin America.* Princeton: Princeton University Press, 1991.

Contreras, Oscar, and Vivienne Bennett. "National Solidarity in the Northern Borderlands: Social Participation and Community Leadership." In *Transforming State-Society Relations in Mexico: The National Solidarity Strategy*, edited by Wayne Cornelius, Ann Craig, and Jonathan Fox. La Jolla, Calif.: UCSD Center for U.S.-Mexican Studies, 1994.

"Convergencias y divergencias en América del Norte." *Este País*, no. 2 (May 1991): 3–8.

Cordera, Rolando, and Carlos Tello. *México: La disputa por la nación.* Mexico City: Siglo Veintiuno, 1981.

Córdova, Arnaldo. *La formación del poder político en México.* Mexico City: Ediciones Era, 1972.

————. "La lucha de tendencias en el Constituyente de 1917 y las tareas actuales para la reforma democrática del estado." In *La revolución mexicana y la lucha actual por la democracia*, edited by Arnaldo Córdova, Gerardo Unzueta, and Edmundo Jardín Arzate. Mexico City: Ediciones de Cultura Popular, 1984.

Cornelius, Wayne. "The Political Economy of Mexico Under De la Madrid: Austerity, Routinized Crisis, and Nascent Recovery." *Mexican Studies* 1 (Winter 1985): 83–124.

————. "Political Liberalization and the 1985 Elections in Mexico." In *Elections and Democratization in Latin America, 1980–1985*, edited by Paul Drake and Eduardo Silva. La Jolla, Calif.: UCSD Center for Iberian and Latin American Studies, 1986.

Cornelius, Wayne, Ann Craig, and Jonathan Fox. *Transforming State-Society*

Relations in Mexico: The National Solidarity Strategy. La Jolla, Calif.: UCSD Center for U.S.-Mexican Studies, 1994.

Cornelius, Wayne, Judith Gentleman, and Peter Smith. "Overview: The Dynamics of Political Change in Mexico." In *Mexico's Alternative Political Futures,* edited by Wayne Cornelius, Judith Gentleman, and Peter Smith. La Jolla, Calif.: UCSD Center for U.S.-Mexican Studies, 1989.

————, eds. *Mexico's Alternative Political Futures.* La Jolla, Calif.: UCSD Center for U.S.-Mexican Studies, 1989.

Corro, Salvador. "De los gobiernos priistas, Emilio Azcárraga ha recibido todos los favores y, como priista confeso, sabe ser agradecido." *Proceso,* no. 922 (4 July 1994): 6–7.

Cosío Villegas, Daniel. *El sistema político mexicano.* Mexico City: Editorial Joaquín Mortiz, 1973.

Craig, Ann, and Wayne Cornelius. "Political Culture in Mexico: Continuities and Revisionist Interpretations." In *The Civic Culture Revisited,* edited by Gabriel Almond and Sidney Verba. Boston: Little, Brown, 1980.

"La crisis de ser gobierno y ser oposición." *Este País,* no. 23 (February 1993): 6–10.

Croan, Melvin. "Is Mexico the Future of East Europe?" In *Authoritarian Politics in Modern Society: The Dynamics of Established One-Party Systems,* edited by Samuel Huntington and Clement Moore. New York: Basic Books, 1970.

Cuéllar Vázquez, Angélica. *La noche es de ustedes, el amanecer es nuestro.* Mexico City: UNAM, 1993.

"De la supervivencia, a la organización." *Este País,* no. 23 (February 1992): 10–15.

Del Castillo, Eduardo, ed. *20 años de búsqueda: Testimonios desde la izquierda.* Mexico City: Ediciones de Cultura Popular, 1991.

De Soto, Hernando. *El otro sendero: La revolución informal.* Buenos Aires: Editorial Sudamericana, 1987.

Diamond, Larry, Juan Linz, and S. M. Lipset, eds. *Politics in Developing Countries: Comparing Experiences with Democracy.* Boulder, Colo.: Lynne Rienner, 1990.

Domínguez, Jorge, and James McCann. "Shaping Mexico's Electoral Arena: The Construction of Partisan Cleavages in the 1988 and 1991 National Elections." *American Political Science Review* 89 (March 1995): 34–48.

Downs, Anthony. *An Economic Theory of Democracy.* New York: Harper & Row, 1957.

Drake, Paul, and Eduardo Silva. *Elections and Democratization in Latin America, 1980–1985.* La Jolla, Calif.: UCSD Center for Iberian and Latin American Studies, 1986.

Dresser, Denise. *Neopopulist Solutions to Neoliberal Problems: Mexico's National Solidarity Program.* La Jolla, Calif.: UCSD Center for U.S.-Mexican Studies, 1991.

Duverger, Maurice. *Political Parties: Their Organization and Activity in the*

Modern State. Translated by Barbara North and Douglas North. New York: John Wiley, 1954.

"La economía de este país." *Este País*, no. 10 (December 1991): 24.

"El ejido ante la opinión pública." *Este País*, no. 10 (January 1992): 34–35.

"Encuestalia: Fraude y los votantes." *Nexos* 14, no. 166 (October 1991): 75–77.

"Encuestalia: El voto en Michoacán." *Nexos* 15, no. 176 (August 1992): 81–85.

Fagen, Richard, and William Tuohy. *Politics and Privilege in a Mexican City*. Stanford, Calif.: Stanford University Press, 1972.

"¡Forjar una alianza democrática y anti-imperialista para actuar en la lucha electoral!" *Política* 3 (15 April 1963): 23–24.

Foweraker, Joe. "Popular Movements and Political Change in Mexico." In *Popular Movements and Political Change in Mexico*, edited by Joe Foweraker and Ann Craig. Boulder, Colo.: Lynne Rienner, 1990.

———. "Popular Organization and Institutional Change." In *Popular Movements and Political Change in Mexico*, edited by Joe Foweraker and Ann Craig. Boulder, Colo.: Lynne Rienner, 1990.

Foweraker, Joe, and Ann Craig, eds. *Popular Movements and Political Change in Mexico*. Boulder, Colo.: Lynne Rienner, 1990.

Fox, Jonathan. "Targeting the Poorest: The Role of the National Indigenous Institute in Mexico's National Solidarity Program." In *Transforming State-Society Relations in Mexico: The National Solidarity Strategy*, edited by Wayne Cornelius, Ann Craig, and Jonathan Fox. La Jolla, Calif.: UCSD Center for U.S.-Mexican Studies, 1994.

García Alba, Pascual, and Jaime Serra Puche. *Causas y efectos de la crisis económica en México*. Mexico City: El Colegio de México, 1984.

Garrido, Luis Javier. "The Crisis of *Presidencialismo*." In *Mexico's Alternative Political Futures*, edited by Wayne Cornelius, Judith Gentleman, and Peter Smith. La Jolla, Calif.: UCSD Center for U.S.-Mexican Studies, 1989.

———. *El Partido de la Revolución Institucionalizada*. Mexico City: Siglo Veintiuno, 1982.

———. "El PRI, o la democracia imposible." In *Democracia emergente y partidos políticos*, edited by Jorge Alonso and Sergio Sánchez Díaz. Vol. 1. Mexico City: Centro de Investigaciones y Estudios Superiores en Antropología Social (CIESAS), 1990.

———. *La ruptura: La Corriente Democrática del PRI*. Mexico City: Editorial Grijalbo, 1993.

Gentleman, Judith. "Mexico After the Oil Boom." In *Mexican Politics in Transition*, edited by Judith Gentleman. Boulder, Colo.: Westview Press, 1987.

Gershberg, Alec Ian. "Distributing Resources in the Education Sector." In *Transforming State-Society Relations in Mexico: The National Solidarity Strategy*, edited by Wayne Cornelius, Ann Craig, and Jonathan Fox. La Jolla, Calif.: UCSD Center for U.S.-Mexican Studies, 1994.

Gilly, Adolfo, ed. *Cartas a Cuauhtémoc Cárdenas*. Mexico City: Ediciones Era, 1989.

Gómez, Leopoldo, and John Bailey. "La transición política y los dilemas del PRI." *Foro Internacional* 31, no. 121 (July–September 1990): 57–87.

Gómez, Pablo. *México 1988: Disputa por la presidencia y lucha parlamentaria.* Mexico City: Ediciones de Cultura Popular, 1989.

Gómez Leyva, Ciro. "Solidaridad gratuita en todas las pantallas." *Este País*, no. 7 (October 1991): 13–16.

Gómez Tagle, Silvia. *De la alquimia al fraude en las elecciones mexicanas.* Mexico City: Garcí y Valadés Editores, 1994.

———. *Las estadísticas electorales de la reforma política.* Mexico City: El Colegio de México, 1990.

González Casanova, Pablo. *Democracy in Mexico.* Translated by Danielle Salti. New York: Oxford University Press, 1970.

———. *El estado y los partidos políticos en México.* Mexico City: Ediciones Era, 1985.

———. *Primer informe sobre la democracia: México 1988.* Mexico City: UNAM, 1988.

González de la Rocha, Mercedes, and Agustín Escobar Latapí, eds. *Social Responses to Mexico's Economic Crisis of the 1980s.* La Jolla, Calif.: UCSD Center for U.S.-Mexican Studies, 1991.

González Graf, Jaime. "La crisis del sistema." In *Las elecciones de 1988 y la crisis del sistema político,* edited by Jaime González Graf. Mexico City: Editorial Diana, 1989.

———, ed. *Las elecciones de 1988 y la crisis del sistema político.* Mexico City: Editorial Diana, 1989.

González Oropeza, Manuel. "Los tribunales electorales." In *Las elecciones federales de 1991,* edited by Alberto Aziz Nassif and Jacqueline Peschard. Mexico City: UNAM, 1992.

González Pedrero, Enrique. *La lección de la elección.* Mexico City: Secretaría de Información y Propaganda, PRI, 1988.

"Los grandes problemas nacionales e internacionales." *Política* 7 (15 July 1966): special section.

Guerra Leal, Mario. *La grilla.* Mexico City: Editorial Diana, 1978.

Guevara N., Alfonso, and Gregorio Santibañez. "Los grupos étnicos autóctonos como motivo de marginación." In *Marginalidad urbana y pobreza rural,* edited by Fernando Serrano Migalló. Mexico City: Editorial Diana, 1990.

Guillen López, Tonatiuh. "Las elecciones de 1991 y transición democrática en Baja California." Unpublished manuscript, 1992.

Gutiérrez Garza, Esthela. "De la relación salarial monopolista a la flexibilidad del trabajo: México, 1960–1986." In *Testimonios de la crisis: La crisis del estado del bienestar,* edited by Esthela Gutiérrez Garza. Vol. 2. Mexico City: Siglo Veintiuno, 1988.

Haber, Paul. "Political Change in Durango: The Role of National Solidarity." In *Transforming State-Society Relations in Mexico: The National Solidarity Strategy,* edited by Wayne Cornelius, Ann Craig, and Jonathan Fox. La Jolla, Calif.: UCSD Center for U.S.-Mexican Studies, 1994.

Harvey, Neil, and Mónica Serrano, eds. *Party Politics in 'an Uncommon Democracy': Political Parties and Elections in Mexico.* London: Institute of Latin American Studies, 1994.

Hauss, Charles, and David Rayside. "The Development of New Parties in Western Democracies Since 1945." In *Political Parties: Development and Decay,* edited by Louis Maisel and Joseph Cooper. Beverly Hills, Calif.: Sage Publications, 1978.

Hernández, Luis. "CDP de Durango, la conquista del futuro." *Pueblo* 11, no. 138 (August 1988): 28–29.

———. "Durango: De la lucha reivindicativa a la democracia social." *Pueblo* 11, no. 125 (May 1988): 29–30.

———. "El Partido del Trabajo: Realidades y perspectivas." *El Cotidiano,* no. 40 (March–April 1991): 21–28.

Hernández Rodríguez, Rogelio. "La reforma interna y los conflictos en el PRI." *Foro Internacional* 32, no. 126 (October–December 1991): 222–49.

Higley, John, and Richard Gunther, eds. *Elites and Democratic Consolidation in Latin America and Southern Europe.* New York: Cambridge University Press, 1992.

Hirschman, Albert. *Exit, Voice, and Loyalty: Responses to Decline in Firms, Organizations, and States.* Cambridge, Mass.: Harvard University Press, 1970.

Huntington, Samuel. *Political Order in Changing Societies.* New Haven: Yale University Press, 1968.

"Implicaciones del voto razonado de Lázaro Cárdenas en pro de Díaz Ordaz." *Política* 5 (15 June 1964): inside front and back cover.

"Instantaneas." *Este País,* no. 21 (December 1992): 38.

"Instantaneas: Gobierno, pendientes, y culpables." *Este País,* no. 38 (May 1994): 2.

"Instantaneas: Hacia las elecciones." *Este País,* no. 40 (July 1994): 2.

"Instantaneas: Pesimismo." *Este País,* no. 39 (June 1994): 2.

"Integración económica y nacionalismo: Canadá, Estados Unidos, y México." *Este País,* no. 1 (April 1991): 3–9.

Karl, Terry. "Dilemmas of Democratization in Latin America." *Comparative Politics* 23 (October 1990): 1–21.

———. "Petroleum and Political Pacts: The Transition to Democracy in Venezuela." *Latin American Research Review* 22, no. 1 (1987): 63–94.

Karl, Terry, and Philippe Schmitter. "Modes of Transition in Latin America, Southern and Eastern Europe." *International Social Science Journal,* no. 128 (May 1991): 269–84.

Keck, Margaret. *The Workers' Party and Democratization in Brazil.* New Haven: Yale University Press, 1992.

Keohane, Robert. *After Hegemony: Cooperation and Discord in the World Political Economy.* Princeton: Princeton University Press, 1984.

Klandermans, Bert, Hanspeter Kriesi, and Sidney Tarrow. *From Structure to Action: Comparing Movement Participation Across Cultures.* Vol. 1. Greenwich, Conn.: JAI Press, 1988.

Klesner, Joseph. "Modernization, Economic Crisis, and Electoral Alignment in Mexico." *Mexican Studies* 9, no. 2 (Summer 1993): 187–223.

———. "The 1994 Mexican Elections: Manifestation of a Divided Society?" *Mexican Studies* 11, no. 1 (Winter 1995): 137–49.

———. "Realignment or Dealignment? Consequences of Economic Crisis and Restructuring for the Mexican Party System." In *The Politics of Economic Restructuring*, edited by Maria Cook, Kevin Middlebrook, and Juan Molinar Horcasitas. La Jolla, Calif.: UCSD Center for U.S.-Mexican Studies, 1994.

Knight, Alan. "Historical Continuities in Social Movements." In *Popular Movements and Political Change in Mexico*, edited by Joe Foweraker and Ann Craig. Boulder, Colo.: Lynne Rienner, 1990.

LaPalombara, Joseph, and Myron Weiner. *Political Parties and Political Development*. Princeton: Princeton University Press, 1966.

Laso de la Vega, Jorge, ed. *La Corriente Democrática: Hablan los protagonistas*. Mexico City: Editorial Posada, 1987.

Leiken, Robert. "Earthquake in Mexico." *National Interest*, no. 14 (Winter 1988-89): 29–42.

León, Samuel. "Del partido de partidos al partido de sectores." In *El partido en el poder: Seis ensayos*. Mexico City: Partido Revolucionario Institucional, IEPES, 1990.

Levy, Daniel. "Mexico: Sustained Civilian Rule Without Democracy." In *Democracy in Developing Countries: Latin America*, edited by Larry Diamond, Juan Linz, and S. M. Lipset. Vol. 4. Boulder, Colo.: Lynne Rienner, 1989.

Levy, Daniel C., and Székely, Gabriel. *Mexico: Paradoxes of Stability and Change*. 2d ed. Boulder, Colo.: Westview Press, 1987.

Lipset, Seymour Martin, and Stein Rokkan, eds. *Party Systems and Voter Alignments: Cross-National Perspectives*. New York: The Free Press, 1967.

López, María Xelhuantzi. "La Corriente Democrática: De la legitimidad y de alianzas." *Estudios Políticos* 7 (April–June 1988): 19–34.

———. "La Corriente Democrática o la defensa de México." In *La Corriente Democrática: Hablan los protagonistas*, edited by Jorge Laso de la Vega. Mexico City: Editorial Posada, 1987.

———. "Una vida nutrida de México: Exclusiva con Cuauhtémoc Cárdenas." *Estudios Políticos* 7 (July–September 1988): 24–26.

López Monjardín, Adriana. "¿Derrota electoral del PRI o inconsistencia sistemática del electorado?" In *Las elecciones federales de 1988 en México*, edited by Juan Felipe Leal, Jacqueline Peschard, and Concepción Rivera. Mexico City: UNAM, 1988.

López Villafañe, Víctor. *La formación del sistema político mexicano*. Mexico City: Siglo Veintiuno, 1986.

Loyola Díaz, Rafael. "1938: El despliegue del corporativismo partidario." In *El partido en el poder: Seis ensayos*. Mexico City: Partido Revolucionario Institucional, IEPES, 1990.

Lugo Chávez, Carlos. *Neocardenismo*. Mexico City: Instituto de Proposiciones Estratégicas, 1989.

Lund, Daniel. "El tratado de libre comercio: Los extremos de la confusión." *Este País*, no. 28 (July 1993): 2–6.

Lustig, Nora. *Mexico: The Remaking of an Economy*. Washington, D.C.: The Brookings Institution, 1992.

Mabry, Donald. *Mexico's Acción Nacional: A Catholic Alternative to Revolution*. New York: Syracuse University Press, 1973.

Mainwaring, Scott. *Transitions to Democracy and Democratic Consolidation: Theoretical and Comparative Issues*. Kellogg Working Papers, no. 130. Notre Dame, Ind.: University of Notre Dame, Helen Kellogg Institute for International Studies, 1989.

Maldonado B., Samuel. *Origenes del Partido de la Revolución Democrática*. Morelia, Michoacán: published by author, 1989.

Martínez, Ifigenia. "La distribución del ingreso en México." In *El perfíl de México en 1980*. Vol. 1. Mexico City: Siglo Veintiuno, 1972.

Martínez Assad, Carlos. *El henriquismo: Una piedra en el camino*. Mexico City: Martin Casillas Editores, 1982.

Martínez Nateras, Arturo. "Solidaridad y Gobernabilidad." In *Solidaridad a debate*. Mexico City: Consejo Consultivo del Programa Nacional de Solidaridad, 1991.

Martínez Verdugo, Arnoldo. *El Partido Comunista Mexicano: Trayectoria y perspectivas*. Mexico City: Fondo de Cultura Popular, 1971.

Marván Laborde, Ignacio. "La dificultad del cambio (1968–1980)." In *El partido en el poder: Seis ensayos*. Mexico City: Partido Revolucionario Institucional, IEPES, 1990.

Meyer, Lorenzo. "La democratización del PRI: ¿Misión imposible?" *Nexos* 11, no. 126 (June 1988): 25–33.

———. "Historical Roots of the Authoritarian State in Mexico." In *Authoritarianism in Mexico*, edited by José Luis Reyna and Richard Weinert. Philadelphia, Pa.: Institute for the Study of Human Issues, 1977.

Michels, Robert. *Political Parties: A Sociological Study of the Oligarchical Tendencies of Modern Democracy*. Translated by Eden and Cedar Paul. New York: The Free Press, 1962.

Middlebrook, Kevin. "Dilemmas of Change in Mexican Politics." *World Politics* 41 (October 1988): 120–41.

———. *The Paradox of Revolution: Labor, the State, and Authoritarianism in Mexico*. Baltimore: Johns Hopkins University Press, 1995.

———. "Political Liberalization in an Authoritarian Regime: The Case of Mexico." In *Elections and Democratization in Latin America, 1980–1985*, edited by Paul Drake and Eduardo Silva. La Jolla, Calif.: UCSD Center for Iberian and Latin American Studies, 1986.

Molinar Horcasitas, Juan. "The Mexican Electoral System: Continuity by Change." In *Elections and Democratization in Latin America, 1980–1985*, edited by Paul Drake and Eduardo Silva. San Diego: UCSD, 1986.

————. "The 1985 Federal Elections in Mexico: The Product of a System." In *Electoral Patterns and Perspectives in Mexico*, edited by Arturo Alvarado. La Jolla, Calif.: UCSD Center for U.S.-Mexican Studies, 1987.

————. "Palabras pronunciadas por Juan Molinar Horcasitas." In *Las elecciones federales de 1988 en México*, edited by Juan Felipe Leal, Jacqueline Peschard, and Concepción Rivera. Mexico City: UNAM, 1988.

————. *El tiempo de la legitimidad*. Mexico City: Cal y Arena, 1991.

Molinar Horcasitas, Juan, and Jeffrey Weldon. "Electoral Determinants and Consequences of National Solidarity." In *Transforming State-Society Relations in Mexico: The National Solidarity Strategy*, edited by Wayne Cornelius, Ann Craig, and Jonathan Fox. La Jolla, Calif.: UCSD Center for U.S.-Mexican Studies, 1994.

"La moneda en el aire." *Voz y Voto*, no. 17 (July 1994): 33–38.

Monnet, Jerome. "Las sorpresas del censo." *Nexos* 13, no. 154 (October 1990): 11–15.

Monsivais, Carlos. "Las repercusiones sociales y culturales del auge." In *El auge petrolero: De la euforia al desencanto*, edited by Rolando Cordera and Carlos Tello. Mexico City: UNAM, 1987.

Morales Sales, Edgar. *Estado de México: Sociedad, economía, política, y cultura*. Series "Biblioteca de las Entidades Federativas." Mexico City: UNAM, 1989.

Moreno, Alejandro. "¿Por qué se votó por el PRI?" *Este País*, no. 33 (December 1993): 26–28.

Mosca, Gaetano. *The Ruling Class*. New York: McGraw-Hill, 1939.

Muñoz Ledo, Porfirio. *Compromisos*. Mexico City: Editorial Posada, 1988.

Needler, Martin C. *Politics and Society in Mexico*. Albuquerque: University of New Mexico Press, 1971.

————. *The Problem of Democracy in Latin America*. Lexington, Mass.: Lexington Books, 1987.

————. "The Significance of Recent Events for the Mexican Political System." In *Mexican Politics in Transition*, edited by Judith Gentleman. Boulder, Colo.: Westview Press, 1987.

O'Donnell, Guillermo, and Philippe Schmitter. *Transitions from Authoritarian Rule: Tentative Conclusions About Uncertain Democracies*. Baltimore: Johns Hopkins University Press, 1986.

Ortega, Jesús. "El padrón electoral: Viejos vicios, nuevas artimañas." *Coyuntura* (August 1991): 11–15.

Ortega, Romeo. *Cárdenas el pequeño*. Mexico City: n.p., 1986.

Ortíz Pinchetti, Francisco. "Acción Nacional no es un partido, sino una federación de organizaciones locales unidas por su anticentralismo: Soledad Loaeza." *Proceso*, no. 969 (29 May 1995): 22–26.

Pacheco Méndez, Guadalupe. "Credenciales y credibilidad." *Nexos: Cuadernos* 14, no. 38 (August 1991): 11–12.

————. "Padrón, credenciales, y distritos en las elecciones de 1991." In *Las elecciones federales de 1991*, edited by Alberto Aziz Nassif and Jacqueline Peschard. Mexico City: UNAM, 1992.

Padgett, Vincent. *The Mexican Political System*. Boston: Houghton Mifflin, 1966.

Palomo, Armando. "Elecciones y movimiento urbano popular." *Pueblo* 11, no. 138 (August 1988): 9–13.

Panebianco, Angelo. *Political Parties: Organization and Power*. Translated by Marc Silver. New York: Cambridge University Press, 1988.

"Panorama nacional." *Política* 2 (15 August 1961): 5–23.

"Panorama nacional." *Política* 2 (15 September 1961): 5–22.

"Panorama nacional." *Política* 3 (15 January 1963): 3–25.

"Panorama nacional." *Política* 5 (15 June 1964): 5–20.

"Panorama nacional." *Política* 5 (15 January 1965): 5–25.

"Panorama nacional." *Política* 8 (November 1967): 5–20.

"Panorama político." *Política* 1 (1 March 1961): 5–24.

Pareto, Vilfredo. *The Rise and Fall of the Elites: An Application of Theoretical Sociology*. New York: Arno Press, 1979.

Pateman, Carole. *Participation and Democratic Theory*. New York: Cambridge University Press, 1970.

Pellicer de Brody, Olga. "La oposición en México: El caso del henriquismo." *Foro Internacional* 17, no. 68 (April–June 1977): 477–89.

Pérez Correa, Fernando. "Modernización y mercado del trabajo: Guión para un diálogo." *Este País*, no. 47 (February 1995): 23–27.

Peschard, Jacqueline. "La organización de las elecciones de 1991: En deuda con la imparcialidad." In *Las elecciones federales de 1991*, edited by Alberto Aziz Nassif and Jacqueline Peschard. Mexico City: UNAM, 1992.

Pinard, Maurice. *The Rise of a Third Party: A Study in Crisis Politics*. Montreal: McGill-Queen's University Press, 1975.

Polo Cheva, Demetrio. "La crisis socialista: Un reto democrático." *Nueva Sociedad*, no. 108 (July–August 1990): 75–85.

Powell, G. Bingham. *Contemporary Democracies: Participation, Stability, and Violence*. Cambridge, Mass.: Harvard University Press, 1982.

"Pronasol." *Este País*, no. 7 (October 1991): 9–11.

Puig Escudero, Antonio, and Jesús Hernández Rivas. "Un modelo de desagregación geográfica: Estimación del PIB por entidad federativa, 1970–1988." Serie de Documentos de Investigación, no. 1. Mexico, D.F.: INEGI, 1989.

"Pulsometro." *Este País*, no. 39 (June 1994): 17.

Ramírez Saíz, Juan Manuel. "Urban Struggles and Their Political Consequences." In *Popular Movements and Political Change in Mexico*, edited by Joe Foweraker and Ann Craig. Boulder, Colo.: Lynne Rienner, 1990.

Las razones y las obras: Gobierno de Miguel De la Madrid. Mexico City: Fondo de Cultura Económica, 1988.

Reding, Andrew. "Mexico: The Crumbling of the 'Perfect Dictatorship.' " *World Policy Journal* 8 (Spring 1991): 255–84.

———. "Mexico at a Crossroads: The 1988 Election and Beyond." *World Policy Journal* 5 (Fall 1988): 615–49.

Reyes del Campillo, Juan. "Candidatos: Hacia una nueva cámara." *Nexos* 14, no. 164 (August 1991): 56–59.

———. "La selección de los candidatos del Partido Revolucionario Institucional." In *Las elecciones federales de 1988 en México*, edited by Juan Felipe Leal, Jacqueline Peschard, and Concepción Rivera. Mexico City: UNAM, 1988.

Reyes Heroles, Federico, and René Delgado. "Empleo e ingreso, reto del Pronasol." *Este País*, no. 7 (October 1991): 3–7.

———. "Pedro Aspe Armella: Una buena noticia . . . y una mala." *Este País*, no. 9 (December 1991): 18–23.

Reyna, José Luis, and Richard Weinert, eds. *Authoritarianism in Mexico*. Philadelphia: Institute for the Study of Human Issues, 1977.

Riding, Alan. *Distant Neighbors: A Portrait of the Mexicans*. New York: Vintage Books, 1986.

Rivera Velázquez, Jaime. "Michoacán: Bipartidismo y abstención." *Nexos: Cuadernos* 14, no. 164 (August 1991): 14–15.

Robles, Manuel. "Manuel Aguilera y Luz Lajous juegan a la lotería . . . electoral." *Proceso*, no. 770 (5 August 1991): 7.

Ros, Jaime. "La crisis económica: Un análisis general." In *México ante la crisis*, edited by Pablo González Casanova and Hector Aguilar Camín. Vol. 1. Mexico City: Siglo Veintiuno, 1985.

———. "La economía y la política macroeconómica durante el auge petrolero: 1978–1982." In *El auge petrolero: De la euforia al desencanto*, edited by Rolando Cordera and Carlos Tello. Mexico City: UNAM, 1987.

Rosas, Javier, et al., eds. *50 años de oposición en México*. Mexico City: UNAM, 1979.

Ross, John. *The Economic System of Mexico*. Stanford, Calif.: California Institute of International Studies, 1971.

Rubio, Luis, and Roberto Blum. "Recent Scholarship on the Mexican Political and Economic System." *Latin American Research Review* 25, no. 1 (1990): 180–92.

Rustow, Dankwart. "Transitions to Democracy." *Comparative Politics* 2 (April 1970): 337–63.

Salinas de Gortari, Carlos. *Political Participation, Public Investment, and Support for the System: A Comparative Study of Rural Communities in Mexico*. Research Report Series, no. 35. La Jolla, Calif.: UCSD Center for U.S.-Mexican Studies, 1982.

Sánchez Gómez, Arturo. "La contienda electoral." In *Las elecciones de 1988 y la crisis del sistema político*, edited by Jaime González Graf. Mexico City: Editorial Diana, 1989.

Sanders, Sol. "The Coming Troubles." *Orbis* 32 (Winter 1988): 49–57.

Sanders, Thomas. *Mexico's Three Modernizations*. Field Staff Reports, no. 9. Indianapolis, Ind.: Universities Field Staff International, 1990.

Sartori, Giovanni. *Parties and Party Systems: A Framework for Analysis*. New York: Cambridge University Press, 1976.

Schmidt, Samuel. *El deterioro del presidencialismo mexicano: Los años de Luis Echeverría*. Mexico City: EDAMEX, 1986.

Schmitter, Philippe. "The Consolidation of Political Democracy in Southern Europe." Unpublished manuscript, 1988.

———. "Still the Century of Corporatism?" In *The New Corporatism: Social-Political Structures in the Iberian World*, edited by Frederick Pike and Thomas Stritch. Notre Dame, Ind.: Notre Dame University Press, 1974.

Scott, Robert. *Mexican Government in Transition*. Rev. ed. Urbana: University of Illinois Press, 1964.

"Sección especial de documentos." *Política* 3 (15 January 1963): 1–14.

Share, Donald. "Transitions to Democracy and Transition Through Transaction." *Comparative Political Studies* 19 (January 1987): 525–48.

Silvestre Méndez, José, and Santiago Zorrilla. *Mexico por entidades federativas*. Mexico City: Ediciones Oceano, 1986.

Skocpol, Theda. *States and Social Revolutions: A Comparative Analysis of France, Russia, and China*. New York: Cambridge University Press, 1979.

Smith, Peter. "Crisis and Democracy in Latin America." *World Politics* 43 (July 1991): 608–34.

———. *Labyrinths of Power: Political Recruitment in Twentieth-Century Mexico*. Princeton: Princeton University Press, 1979.

———. "Leadership and Change: Intellectuals and Technocrats in Mexico." In *Mexico's Political Stability: The Next Five Years*, edited by Roderic Camp. Boulder, Colo.: Westview Press, 1986.

Snow, David, and Robert Benford. "Master Frames and Cycles of Protest." In *Frontiers in Social Movement Theory*, edited by Aldon Morris and Carol McClurg Mueller. New Haven: Yale University Press, 1992.

Statistical Abstract of Latin America. Edited by James Wilkie. Vol. 26. Los Angeles: UCLA, 1988.

Stepan, Alfred. "Paths Toward Redemocratization: Theoretical and Comparative Considerations." In *Transitions from Authoritarian Rule: Comparative Perspectives*, edited by Guillermo O'Donnell, Philippe Schmitter, and Laurence Whitehead. Baltimore: Johns Hopkins University Press, 1986.

Story, Dale. *The Mexican Ruling Party*. New York: Praeger, 1986.

Székely, Gabriel. "La crisis de los precios del petróleo." In *México ante la crisis*, edited by Pablo González Casanova and Hector Aguilar Camín. Vol. 1. Mexico City: Siglo Veintiuno, 1985.

Tamayo, Jaime. "Neoliberalism Encounters *Neocardenismo*." In *Popular Movements and Political Change in Mexico*, edited by Joe Foweraker and Ann Craig. Boulder, Colo.: Lynne Rienner, 1990.

Tarrow, Sidney. "Mentalities, Political Cultures, and Collective Action Frames: Constructing Meanings Through Action." In *Frontiers in Social Movement Theory*, edited by Aldon Morris and Carol McClurg Mueller. New Haven, Conn.: Yale University Press, 1992.

Thorup, Cathryn. "México-E.U.: La democratización y la agenda bilateral." *Nexos* 14, no. 162 (June 1991): 57–60.

——. "Tratado de libre comercio: Valores y culturas entrelazadas." *Este País*, no. 28 (July 1993): 7–29.

Tucker, Robert C. "The Theory of Charismatic Leadership." In *Philosophers and Kings: Studies in Leadership*, edited by Dankwart Rustow. New York: George Braziller, 1970.

Valdés, Leonardo. "Partido de la Revolución Democrática: The Third Option in Mexico." In *Party Politics in 'an Uncommon Democracy': Political Parties and Elections in Mexico*, edited by Neil Harvey and Mónica Serrano. London: Institute of Latin American Studies, 1994.

Ward, Peter. "Social Welfare Policy and Political Opening in Mexico." *Journal of Latin American Studies*, no. 25 (October 1993): 613–28.

Weber, Max. *The Theory of Social and Economic Organization*. Translated by A. M. Henderson and Talcott Parsons. New York: The Free Press, 1964.

Weintraub, Sidney. *Transforming the Mexican Economy: The Salinas Sexenio*. Washington, D.C.: National Planning Association, 1993.

Williams, Geoffrey Lee, and Alan Lee Williams. *Labour's Decline and the Social Democrats' Fall*. London: Macmillan, 1989.

Wilson, Michael. "Political Reform in Mexico: Salinas's Other Revolution." *The Backgrounder*. Heritage Foundation, no. 858 (11 October 1991).

Wyman, Donald. "The Mexican Economy: Problems and Prospects." In *Mexico's Economic Crisis: Challenges and Opportunities*, edited by Donald Wyman. Monograph Series, no. 12. La Jolla, Calif.: UCSD Center for U.S.-Mexican Studies, 1983.

Yo Manuel: Memorias ¿apócrifas? de un comisionado. Mexico City: Rayuela Editores, 1995.

Yúñez Naude, Antonio. *Crisis de la agricultura mexicana*. Mexico City: El Colegio de México/Fondo de Cultura Económica, 1988.

Zald, Mayer, and Roberta Ash. "Social Movement Organizations: Growth, Decay, and Change." In *Protest, Reform, and Revolt: A Reader in Social Movements*, edited by Joseph R. Gusfield. New York: Wiley, 1970.

Zapata, Francisco. *El sindicalismo mexicano frente a la restructuración*. Mexico City: El Colegio de México, 1995.

Zazueta, César, and Ricardo de la Peña. *La estructura del Congreso del Trabajo: Estado, trabajo, y capital en México*. Mexico City: Fondo de Cultura Económica, 1984.

Zepeda Patterson, Jorge. *Michoacán*. Series "Biblioteca de las Entidades Federativas." Mexico City: UNAM, 1988.

Zermeño, Sergio. "Crisis, Neoliberalism, and Disorder." In *Popular Movements and Political Change in Mexico*, edited by Joe Foweraker and Ann Craig. Boulder, Colo.: Lynne Rienner, 1990.

Index

Kathleen Bruhn is Assistant Professor of Political Science at the University of California, Santa Barbara. The dissertation on which this book is based won the Hubert Herring Award of the Pacific Coast Council on Latin American Studies for best dissertation in 1993.